GRAMMAR AND BEYOND

Randi Reppen
with Deborah Gordon

2

CAMBRIDGE
UNIVERSITY PRESS

CAMBRIDGE UNIVERSITY PRESS
Cambridge, New York, Melbourne, Madrid, Cape Town,
Singapore, São Paulo, Delhi, Mexico City

Cambridge University Press
32 Avenue of the Americas, New York, NY 10013-2473, USA

www.cambridge.org
Information on this title: www.cambridge.org/9780521142960

First published 2012
3rd printing 2013

Printed in the United States of America.

A catalog record for this publication is available from the British Library.

ISBN 978-0-521-14296-0 Student's Book 2
ISBN 978-0-521-14310-3 Student's Book 2A
ISBN 978-0-521-14312-7 Student's Book 2B
ISBN 978-0-521-27991-8 Workbook 2
ISBN 978-0-521-27992-5 Workbook 2A
ISBN 978-0-521-27993-2 Workbook 2B
ISBN 978-1-107-67653-4 Teacher Support Resource 2
ISBN 978-0-521-14335-6 Class Audio 2
ISBN 978-1-139-06186-5 Writing Skills Interactive 2

Art direction, book design, and layout services: Adventure House, NYC
Audio production: John Marshall Media

Contents

PART 1 The Present

PART 2 The Past

PART 5 Adjectives, Adverbs, and Prepositions

PART 6 The Future

Appendices

Introduction to *Grammar and Beyond*

Grammar and Beyond is a research-based and content-rich grammar series for beginning- to advanced-level students of North American English. The series focuses on the grammar structures most commonly used in North American English, with an emphasis on the application of these grammar structures to academic writing. The series practices all four skills in a variety of authentic and communicative contexts. It is designed for use both in the classroom and as a self-study learning tool.

Grammar and Beyond Is Research-Based

The grammar presented in this series is informed by years of research on the grammar of written and spoken North American English as it is used in college lectures, textbooks, academic essays, high school classrooms, and conversations between instructors and students. This research, and the analysis of over one billion words of authentic written and spoken language data known as the *Cambridge International Corpus*, has enabled the authors to:

- Present grammar rules that accurately represent how North American English is actually spoken and written

- Identify and teach differences between the grammar of written and spoken English

- Focus more attention on the structures that are commonly used, and less attention on those that are rarely used, in written and spoken North American English

- Help students avoid the most common mistakes that English language learners make

- Choose reading and writing topics that will naturally elicit examples of the target grammar structure

- Introduce important vocabulary from the Academic Word List

Grammar and Beyond Teaches Academic Writing Skills

Grammar and Beyond helps students make the transition from understanding grammar structures to applying them in their academic writing.

In the Student's Books

At Levels 1 through 3 of the series, every Student's Book unit ends with a section devoted to the hands-on application of grammar to writing. This section, called Grammar for Writing, explores how and where the target grammar structures function in writing and offers controlled practice, exposure to writing models, and a guided but open-ended writing task.

At Level 4, the most advanced level, the syllabus is organized around the academic essay types that college students write (e.g., persuasive, cause and effect) and is aimed at teaching students the grammar, vocabulary, and writing skills that they need in order to be successful at writing those kinds of essays.

Online

Grammar and Beyond also offers *Writing Skills Interactive*, an interactive online course in academic writing skills and vocabulary that correlates with the Student's Books. Each unit of the writing skills course focuses on a specific writing skill, such as avoiding sentence fragments or developing strong topic sentences.

Special Features of *Grammar and Beyond*

Realistic Grammar Presentations

Grammar is presented in clear and simple charts. The grammar points presented in these charts have been tested against real-world data from the *Cambridge International Corpus* to ensure that they are authentic representations of actual usage of North American English.

Data from the Real World

Many of the grammar presentations and application sections in the Student's Book include a feature called Data from the Real World, in which concrete and useful points discovered through analysis of corpus data are presented. These points are practiced in the exercises that follow.

Avoid Common Mistakes

Each Student's Book unit features an Avoid Common Mistakes section that develops students' awareness of the most common mistakes made by English language learners and gives them an opportunity to practice detecting and correcting these errors in running text. This section helps students avoid these mistakes in their own work. The mistakes highlighted in this section are drawn from a body of authentic data on learner English known as the *Cambridge Learner Corpus*, a database of over 35 million words from student essays written by nonnative speakers of English and information from experienced classroom teachers.

Academic Vocabulary

Every unit in *Grammar and Beyond* includes words from the Academic Word List (AWL), a research-based list of words and word families that appear with high frequency in English-language academic texts. These words are introduced in the opening text of the unit, recycled in the charts and exercises, and used to support the theme throughout the unit. The same vocabulary items are reviewed and practiced in *Writing Skills Interactive*, the online writing skills course. By the time students finish each level, they will have been exposed several times to a carefully selected set of level-appropriate AWL words, as well as content words from a variety of academic disciplines.

Series Levels

The following table provides a general idea of the difficulty of the material at each level of *Grammar and Beyond*. These are not meant to be interpreted as precise correlations.

	Description	TOEFL IBT	CEFR Levels
Level 1	beginning	20 – 34	A1 – A2
Level 2	low intermediate to intermediate	35 – 54	A2 – B1
Level 3	high intermediate	55 – 74	B1 – B2
Level 4	advanced	75 – 95	B2 – C1

Components for Students

Student's Book

The Student's Books for Levels 1 through 3 teach all of the grammar points appropriate at each level in short, manageable cycles of presentation and practice organized around a high-interest unit theme. The Level 4 Student's Book focuses on the structure of the academic essay in addition to the grammar rules, conventions, and structures that students need to master in order to be successful college writers. Please see the Tour of a Unit on pages xvi–xix for a more detailed view of the contents and structure of the Student's Book units.

Workbook

The Workbook provides additional practice of the grammar presented in each unit of the Student's Book. The exercises offer both discrete and consolidated practice of grammar points and can be used for homework or in class. Each unit also offers practice correcting the errors highlighted in the Avoid Common Mistakes section in the Student's Book to help students master these troublesome errors. Self-Assessment sections at the end of each unit allow students to test their mastery of what they have learned.

Writing Skills Interactive

This online course provides graduated instruction and practice in writing skills, while reinforcing vocabulary presented in the Student's Books. Each unit includes a vocabulary review activity, followed by a short text that builds on the theme presented in the Student's Book and provides an additional context for the vocabulary. The text is followed by an animated interactive presentation of the target writing skill of the unit, after which students have the opportunity to practice the target skill in three different activities. Each unit closes with a quiz, which allows students to assess their progress.

Teacher Resources

Teacher Support Resource Book

This comprehensive book provides a range of support materials for instructors, including:

- Suggestions for applying the target grammar to all four major skill areas, helping instructors facilitate dynamic and comprehensive grammar classes
- An answer key and audio script for the Student's Book
- A CD-ROM containing:
  - Ready-made, easily scored Unit Tests
  - PowerPoint presentations to streamline lesson preparation and encourage lively heads-up interaction

Class Audio CDs

The class audio CDs for each level provide the Student's Book listening material for in-class use.

Teacher Support Website

www.cambridge.org/grammarandbeyond

The website for *Grammar and Beyond* contains even more resources for instructors, including:

- Unit-by-unit teaching tips, helping instructors plan their lessons
- Downloadable communicative activities to add more in-class speaking practice
- A monthly newsletter on grammar teaching, providing ongoing professional development

We hope you enjoy using this series, and we welcome your feedback! Please send any comments to the authors and editorial staff at Cambridge University Press, at grammarandbeyond@cambridge.org.

About the Authors

Randi Reppen is Professor of Applied Linguistics and TESL at Northern Arizona University (NAU) in Flagstaff, Arizona. She has over 20 years experience teaching ESL students and training ESL teachers, including 11 years as the Director of NAU's Program in Intensive English. Randi's research interests focus on the use of corpora for language teaching and materials development. In addition to numerous academic articles and books, she is the author of *Using Corpora in the Language Classroom* and a co-author of *Basic Vocabulary in Use*, 2nd edition, both published by Cambridge University Press.

Deborah Gordon, creator of the Grammar for Writing sections, has more than 25 years' experience teaching ESL students and training ESL teachers in the United States and abroad. She is currently an ESL instructor at Santa Barbara City College and a TESOL Certificate instructor at the University of California, Santa Barbara Extension. Deborah is coauthor of *Writers at Work: From Sentence to Paragraph*, published by Cambridge University Press, among many other titles.

Corpus Consultants

Michael McCarthy is Emeritus Professor of Applied Linguistics at the University of Nottingham, UK, and Adjunct Professor of Applied Linguistics at the Pennsylvania State University. He is a co-author of the corpus-informed *Touchstone* series and the award-winning *Cambridge Grammar of English*, both published by Cambridge University Press, among many other titles, and is known throughout the world as an expert on grammar, vocabulary, and corpus linguistics.

Jeanne McCarten has over 30 years of experience in ELT/ESL as a teacher, publisher, and author. She has been closely involved in the development of the spoken English sections of the *Cambridge International Corpus*. Now a freelance writer, she is co-author of the corpus-informed *Touchstone* series and *Grammar for Business*, both published by Cambridge University Press.

Advisory Panel

The ESL advisory panel has helped to guide the development of this series and provided invaluable information about the needs of ESL students and teachers in high schools, colleges, universities, and private language schools throughout North America.

Neta Simpkins Cahill, Skagit Valley College, Mount Vernon, WA

Shelly Hedstrom, Palm Beach State College, Lake Worth, FL

Richard Morasci, Foothill College, Los Altos Hills, CA

Stacey Russo, East Hampton High School, East Hampton, NY

Alice Savage, North Harris College, Houston, TX

Acknowledgments

The publisher and authors would like to thank these reviewers and consultants for their insights and participation:

Marty Attiyeh, The College of DuPage, Glen Ellyn, IL

Shannon Bailey, Austin Community College, Austin, TX

Jamila Barton, North Seattle Community College, Seattle, WA

Kim Bayer, Hunter College IELI, New York, NY

Linda Berendsen, Oakton Community College, Skokie, IL

Anita Biber, Tarrant County College Northwest, Fort Worth, TX

Jane Breaux, Community College of Aurora, Aurora, CO

Anna Budzinski, San Antonio College, San Antonio, TX

Britta Burton, Mission College, Santa Clara, CA

Jean Carroll, Fresno City College, Fresno, CA

Chris Cashman, Oak Park High School and Elmwood Park High School, Chicago, IL

Annette M. Charron, Bakersfield College, Bakersfield, CA

Patrick Colabucci, ALI at San Diego State University, San Diego, CA

Lin Cui, Harper College, Palatine, IL

Jennifer Duclos, Boston University CELOP, Boston, MA

Joy Durighello, San Francisco City College, San Francisco, CA

Kathleen Flynn, Glendale Community College, Glendale, CA

Raquel Fundora, Miami Dade College, Miami, FL

Patricia Gillie, New Trier Township High School District, Winnetka, IL

Laurie Gluck, LaGuardia Community College, Long Island City, NY

Kathleen Golata, Galileo Academy of Science & Technology, San Francisco, CA

Ellen Goldman, Mission College, Santa Clara, CA

Ekaterina Goussakova, Seminole Community College, Sanford, FL

Marianne Grayston, Prince George's Community College, Largo, MD

Mary Greiss Shipley, Georgia Gwinnett College, Lawrenceville, GA

Sudeepa Gulati, Long Beach City College, Long Beach, CA

Nicole Hammond Carrasquel, University of Central Florida, Orlando, FL

Vicki Hendricks, Broward College, Fort Lauderdale, FL

Kelly Hernandez, Miami Dade College, Miami, FL

Ann Johnston, Tidewater Community College, Virginia Beach, VA

Julia Karet, Chaffey College, Claremont, CA

Jeanne Lachowski, English Language Institute, University of Utah, Salt Lake City, UT

Noga Laor, Rennert, New York, NY

Min Lu, Central Florida Community College, Ocala, FL

Michael Luchuk, Kaplan International Centers, New York, NY

Craig Machado, Norwalk Community College, Norwalk, CT

Denise Maduli-Williams, City College of San Francisco, San Francisco, CA

Diane Mahin, University of Miami, Coral Gables, FL

Melanie Majeski, Naugatuck Valley Community College, Waterbury, CT

Jeanne Malcolm, University of North Carolina at Charlotte, Charlotte, NC

Lourdes Marx, Palm Beach State College, Boca Raton, FL

Susan G. McFalls, Maryville College, Maryville, TN

Nancy McKay, Cuyahoga Community College, Cleveland, OH

Dominika McPartland, Long Island Business Institute, Flushing, NY

Amy Metcalf, UNR/Intensive English Language Center, University of Nevada, Reno, NV

Robert Miller, EF International Language School San Francisco – Mills, San Francisco, CA

Marcie Pachino, Jordan High School, Durham, NC

Myshie Pagel, El Paso Community College, El Paso, TX

Bernadette Pedagno, University of San Francisco, San Francisco, CA

Tam Q Pham, Dallas Theological Seminary, Fort Smith, AR

Mary Beth Pickett, Global-LT, Rochester, MI

Maria Reamore, Baltimore City Public Schools, Baltimore, MD

Alison M. Rice, Hunter College IELI, New York, NY

Sydney Rice, Imperial Valley College, Imperial, CA

Kathleen Romstedt, Ohio State University, Columbus, OH

Alexandra Rowe, University of South Carolina, Columbia, SC

Irma Sanders, Baldwin Park Adult and Community Education, Baldwin Park, CA

Caren Shoup, Lone Star College – CyFair, Cypress, TX

Karen Sid, Mission College, Foothill College, De Anza College, Santa Clara, CA

Michelle Thomas, Miami Dade College, Miami, FL

Sharon Van Houte, Lorain County Community College, Elyria, OH

Margi Wald, UC Berkeley, Berkeley, CA

Walli Weitz, Riverside County Office of Ed., Indio, CA

Bart Weyand, University of Southern Maine, Portland, ME

Donna Weyrich, Columbus State Community College, Columbus, OH

Marilyn Whitehorse, Santa Barbara City College, Ojai, CA

Jessica Wilson, Rutgers University – Newark, Newark, NJ

Sue Wilson, San Jose City College, San Jose, CA

Margaret Wilster, Mid-Florida Tech, Orlando, FL

Anne York-Herjeczki, Santa Monica College, Santa Monica, CA

Hoda Zaki, Camden County College, Camden, NJ

We would also like to thank these teachers and programs for allowing us to visit:

Richard Appelbaum, Broward College, Fort Lauderdale, FL

Carmela Arnoldt, Glendale Community College, Glendale, AZ

JaNae Barrow, Desert Vista High School, Phoenix, AZ

Ted Christensen, Mesa Community College, Mesa, AZ

Richard Ciriello, Lower East Side Preparatory High School, New York, NY

Virginia Edwards, Chandler-Gilbert Community College, Chandler, AZ

Nusia Frankel, Miami Dade College, Miami, FL

Raquel Fundora, Miami Dade College, Miami, FL

Vicki Hendricks, Broward College, Fort Lauderdale, FL

Kelly Hernandez, Miami Dade College, Miami, FL

Stephen Johnson, Miami Dade College, Miami, FL

Barbara Jordan, Mesa Community College, Mesa, AZ

Nancy Kersten, GateWay Community College, Phoenix, AZ

Lewis Levine, Hostos Community College, Bronx, NY

John Liffiton, Scottsdale Community College, Scottsdale, AZ

Cheryl Lira-Layne, Gilbert Public School District, Gilbert, AZ

Mary Livingston, Arizona State University, Tempe, AZ

Elizabeth Macdonald, Thunderbird School of Global Management, Glendale, AZ

Terri Martinez, Mesa Community College, Mesa, AZ

Lourdes Marx, Palm Beach State College, Boca Raton, FL

Paul Kei Matsuda, Arizona State University, Tempe, AZ

David Miller, Glendale Community College, Glendale, AZ

Martha Polin, Lower East Side Preparatory High School, New York, NY

Patricia Pullenza, Mesa Community College, Mesa, AZ

Victoria Rasinskaya, Lower East Side Preparatory High School, New York, NY

Vanda Salls, Tempe Union High School District, Tempe, AZ

Kim Sanabria, Hostos Community College, Bronx, NY

Cynthia Schuemann, Miami Dade College, Miami, FL

Michelle Thomas, Miami Dade College, Miami, FL

Dongmei Zeng, Borough of Manhattan Community College, New York, NY

Tour of a Unit

Grammar in the Real World presents the unit's grammar in a **realistic** context using **contemporary** texts.

Notice activities draw students' attention to the **structure**, guiding their own **analysis** of form, meaning, and use.

UNIT
4

Simple Past
Entrepreneurs

1 | Grammar in the Real World

A What is the best way to find information today? Read the article from a technology magazine. How did Google start?

The Story of Google

Who started Google?
Sergey Brin and Larry Page **started** the company. Sergey **came** from Moscow, Russia. He **moved** to the United States as a young child
5 and later **studied** mathematics and computer science. Larry **was** born in Michigan and **became** interested in computers as a child.

How did they meet?
They **met** in 1995 at Stanford University,
10 in California, where they **were** both computer science students. They **did not get along** at first, but they soon **became** friends.

What happened next?
They **designed** a new Internet search engine. At first, they **worked** in their
15 rooms in college. Then they **rented** a friend's garage because Sergey's roommate **complained** about the noise from his computers. Three years later, they **started** Google.

Was it an immediate success?
The company **was** an immediate success. Before Google, **there were** other search
20 engines, but Google soon **became** the most popular one. The company **grew** quickly. They **did not stop** at just one product. Very soon, **there were** other Google products, like Google Maps and Gmail. Ten years later, Google **earned** over $10 billion and **had** about 20,000 employees.

So what did people do before Google?
25 Before Google, people **went** to libraries. They **got** information from books. These days, they just "google" for information.

40

Simple Past

B *Comprehension Check* Answer the questions.
1. Where did Larry Page and Sergey Brin meet?
2. Why did they work in a garage?
3. What other products did Google start?
4. How many people worked at Google after 10 years?

C *Notice* Look at the article. Find the simple past forms of these verbs.

Group A		Group B	
1. start	_____	5. come	_____
2. move	_____	6. be	_____ , _____ (two forms)
3. study	_____	7. become	_____
4. happen	_____	8. meet	_____

How are the two groups of verbs different?

2 | Simple Past

▶ Grammar Presentation

You can use the simple past to talk about completed events in the past.	Brin and Page **started** Google in 1998. They **did not get along** at first.

2.1 Affirmative Statements

Subject	Verb + -ed (Regular Verbs)		Subject	Irregular Verb
I You He / She / It We They	**started** in 1998. **employed** 20,000 people.		I You He / She / It We They	**grew** quickly. **became** successful.

▸ Spelling Rules for Regular Verbs in Simple Past: See page 403.   ▸ Irregular Verbs: See page 402.

Data from the Real World

Research shows that these are six of the most common **regular** simple past verbs.	work start call	worked started called	live try plan	lived tried planned
Research shows that these are eight of the most common **irregular** simple past verbs.	have get do say	**had** **got** **did** **said**	go come take make	**went** **came** **took** **made**

Entrepreneurs **41**

The *Grammar Presentation* begins with an **overview** that describes the grammar in an **easy-to-understand** summary.

xvi

Charts provide clear guidance on the form, meaning, and use of the target grammar, for **ease of instruction and reference**.

Data from the Real World, a feature **unique** to this series, takes students **beyond traditional information** and teaches them how the unit's grammar is used in authentic situations, including differences between spoken and written use.

Theme-related exercises allow students to **apply the grammar** in a variety of natural contexts.

Simple Past

2.5 Using Simple Past

a. Use the simple past to talk or write about:

- a single action that started and ended in the past.

They **started** Google in 1998.
×
past ————————————— now

- a repeated action or habit in the past.

They **worked** in their rooms every day.
× × ×
past ————————————— now

- a state, situation, or feeling in the past.

They **didn't get along**.
past ▬▬▬▬ now

b. Time expressions can come at the start or end of a statement. Examples: *last week / month / year, 10 years ago, in 1998, yesterday*

Last year, I joined a new company.
I joined a new company *last year*.

Two years ago, I graduated.
I graduated *two years ago*.

c. Remember to use a comma when the time expression comes at the beginning of the sentence.

In 1998, they started Google.
They started Google *in 1998*.

d. Adverbs of frequency often come before the main verb in simple past statements. Some examples of adverbs of frequency are *never, rarely, sometimes, often, usually,* and *always*.

They **often had** meetings at a pizza parlor.
They **sometimes worked** in their room.

Data from the Real World

Research shows that *didn't* is not common in formal writing. Use *did not* instead. Writers sometimes use *didn't* in quotes of people speaking.

Use *didn't* in conversation and informal writing. In conversation, *did not* can sound formal, emphatic, or argumentative.

Formal writing
didn't
did not

Conversation
didn't
did not

Entrepreneurs **43**

▶ **Grammar Application**

Exercise 2.1 Statements and Questions

A Complete the article with the simple past form of the verbs in parentheses.

Ben Cohen and Jerry Greenfield _grew up_ (grow up)
(1)
in Merrick, Long Island. They _____
(2)
(meet) in middle school, and they _____
(3)
(graduate) from high school together. Their connections to
ice cream _____ (begin) at an early age.
(4)
Ben _____ (drive) an ice cream truck in
(5)
high school. Jerry _____ (work) in his
(6)
college cafeteria as an ice cream scooper.

Ben _____ (try) different colleges, but he _____
(7)   (8)
(not graduate). At one time, he _____ (teach) crafts in a school. At
(9)
the school, he sometimes _____ (make) ice cream with his students.
(10)
Jerry _____ (want) to be a doctor. After he _____
(11)   (12)
(graduate) from college, he _____ (apply) to medical school, but he was not
(13)
successful. During those years, Ben and Jerry _____ (stay) friends.
(14)

After a few years, Ben and Jerry _____ (go) into the food business
(15)
together. At first, they _____ (think) about making bagels, but the
(16)
equipment was expensive. So they _____ (choose) ice cream and
(17)
_____ (take) a $5 class on ice-cream making.
(18)
Ben and Jerry _____ (see) an opportunity in Burlington,
(19)
Vermont. This college town _____ (not have) an ice cream shop. They
(20)
_____ (find) an old gas station, and in 1978 they _____
(21)   (22)
(open) the first Ben & Jerry's store.

Ben & Jerry's quickly _____ (become) popular because it
(23)
_____ (have) great ice cream and a caring approach to the community.
(24)
On their first anniversary, they _____ (give) everyone free ice cream
(25)
as a "thank you." They still give away free ice cream every year on their anniversary.

44 Unit 4 Simple Past

xvii

Tour of a Unit

A **wide variety** of exercises introduce new and stimulating content to keep students engaged with the material.

Students learn to *Avoid Common Mistakes* based on research in student writing.

C *Over to You* Write six sentences about your own life. Use the ideas in B or your own ideas. Compare sentences with a partner. Ask your partner for more information.

A *My family moved here in 1998.*
B *Really? Where did you live before that?*

Exercise 2.3 Questions and Answers

A Complete the article with the simple past form of the verbs in parentheses.

Today Oprah Winfrey is one of the most successful broadcasters, publishers, and entrepreneurs in the world. However, she did not have an easy start in life. Oprah _had_ (1) (have) a difficult childhood. She _____ (2) (not have) a lot of opportunities as a child, but she was very intelligent. She _____ (3) (learn) to read before the age of 3. Her broadcasting career _____ (4) (begin) in high school. In 1971, she _____ (5) (go) to Tennessee State University. During high school and college, she _____ (6) (work) on a radio show. She also _____ (7) (work) at a TV station in Nashville as a student. At the age of 19, she _____ (8) (become) the first African-American woman news anchor[1] at the station.

In 1976, she _____ (9) (graduate) from college. That year, she _____ (10) (move) to Baltimore. There she _____ (11) (host) a TV talk show called *People Are Talking*. Eight years later, she _____ (12) (start) working on a morning show in Chicago. It _____ (13) (become) *The Oprah Winfrey Show*. Oprah's popularity _____ (14) (grow) quickly, and in 1986, it _____ (15) (become) a national show.

[1]**anchor:** a person who reports the news

B *Pair Work* Complete the questions about Oprah Winfrey. Use the information in the article. Then ask and answer the questions with a partner.

1. What kind of childhood _____ ?
2. What _____ before the age of 3?
3. Which university _____ ?
4. What _____ during high school and college?

Exercise 3.2 Questions with *Be* and Other Verbs

A *Pair Work* Write the simple past questions. Then interview a classmate. Ask for more information as you talk.

1. What / be / your first job
   What was your first job?

2. be / it / a good job
   _____

3. What / be / your co-workers like
   _____

4. What / you / do there
   _____

5. Why / you / leave   _____
6. What / be / your best job   _____
7. Why / you / like it   _____
8. Where / be / your worst job _____

B *Pair Work* Write a short work history of your classmate.

Luis's first job was in a hotel in San Diego. He worked there from 2008 to 2009.

4 Avoid Common Mistakes ⚠

1. **Use the simple past, not the simple present, when you write about the past.**
   started
   I start my first job in 2008.

2. **After *did not* or *didn't*, use the base form of the verb, not the past form.**
   They didn't earned a lot of money.

3. **Put time expressions at the beginning or end of a statement, not between the subject and the verb, and not between the verb and the object.**
   yesterday
   I bought yesterday a computer.
   OR
   Yesterday
   I bought yesterday a computer.

4. **Use *there were* with plural nouns. Use *there was* with singular or noncount nouns.**
   were
   There was a lot of people. There were no information.
   was

Editing Task

Find and correct nine more mistakes in the blog.

```
○ ○ ○                                                              ⊡
              moved
        My family move from Mexico City to the United States in 1998. I went to Hamilton

High School in Los Angeles. I did not knew anybody, and I did not had any friends

here. I in 1999 met Jun. He became my first friend.

        We in 2001 graduated. I got a job at a nice restaurant, but I did not enjoyed my

job. Jun drove a taco truck, but he did not liked the food. I wanted to be my own boss,

and I always liked food and cooking. Jun wanted his own business, too. Jun saw an

opportunity. There was hungry office workers downtown at noon, but there weren't

a nice place to eat. We bought a food truck and we start Food on the Move in 2003.

Today, we have 5 trucks and 15 employees.
```

5 | Grammar for Writing ✎

Using Simple Past

Writers use the simple past to describe single actions, repeated actions, or states in the past. In a story about a person's life, the verbs that tell about past events, actions, or states should be in the past.

    STATE   STATE   SINGLE ACTION
He *wanted* his own business, but he *did not have* the money for it. He *went* to the bank to ask for a loan.

Writers often use the simple present at the end of a story to say what is different now.

               PRESENT
. . . Today my uncle *has* a successful business.

Remember:

Check the spelling of irregular verbs.

      got   paid
He *getted* a loan from the bank. Then he *payed* a lot of money to start the business.

Pre-writing Task

1 Read the paragraph below. Notice how the writer uses the simple past to describe the single actions, repeated actions, and states in a person's life.

My Boss Missolle

    My boss, Missolle, came to the United States from Haiti 12 years ago. When she came here, she was very sad because her children were still in Haiti. She wanted them to come here, so she worked very hard. She practiced her English all the time. She worked during the day in a hair salon, and at night she cooked for people. She always thought about her children. When I met her five years ago, she was always happy and enthusiastic. I did not know her life was difficult. She told me that she did not want to show her true feelings. Now she is very happy because her children are here, and her life is good.

2 Read the paragraph again. Circle the verbs in the simple past, and underline the verbs in the simple present.

Writing Task

1 *Write* Use the paragraph in the Pre-writing Task to help you write about the life events of a person you know. What are some important past events in this person's life? How is this person's life different today?

2 *Self-Edit* Use the editing tips to improve your paragraph. Make any necessary changes.

    1. Did you use the simple past for all single actions, repeated actions, and states?
    2. Did you use the correct form for irregular verbs?
    3. Did you avoid the mistakes in the Avoid Common Mistakes chart on page 51?

Simple Present

Are You Often Online?

1 | Grammar in the Real World

A What kinds of things do you do on the Internet? Read the magazine article. What is one good thing and one bad thing about spending time online?

Balancing Time Online and Time with People

In today's busy world, people **spend** a lot of time with computers, and they **spend** less and less time with people. **Does** this **change** how people
5 interact with family and friends? **Does** it **help** or **hurt** people and relationships? Sociologists[1] **disagree** about this. Some **worry** about the Internet's effect on our friends and family. Others **think**
10 this is not a problem.

Studies **show** that people spend less face-to-face[2] time with family and friends than they did a few years ago. Instead, they **play** online games,
15 **shop** online, and also **look** at social networking sites. In the United States, the average person **spends** 13 hours a week online. They **interact** face-to-face less, and this sometimes **has** bad
20 effects. For example, some people **do not spend time** together as a family very often. They **talk** less because they spend more time online.

Sometimes technology **helps**
25 people improve their relationships with

others. For example, social networking sites **help** people stay in touch with friends and family who live far away. They enable people to reconnect with old friends and classmates. 30

Are you worried about the time you spend online? If so, try to make a schedule. Schedule time away from the computer to be with family and friends. Try to balance online time with 35 face-to-face time.

[1]**sociologist:** someone who studies people and society | [2]**face-to-face:** meeting with someone in the same place directly

B *Comprehension Check* Answer the questions.

1. What do sociologists disagree about?
2. How much time does the average person in the United States spend online per week?
3. What is face-to-face time? What are some examples of face-to-face time?
4. Does the article say not to use computers?

C *Notice* Find the sentences in the article and complete them.

1. In today's busy world, people _____ a lot of time with computers, and they _____ less and less time with people.

2. Sociologists _____ about this.

3. In the United States, the average person _____ 13 hours a week online.

4. Sometimes technology _____ people improve their relationships with others.

Look at the words you wrote in the blanks. Which of the verbs end in -*s*?

2 | Simple Present

▶ Grammar Presentation

The simple present describes habits, general truths, feelings, or thoughts.	Many people **spend** up to 8 hours a day online. I **play** games online every night. My sister **loves** to shop online.

2.1 Affirmative and Negative Statements

AFFIRMATIVE			NEGATIVE			
Subject	**Verb**		**Subject**	**Do / Does + Not**	**Base Form of Verb**	
I You We They	**shop**	online.	I You We They	**do not** **don't**	**shop**	online.
He / She / It	**shops**		He / She / It	**does not** **doesn't**		

2.2 Affirmative and Negative Statements with *Be*

AFFIRMATIVE		
Subject	***Be***	
I	**am**	
You We They	**are**	online.
He / She / It	**is**	

NEGATIVE		
Subject	***Be + Not***	
I	**am not**	
You We They	**are not**	online.
He / She / It	**is not**	

CONTRACTIONS		
Affirmative	**Negative**	
I**'m**	I**'m not**	
You**'re** We**'re** They**'re**	You**'re not** We**'re not** They**'re not**	You **aren't** We **aren't** They **aren't**
He**'s** She**'s** It**'s**	He**'s not** She**'s not** It**'s not**	He **isn't** She **isn't** It **isn't**

Data from the Real World

Research shows the contractions *'s not* and *'re not* are more common after pronouns (*he*, *she*, *you*, etc.) than *isn't* and *aren't*.	*'s not / 're not* ▬▬▬▬▬▬▬▬▬▬▬▬▬ *isn't / aren't* ▬▬
Be careful not to use contractions in formal writing.	Say: *"He's not feeling well today."* Write: *He is not feeling well today.*

2.3 *Yes / No* Questions and Short Answers

Do / Does	Subject	Base Form of Verb		Short Answers	
Do	I you we they	**shop**	online?	Yes, I **do**. Yes, you **do**. Yes, we **do**. Yes, they **do**.	No, I **don't**. No, you **don't**. No, we **don't**. No, they **don't**.
Does	he / she / it			Yes, he / she / it **does**.	No, he / she / it **doesn't**.

2.4 Information Questions and Answers

Wh- Word	Do / Does	Subject	Base Form of Verb	Answers
Where **When** **How often**	**do**	I you we they	**shop**?	I **shop** online. You **shop** at night. We **shop** once a week. They **shop** every day.
	does	he / she / it		He **shops** every night.

Wh- Word	Verb		Answers
Who	**uses**	e-mail?	Everyone **uses** e-mail!
What	**helps**	people reconnect?	The Internet **helps** people reconnect.

2.5 Using Simple Present Statements

a. Use the simple present to describe habits and routines (usual and regular activities).

*I usually **read** the news online.*
*We **eat** together as a family on weekends.*

b. Use the simple present to describe facts, general truths, feelings, or thoughts.

*The average person **spends** 13 hours a week online.*
*Some people **worry** about the effects of the Internet.*

c. Use the simple present with adverbs of frequency to say how often something happens.

0%   100%

never	seldom hardly ever* rarely	occasionally sometimes	often	usually almost always normally	always

*ever: at any time

d. Adverbs of frequency come before the main verb in affirmative statements but after the verb *be*.	*I **occasionally** play online games.* *I am **hardly ever** free.*
e. Do not use *sometimes* after *not*. Note that meaning can change in negative statements with adverbs of frequency.	***Sometimes** people do not check e-mail.* *People ~~do not sometimes~~ check e-mail.* *I don't **always** check e-mail.* (Does *not* mean "I never check e-mail.")
f. *Sometimes, occasionally, normally, often, usually,* and *almost always* can come before the verb or at the beginning or end of a sentence.	*I **usually** check my e-mail at home.* ***Usually,** I check my e-mail at home.* *I check my e-mail at home **usually**.*
g. Adverbs of frequency come before the main verb in questions.	*Do you **always** <u>study</u> at night? Yes, I do.* *Do you **ever** <u>watch</u> YouTube? No, I don't.*
h. Do not use negative adverbs of frequency in negative sentences.	*I **don't usually** shop online.* *~~I don't never shop online.~~*

2.6 Using Simple Present Questions

a. Answer *when* or *what time* questions with **time expressions**.	*What time do you shop online? I shop online **at night**.* *When do you check e-mail? I check e-mail **during the day**.* *When do you call your family? I call my family **on Sunday night**.* *When do you shop at the mall? I shop at the mall **in December**.*
b. Answer *how often* questions with **frequency expressions**.	*How often do you shop? I shop **once a week**.* *How often do you check e-mail? I check e-mail **three times a day**.*

▶ Grammar Application

Exercise 2.1 Statements

A Complete the sentences. Use the correct form of the verbs in parentheses. Use contractions when possible.

1. My family and friends _use_ (use) the computer for all sorts of things.
2. I _____ (use) an online dictionary for my classes.
3. My friend Mark _____ (shop) for clothes online.
4. Our classmates Marta and Raul _____ (check) their e-mail at the library.
5. My best friend Ana _____ (not be) on any social networking sites.
6. Ana and her sister Claudia _____ (not buy) groceries online.
7. My family _____ (spend) a lot of time online.
8. My brother Sam is online a lot, but he also _____ (interact) with our family.
9. Technology _____ (not hurt) my relationships.

B *Over to You* Rewrite three sentences in A so they are true about you. Then compare your sentences with a partner.

A I don't use an online dictionary. How about you?
B No, I don't, but I shop for clothes online.

Exercise 2.2 Frequency Adverbs

🔊 Listen to Alex and Karen talk about their online activities. Complete the sentences with the correct adverb of frequency.

1. Karen _hardly ever_ shops at the mall.
2. Karen _____ shops online.
3. Alex _____ shops online.
4. Karen _____ buys clothes online.
5. Karen _____ buys shoes online.
6. Karen _____ pays her bills online.
7. Karen _____ uses stamps.
8. Alex _____ goes to the post office.

Exercise 2.3 Time Expressions and Frequency Adverbs

Look at the things Brandon does online. Then complete the sentences. Circle the correct answer.

	Sun.	Mon.	Tue.	Wed.	Thu.	Fri.	Sat.
Watch videos	✓						
Read the news	✓	✓	✓	✓	✓	✓	
Shop for groceries	✓	✓					
Play games						✓	✓
Check e-mail	✓	✓	✓	✓	✓	✓	✓
Shop for clothes							

1. Brandon **occasionally** / **never** watches videos online.

2. He checks e-mail **sometimes / every day**.

3. He **seldom / often** reads the news online.

4. Brandon always plays games **on Thursday / on Saturday**.

5. He shops for groceries online **twice / once** a week.

6. He **hardly ever / never** plays games.

7. Brandon **always / rarely** checks e-mail.

8. He **never / sometimes** shops for clothes online.

Exercise 2.4 Questions

A Unscramble the words to make questions. Then write two questions of your own.

1. own / Do / a computer? / you   *Do you own a computer?*

2. the news / Do / read / you / online?   _____

3. often / shop online? / do / How / you   _____

4. usually / check / do / you / your / Where / e-mail?   _____

5. website? / your / favorite / is / What   _____

6. music? / you / Do / download / sometimes   _____

7. _____   _____

8. _____   _____

B *Group Work* Ask three classmates the questions in A. Answer your classmates' questions. Give extra information.

A *Do you own a computer?*

B *No, I don't. But I use the computers at the library. They're free!*

C *Pair Work* Tell a partner some things you learned in B.

I own a computer, but Peter doesn't. He uses the computers at the library.
Peter doesn't shop online, but I do.

3 | Time Clauses and Factual Conditionals

▶ Grammar Presentation

Time clauses in the present tense show the sequence of events. Factual conditionals describe things that are generally true in a certain situation.	***When I get home,*** *I check my e-mail.* ***If*** *it's late, I don't stay online for a long time.*

3.1 Time Clauses

Time Clause		Main Clause	Main Clause	Time Clause	
Before **After** **As soon as** **When**	**I get to work,**	I check my e-mail.	I check my e-mail	**before** **after** **as soon as** **when**	**I get to work.**

3.2 Factual Conditionals

Condition		Main Clause	Main Clause	Condition	
If	**I get an e-mail,**	I feel great!	I feel great	**if**	**I get an e-mail.**

3.3 Using Time Clauses

a. Use time clauses to say when the main clause happens.
Use *after* to introduce the first event.

SECOND EVENT   FIRST EVENT
*I check my e-mail **after** I get home.*

b. Use *as soon as* to introduce the first event when the second event happens immediately after.

FIRST EVENT   SECOND EVENT
***As soon as** I change my password, I forget it.*

c. Use *while* when events happen at the same time.

***While** I'm online, I check my e-mail.*

3.3 Using Time Clauses *(continued)*

d. *When* means "at almost the same time." Use *when* to introduce the first event.

SECOND EVENT   FIRST EVENT

*I visit social networking sites **when** I get home.*

e. Use *before* to introduce the second event.

SECOND EVENT   FIRST EVENT

***Before** I go to work, I check my e-mail.*

f. Use a comma if the time clause comes first.

***Before I go out,** I check my e-mail.*
***After I check my e-mail,** I read the news.*

g. A time clause by itself is not a complete sentence.

Before I go out, I turn off my computer.
~~Before I go out.~~ I turn off my computer.

3.4 Using Factual Conditionals

a. Use factual conditionals to describe things that are generally true in certain situations. The condition describes a situation. The main clause describes the result of the situation.

CONDITION   MAIN CLAUSE (RESULT)

***If I need a recipe,** I go to a cooking site.*

b. Use *if* when one event depends on another one happening.

If I need directions, I go to a map site.
(I go to a map site only because I need directions.)

c. A condition by itself is not a complete sentence.

***If I need directions,** I go to a map site.*
~~If I need directions.~~ I go to a map site.

▶ Grammar Application

Exercise 3.1 Time Clauses

A Read about Dave. Then complete the sentences. Circle the correct words.

- Dave gets out of bed and immediately turns on his computer.
- Then he checks his e-mail.
- He plays an online game. Then he goes to work.
- At work, Dave checks his e-mail many times a day.
- He gets home and immediately turns on his computer.
- He stays at home all evening and plays online games.
- He sometimes eats dinner and sits in front of his computer.
- He visits a social networking site. Then he goes to bed.

1. **As soon as**/ **Before** he gets out of bed in the morning, Dave turns on his computer.

2. **After / Before** he turns on his computer, he checks his e-mail.

3. He plays an online game **when / before** he goes to work.

4. **As soon as / While** he is at work, Dave checks his e-mail many times a day.

5. **Before / As soon as** Dave gets home, he turns on his computer again.

6. Dave usually plays online games **after / while** he is at home in the evening.

7. Dave sometimes eats dinner **while / after** he sits in front of his computer.

8. Dave visits a social networking site **before / as soon as** he goes to bed.

B *Pair Work*   Compare your behavior with Dave's. Discuss it with a partner.

A *As soon as I get out of bed in the morning, I turn on my computer. How about you?*
B *I turn my computer on after I make coffee.*

Exercise 3.2 Time Clauses and Factual Conditionals

Read the sentences about Internet research. Underline the time clause or condition. Circle the main clause.

1. When Dani has a school assignment, she often does research on the Internet.

2. She usually starts with a search engine when she does research.

3. If the topic is general, Dani thinks about the best words to put into the search engine.

4. For example, if the topic is "How to avoid identity theft," Dani uses *avoid identity theft*.

5. If she gets too many results, she puts quotation marks around the words "identity theft."

6. She clicks on a result if it comes from a useful site.

7. When she gets to the page, she usually skims the information first.

8. She reads the entire page if the information seems useful.

Exercise 3.3 More Factual Conditionals

A Match the task with the website you go to.

If you . . .

1. forget the actors in an old movie, __e__

2. need the definitions of some words, _____

3. want to know the score of a soccer game, _____

4. need to know the temperature in Chicago today, _____

5. need a book at the library, _____

6. drive to a new friend's house, _____

7. want to cook something new for dinner, _____

8. forget the birth date of a famous person, _____

you go to . . .

a. a sports site.

b. an online encyclopedia.

c. a recipe site.

d. your library's website.

e. a movie site.

f. an online dictionary.

g. a weather site.

h. a map site.

B *Over to You* Write conditional sentences about your own Internet research. Use the ideas in A or your own ideas. Then compare your sentences with a partner.

1. If I _forget the title of a book,_ I _go to an online bookstore_ .

2. If I _____
   I _____ .

3. If I _____
   I _____ .

4. I _____
   if I _____ .

5. I _____
   if I _____ .

4 Avoid Common Mistakes ⚠

1. Do not contract *not* with *am*.

I'm not
~~I amn't~~ online every day.

2. Use the correct form of *do* with singular and plural subjects.

doesn't
He ~~don't~~ own a computer.

3. Remember to form information questions correctly.

does the professor
Where ~~the professor does~~ post his comments?

4. Do not use *sometimes* after *not*.

Sometimes I do not check
~~I do not sometimes check~~ e-mail on the weekends.

5. Always use a comma if a time clause or a condition clause begins a sentence.

When I change my password, I write it down.
~~When I change my password I write it down.~~

Editing Task

Find and correct 10 more mistakes in this blog entry.

doesn't
My roommate Mark plays online games. He ~~don't~~ own a computer, so he goes to a computer lab. How often he does play? He plays every night! As soon as he finishes his homework he goes to the lab. He does not sometimes come home until midnight. He usually plays with people from around the world. He don't know the other players, but it doesn't matter. When Mark gets home he always has stories about the games he plays. Why people play these games? I do not understand. I amn't like Mark. I always play with people face-to-face when I play a game. When I play a game I know the people. Does many people play online games? How often you do play online games?

5 | Grammar for Writing

Using Simple Present with Time Clauses

Writers often use the simple present to talk about habits and routines. They use adverbs of frequency and time clauses to explain when these habits and routines happen. This helps to guide readers through an essay or through a process, such as a description of things we regularly do.

Remember:

- **Use the simple present to talk about habits, general truths, feelings, or thoughts.**

  My cell phone does not work well in this area.

- **Time clauses with *before, after, as soon as*, and *when* help show the order of ideas.**

  Before she has breakfast, she usually goes for a run.

  After she finishes work, Susie meets her friends.

- **Adverbs of frequency such as *never, sometimes*, and *often*, and frequency and time expressions such as *at night, during the day*, and *twice a day* show when and how often things happen.**

  He often checks his e-mail at work.

  Franco works from home three days a week.

Pre-writing Task

1 Read the paragraph below. When do the writer's friends use their cell phones? Is the writer the same or different?

My Friends and Their Cell Phones

My friends can't live without their cell phones. When they lose their cell phones, they become very nervous and upset. When I am with my friends, I feel that they do not always listen to me. I think it is because they text wherever they are. They text at restaurants, at parties, in class, and they even text on dates. Some of my friends send texts after they go to bed. As soon as they wake up, they check their messages. I rarely text. I prefer talking with people face-to-face.

2 Read the paragraph again. Underline the adverbs of frequency, the frequency expressions, and the time expression. Circle the time clauses.

Writing Task

1 *Write*   Use the paragraph in the Pre-writing Task to help you write about a habit or routine that your friends have. Use adverbs of frequency, frequency expressions, and time expressions. You can write about these things or use your own ideas.

- cell phone, Internet, or computer use
- eating or cooking habits
- exercise habits
- study habits
- TV habits
- weekend habits

Use these sentence starters to help you.

- My friends _____ as soon as they _____ .
- When they _____ , they _____ .
- After they _____ , they _____ .

2 *Self-Edit*   Use the editing tips below to improve your paragraph. Make any necessary changes.

1. Did you use the simple present to talk about habits and routines that happen frequently?
2. Did you use time clauses to show the order of ideas?
3. Did you use adverbs of frequency and time and frequency expressions to show when and how often things happen?
4. Did you avoid the mistakes in the Avoid Common Mistakes chart on page 13?

Present Progressive and Simple Present

Brainpower

1 Grammar in the Real World

A What do you do to improve your brain? Read the article from a health magazine. How are the people in the article improving their brains?

A Healthy Brain

It is 9:00 a.m. in Portland, Oregon. Hannah Lewis **is sitting** at her computer. She **is looking** at websites that interest her. Bill Green **is doing** a word puzzle at his
5 kitchen table. Kelly South **is eating** a bowl of cereal with blueberries. Nina Ritch **is brushing** her teeth after breakfast. Anthony Owens **is jogging** in the park. Olga Prince **is sitting** on the floor of her apartment with her
10 eyes closed. She **is thinking** beautiful, calm thoughts.

What do these people have in common? They all **live** in Portland, of course. In addition, they **are** all **improving** their brains. We **are learning** more about the brain every day. Do things like word puzzles and blueberries help
15 your brain? Many scientists **think** so. They **believe** that exercise, food, and other activities give people sharper memory and stronger, healthier brains.

These things **help** the brain in different ways. For example, the chemicals in blueberries **improve** your memory and your ability to learn. Calm thoughts **are** also good for your memory. Using interesting websites **makes** your brain stronger, and word puzzles 20 **make** it younger. Take Bill Green, the word-puzzle lover. He **is** 60, but his brain **is** like the brain of a 40-year-old. Exercise **helps** the brain, not just the body. Even oral health **is** connected to the health of the brain, so don't forget to brush your teeth!

Improving your brain **does not stop** at any particular time. 25 It can continue for life.

B *Comprehension Check* Match each item with its benefit.

1. Chemicals in blueberries _b_   a. helps the brain, not just the body.

2. Calm thoughts _____   b. improve your memory and ability to learn.

3. Word puzzles _____   c. are good for your memory.

4. Exercise _____   d. make your brain younger.

C *Notice* Find the sentences in the article. Circle the answer you find in the article.

1. It is 9:00 a.m. in Portland, Oregon. Hannah Lewis **sits / is sitting** at her computer.

2. They all **live / are living** in Portland, of course.

3. Exercise **helps / is helping** the brain, not just the body.

Which sentences describe things that are true in general? Which describe things in progress now or around the present time?

2 | Present Progressive

▶ Grammar Presentation

| The present progressive describes things that are in progress now or around the present time. | *Hannah **is sitting** at her computer.*
 *She **is exercising** a lot these days.* |

2.1 Affirmative and Negative Statements

AFFIRMATIVE			NEGATIVE			CONTRACTIONS		
Subject	*Be*	Verb + *-ing*	Subject	*Be + Not*	Verb + *-ing*	Affirmative	Negative	
I	am		I	am not		I'm	I'm not	
You We They	are	thinking.	You We They	are not	working.	You're We're They're	You're not We're not They're not	You aren't We aren't They aren't
He She It	is		He She It	is not		He's She's It's	He's not She's not It's not	He isn't She isn't It isn't

▶▶ Spelling Rules for Verbs Ending in *-ing*: See page A4.

Data from the Real World

| *Isn't* and *aren't* are more common after nouns than *'s not* and *'re not*. | *Bill and Olga **aren't** exercising.* |

2.2 Yes / No Questions and Short Answers

Be	Subject	Verb + -ing	Short Answers		
Am	I		Yes, I **am**.	No, I**'m not**.	
Are	you we they	**thinking**?	Yes, you **are**. Yes, we **are**. Yes, they **are**.	No, you**'re not**. No, we**'re not**. No, they**'re not**.	No, you **aren't**. No, we **aren't**. No, they **aren't**.
Is	he she it		Yes, he **is**. Yes, she **is**. Yes, it **is**.	No, he**'s not**. No, she**'s not**. No, it**'s not**.	No, he **isn't**. No, she **isn't**. No, it **isn't**.

Data from the Real World

The *'s not* and *'re not* contractions are more common in short answers than the *isn't* and *aren't* contractions.	*Are they exercising?* *No, they***'re not***.*

2.3 Information Questions and Answers

Wh- Word	Be	Subject	Verb + -ing	Answers
Who	**are**	you	**helping**?	I**'m helping** my brother.
What	**is**	your brother	**reading**?	He**'s reading** a news article.
Why	**are**	you	**jogging**?	Because I**'m trying** to improve my brainpower.

Wh- Word	Be	Verb + -ing	Answers
Who	**is**	**doing** a word puzzle?	Bill **is doing** a word puzzle.
What		**happening** at Kelly's house?	She**'s eating** blueberries.

2.4 Using Present Progressive

a. Use the present progressive for things in progress now or around the present time.

*Lorna***'s doing** *a puzzle right now.*
*I***'m reading** *a great book about brain training exercises.*

b. You can use the present progressive with time expressions that mean "right now" and "around now": *now, right now, at the moment, this week, these days, this month.*

She's working on her essay ***right now***.
He's exercising at the gym ***now***.
What's Felipe reading ***these days***?
I'm not doing anything interesting ***this week***.

2.4 Using Present Progressive *(continued)*

c. Use the full forms when writing in class. Use contractions in everyday speaking.	*Anthony **is not running** today.* *I'**m improving** my brainpower.*
d. You can contract *Wh-* words + *is* in informal speaking and writing.	***Who's** she working for?* ***Why's** the printer not working?*
You can contract *Wh-* words + *are* in speaking but **not** in formal writing.	*Say: "**What're** you doing?"* *Write: What **are** you doing?*

▶ # Grammar Application

Exercise 2.1 Statements

A Complete the article about improving brainpower. Use the correct form of the verb in parentheses. Use full forms.

There are a lot of ways to improve brainpower, such as doing word puzzles and exercising. Here are a few more things our readers are doing.

    Jane R., from Chicago, usually wears her watch on her right arm. This week she _is wearing_ (wear) it on
(1)
her left arm. Jane uses her right hand a lot, but now she

_____ (use) her left hand more.
(2)

    Joe M., from Dallas, usually drives to work. This month he _____
(3)
(not drive). Instead, he _____ (walk) to work every day. Also, he
(4)

_____ (run) three times a week this month.
(5)

    Isabel and Max V., from Los Angeles, _____ (go) to the gym together
(6)
every day this week. They _____ (try) to improve their mental and physical
(7)
health, too.

    Mario S., from Boston, always goes to bed after midnight, but this week he

_____ (not go) to bed so late. Also, he _____ (not eat)
(8)   (9)
junk food this week.

B *Over to You* Here are more things people do to improve their brainpower. Are you or people you know doing any of these things? Use the words to write sentences about you and people you know.

1. I / learn / a musical instrument   *I'm not learning a musical instrument.*

2. My best friend / learn / a musical instrument   _____

3. I / improve / my vocabulary   _____

4. My friends / improve / their vocabulary   _____

5. I / eat / less junk food   _____

6. My family / eat / less junk food   _____

7. I / study / math   _____

8. My co-workers / study / math   _____

Exercise 2.2 Questions and Answers

A Complete the questionnaire with the present progressive. Then write true answers.

1. a. _Are_ you _doing_ (do) anything to improve your brainpower right now?

Yes, I am. _____

  b. If yes, what _____ you _____ (do)? _____

2. a. _____ you _____ (try) to improve your health? _____

  b. If yes, what _____ you _____ (do)? _____

3. a. _____ you _____ (read) an interesting book? _____

  b. If yes, what _____ you _____ (read)? _____

  c. If no, _____ you _____ (read) anything else? _____

4. a. _____ you _____ (get) enough exercise right now? _____

  b. _____ you _____ (eat) the right kinds of food? _____

5. a. _____ your friends also _____ (take) classes? _____

  b. If yes, what _____ they _____ (study)? _____

6. a. _____ you and your classmates _____ (work) hard this semester?

_____

  b. _____ you all _____ (get) good grades? _____

B *Pair Work* Ask and answer the questions with a partner. How many of your answers are the same?

C *Pair Work* Change partners. Ask and answer questions about your first partner.

  A *Is Andrea doing anything to improve her brainpower right now?*

  B *Yes, she is. She's doing a lot! She's . . .*

3 | Simple Present and Present Progressive Compared

▶ Grammar Presentation

The simple present describes actions that are true in general or that happen regularly. The present progressive describes things that are happening now or around the present time.	*He **runs** every evening.* *He**'s running** right now.*

3.1 Using Simple Present and Present Progressive

a. Use the simple present to describe habits, routines, facts, or general truths.	*He **runs** in the park every day.* *Physical exercise **improves** the brain.*
Use the present progressive when an action is happening right now or around the present time.	*Mark **is doing** brain exercises these days.* *Right now, he**'s improving** his memory.* *He**'s** not **running** today.*
b. Use the simple present for situations that are true in general. The situations are settled, and we do not expect them to change.	*Exercise **helps** the brain, not just the body.* *Many people **don't get** enough exercise.*
The present progressive often describes temporary or changing actions.	*Lara **is eating** fish this week. (She's trying fish just for this week.)* *I**'m reading** a lot these days because I have an exam next week. (I'm reading a lot, but it's just for the exam.)*
c. Use the simple present with stative verbs, such as *like*, *know*, and *want*. Stative verbs do not describe actions. They describe states or situations.	*I **like** your new laptop.* *I don't **know** her e-mail address.* *I **want** a new cell phone.*
d. We do not usually use stative verbs in the present progressive, even if we are talking about right now.	*I'm liking your new laptop.* *I'm not knowing her e-mail address.* *I'm wanting a new cell phone.*
Exception Some stative verbs can be used in the present progressive. These verbs have an action meaning as well as a stative meaning.	*I **have** a new puzzle book. (have = own)* *He's **having** fish for lunch these days. (have = eat)* *I **think** blueberries are good for brain health. (think = believe)* *I'm **thinking** about a word problem. (think = using my mind)*

▶ Grammar Application

Exercise 3.1 Simple Present or Present Progressive?

Complete the article. Use the correct form of the verbs in parentheses. Use the simple present or the present progressive.

Rafael Sosa is only 12 years old, but he _*is getting ready*_ (get ready) (1) to go to college this week. At 12 years old, Rafael _____ (seem) (2) young for college, but Rafael is not a typical child. He _____ (3) (have) high intelligence-test scores, and he easily _____ (4) (understand) difficult ideas. He _____ (love) both science and music. (5)

Rafael _____ (write) music and _____ (design) (6) (7) electronic devices. He _____ (own) a lot of college textbooks, and (8) he _____ (read) engineering textbooks every day. These days, he (9) _____ (study) Japanese and Chinese. Rafael _____ (10) (11) (look) like a normal child, and he _____ (like) normal activities, too. (12)

He _____ (not spend) all his time reading and studying. Right now, he (13) _____ (play) soccer with a group of friends and _____ (14) (15) (have) a great time.

Exercise 3.2 Stative or Active?

Complete the conversation with the correct form of *have*, *look*, or *think*.
Use the simple present or the present progressive.

Clerk Can I help you?

Sally Yes. I *'m looking* for some brain-training software. What do you have?
$\qquad$ (1)

Clerk We _____ several good products for brain training. Here's one:
$\qquad$ (2)
Memory Plus.

Sally That _____ good. Does it work?
$\qquad$ (3)

Clerk I _____ all these products work well.
$\qquad$ (4)

Sally We're also _____ about our eight-year-old son. What do you
$\qquad$ (5)
_____ for children?
$\qquad$ (6)

Clerk Here's *Memory Plus Kids*.

Sally OK . . . I'm _____ for the
$\qquad$ (7)
price. . . .

Clerk Here it is: $25.

Sally That's not bad.

Clerk And we're _____ a sale
$\qquad$ (8)
this week, too. Twenty percent off
all week.

Sally OK. These _____ perfect.
$\qquad$ (9)
I'll take them.

Exercise 3.3 More Simple Present or Present Progressive?

A 🔊 Complete the text about a company's idea for market research with the correct form of the verbs in parentheses. Use the simple present or the present progressive. Then listen and check your answers.

Large corporations often _need_ (need) to
make decisions about new products. _Do_ people
(2)
want (want) this product? At the present
(2)
moment, _____ people _____ (look) for
(3)   (3)
a product like this in the stores? New products
_____ (cost) a lot of money and
(4)
_____ (need) a lot of research.
(5)
Corporations usually _____
(6)
(pay) experts to do market research. But
there is another way. One large corporation
_____ (try) a new idea this year. Every time the company _____
(7)   (8)
(need) market information for a new product, managers _____ (ask) the
(9)
employees for their opinions. The employees _____ (vote) yes or no on the
(10)
new idea. They _____ (tell) the managers, "I _____ (like) the
(11)   (12)
idea" or "I _____ (not like) the idea."
(13)
Manager Rick Jons said, "Right now we _____ (use) the collective
(14)
brain of our employees, and it _____ (seem) to work. The results are
(15)
more reliable than expensive market research."

B Imagine you are doing market research for a new dictionary. Write market research questions about dictionary use. Use the simple present or the present progressive.

1. how often / use a dictionary? _How often do you use a dictionary?_
2. look for / a better dictionary right now? _____
3. use a dictionary / in this class today? _____
4. prefer / an online dictionary or a paper one? _____
5. use a dictionary / when you prepare for tests? _____
6. prepare / for a test at the moment? _____

C *Group Work* Ask and answer the questions in B. Based on the results, what is the best dictionary for your group?

The best dictionary is an electronic one, like the one Sam is using in this class.

4 | Avoid Common Mistakes ⚠

1. Use a form of *be* with the present progressive.

am listening
I ~~listening~~ to the radio.

2. Use the *-ing* form of the verb with the present progressive.

is studying.
Fred ~~is study.~~

3. Spell the *-ing* form of the verb correctly. (See page 403 for more information.)

planning   *writing*   *enjoying*
plan → ~~planing~~   write → ~~writting~~   enjoy → ~~enjoing~~

4. Do not use the present progressive with verbs of stative meaning.

I have
~~I'm having~~ a very smart brother.

5. Use the simple present for habits, routines, and general truths. Use the present progressive for actions in progress now or around the present time.

I'm watching
Can you call me back later? I ~~watch~~ the news right now.

improves
Exercise ~~is improving~~ physical and mental health.

Editing Task

Find and correct nine more mistakes in this article about the brain.

resembles
      The human brain ~~is resembling~~ a computer. It stores a lot of information. But

humans are smarter than computers because we store things outside of our brains

that we do not need to store *in* our brains. For example, we ~~are~~ *store* storing information

in books, newspapers, images, and of course, computers. Another example is this *the*

5 text. At this moment, you are *reading* ~~read~~ this text. You are not needing to remember all

the information in it. The book is having the information, and you read it when you

need it. If you are *planning* ~~planing~~ an essay, you can make notes on paper or on a computer.

When you are *writing* ~~writting~~ the essay, you can read those notes again. If you are ~~studing~~ *studying*

a subject, you can go online and find information about it. The information is on the

10 Internet. We do not look into people's brains to see it. When we are *enjoying* ~~enjoing~~ an online

video, we *watch* ~~watching~~ something that is outside of the human brain. So computers are

like extensions[1] of our brains.

[1]**extension:** something added or extra

5 | Grammar for Writing ✏

Using Simple Present and Present Progressive Together

Writers often use the simple present and the present progressive together to compare the way things usually are with the way things are at the present time. They often use them in writing about a change in routine or habits.
Remember:

- **Use the simple present to describe habits or situations that are true not *only* at the present time. These things often happen or are general truths.**

  She usually <u>walks</u> to work. She <u>works</u> at a bank.

- **Use the present progressive to describe things that are happening *now* or around the present time.**

  He is <u>working</u> at the bank part-time while he goes to school. He usually works full-time.

- **Use the simple present with verbs of stative meaning.**

  Your idea <u>seems</u> good to me, and my husband <u>agrees</u> with me about that.

Pre-writing Task

1 Read the paragraph below. Write *SP* (simple present) or *PP* (present progressive) over each of the verbs in **bold**.

Unhealthy Holidays

> *PP*

These days I **am not taking** good care of myself. Most of the time I **eat** healthy

foods and I **exercise**, but currently I **am not living** a healthy lifestyle. I **work** at a big

department store. During the holidays, the store **gets** very busy. I **do not usually work**

overtime, but this holiday season I **am working** 16 hours every day. I **am making** more

money, but I **am not getting** enough sleep because I **am working** so much. I always

feel tired these days. Usually, I **enjoy** this time of year, but I **do not like** it this year. I **am**

looking forward to the end of the holiday season.

2 Read the paragraph again. Which of the verbs in **bold** are in progress now? Which describe habits?

in progress now		habits	
am not taking	_____	_____	_____
_____	_____	_____	_____
_____	_____	_____	_____
_____	_____	_____	

Writing Task

1 *Write* Use the paragraph in the Pre-writing Task to help you write about a change in routine or habits that you are experiencing these days. Use these sentence starters to help you.

- Usually I _____ , but these days _____ .
- Most of the time I _____ , but right now _____ .

2 *Self-Edit* Use the editing tips to improve your paragraph. Make any necessary changes.

1. Did you use the simple present and the present progressive to compare the way things usually are with the way things are now?
2. Did you use the simple present for things that often happen or are general truths?
3. Did you use the present progressive for things that are happening now?
4. Did you use the simple present for stative verbs or verbs with stative meaning?
5. Did you avoid the mistakes in the Avoid Common Mistakes chart on page 25?

Imperatives

What's Appropriate?

1 | Grammar in the Real World

A Who do you usually send e-mails to – friends, family, your professors? Do you write the same way to all of them? Read the web article about e-mailing. What are some good rules to follow in an e-mail to a professor?

How to Write an E-mail to a Professor

At some point in the school year, you may need to e-mail a professor. **Make sure** that you create a positive impression[1] by following these simple rules.

1. **Use** an e-mail address that shows your name. A fun e-mail address like soccerfan@cambridge.org does not look professional. Your e-mail may go to the professor's spam folder if there is no name in the e-mail address. **Use** your name or your school e-mail address instead.

2. **Write** the purpose of your e-mail in the subject line. **Do not write** "Hi" or "Question." **Include** your class name and time so your professor can immediately see this information.

3. **Always start** with a greeting, for example, "Dear Prof. Smith." **Never send** an e-mail, especially a request, without one. Your professor might be friendly and informal in class. However, it is not appropriate[2] to be informal in an e-mail to him or her, so **don't start** an e-mail with "Hi there!" or "What's up?"

4. **Be** brief,[3] clear, and specific. **Do not write** pages and pages of text. Remember, your professor is very busy. **Do not write** more than one screen.

5. **Always be** polite. **Say** "please" and "thank you." **Don't tell** your professor what to do. For example, **don't say** "Reply ASAP,[4]" "Please respond immediately," or "Urgent!!!" **Do not write** "I need the assignment. Please send it." Instead, **write** "Could you please e-mail me the assignment?" →

---

[1]**a positive impression:** a good opinion | [2]**appropriate:** right for a particular situation | [3]**be brief:** do not write a lot | [4]**ASAP:** an abbreviation for "as soon as possible"

6. **Don't use** text messaging abbreviations. This is an e-mail to a professor, not a friend, so **avoid** "LOL" (laughing out loud), "TTYL" (talk to you later), or smileys (☺).

7. **Thank** your professor at the end of the e-mail. **Write** something like "Thanks" or "Thanks for your time" and a polite ending like "See you in class on Tuesday" or "Best regards." **Remember** to type your name.

8. Finally, **don't forget** to check your grammar and spelling.

If you follow these rules, you will always communicate appropriately with your professors.

B *Comprehension Check* Read the e-mail. Label the parts *A* for appropriate or *NA* for not appropriate.

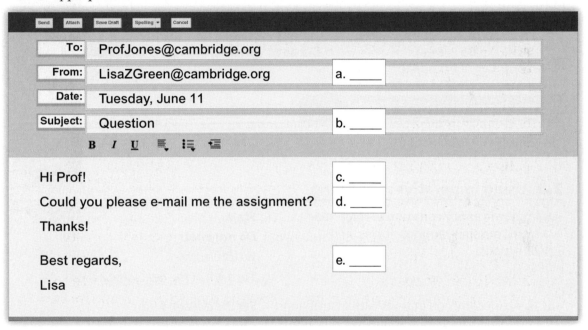

C *Notice* Find and write the sentences from the article with these meanings.

1. You need an e-mail address that shows your name.

_____

2. You need to write a greeting.

_____

3. It is not good to write pages and pages of text.

_____

4. Text messaging abbreviations are not appropriate.

_____

2 | Imperatives

▶ Grammar Presentation

Imperatives tell people to do things. For example, they can give instructions, directions to a place, or advice.	**Write** the purpose of your e-mail in the subject line. **Don't use** text messaging abbreviations.

2.1 Affirmative and Negative Statements

AFFIRMATIVE		NEGATIVE		
Base Form of Verb		**Do + Not**	**Base Form of Verb**	
Avoid	abbreviations.	**Don't**	**make**	demands.
Be	clear.	**Do not**	**write**	pages and pages of text.

Data from the Real World

Don't is much more common than *do not* in conversation. *Do not* is also very strong.

2.2 Using Imperatives in Writing

a. Imperatives are common in rules, road signs, orders, warnings, forms, and directions.	**Stop**. **Do not enter**. **Write** clearly. **Turn** left at the next intersection.
b. They are common in texts with instructions and advice, such as manuals, recipes, and magazine articles.	**Set** the date and time. **Chop** the onions. **Finish** your e-mail with something polite.
c. You can use *always* and *never* to give emphasis in writing.	**Always start** with a greeting. **Never send** an e-mail without one. (= Don't send.)
d. You can use imperatives with time clauses and with *if* clauses.	*Check the e-mail for spelling errors* **before you send it**.
Use a comma when the main clause is second.	**If you e-mail a professor,** *do not use texting language.*

2.3 Using Imperatives in Speaking and Informal Writing

a. Don't use imperatives to tell people you don't know well what to do. It can sound rude. Saying *please* doesn't make it polite.	***Send me*** ~~*the assignment,*~~ ***please.*** ***Could you please send me*** *the assignment?*
b. When you know people very well, you can use imperatives in everyday situations to ask for things, give instructions or advice, and to make offers or invitations.	***Give*** *me that pen.* ***Have*** *a cookie.* ***Call*** *the doctor.* ***Come over*** *Saturday.* ***Don't forget.***

▶ Grammar Application

Exercise 2.1 Forming Imperatives

A Complete the sentences in this advice column about using cell phones. Use the affirmative or negative imperative form of the verbs in the box.

answer	find	keep	leave	let	send	take	~~turn~~	~~use~~

Rules for Using Cell Phones

What is appropriate use of a cell phone at the office? Here are some simple rules to follow so that you do not upset your friends, co-workers, business clients, and most of all, your boss!

1. _Turn_ your cell phone ringer off in the office, or put it on vibrate.

2. _Don't use_ a pop song for a ring tone. It is not professional.

3. _____ unimportant calls go to voice mail. Your co-workers do not want to know what you are having for dinner tonight.

4. If your cell phone rings in a restroom, _____ it! People can hear you.

5. _____ your voice down. On a modern cell phone, there is no need to shout.

6. _____ text messages instead of making phone calls in the office. They are less annoying to other people.

7. _____ a quiet, private place to take calls, and be brief.

8. _____ a call in a meeting. Just _____ the room and take the call outside.

B *Over to You*   Rewrite two of the imperatives above using *Always* and two with *Never*. Compare with a partner.

I wrote, "Always turn your cell phone ringer off." How about you?

Exercise 2.2 Time Clauses and *If* Clauses

Use the words to write sentences about appropriate cell phone use. Use affirmative or negative imperatives. Write each sentence two different ways.

1. go into a meeting / turn your cell phone off

   Before *you go into a meeting, turn your cell phone off* .

   Turn your cell phone off before *you go into a meeting* .

2. be in a face-to-face meeting / check your messages

   When _____ .

   _____ when _____ .

3. be in a meeting / keep checking your messages

   If _____ .

   _____ if _____ .

4. be in a presentation / reply to a call or an e-mail

   When _____ .

   _____ when _____ .

5. be expecting a call / tell the other people in a meeting

   If _____ .

   _____ if _____ .

6. take a phone call in a meeting / leave the room to talk

   If _____ .

   _____ if _____ .

7. leave the room to take a call / be brief

   If _____ .

   _____ if _____ .

8. finish your call and come back to the room / apologize

   After _____ .

   _____ after _____ .

Exercise 2.3 Making Rules with Imperatives

A *Group Work* Discuss the questions about cell phone use. Do you all do the same things?

- When do you turn off your phone?
- When do you set it to vibrate?
- Do you take calls during dinner? At a restaurant?
- Do you talk on the phone when you're out with friends?
- Do you sometimes go someplace quiet to talk?
- Do you always answer your phone when someone calls you?

B *Group Work* Agree on four rules for using a cell phone appropriately. Write four rules with imperatives. Use time clauses and *if* clauses. Share your ideas with the class.

When you're in class, turn off your cell phone.

Exercise 2.4 Imperatives with Subject Pronouns

Data from the Real World

You can use *You* with imperatives in informal situations, for example, to decide who does what or to add emphasis and make the imperative stronger.	***You write*** the e-mail, and I'll check it. ***You take*** care now. ***Don't you scare*** me like that again!
You can use *somebody*, *someone*, *everybody*, and *everyone* with imperatives when there are a lot of people, for example, in class or at a party. Use *someone / somebody* to refer to one person. Use *everyone / everybody* to refer to a group.	***Someone*** turn off the lights. ***Everybody*** please sit down. ***Everyone*** please take your seats.

A Complete these sentences people might say while doing group activities in class. Use *you* and the imperative form of the verbs in parentheses.

1. _You write_____ (write) the questionnaire, and
   I'll write the answers. Does that sound fair?

2. Kate, _____ (do) some research on the Internet.

3. Dale, _____ (be) the salesperson, and Josh,
   _____ (play) the role of the customer.

4. We'll get a good grade, _____ (not worry).

5. Who's going to be A and B? I'll be A, and _____ (be) B.

6. Binh, _____ (be) the group leader, and Ana,
   _____ (take) notes.

7. Claudia, _____ (think) of a clever title for our report.

8. Asha, _____ (find) the pictures, and I'll print them.

B Complete the sentences from a student's presentation with *somebody/someone* or *everybody/everyone*.

1. _Everybody/Everyone_ take a seat, please.

2. _____ pass out the worksheet, OK?

3. Now, before I start, _____ choose a partner. We're going to do some pair work.

4. Do you need a pencil, Raffi? _____ hand this pencil to Raffi, please.

5. I want to use the projector now, so _____ turn off the lights, please.

6. _____ please write the answer on the board.

7. Now, _____ go back to your first partner and discuss the questions.

8. Before you leave the room, _____ take a handout.

3 | *Let's . . .*

▶ Grammar Presentation

Let's is a kind of imperative that makes suggestions or gives instructions to other people in a group you are in.	***Let's stop*** *there and talk about this in the next class.*

3.1 Affirmative and Negative Statements

AFFIRMATIVE	NEGATIVE
Let's + Base Form of Verb	***Let's not*** + Base Form of Verb
Let's stop there. **Let's be** clear.	**Let's not talk** about that now. **Let's not confuse** writing to friends and writing to professors.

Data from the Real World 🌐	
In very formal academic writing, people use *Let us*. Research shows that the negative form, *Let's not*, is not very common in academic writing or conversation.	***Let us*** *now* **look** *at the use of smart phones.*

3.2 Using Imperatives with *Let's*

a. You can use *Let's* to make suggestions to do things with other people.	***Let's meet*** *after class today.*
b. You can also use *Let's* to give instructions, for example, in class.	***Let's get started****.* ***Let's stop*** *there.* ***Let's discuss*** *this in the next class.*
c. You can soften (say in a nice way) *Let's* imperatives with *just* in speaking.	***Let's just*** *do this exercise, and then we can stop for today.*

Data from the Real World

Research shows that the most common expressions with *Let's* in formal academic speaking are *Let's say*, *Let's see*, and *Let's look at*. *Let's say* often means "imagine." *Let's see* gives you time to think.	***Let's say*** *you're writing to a professor. How do you start your e-mail?* *You can say this in several ways.* ***Let's see****, you can say . . .* *Are you still confused?* ***Let's look at*** *page 12.*

▶ Grammar Application

Exercise 3.1 Imperatives with *Let's* and *Let's Not*

A Some students are creating a questionnaire on text messaging. Complete the conversation with *Let's* or *Let's not* and the words in the box.

ask	put it first	~~start~~
choose a topic	see	write down

A OK. <u>Let's start</u> .
　　　　　(1)

B Right. _____ . How about text messaging?
　　　　　　　　(2)

A Yeah. That's a good topic for a questionnaire.

B All right. First, _____ some questions. What
　　　　　　　　　　　(3)
can we ask?

A _____ . Oh, here's one: "Do you ever text
　　　　(4)
friends when you're in class?"

B Yes, that sounds good, but _____ . It can be
　　　　　　　　　　　　　(5)
second. The first question can be: "Do you turn off your cell

phone in class?" What do you think?

A OK. So that's two questions. For question three, _____ : "Do you

(6)

ever text your instructors?"

B Sounds good!

B 🔊)) Listen to the rest of the conversation and write the missing words with
Let's / Let's not.

A OK, group, <u>*let's think*</u> of two more questions.

(1)

B Wait a minute. How will we distribute the questionnaire to everyone?

A _____ about that now. We can ask the teacher for help when

(2)

we're ready.

B I have some ideas for the presentation. _____ about that.

(3)

A _____ the questionnaire first. We still need two more questions.

(4)

C _____ How about: How many text messages do you send in a day?

(5)

A Great question. One more.

B What about: Do you sleep with your cell phone near you?

A I love it! That's six questions. _____ there for today, OK? Can we

(6)

meet again on Thursday or Friday?

C _____ on Friday. I have to work all day. Thursday's good.

(7)

Same time?

A OK, _____ on Thursday.

(8)

Exercise 3.2 Imperatives with *Let's* and *Let's Not*

Read the situations for preparing a group presentation on appropriate work
behavior. Write suggestions using *Let's / Let's not.*

1. You arrive at school to meet with your group. You are the group leader. Everyone is talking.
    You want to start the meeting. You say: OK, everybody, <u>*let's start the meeting.*</u>

2. One member wants to talk about handouts. You don't want to think about that until later.
    You say: <u>*Let's not think about that until later.*</u>

3. The group isn't sure what to do. You want to try brainstorming ideas. You say:
    Well, _____

4. The group thinks of many ideas. You want to divide the ideas up so that everyone presents
    something. You say: _____

5. A member thinks that the presentation might be too long. You don't want to worry about that now. You say: _____

6. Your group is deciding who will introduce the presentation. You want to vote on it. You say: I have an idea. _____

7. It's getting late and everyone seems tired. You want to stop for now and meet tomorrow. You say: It's getting late. _____

4 | Avoid Common Mistakes ⚠️

1. Negative imperatives are *Don't / Do not* + base form. *No* is not used in imperatives.

Don't use
~~No use~~ text messaging abbreviations.

2. *Do not* is two words, not one.

Do not
~~Donot~~ write pages and pages of text.

3. There is an apostrophe in *Don't* and *Let's*.

Don't
~~Dont~~ send text messages during class.

Editing Task

Find and correct four more mistakes in this article about how to set up a professional social networking profile.

Your Profile

What are the rules for making an appropriate social networking profile? First,
don't
~~dont~~ use a silly photo of yourself. Choose a professional-looking photo. For example, no use a picture of yourself at a party or at the beach. And dont use a photo that is too old. Update your photo every few years.

For your profile, donot give too much information. Always remember: Strangers are looking at your profile. Include details that can give possible employers a good impression.

A professional social networking profile is like a résumé, so no lie in your profile. Always be honest about your experience and your skills.

5 | Grammar for Writing

Using Imperatives with Time Clauses, *If*, *Always*, and *Never*

Writers often use imperatives with time clauses or with *if*, *always*, and *never* when writing instructions, directions, or advice. These signal to the reader what things to do and what to avoid in certain situations.

Remember:

- **Always and *never* make an imperative stronger.**

  Always turn your phone off before a business meeting. Never send text messages during the meeting.

- **Use imperatives with time clauses and *if* to explain when the instruction in your imperative is appropriate.**

  Don't call me when I'm in a meeting. If I'm in a meeting, send me an e-mail instead.

Pre-writing Task

1 Read the e-mail below. Underline the imperatives. Circle the imperatives with *always* and *never*.

Hi Matt,

Your trip to Japan next month sounds wonderful. There are some things you need to know about meeting people and communicating in Japan. Read these instructions. If you have any questions, call me.

1. Always bring a gift when you are invited to someone's home. Wrap the gift, and hand it to your hosts with both hands. If your hosts give you a gift, always accept it with both hands.

2. If someone invites you to their home, never wear shoes inside. Wear socks, and if your hosts give you slippers, put them on. When you put your shoes down, make the toes face the door. Always take off the slippers before you go into the bathroom, though, and put on the special bathroom slippers from your hosts.

3. If you take a train or bus in Japan, always set your cell phone to silent mode, or as the Japanese call it, "Manner Mode." Never talk loudly on the phone when you are on the train. It will annoy the other passengers. Instead, use e-mail or text messages.

> 4. If you are near elderly people on public transportation, always turn off your cell phone. The electromagnetic waves from the cell phone could affect medical equipment like pacemakers.
>
> Have a fantastic trip! Call me as soon as you get back.
>
> Hikumi

2 Rewrite these sentences from the e-mail in the Pre-writing Task. For sentences with *always*, use *never*. For sentences with *never*, use *always*.

1. Always bring a gift.

   Never go to a house without a gift.

2. Always accept the gift with both hands.

   _____

3. Never wear shoes inside.

   _____

4. Never talk loudly on the phone.

   _____

Writing Task

1 *Write* Use the e-mail in the Pre-writing Task to help you write an advice e-mail to a friend. Use *always*, *never*, *if*, and time clauses with *before*, *after*, *when*, or *as soon as*. You can write about:

- cell phone etiquette in another country.
- how to behave at meetings, business meals, or other situations.
- rules and etiquette for speaking and participating in class.

2 *Self-Edit* Use the editing tips to improve your e-mail. Make any necessary changes.

1. Did you use imperatives to signal what to do and what to avoid?
2. Did you use *always* and *never* to make your imperatives stronger?
3. Did you use time clauses and *if* to explain when to do something?
4. Did you avoid the mistakes in the Avoid Common Mistakes chart on page 37?

Simple Past
Entrepreneurs

1 Grammar in the Real World

A What is the best way to find information today? Read the article from a technology magazine. How did Google start?

The Story of Google

Who **started** Google?

Sergey Brin and Larry Page **started** the company. Sergey **came** from Moscow, Russia. He **moved** to the United States as a young
5 child and later **studied** mathematics and computer science. Larry **was** born in Michigan and **became** interested in computers as a child.

How **did** they **meet**?

They **met** in 1995 at Stanford University,
10 in California, where they **were** both computer science students. They **did not get along** at first, but they soon **became** friends.

What **happened** next?

They **designed** a new Internet search engine. At first, they **worked** in their
15 rooms in college. Then they **rented** a friend's garage because Sergey's roommate **complained** about the noise from his computers. Three years later, they **started** Google.

Was it an immediate success?

The company **was** an immediate success. Before Google, **there were** other search
20 engines, but Google soon **became** the most popular one. The company **grew** quickly. They **did not stop** at just one product. Very soon, **there were** other Google products, like Google Maps and Gmail. Ten years later, Google **earned** over $10 billion and **had** about 20,000 employees.

So what **did** people **do** before Google?

25 Before Google, people **went** to libraries. They **got** information from books. These days, they just "google" for information.

B *Comprehension Check* Answer the questions.

1. Where did Larry Page and Sergey Brin meet?
2. Why did they work in a garage?
3. What other products did Google start?
4. How many people worked at Google after 10 years?

C *Notice* Look at the article. Find the simple past forms of these verbs.

Group A

1. start _____
2. move _____
3. study _____
4. happen _____

Group B

5. come _____
6. be _____ , _____ (two forms)
7. become _____
8. meet _____

How are the two groups of verbs different?

2 | Simple Past

▶ Grammar Presentation

You can use the simple past to talk about completed events in the past.	*Brin and Page* **started** *Google in 1998.* *They* **did not get along** *at first.*

2.1 Affirmative Statements

Subject	Verb + -*ed* (Regular Verbs)
I You He / She / It We They	**started** in 1998. **employed** 20,000 people.

Subject	Irregular Verb
I You He / She / It We They	**grew** quickly. **became** successful.

▸▸ Spelling Rules for Regular Verbs in Simple Past: See page A4.   ▸▸ Irregular Verbs: See page A3.

Data from the Real World

Research shows that these are six of the most common **regular** simple past verbs.	work	work**ed**	live	live**d**
	start	start**ed**	try	tri**ed**
	call	call**ed**	plan	plan**ned**
Research shows that these are eight of the most common **irregular** simple past verbs.	have	**had**	go	**went**
	get	**got**	come	**came**
	do	**did**	take	**took**
	say	**said**	make	**made**

2.2 Negative Statements

Subject	Did + Not	Base Form of Verb	
I You He / She / It We They	**did not** **didn't**	**start**	slowly.

2.3 *Yes / No* Questions and Short Answers

Did	Subject	Base Form of Verb	
Did	I you he / she / it we they	**work** **start**	every day? quickly?

Short Answers	
Yes, I **did**. Yes, you **did**. Yes, he / she / it **did**. Yes, we **did**. Yes, they **did**.	No, I **didn't**. No, you **didn't**. No, he / she / it **didn't**. No, we **didn't**. No, they **didn't**.

2.4 Information Questions

Wh- Word	Did	Subject	Base Form of Verb
What **Where** **When** **Who** **Why**	**did**	I you he / she / it we they	**study**?

Wh- Word	Simple Past Verb	
What **Who**	**happened** **started**	next? the company?

2.5 Using Simple Past

a. Use the simple past to talk or write about:

- a single action that started and ended in the past.

*They **started** Google in 1998.*

×

past   now

- a repeated action or habit in the past.

*They **worked** in their rooms every day.*

× × ×

past   now

- a state, situation, or feeling in the past.

*They **didn't get along**.*

past   now

b. Time expressions can come at the start or end of a statement. Examples: *last week / month / year, 10 years ago, in 1998, yesterday*

Last year, *I joined a new company.*
*I joined a new company **last year**.*

Two years ago, *I graduated.*
*I graduated **two years ago**.*

c. Remember to use a comma when the time expression comes at the beginning of the sentence.

In 1998, *they started Google.*
*They started Google **in 1998**.*

d. Adverbs of frequency often come before the main verb in simple past statements. Some examples of adverbs of frequency are *never, rarely, sometimes, often, usually,* and *always*.

*They **often had** meetings at a pizza parlor.*
*They **sometimes worked** in their room.*

Data from the Real World

Research shows that *didn't* is not common in formal writing. Use *did not* instead. Writers sometimes use *didn't* in quotes of people speaking.

Formal writing
didn't
did not

Use *didn't* in conversation and informal writing. In conversation, *did not* can sound formal, emphatic, or argumentative.

Conversation
didn't
did not

▶ Grammar Application

Exercise 2.1 Statements and Questions

A Complete the article with the simple past form of the verbs in parentheses.

Ben Cohen and Jerry Greenfield _grew up_ (grow up)
(1)
in Merrick, Long Island. They _____met_____
(2)
(meet) in middle school, and they _____graduated_____
(3)
(graduate) from high school together. Their connections to
ice cream _____began_____ (begin) at an early age.
(4)
Ben _____drove_____ (drive) an ice cream truck in
(5)
high school. Jerry _____worked_____ (work) in his
(6)
college cafeteria as an ice cream scooper.

Ben _____tried_____ (try) different colleges, but he _____didn't graduate_____
(7)   (8)
(not graduate). At one time, he _____taught_____ (teach) crafts in a school. At
(9)
the school, he sometimes _____made_____ (make) ice cream with his students.
(10)
Jerry _____wanted_____ (want) to be a doctor. After he _____graduated_____
(11)   (12)
(graduate) from college, he _____applied_____ (apply) to medical school, but he was not
(13)
successful. During those years, Ben and Jerry _____stayed_____ (stay) friends.
(14)

After a few years, Ben and Jerry _____got_____ (go) into the food business
(15)
together. At first, they _____thought_____ (think) about making bagels, but the
(16)
equipment was expensive. So they _____chose_____ (choose) ice cream and
(17)
_____took_____ (take) a $5 class on ice-cream making.
(18)
Ben and Jerry _____saw_____ (see) an opportunity in Burlington,
(19)
Vermont. This college town _____didn't have_____ (not have) an ice cream shop. They
(20)
_____found_____ (find) an old gas station, and in 1978 they _____opened_____
(21)   (22)
(open) the first Ben & Jerry's store.

Ben & Jerry's quickly _____became_____ (become) popular because it
(23)
_____had_____ (have) great ice cream and a caring approach to the community.
(24)
On their first anniversary, they _____gave_____ (give) everyone free ice cream
(25)
as a "thank you." They still give away free ice cream every year on their anniversary.

B *Pair Work* Complete the *Yes/No* questions and answers about Ben and Jerry. Then ask and answer the questions with a partner. Give more information.

1. _Did_ Ben and Jerry _grow up_ (grow up) on Long Island?
   Yes, they did.

2. _____Did_____ they _____meet_____ (meet) in college?
   Yes, they did meet in college.

3. _____Did_____ Ben _____graduate_____ (graduate) from college?
   Ben did not graduatee

4. _____ Ben _____ (teach) in a school?
   _____

5. _____ Jerry _____ (go) to college?
   _____

6. _____ Jerry _____ (apply) to law school?
   _____

7. _____ they _____ (think) about making ice cream at first?
   _____

8. _____ they _____ (open) their first store in 1978?
   _____

A Did Ben and Jerry grow up on Long Island?
B Yes, they did. They grew up in Merrick, Long Island.

C Complete the information questions about Ben and Jerry. Use the answers to help you.

1. *A* Where _did Ben and Jerry grow up_ ?   *B* On Long Island.
2. *A* Where _____ ?   *B* In middle school.
3. *A* What _____ ?   *B* Crafts.
4. *A* What kind of course _____ ? *B* An ice cream-making course.
5. *A* How much _____ ?   *B* $5.
6. *A* When _____ ?   *B* In 1978.
7. *A* Why _____ ?   *B* The ice cream was good.
8. *A* What _____ ?   *B* Free ice cream.

D *Pair Work* Complete the information questions about Ben and Jerry. Write *did* in the blank, if necessary. If *did* is not necessary, write an **X**. Then take turns asking and answering the questions with a partner.

1. Who ____X____ drove an ice-cream truck in high school?

2. Who _____ worked in the college cafeteria?

3. What _____ he do in the cafeteria?

4. Who _____ graduated from college?

5. What _____ he want to study after college?

6. Who _____ taught in a school?

7. What _____ happened on their first anniversary?

8. Why _____ they open a store in Burlington?

Exercise 2.2 ◀)) Pronunciation Focus: Simple Past -*ed* Endings

Verbs ending in /t/ or /d/	/ɪd/ or /əd/	
If the base form of the verb ends with the sound /t/ or /d/, say -*ed* as an extra syllable /ɪd/ or /əd/.	/t/ ren**t** – rented	/d/ deci**de** – decided
Verbs ending in voiceless consonants	/t/	
If the base form of the verb ends in /f/, /k/, /p/, /s/, /ʃ/, and /tʃ/, say the -*ed* as /t/.	/f/ lau**gh** – laughed /s/ mi**ss** – missed /k/ loo**k** – looked /ʃ/ fini**sh** – finished /p/ sto**p** – stopped /tʃ/ wat**ch** – watched	
Verbs ending in voiced consonants or vowels	/d/	
If the base form of the verb ends in a voiced consonant or vowel, say the -*ed* endings as /d/.	li**ve** – lived lea**rn** – learned cha**nge** – changed pla**y** – played	

A ◀)) Listen and repeat the verbs with -*ed* endings in the chart above.

B ◀)) Circle the -*ed* endings that have an extra syllable (/ɪd/ or /əd/) in these sentences. Then listen, check, and repeat.

1. My family moved here six years ago.

2. I needed to earn some money, so I decided to get a job in a factory.

3. I earned a lot of money, but I wanted to be my own boss.

4. I studied business and learned how to start a company.

5. I finished the program and graduated two years ago.

6. Finally, I started my own business.

C *Over to You* Write six sentences about your own life. Use the ideas in B or your own ideas. Compare sentences with a partner. Ask your partner for more information.

> A *My family moved here in 1998.*
> B *Really? Where did you live before that?*

Exercise 2.3 Questions and Answers

A Complete the article with the simple past form of the verbs in parentheses.

Today Oprah Winfrey is one of the most successful broadcasters, publishers, and entrepreneurs in the world. However, she did not have an easy start in life. Oprah __had__ (1) (have) a difficult childhood. She _____ (2) (not have) a lot of opportunities as a child, but she was very intelligent. She _____ (3) (learn) to read before the age of 3. Her broadcasting career _____ (4) (begin) in high school. In 1971, she _____ (5) (go) to Tennessee State University. During high school and college, she _____ (6) (work) on a radio show. She also _____ (7) (work) at a TV station in Nashville as a student. At the age of 19, she _____ (8) (become) the first African-American woman news anchor[1] at the station.

In 1976, she _____ (9) (graduate) from college. That year, she _____ (10) (move) to Baltimore. There she _____ (11) (host) a TV talk show called *People Are Talking*. Eight years later, she _____ (12) (start) working on a morning show in Chicago. It _____ (13) (become) *The Oprah Winfrey Show*. Oprah's popularity _____ (14) (grow) quickly, and in 1986, it _____ (15) (become) a national show.

[1]**anchor:** a person who reports the news

B *Pair Work* Complete the questions about Oprah Winfrey. Use the information in the article. Then ask and answer the questions with a partner.

1. What kind of childhood _____ ?

2. What _____ before the age of 3?

3. Which university _____ ?

4. What _____ during high school and college?

5. What else _____ as a student?

6. Where _____ after college?

7. What _____ working on in Chicago?

8. When _____ a national show?

A *What kind of childhood did Oprah Winfrey have?*

B *She had a difficult childhood.*

3 | Simple Past of *Be* and *There Was / There Were*

▶ # Grammar Presentation

The simple past of *be* and *There was / There were* describe people, places, and things in the past.	*Oprah Winfrey* **was** *an intelligent child.* ***There were*** *millions of visitors to Oprah's website last month.*

3.1 Simple Past of *Be*: Affirmative and Negative Statements

AFFIRMATIVE			NEGATIVE		
Subject	***Was / Were***		**Subject**	***Was / Were + Not***	
I He / She / It	**was**	at Stanford University.	I He / She / It	**was not** **wasn't**	in Chicago.
You We They	**were**		You We They	**were not** **weren't**	

Data from the Real World 🌐

Research shows that *wasn't* and *weren't* are not common in academic writing. Use *was not* and *were not* instead.	**Academic writing** *wasn't / weren't* ▮ *was not / were not* ▬▬▬▬▬▬▬▬▬▬▬▬▬
Use *wasn't* and *weren't* in conversation, where they are very common.	**Conversation** *wasn't / weren't* ▬▬▬▬▬▬▬ *was not / were not* ▬▬

3.2 Simple Past of *Be*: *Yes* / *No* Questions and Short Answers

Was / *Were*	Subject		Short Answers	
Was	I he / she / it	popular?	Yes, I **was**. Yes, he / she / it **was**.	No, I **wasn't**. No, he / she / it **wasn't**.
Were	you we they		Yes, you **were**. Yes, we **were**. Yes, they **were**.	No, you **weren't**. No, we **weren't**. No, they **weren't**.

3.3 Information Questions with Simple Past of *Be*

Wh- Word	*Was* / *Were*	Subject
Who **Where** **What** **How**	**was**	I? he / she / it?
	were	you? we? they?

Wh- Word	*Was*	
Who **What**	**was**	there at the beginning? next for the company?

3.4 *There Was* / *There Were*

There Was / *Wasn't* + Singular or Noncount Noun	*There Were* / *Weren't* + Plural Noun
There was a problem. **There wasn't any** software. **There was no** software.	**There were** some problems. **There weren't any** programs. **There were no** programs.

3.5 Using *There Was* / *There Were*

a. Use *There was* (*not*) / *There were* (*not*) to talk about things that did or did not exist in the past.

Before Google, **there were** *other search engines.*

There was *no software.*

 Research shows that *There was* / *were no* is more common than *There wasn't* / *weren't any*.

b. The form of *be* always agrees with the noun that follows it.

There were *other search engines.*

There ~~was~~ *other search engines.*

▶ Grammar Application

Exercise 3.1 Statements

A Complete the lecture about Sarah Breedlove McWilliams Walker (1867–1919). Use the affirmative or negative form of *was*, *were*, *there was*, and *there were*.

Sarah Breedlove McWilliams Walker _was_ the first
₍₁₎
American female self-made millionaire. However, before she

became a millionaire, life _____ easy for young
₍₂₎

Sarah. Her parents died, and Sarah _____
₍₃₎

an orphan at the age of 7. For a time, Sarah and her sister

_____ cotton pickers. By the age of 14, Sarah
₍₄₎

_____ already married. Her husband died
₍₅₎

two years later, and she went to live with her brothers. They

_____ barbers.
₍₆₎

In the 1890s, Sarah lost some of her hair. At that time,

_____ no good products in the stores for this
₍₇₎

problem. In fact, _____ a lot of hair care
₍₈₎

products for African Americans in those days. Sarah saw that

_____ an opportunity for a new business, so
₍₉₎

she invented "Madam Walker's Wonderful Hair Grower."

The business grew. Soon _____ other "Madam
₍₁₀₎

Walker" products, such as shampoos and cosmetics. She

_____ very successful and eventually became
₍₁₁₎
a millionaire.

B 🔊 *Pair Work* Now listen to the lecture. It has some extra information about Madam Walker. Write down three new things you hear. Then tell your partner.

1. _____

2. _____

3. _____

A Her brothers were barbers in St. Louis.

B Right. And she worked for . . .

Exercise 3.2 Questions with *Be* and Other Verbs

A *Pair Work* Write the simple past questions. Then interview a classmate. Ask for more information as you talk.

1. What / be / your first job

   What was your first job?

2. be / it / a good job

   _____

3. What / be / your co-workers like

   _____

4. What / you / do there

   _____

5. Why / you / leave   _____

6. What / be / your best job   _____

7. Why / you / like it   _____

8. Where / be / your worst job _____

B *Pair Work* Write a short work history of your classmate.

Luis's first job was in a hotel in San Diego. He worked there from 2008 to 2009.

4 Avoid Common Mistakes ⚠

1. Use the simple past, not the simple present, when you write about the past.

    started
I start my first job in 2008.

2. After *did not* or *didn't*, use the base form of the verb, not the past form.

They didn't earned a lot of money.

3. Put time expressions at the beginning or end of a statement, not between the subject and the verb, and not between the verb and the object.

        yesterday
I bought yesterday a computer⌃.

   OR

Yesterday
⌃I bought yesterday a computer.

4. Use *there were* with plural nouns. Use *there was* with singular or noncount nouns.

   were   *was*
There was a lot of people. There were no information.

Editing Task

Find and correct nine more mistakes in the blog.

>   *moved*
>
> My family ~~move~~ from Mexico City to the United States in 1998. I went to Hamilton High School in Los Angeles. I did not knew anybody, and I did not had any friends here. I in 1999 met Jun. He became my first friend.
>
>   We in 2001 graduated. I got a job at a nice restaurant, but I did not enjoyed my job. Jun drove a taco truck, but he did not liked the food. I wanted to be my own boss, and I always liked food and cooking. Jun wanted his own business, too. Jun saw an opportunity. There was hungry office workers downtown at noon, but there weren't a nice place to eat. We bought a food truck and we start Food on the Move in 2003. Today, we have 5 trucks and 15 employees.

5 Grammar for Writing

Using Simple Past

Writers use the simple past to describe single actions, repeated actions, or states in the past. In a story about a person's life, the verbs that tell about past events, actions, or states should be in the past.

>   STATE   STATE   SINGLE ACTION
> *He <u>wanted</u> his own business, but he <u>did not have</u> the money for it. He <u>went</u> to the bank to ask for a loan.*

Writers often use the simple present at the end of a story to say what is different now.

>   PRESENT
> *... Today my uncle <u>has</u> a successful business.*

Remember:

Check the spelling of irregular verbs.

>   *got*   *paid*
> *He ~~getted~~ a loan from the bank. Then he ~~payed~~ a lot of money to start the business.*

Pre-writing Task

1 Read the paragraph below. Notice how the writer uses the simple past to describe the single actions, repeated actions, and states in a person's life.

My Boss Missolle

My boss, Missolle, came to the United States from Haiti 12 years ago. When she came here, she was very sad because her children were still in Haiti. She wanted them to come here, so she worked very hard. She practiced her English all the time. She worked during the day in a hair salon, and at night she cooked for people. She always thought about her children. When I met her five years ago, she was always happy and enthusiastic. I did not know her life was difficult. She told me that she did not want to show her true feelings. Now she is very happy because her children are here, and her life is good.

2 Read the paragraph again. Circle the verbs in the simple past, and underline the verbs in the simple present.

Writing Task

1 *Write* Use the paragraph in the Pre-writing Task to help you write about the life events of a person you know. What are some important past events in this person's life? How is this person's life different today?

2 *Self-Edit* Use the editing tips to improve your paragraph. Make any necessary changes.

1. Did you use the simple past for all single actions, repeated actions, and states?
2. Did you use the correct form for irregular verbs?
3. Did you avoid the mistakes in the Avoid Common Mistakes chart on page 51?

Simple Past, Time Clauses, *Used To*, and *Would*

Science and Society

1 | Grammar in the Real World

A What is your favorite ice cream flavor? Read the article from a textbook. How is ice cream today different from ice cream in the past?

Ice Cream: A Food Revolution

Science can have a great effect on society. Take ice cream, for example. Today, people 5 all over the world, rich or poor, eat ice cream. **Before there were modern refrigerators**, however, ice cream was a 10 luxury food.

Ice Cream Maker, 1800s

The history of ice cream goes back to ancient times. In 400 BCE,[1] Persians made a frozen dessert with noodles and fruit. There are early records of frozen milk and rice 15 in China from around 200 BCE. In 618 CE, King Tang of Shang (China) ate frozen buffalo milk.

Before refrigeration existed, people needed ice to make frozen desserts. For 20 example, in ancient Rome, people would go into the mountains and collect snow. They would bring it to the city and mix the snow with fruit. This was later called "sorbet."

When an Italian duchess[2] moved to France, she brought sorbet and other 25 frozen desserts with her. **After sorbet and ice cream became popular in France**, they spread to the rest of Europe. However, only the rich ate them.

In the twentieth century, ice cream 30 became easier to make and keep. **After scientists found better processes for freezing things**, ice cream became popular with all classes, rich and poor. Then, in the 1940s and 1950s, British chemists 35 discovered a new way to make ice cream. They put air into it. This made the ice cream bigger and softer. Now, ice cream was less expensive. It lasted longer, too. **As soon as ice cream became more available**, 40 people began to buy it more often.

Today, almost anyone, rich or poor, can buy ice cream and keep it at home. Ice cream is a universal dessert, popular all over the world. Together, traditional 45 ice cream makers and scientists created a food revolution.

[1]**BCE:** before common era | [2]**duchess:** a woman of very high social rank in some European countries

B *Comprehension Check* Circle the correct answer.

1. Persians made a frozen dessert with **noodles / buffalo milk**.

2. In ancient Rome, people mixed snow with **fruit / cream**.

3. A duchess brought sorbet to **Italy / France**.

4. British chemists invented ice cream that **lasted longer / had no air in it**.

C *Notice* Find the sentences in the article. Complete them with *after*, *before*, or *as soon as*.

1. _____ refrigeration existed, people needed ice to make frozen desserts.

2. _____ scientists found better processes for freezing things, ice cream became popular with all classes, rich and poor.

3. _____ ice cream became more available, people began to buy it more often.

In each sentence, two events happen. Circle the event that happened first.

2 | Time Clauses and the Order of Past Events

▶ Grammar Presentation

Time clauses can show the order of events in the past.	*After* scientists developed better processes for freezing things, ice cream became popular with everyone.

2.1 Time Clauses

a. A time clause can come first in a sentence. When it comes first, use a comma after it.

A time clause can also come second in a sentence. No comma is needed.

┌──────────── TIME CLAUSE ────────────┐ ┌── MAIN CLAUSE ──┐
After sorbet became popular in France, it spread to the rest of Europe.

┌──── MAIN CLAUSE ────┐ ┌──── TIME CLAUSE ────┐
Sorbet spread to the rest of Europe after it became popular in France.

b. Use *after* to introduce the first event.

                  FIRST EVENT   SECOND EVENT
After an Italian duchess brought ice cream to France, it became popular.

    SECOND EVENT   FIRST EVENT
Ice cream became popular after an Italian duchess brought it to France.

2.1 Time Clauses *(continued)*

c. Use *before* to introduce the second event.	SECOND EVENT FIRST EVENT **Before** *there were freezers, people needed ice to make frozen desserts.* FIRST EVENT SECOND EVENT *People needed ice to make frozen desserts* **before** *there were freezers.*
d. Use *when* to refer to the time that something started.	**When** *scientists found new ways to make ice cream, it became cheaper.* *Ice cream became cheaper* **when** *scientists found new ways to make it.*
e. Use *as soon as* to refer to something that happened right after or immediately after.	FIRST EVENT SECOND EVENT **As soon as** *scientists found ways to freeze things, people began buying more ice cream.* (Scientists invented ways to freeze things. Soon after, people started buying ice cream more often.)
f. Use *until* to refer to things that continued up to a certain time.	**Until** *people had refrigerators, it was difficult to keep food for a long time.* (Up to the time when people got refrigerators, it was difficult to keep food for a long time.)

▶ Grammar Application

Exercise 2.1 Time Clauses

Read the sentences about Ernest Hamwi, the possible inventor of the ice cream cone. Label the first event *1*, and the second event *2*.

                   2.   *1*

1. (Until Ernest Hamwi invented the ice cream cone,) (most people ate ice cream in a dish.)

2. Hamwi was a waffle seller at the 1904 World's Fair when he invented the ice cream cone.

3. When an ice-cream seller at the fair ran out of dishes, Hamwi rolled up a waffle.

4. The warm waffle turned hard when Hamwi filled it with ice cream.

5. As soon as they saw Hamwi's cones, all the other ice cream sellers started using them.

6. Before Hamwi started an ice cream cone business, he returned from the fair.

7. After Hamwi's story became popular, many people said that *they* invented the ice cream cone.

8. Another man, Italo Marchiony, invented an edible ice cream *cup* before Hamwi invented his cone.

Exercise 2.2 Time Words

Complete the sentences. Circle the correct answer.

1. **Before** / **After** people drove cars, they rode horses.

2. **When** / **Until** the Internet became popular, people wrote letters and sent faxes.

3. **Before** / **After** the first men landed on the moon in 1969, U.S. astronauts made five more trips to the moon between 1969 and 1972.

4. **As soon as** / **Before** people used digital cameras, they took photographs using film.

5. Public transportation changed completely **until** / **when** the first airlines began to operate.

6. People did not understand the solar system **when** / **until** scientists invented telescopes.[1]

7. **Before** / **As soon as** telephones existed, communication was very slow.

8. **As soon as** / **Until** scientists developed medicines such as vaccines,[2] public health improved rapidly.

[1]**telescope:** a device you look through to make objects that are far away look bigger | [2]**vaccine:** a special substance that you take into your body to prevent disease and that has a weak or dead form of the disease-causing organism

Exercise 2.3 Answering Questions with Time Clauses

Data from the Real World

We often answer information questions about time (e.g., *When...?*, *What time...?*, and *How long...?*) with time clauses. In conversation, these answers do not usually contain a main clause.	A *When did you start studying English?* B **After** *I got my job at the museum.* A *How long did you study at a community college?* B **Until** *I got my degree.*

A Listen to a radio interview with an inventor of a new printer. Match the interview questions with the answers.

1. When did you come to the United States? ___d___
2. So, when did you get the idea for your invention? _____
3. And how long did you study at college? _____
4. When did you build your first printer? _____
5. And when did you start your printer company? _____
6. So, when did you get the money for your company? _____
7. And when did the company start making a profit? _____

a. As soon as my first printer reached the stores.
b. After I graduated from college.
c. As soon as we got the money to start.
d. After I graduated from high school.
e. Until I got my degree.
f. When I was a student in college.
g. After I presented my idea to some banks and investors.

B 🔊 Listen again and check your answers.

Exercise 2.4 More Time Clauses

A Write sentences in the simple past about inventions and discoveries. Use an event in Column A, an event in Column B, and *after*, *before*, *when*, *until*, or *as soon as*.

A	**B**
1. TV / exist	people / start to fly more
2. cheap air travel / become possible	credit cards / become popular
3. everyone / have a cell phone	families / listen to the radio together
4. people / pay for things with cash or checks	millions of people / learn to drive
5. free education / be available	roads / become safer
6. traffic lights / come into our cities	people / buy food from small local stores
7. Ford / make the first mass-produced car	people / make calls from pay phones
8. the first supermarket / open	most people / not read or write

1. *Before TV existed, families listened to the radio together.*
2. Cheape air travel become possibl when people started to fly
3. Before everyone had a cell phone people made calls from pay phones
4. People paid for things with cash or checks until credit cards beconed
5. Free education was available when most people didn't read a write
6. *as soon* Traffic lights came into our cities, roads become safer
7. Ford made the first mass. produced car after millions of people learned
8. _____

B *Pair Work* Compare your sentences with a partner. How many different ways are there to say the same thing?

    A I wrote, "Before free education was available, most people did not read or write." What did you write?

    B I wrote, "Until free education was available, most people did not read or write."

C *Over to You* Think of three more sentences like the ones in B. Use your own ideas and the words *after*, *before*, *when*, *until*, or *as soon as*. Share your sentences with a partner.

Before there were microwave ovens, it took a long time to heat up food.

3 | Past with *Used To* and *Would*

▶ Grammar Presentation

Used to and *would* describe repeated past actions, habits, and situations.	Before we had the Internet, we **used to** go to the library a lot. Before there was refrigeration, people **would** use ice to keep food cool.

3.1 Statements with *Used To*

AFFIRMATIVE				NEGATIVE				
Subject	*Used To*	Base Form of Verb		Subject	*Did + Not*	*Use To*	Base Form of Verb	
I You He / She / It We They	**used to**	**listen**	to the radio.	I You He / She / It We They	**did not didn't**	**use to**	**watch**	TV.

Data from the Real World

Research shows that statements about the past with *didn't use to* are not very common. Instead, you can use the negative form of the simple past.	*I didn't watch a lot of TV when I was younger.*

3.2 *Yes / No* Questions and Short Answers with *Use To*

Did	Subject	*Use To*	Base Form of Verb		Short Answers		
Did	I you he / she / it we they	**use to**	**keep**	food cool with ice?	Yes, I **did**. Yes, you **did**. Yes, he / she / it **did**. Yes, we **did**. Yes, they **did**.	No, I **didn't**. No, you **didn't**. No, he / she / it **didn't**. No, we **didn't**. No, they **didn't**.	

Data from the Real World

Research shows that questions with *use to* are very rare. Instead, you can use questions with the simple past.	*In those days, did you keep food cool with ice?*

3.3 Information Questions with *Used To*

Wh- Word	*Did*	Subject	*Use To*	Base Form of Verb	
When **Why** **Where** **How often**	**did**	I you he / she / it we they	**use to**	**keep**	food cool with ice?

Wh- Word	*Used To*	Base Form of Verb	
Who	**used to**	**keep**	food cool with ice?

3.4 Statements with *Would*

AFFIRMATIVE			
	Subject	*Would*	Base Form of Verb	
In the past,	I you he / she / it we they	**would**	**build**	a fire to heat water.

NEGATIVE			
	Subject	*Would + Not*	Base Form of Verb	
In the past,	I you he / she / it we they	**would not** **wouldn't**	**bathe**	often.

Data from the Real World

Research shows that statements about the past with *wouldn't* are not very common. Instead, you can use the negative form of the simple past.	*In the past, they didn't bathe often.*

3.5 Information Questions with *Would*

Time Context	*Wh-* Word	*Would*	Subject	Base Form of Verb	
In the past,	**how** **where**	**would**	I you he/she/it we they	**heat**	the water?

Time Context	*Wh-* Word	*Would*	Base Form of Verb	
In the past,	**who**	**would**	**heat**	the water?

Data from the Real World

Research shows that *Yes/No* questions with *would* are very rare. Instead, you can use *Yes/No* questions with the simple past.	*In the past, did you always get information from the library?*

3.6 Using *Used To*

a. You can use *used to* for actions that happened regularly in the past. These actions do not happen now.	*My grandmother **used to wash** clothes by hand.*
b. You can use *used to* for states that were true in the past. These states are not true anymore.	*Air travel **used to be** very expensive. It is less expensive now.*
c. Do not use *used to* for things that happened only once.	*In the 1940s, chemists discovered a new way to make ice cream.* *In the 1940s, chemists used to discover a new way to make ice cream.*

3.7 Using *Would*

a. You can use *would* for actions that happened regularly in the past.	*When my grandparents were children, they **would listen** to the radio every night.*
b. Before you use *would*, first make the past time clear. Use a time expression, a simple past verb, or *used to*.	*In the old days, people **would wash** clothes by hand. They **would hang** them outside to dry. It used to be a day or more before the clothes **would dry**.*
c. With stative verbs, use *used to*, not *would*, to talk about the past. Some examples of stative verbs are *be, love, know*, and *want*.	*We **used to love** to eat ice cream. We would love to eat ice cream. Ice cream **used to be** a luxury. Ice cream would be a luxury.*

3.7 Using *Would* (continued)

d. Do not use *would* to talk about things that happened only once.	*Last week, Joe* **made** *green tea ice cream at home.* *Last week, Joe* ~~would make~~ *green tea ice cream at home.*
e. Use full forms in writing. Use contractions in speaking.	*In writing: We* **would sing** *songs or* **play** *games in the evening.* *In speaking: We***'d go** *to bed early.*

▶ Grammar Application

Exercise 3.1 *Used To*: Statements and Questions

A Complete the article. Use the correct form of *use to* or *used to* and the verbs in parentheses.

The Wisdom of Our Grandparents

College Weekly spoke to Joseph Green, an 87-year-old retired teacher, about the old days.

College Weekly What <u>did</u> people <u>use to do</u> (do) for
                                   (1)   (1)
fun before there was television?

Joseph Green Well, we <u>used to listen</u>
                                        (2)
(listen) to the radio in the evening.

    CW How <u>did</u> you <u>use to spend</u> (spend) your free time?
                          (3)   (3)

    JG Well, because there was no television, we <u>used to play</u>
                                                                    (4)
(play) games a lot.

    CW Who <u>did used to play</u> (play) with you?
                            (5)

    JG My brothers.

    CW It seems like people <u>used to have</u> (have) more free
                                          (6)
time in those days. . . .

    JG Not really. In fact, people <u>didn't use to have</u> (not have) a
                                              (7)
lot of free time. For example, my parents <u>used to work</u>
                                                      (8)
(work) six days a week.

    CW What was school like?

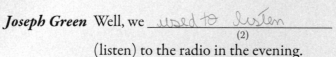
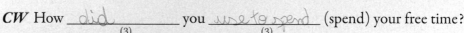

JG We ___used to write___ (write) with pencils and paper. And
   (9)
when I was in college, we ___used to take___ (take) notes in
                                    (10)
real notebooks, not on notebook computers!

CW ___Did___ you ___use to type___ (type) your papers?
      (11)   (11)

JG No, I didn't. Typewriters were too expensive. I

___used to write___ (write) all my papers in ink on lined paper.
      (12)

I ___used to get___ (get) so frustrated if I made a mistake
      (13)
because I had to start all over again!

B Write three affirmative sentences and one negative sentence about Mr. Green's life
before computers and TV. Compare your sentences with a partner.

1. _He used to play games in the evenings._

2. _His parents used to work six days a week_

3. _He didn't use To Type your parents_

4. _He used to listen radio_

5. _____

Exercise 3.2 *Would*, *Used To*, or *Simple Past*?

Complete the article about life before electricity. Use *used to* or *would* and the
verbs in parentheses, or use the simple past form of the verbs. Sometimes more
than one answer is correct.

Voltaic battery

Alessandro Volta ___invented___ (invent) the first battery in 1800.
                        (1)
How ___did___ people ___use to live___ (live) in the days before electricity?
      (2)   (2)
Most people ___used to burn___ (burn) oil lamps or candles for
                    (3)
light. When it got cold, they ___would make___ (make) open fires to
                                    (4)
keep warm. People ___would not travel___ (not travel) long distances.
                        (5)
Most people only ___used to visit___ (visit) neighbors or nearby relatives.
                        (6)

Before Volta's battery, many scientists ___didn't use to think___ (not think) that
                                                (7)
electricity was useful. And in the early days of electricity, some people ___used to think___
                                                                              (8)
(think) it was dangerous. They ___would be___ (be) afraid of it. Some people
                                    (9)
even ___used to believe___ (believe) that electricity had a bad effect on society. They
          (10)

would prefer (prefer) the simple life of the past. Soon, however, electricity
(11)
made (make) the world brighter, faster, and more comfortable.
(12)
Electricity in homes and industry _changed_ (change) the world in
(13)
many ways.

Exercise 3.3 *Would*: Questions and Statements

A Imagine that you can talk to a person who lived before there was electricity. Use the words
to make questions with *would*. Then add two questions of your own with *would*.

1. how / heat / your house? _Before electricity, how would you heat your house?_

2. how / light / your house? _Before electricity, how would you light your ―_

3. how / clean / your house? _" " how would you clean your house._

4. what / do / in the evenings? _" " what would you do in the_

5. what / play / with? _____

6. how / get / to work or school? _____

7. _____

8. _____

B *Over to You* Now write answers with *would* to the questions. Use your imagination.
When you finish, compare your answers with a partner.

We would build a fire to heat our house.

C *Group Work* Discuss how people used to live before the following inventions
changed society. Was life better or worse? Was it safer or more dangerous?
In what ways?

- computers
- cold medicine
- cars
- microwave ovens
- airplanes
- TV

*A Before computers existed, students used to write everything down with a
pencil or pen.*

B And they would copy everything again when they revised their papers.

C Student life was hard!

4 Avoid Common Mistakes ⚠

1. Use a subject in the time clause.

they
Before ⌃ invented electricity, people used candles.

2. Do not forget the *-d* in *used to* in affirmative statements.

used
When I was living in New York, I ~~use~~ to play in a rock band.

3. Use *use to* (without *-d*) in negative statements and in questions with *did*.

use
How did you ~~used~~ to heat your home?

Editing Task

Find and correct six more mistakes in this article from a magazine.

A New Invention

use
How did people ~~used~~ to wash dishes? People did not ~~used~~ to have dishwashers

before invented electricity, so they would wash dishes by hand. But did men and women

used to share the dishwashing equally? Not usually. Mostly it was women who did it.

used
Before there was electricity, women ~~use~~ to heat up water on the stove and use it for

5   washing dishes. It took hours and hours, and dishes often broke or chipped.

In 1886, one woman finally got tired of washing dishes by hand. "If nobody else

is going to invent a dishwashing machine," she said, "I'll do it myself." Her name was

Josephine Cochrane, a housewife and engineer's daughter who was tired of washing –

and sometimes breaking – her favorite dishes after dinner parties. Cochrane worked and

10   worked on her invention until 1893 when finally created a machine that washed dishes.

She showed the machine at the World's Fair that year. People operated it by hand, so it

was still hard work. After the fair ended, she started a company to make the machines.

When first tried to sell dishwashers, only restaurants and hotels bought them from

her. However, after electricity became more easily available, her company built electric

15   dishwashers for people to use in their homes. Today, homes around the world have

electric dishwashers.

5 | Grammar for Writing ✒

Using Past with *Used To* and *Would*

Writers use *used to* and *would* in texts where the past is contrasted with the present.
Remember:

- **Use time clauses to explain the order of events.**

  <u>Before there were computers,</u> students wrote their papers with pens.

- **Use *would* or *used to* to talk about things people did regularly.**

  When people wanted to listen to music, they <u>used to</u> put a cassette into a cassette player.
  Now, they listen on MP3 players.

Pre-writing Task

1 Read the paragraph below. Underline the past forms. <u>Double underline</u> the present forms.

Life Before Cell Phones

Because of cell phones, our lives are very different than they used to be. Today,
when we want to talk to someone, we can call them anytime. Before we had cell
phones, however, we had to wait until we were at home. In addition, before there were
cell phones, we did not know who called us. Now, we always know because cell phones
5 show the caller's number or name. Another change is that parents expect to be in
contact with their children more often. Before I had a cell phone, my parents would
not call me very frequently. After I purchased one, they used to call me many times
a day. They would always ask me, "Where are you?" Sometimes, I would not answer
my phone. This used to make my parents very angry! They would threaten to take
10 the phone away, but they never did. I am glad that things are different today, but cell
phones do not make everything easier.

2 Read the paragraph again and circle all the time clauses.

Writing Task

1 *Write* Use the paragraph in the Pre-writing Task to help you write about something that used to be different. How is life now? How was life different before? Use past forms, *used to* and *would*, and time clauses. You can write about one of these things or use your own ideas.

- the Internet
- MP3 players
- text messages
- social networking sites
- Internet dating
- air travel

2 *Self-Edit* Use the editing tips to improve your paragraph. Make any necessary changes.

1. Did you check that you used the past forms of your verbs correctly?
2. Did you use *used to* and *would*?
3. Did you use time phrases and time clauses?
4. Did you avoid the mistakes in the Avoid Common Mistakes chart on page 65?

Past Progressive

Memorable Events

1 Grammar in the Real World

A What were you doing on New Year's Eve, 1999? Read the blog. What were the bloggers doing?

The New Millennium - What Were You Doing?

January 1

I remember when we entered the new millennium[1] in 2000. At the end of 1999, some people **were worrying** about the Y2K bug. The Y2K bug was a concern because many computers **were using** only two digits for the year. So "00" could mean the year 1900 or the year 2000, for example. Anyway, I remember companies around the world
5 **were checking** their computer systems just in case there were problems. In the end, nothing happened!

Were you worrying about Y2K? I wasn't. Actually, I think most people **weren't worrying** about it much. In fact, I think on New Year's Eve, 1999, most people **were having** fun. So, that brings me to today's question: **What were *you* doing when the**
10 **new millennium arrived?**

posted by Claire Sanchez

---

3 Responses   leave a comment

Emily: I **was watching** TV with my family **when the millennium arrived**. We **were watching** a show about millennium celebrations in different parts of the world. The images were fantastic! In France, people **were watching** fireworks at the
15 Eiffel Tower. In Egypt, people **were attending** a concert at the pyramids. In Greece, people **were singing** and **dancing** in the streets.

Steve: In 1999, I **was going** to college in New York City. On New Year's Eve, my friends and I **were standing** in Times Square.
20 Over 2 million people were there, too! We **were** all **watching** the New Year's Eve ball drop **when 1999 became 2000**. The crowd was happy. Everyone **was feeling** very positive about the new millennium.

[1]**millennium:** a 1,000-year period; 2000 was the "new millennium"

> **Bao:** I **was working on December 31, 1999**. I **wasn't having** fun! I had a job as a
> 25 computer technician, and I **was working** from 6:00 p.m. to 2:00 a.m. on New Year's Eve.
> I **was sitting** by the phones in case the company's computers shut down. But nothing
> happened that night. **While I was sitting** at my desk, **I got** only one call. It was just my
> co-worker. He **wasn't doing** anything, either.

B *Comprehension Check* Answer the questions.

1. What were some people worrying about at the end of 1999?
2. What were people doing in Egypt when the millennium arrived?
3. How many people were standing in Times Square when the millennium arrived?
4. Why was Bao working on New Year's Eve, 1999?

C *Notice* Find the sentences in the blog. Circle the correct words.

1. I <u>watched / was watching</u> TV with my family when the millennium arrived.

2. On New Year's Eve, my friends and I <u>stood / were standing</u> in Times Square.

3. I <u>sat / was sitting</u> by the phones in case the company's computers shut down.

Do the sentences show an action that was in progress in the past or an action that happened only one time in the past?

2 | Past Progressive

▶ Grammar Presentation

The past progressive describes actions that were in progress at a time in the past.	*On December 31, we **were standing** in Times Square.*

2.1 Affirmative and Negative Statements

AFFIRMATIVE				NEGATIVE			
Subject	*Was / Were*	**Verb + -ing**		**Subject**	*Was / Were + Not*	**Verb + -ing**	
I He / She / It	**was**	**standing**	in Times Square.	I He / She / It	**was not** **wasn't**	**working**	in New York.
You We They	**were**			You We They	**were not** **weren't**		

▸▸ Spelling Rules for Verbs Ending in *-ing*: See page A4.

2.2 *Yes/No* Questions and Short Answers

Was/Were	Subject	Verb + -ing	
Was	I he/she/it		
Were	you we they	**standing**	in Times Square?

Short Answers		
Yes, I **was**. Yes, he/she/it **was**.	No, I **wasn't**. No, he/she/it **wasn't**.
Yes, you **were**. Yes, we **were**. Yes, they **were**.	No, you **weren't**. No, we **weren't**. No, they **weren't**.

2.3 Information Questions

Wh- Word	*Was/Were*	Subject	Verb + -ing
What How	**was**	I he/she/it	**doing**?
	were	you we they	

Wh- Word	*Was/Were*	Verb + -ing
Who What	**was**	**dancing** at the club? **happening** at 11 p.m.?

2.4 Using Past Progressive

a. Use the past progressive to talk about events in progress at a time in the past.

*They **were watching** TV at dinner time.*

b. Use time expressions with *in*, *at*, *on*, and *last* to talk about events in progress at specific times in the past.

*In 1999**, I was going to school.*
*We were shopping a lot **in December**.*
*We were standing in Times Square **at midnight**.*
*She wasn't working **on New Year's Eve**.*
*I wasn't working **on May 4**.*
*They weren't watching the game **last night**.*

Data from the Real World

Research shows that these are the verbs most frequently used with the past progressive in formal and informal writing and speaking. The verbs in **bold** are very frequent.

say	**wonder**	try	come	take	make
think	**ask**	look	work	watch	drive
talk	do	get	sit	read	wear

▶ Grammar Application

Exercise 2.1 Statements and Questions

A Complete the interview about New Year's Eve activities. Use the words in parentheses with the past progressive.

New Year's Eve Roundup

The *Morning Sun* asked three people:
"What were you doing last New Year's Eve?"

Sandy L., 25, Personal Trainer

Q What _were_ you _doing_ (do) last New Year's Eve?
    (1)   (1)

A I _was dancing_ (dance) and I _____ (have) a great time.
    (2)   (3)

Q Who _____ you _____ (celebrate) with?
         (4)   (4)

A My best friends and I _____ (celebrate) New Year's Eve at a party.
                          (5)

Amir A., 20, Salesperson

Q What _____ you _____ (do) last New Year's Eve?
          (6)   (6)

A I _____ (not have) fun! I _____ (sleep) last New Year's Eve!
       (7)   (8)

Q Why _____ you _____ (sleep)?
         (9)   (9)

A I was tired! At that time, I _____ (work) for several hours a day at a
                                 (10)

department store. The store _____ (have) a big sale on December 31.
                            (11)

Roberto R., 34, Computer Technician

Q _____ you _____ (do) anything fun last
      (12)   (12)
New Year's Eve?

A Not really. I _____ (drive) from New York to Chicago. My wife and
                  (13)

I _____ (move) to Chicago. We _____ (start) new jobs
  (14)   (15)
there.

Q That's too bad. Who _____ (drive)?
                         (16)

A I _____ (be). But we _____ (not feel) bad. In fact, we
       (17)   (18)

_____ (feel) very good about our new life in Chicago.
(19)

B *Group Work* Talk in groups about what you were doing last New Year's Eve. Ask *Yes / No* and information questions to get as many details as you can.

A *What were you doing last New Year's Eve?*
B *I was watching TV.*
C *Were you watching TV alone?*
B *No, I wasn't. I was watching TV with . . .*

Exercise 2.2 Time Expressions

A *Over to You* Complete the questions. Circle the correct words. Then answer the questions about yourself.

1. What were you doing **last** / **in** year?

   I was going to school and working part-time.

2. Where were you living **at** / **in** 2009?

   _____

3. What were you doing **on** / **in** the Fourth of July?

   _____

4. What were you doing **at** / **on** 9:00 a.m. yesterday?

   _____

5. Were you studying English **in** / **last** month?

   _____

6. Was your family living in the United States **on** / **in** 2000?

   _____

7. Who were you living with **at** / **in** the winter of 2010?

   _____

8. Were you working **at** / **on** 6:00 p.m. yesterday?

   _____

B *Pair Work* Compare the words you circled with a partner. Then discuss your answers to the questions.

A *What were you doing last year?*
B *I was studying English and living with my cousin.*

Exercise 2.3 More Statements and Questions

A 🔊 Listen to people talking about the most important time in their lives. When was the day or time? What were they doing? How were they feeling? Complete the chart.

Name	Day/Time	What he or she was doing	What he or she was feeling or thinking
1. Wei	*April 25, 2005*	1. 2.	1. 2.
2. Nick		1. *getting his driver's license*	1.
3. Ana	*the spring of 1999*	1. 2.	1. *thinking about her family* 2.

B *Pair Work* Now take turns telling your partner about the people in A.

A On April 25, 2005, Wei was . . .

B On . . . , Nick was getting his driver's license. He was feeling . . .

C *Over to You* What was an important day or time in your life? What were you doing? What were you thinking or feeling? Tell your partner.

An important day in my life was in July 2008, the first day of my new job. I was starting a new career, and I was feeling very . . .

3 | Using *When* and *While* with Past Progressive

▶ Grammar Presentation

Time clauses with *when* and *while* and the past progressive show something that was in progress; the main clause shows that something happened.	**The millennium arrived when I was watching TV** with my family. **While I was sitting** at my desk, **I got** only one call.

3.1 Past Progressive or Simple Past?

a. Use the past progressive for an action in progress in the past.	*On the day of the earthquake, we **were living** in San Francisco.*
b. Use the simple past for an action that happened one time and was completed.	*On the day of the earthquake, the power **went out**.*

3.2 Using Past Progressive and Simple Past with Time Clauses

a. Time clauses with *when* or *while* show when events happened.

MAIN CLAUSE   TIME CLAUSE
*The power went out **while we were riding the elevator**.*

MAIN CLAUSE   TIME CLAUSE
*We were riding the elevator **when the power went out**.*

b. Use *when* or *while* in a past progressive time clause to show an event that was in progress when a second event happened. Use the simple past in the main clause.

MAIN CLAUSE   TIME CLAUSE
SECOND EVENT   EVENT IN PROGRESS
*The power **went** out **when/while** we **were riding** the elevator.*

TIME CLAUSE   MAIN CLAUSE
EVENT IN PROGRESS   SECOND EVENT
***When/While** we **were riding** the elevator, the power **went** out.*

c. Use *when*, but not *while*, in a simple past time clause to show an event that happened while an event was already in progress. Use the past progressive in the main clause.

MAIN CLAUSE   TIME CLAUSE
EVENT IN PROGRESS   SECOND EVENT
*We **were riding** the elevator **when** the power **went** out.*

TIME CLAUSE   MAIN CLAUSE
SECOND EVENT   EVENT IN PROGRESS
***When** the power **went** out, we **were riding** the elevator.*

d. Time clauses usually come second.

When they come first, remember to use a comma.

Do not use a period after a time clause. It is not a complete sentence.

*We were riding the elevator **when the power went out**.*

***When the power went out,** we were riding the elevator.*

~~When the power went out.~~ We were riding the elevator.

e. You can also use time clauses in questions. Notice that the word order does not change.

SUBJECT   VERB
*Were you having fun **when the new millennium came**?*
*What was he doing **when the earthquake hit**?*
*Where were you sitting **when the power went out**?*

▶ # Grammar Application

Exercise 3.1 Past Progressive or Simple Past?

Complete the paragraph about a memorable event. Circle the correct verb.

    My most memorable experience (**was**)/ **was being**
                              (1)
the solar eclipse of 2009. In the summer of 2009, I

traveled / was traveling around Turkey. One day when
      (2)
I **read / was reading** the newspaper, I **saw / was seeing**
      (3)   (4)
an article about the eclipse. I **decided / was deciding** to
                     (5)

go to the town of Amasya because the article **said / was saying** it was the best place to
see it. I **arrived / was arriving** in town on the day of the eclipse. I **walked / was walking**
down the street when I **saw / was seeing** a group of people in the town square.
They **waited / were waiting** for the eclipse to start. I **decided / was deciding** to join
them. Then the eclipse **started / was starting** at around 2:00 in the afternoon. The shadow
of the moon moved across the sun, and the sky started to get dark. By 3:00, the sun was
completely covered. Everyone was quiet and amazed. Unfortunately, while the eclipse
happened / was happening, my cell phone rang! I was so embarrassed!

Exercise 3.2 Time Clauses

Correct the punctuation mistakes in these sentences.

1. When the power went out, I was cooking a big dinner.
2. When the millennium arrived. Bao was working for a computer company.
3. When the power went out we were riding home on the subway.
4. While we were standing in a doorway the ground started to shake.
5. When the earthquake hit she was driving across the bridge.
6. Asha was standing in the town square. When the sky got dark.
7. Rob was shopping. When the lights went out.
8. While we were working. The hurricane hit.

Exercise 3.3 More Time Clauses

A Complete the reader stories. Use the past progressive or simple past form of the
verbs in parentheses.

Reader Stories: A Day I Will Never Forget

I will never forget the 1989 San Francisco earthquake. My wife and I _were eating_ (eat) at a restaurant when the earthquake _____ (hit). We _____ (wait) for our food when the waiter _____ (shout), "It's a big one! Get under the table!" We _____ (stay) under the table and _____ (eat) our dinner while the ground _____ (shake).

– Samir N., Oakland, California

I will never forget Hurricane Henriette.

It wasn't dangerous, but it was very exciting. I

_____ (walk) on the beach when
(8)

a lifeguard _____ (tell) me to go
(9)

home. When I _____ (get) home,
(10)

my mother _____ (wait) for me.
(11)

She _____ (make) dinner when the electricity _____ (go)
(12)   (13)

out. We _____ (stay) inside and _____ (play) games by
(14)   (15)

candlelight while the storm _____ (crash) all around us.
(16)

– Luisa F., Acapulco, Mexico

B Use the words to write questions about the stories in A. Use the past progressive.

For Samir N.

1. What / do / ?   *What was Samir doing when the earthquake hit?*

2. Where / eat / ?   _____

3. What / eat / ?   _____

For Luisa F.

4. What / do / ?   _____

5. Where / walk / ?   _____

6. What / mother / do / ?   _____

C *Group Work* Talk about a memorable event in your life. What happened? What were you doing? Ask and answer questions about the event. Use information questions.

A *My most memorable experience was the snowstorm of 2010.*

B *What were you doing when it started snowing?*

A *When it started snowing, I was . . .*

C *Then what did you do?*

4 Avoid Common Mistakes ⚠

1. Use the correct form of *be* in the past progressive.

   were
   They ~~was~~ watching fireworks on New Year's Eve.

2. Use the correct word order in information questions in the past progressive.

   were the people
   Where ~~the people were~~ standing?

3. Use the past progressive for an event in progress.

   went   *were riding*
   The power ~~was going~~ out while they ~~rode~~ the elevator.

4. A time clause by itself is not a complete sentence.

   We stayed in the car while the ground was shaking.

   We stayed in the car. ~~While the ground was shaking.~~

5. If the time clause comes first in a sentence, use a comma.

   While they were looking at the map‚ they found their hotel.

Editing Task

Find and correct nine more mistakes in this excerpt of an interview with some people who remember the moon landing in 1969.

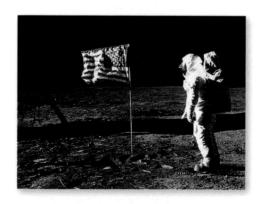

Interviewer   Where ~~you were~~ *were you* when *Apollo 11* landed

on the moon?

Maria   Well, in the summer of 1969 I was 19. I

was living in Mexico. On July 20, I was

5   sitting on the beach with an American

couple. We was listening to the radio.

When the speaker was announcing

the landing.

Interviewer   What you were doing when the astronauts landed on the moon?

10   **Tom**   At that time, my wife and I moved from Chicago to San Diego. To save money, we

stayed in campgrounds every night. We listened to the car radio at our campsite

when the astronauts stepped on the moon. That night, while we was lying on the

ground we looked up at the moon. We were being amazed!

5 | Grammar for Writing ✎

Using Past Progressive and Simple Past Together

Writers often use the past progressive to talk about things that were in progress at a certain time. They use the simple past to talk about things that happened one time and then were over. The past progressive provides readers with background information about the main events, which are in the simple past.
Remember:

- **Use the past progressive to talk about actions in progress in the past and the simple past to talk about completed actions.**

  *In the fall of 2007, Maria was studying English in her hometown.
  She came to Miami in 2008.*

- **Use the past progressive with *when* and *while* time clauses.**

  He suddenly arrived when they were talking about him. While they were eating dinner, José came to the door.

Pre-writing Task

1 Read the paragraph below. Underline the past progressive forms and circle the simple past forms.

When I Met My Husband

I was living in Chicago when I met my husband. We were both taking classes at the community college there. We were not in many classes together, but we were both taking the same math class. I was also working at a coffee shop near the college. One day, my husband walked in when I was working. I recognized him from our class, but we did not know each other's names. We said "Hi," but we did not say anything else. After that, he came in every day. Then, a few weeks later, I was walking out of class when he asked me for help with his homework. While I was helping him, we realized that we liked each other.

2 Read the paragraph again and double underline *while* and *when*. Notice what verb form follows *while*. What verb form follows *when*?

Writing Task

1 *Write*   Use the paragraph in the Pre-writing Task to help you write about a day when something special happened. What were you doing around that time? What were you doing at the exact time that thing happened? Use the past progressive, the simple past, and *when* and *while*. You can write about these things or use your own ideas.

- when you met an important person in your life
- when you started at a new school or company
- when you moved to a new place
- when you met someone famous or important

2 *Self-Edit*   Use the editing tips to improve your paragraph. Make any necessary changes.

1. Did you use the past progressive and the simple past to give background information in your story?
2. Did you use past progressive for actions in progress in the past and simple past for one-time, completed actions?
3. Did you use *when* and *while* time clauses with the past progressive?
4. Did you avoid the mistakes in the Avoid Common Mistakes chart on page 77?

Count and Noncount Nouns

Privacy Matters

1 | Grammar in the Real World

A What information about yourself do you want to keep private? Read the article from a website. What are some ways you can protect your personal information?

Identity Theft

Keep your identity private! Here are some facts about identity (ID) theft.

What Is Identity Theft?

Identity theft is the act of using someone's personal **information** without **permission**. ID thieves use the **information** to buy things. They also use it to get credit cards or to open other
5 types of accounts. Personal **information** includes your name and address. It also includes your Social Security number or credit card numbers. You can lose **money** because of ID theft. ID theft also causes **damage** to your reputation. Sometimes, people cannot get **work** or loans for school because of ID theft.

How Do Thieves Steal Your Identity?

10 • ID thieves go through your garbage and look for papers with **information** about you, such as bills.

• They steal your credit card number when you are buying something. This can happen with online shopping or in stores.

• They "phish" for **information**. Phishing is sending an e-mail that asks for your personal
15 **information**. The e-mail looks like it is from a bank or credit card company. It often asks you to go to a website and give your personal **information**.

How Can You Avoid ID Theft?

• Shred[1] bills and other documents that have personal **information** before you throw them away.

20 • If you shop online, only shop at well-known shopping sites. Only pay on secure[2] Web pages. URLs on secure pages begin with "https." (The s means "secure.")

• Never answer an unsolicited[3] e-mail. This is especially true if the e-mail looks like it is from a bank or a credit card company.

25 Follow this **advice**, and you can protect yourself from ID theft.

[1]**shred:** cut into very small pieces | [2]**secure:** safe | [3]**unsolicited:** not asked for

B *Comprehension Check* Match the kind of ID theft with the way to avoid it.

ID thieves . . .
1. take information from your garbage. _____
2. steal your credit card number online. _____
3. "phish" for information. _____

But you can . . .
a. only pay on secure websites.
b. not respond to an unsolicited e-mail.
c. shred your bills before you throw them away.

C *Notice* Find the sentences in the article and complete them with *a* or *an*. If no word goes in the blank, write **X**.

1. Identity theft is the act of using someone's personal information without

   ____*X*____ permission.

2. ID thieves go through your garbage and look for _____ papers.

3. They "phish" for _____ information.

4. Phishing is sending _____ e-mail that asks you for your personal information.

5. The e-mail looks like it is from _____ bank.

Which of the nouns are things you can count? Which are things you cannot count? Which noun is plural?

2 | Count Nouns and Noncount Nouns

▶ Grammar Presentation

Nouns are the names of people, places, and things. You can count most nouns (*an e-mail, three e-mails*); you cannot count certain nouns (*information, money*).	*A **website** gave us **information** about ID theft.*

2.1 Count Nouns

Count nouns refer to things you can count with numbers. They have a plural form.	*I do not have a credit card **account**.* *An ID thief opened two **accounts** in my name.* *The **bank** on First Street is closed.* *There are three **banks** on Oak Street.*

2.2 Noncount Nouns

Noncount nouns refer to things you *cannot* count with numbers. They have only one form.	*ID theft causes **damage** to your reputation.* *The computer records how much **money** you spend.* *I need some **advice**.*

2.3 Using Count Nouns

a. Singular count nouns always have a determiner before them. Determiners are words like *a, an, the, that, this, my,* or *our.*	I have ***a brother***. I have ~~brother~~. ***This computer*** is fast. ~~Computer~~ is fast.
b. You can use plural count nouns with or without a determiner. However, do not use *a* or *an* with plural nouns.	***Computers*** are not very expensive nowadays. ***These computers*** are not very expensive. Credit ***cards*** are convenient. I can't find ***my*** credit ***cards***. I can't find ~~a credit cards~~.

2.4 Using Noncount Nouns

a. Do not use plural forms like *-s* with noncount nouns.	They gave us ***information*** about ID theft. They gave us ~~informations~~ about ID theft.
b. Do not use numbers with noncount nouns.	She gave me ***advice*** about using my credit card. She gave me ~~two advices~~.
c. Do not use *a / an* with noncount nouns.	Because of ID theft, he can't get ***work***. Because of ID theft, he can't get ~~a work~~.
d. You can use other determiners (*my, some, this,* etc.) with noncount nouns.	They found ***some information*** on the Internet. ***Her advice*** was useful.
e. Use a singular verb form with noncount nouns.	***Safety is*** important to everyone. There ***was information*** about ID theft online.
f. Some noncount nouns also have a countable meaning. **Noncount Noun** / **Count Noun** coffee / coffees experience / experiences paper / papers	***Coffee*** is delicious. *(coffee as a drink)* We ordered two ***coffees***. *(two cups or orders of coffee)* They hired someone with ***experience***. *(knowledge about a job)* He has had a lot of interesting ***experiences***. *(things that he did or that happened to him)* She needed some ***paper*** to print on. *(material for writing or printing on)* She threw away some important ***papers***. *(individual documents)*

Data from the Real World

Some common noncount nouns in speaking and writing are:

advice	equipment	information	music	research	stuff
bread	evidence	knowledge	news	rice	traffic
cash	fun	luck	permission	safety	water
coffee	furniture	milk	progress	security	weather
damage	health	money	publicity	software	work

▶ Grammar Application

Exercise 2.1 Count or Noncount?

A Complete the chart. Check (✓) *Count* or *Noncount*. Then write the plural form of the count nouns.

Noun	Count	Noncount	Plural Form
1. passport	✓		*passports*
2. document			
3. information			
4. research			
5. equipment			
6. computer			
7. software			
8. credit card			
9. identity			
10. safety			
11. privacy			
12. e-mail			

B Complete the article. Where needed, write -s, -es, or -ies to make the nouns plural. Write ✗ if a plural form is not needed.

ID thieves use other people's identity*ies* without their permission _**✗**_ . Some ID
(1)   (2)
thieves look in the garbage for information_____ about you. Others use software_____ and
(3)   (4)
high-tech equipment_____ to steal your identity. (This is why Internet security_____ is so
(5)   (6)
important on home computer_____ today.) In addition, some ID thieves just steal your bag.
(7)
These thieves do not just take your money_____ . They also steal document_____ like your
(8)   (9)
driver's license and one or more of your credit card_____ . ID thieves love these!
(10)

If you want to protect your privacy _____ and avoid
₍₁₁₎
identity theft, do not carry these things in your wallet, pocket,
or purse:

- Your Social Security card or number.

- Your passport. If someone steals this, they could use it to
  commit a serious crime. These criminals threaten everyone's
  safety _____ .
  ₍₁₂₎

- Your computer, e-mail, and other password _____ . A lot of people keep this
  ₍₁₃₎
  information in their wallets, but it is a bad idea!

- Your birth certificate. With a little research _____ about you, a thief can use
  ₍₁₄₎
  your birth certificate to get a driver's license, credit cards, and even bank loans.

C *Pair Work* Think about an ID card you have (for example, your student ID card or
your driver's license), and discuss it with your partner. When do you use this card?
What kind of information does it have about you? How easy is it to steal or copy the
information on it?

Exercise 2.2 Count and Noncount Meanings

Complete the sentences. Use the correct form of the nouns in the box. Then write
C if the noun is a count noun or *NC* if it is a noncount noun.

crime	experience	life	paper

1. Marc had a bad _experience_ with ID theft. It damaged his reputation.   _C_

2. Now he can't get a job, even though he has a lot of _____ in   _____
   his field.

3. How did it happen? There were _____ in Marc's garbage that   _____
   had a lot of personal details about him.

4. In addition, he put his passwords down on _____ instead of   _____
   memorizing them.

5. Marc is not alone – there is a lot of Internet _____ nowadays.   _____

6. Some _____ affect us financially, but ID theft can hurt us   _____
   emotionally, too.

7. _____ is difficult for Marc right now.   _____

8. We all have difficult times in our _____ , but we can learn   _____
   from our mistakes.

Exercise 2.3 More Noncount Nouns

A Write these count nouns in the correct categories.

backpacks	CDs	jeans	soccer balls	sweaters
basketballs	computer games	movies	sofas	tables
briefcases	~~desks~~	shirts	suitcases	tennis rackets

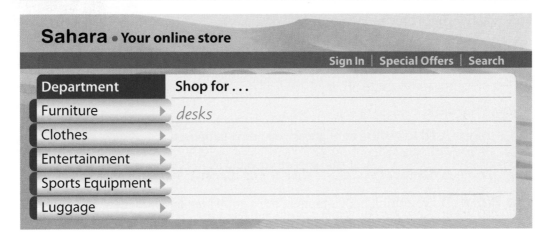

Sahara • Your online store

Sign In | Special Offers | Search

Department	Shop for . . .
Furniture ▶	*desks*
Clothes ▶	
Entertainment ▶	
Sports Equipment ▶	
Luggage ▶	

B *Pair Work* Now ask and answer questions with a partner about where things are in the store.

A *Where do you shop for sofas?*
B *You shop for sofas in the furniture department.*

Exercise 2.4 Common Noncount Nouns

A Complete the conversation about full-body scanners (machines that show what is on a person's body) with the correct form of the words in the box.

airport	fun	person	publicity	traveler
evidence	~~news~~	progress	traffic	

A There was a report on the *news* last night about those full-body scanners
    (1)
    at _____ . People were complaining about them. Do you know
          (2)
    anything about them?

B Not much, but there's a lot of _____ about them these days in the
                                  (3)
    media. I know some people are worried about the health issues. I mean, is the
    technology safe?

A Well, so far, there's no _____ that body scanners are dangerous.
                          (4)
    There's no real proof. In fact, I was reading somewhere that they're pretty safe.

B Hmm. Maybe they're better than what we had before. I guess

we're making _____ in keeping airports safe, but

                  (5)

what about the privacy issues?

A Right! Scanners can give some pretty personal information

about _____ . They're like an X-ray. They can

           (6)

show exactly what's on your body.

B And there are millions of _____ these days! With

                (7)

all the _____ at airports nowadays, security is

       (8)

taking a lot longer.

A Yeah. Airports used to be fun, but I guess you aren't supposed

to have _____ at the airport nowadays!

       (9)

B *Group Work* Do you think body scanners are a good idea or a bad idea? Use these
words to give your opinion.

Body scanners are good for . . .	security	convenience
Body scanners are bad for . . .	safety	personal information
I worry about . . .	privacy	my health
. . . is important to me.	crime	the government

I think they're a good idea. I worry about privacy, but safety is important to me.

3 | Noncount Nouns: Determiners and Measurement Words

▶ Grammar Presentation

You can use certain determiners and measurement words with noncount nouns.	*Can you give me **some advice** about spyware programs?* *She told me two interesting **pieces of news**.*

3.1 Noncount Nouns with Determiners

a. Use *a lot of, some,* and *a little* with noncount nouns in affirmative statements.	*There was **a lot of milk** in the refrigerator.* *I have **some** important **information** for you.* *Could I have **a little cream** in my coffee, please?*

3.1 Noncount Nouns with Determiners (continued)

b. Use *much*, *a lot of*, and *any* with noncount nouns in questions.	Was there **much furniture** in the apartment?
	Is there **a lot of traffic** at 5:00 p.m.?
	Are you making **any progress** with your English these days?
c. Use *some* and *a little* for questions that are offers and requests.	Would you like **some tea**?
	Would you like **a little sugar** in your coffee?
d. Use *not much*, *not a lot*, and *not any* with noncount nouns in negative statements.	There's **not much juice** left in your glass.
	She does**n't** earn **a lot of money** in her present job.
	We did**n't** do **any work** yesterday.
e. Do not use *much* or *a little* with count nouns.	We don't have **much time** left.
	We don't have ~~much hours~~ left.
	There's **a little coffee** in the cup.
	There's ~~a little cups~~ on the table.
f. Do not use *many* or *a few* with noncount nouns.	There is **not much news** today.
	There is ~~not many news~~ today.
	I sold **some furniture** that I didn't need.
	I sold ~~a few furniture~~.
g. You can use *a lot of*, *some*, and *any* with both count and noncount nouns.	There is **a lot of** Internet **crime** nowadays.
	They caught **a lot of** ID **thieves** last year.
	There's **some** new **furniture** at the apartment.
	We bought **some** new **chairs**.
	We don't have **any** new **equipment**.
	There aren't **any** new **computers** at the school.

3.2 *Too Many / Much* and *Enough*

a. Use *too many* with count nouns and *too much* with noncount nouns to say "more than you want."	**Too many people** came to the lecture on Internet privacy. Some of them had to stand.
	There is **too much information** about us on databases. It's scary!
b. Use *enough* with count and noncount nouns to say "the amount you need."	We have **enough eggs** in the refrigerator.
	We have **enough information** on the problem.
	We don't have **enough potatoes**.
	We don't have **enough milk**. We need to buy some.

3.3 Noncount Nouns with Measurement Words

a. Containers

a **box** of	cereal pasta
a **package** of	sugar rice coffee
a **can** of	soup tuna

a **bottle** of	water juice
a **glass** of	milk juice water
a **carton** of	milk juice

Portions

a **piece** of	cake bread pie candy
a **slice** of	pizza bread cake cheese turkey
a **scoop** of	ice cream sorbet

Measurements

a **gallon** of	milk gas
a **pound** of	butter sugar coffee meat
a **cup** of	sugar milk coffee tea

Shapes

a **bar** of	soap chocolate
a **loaf** of	bread
a **sheet** of	paper
a **tube** of	toothpaste

b. You can also use *piece* with non-food items, such as *advice, information, news, music, equipment, evidence, furniture, tape*, and *research*.

*He told us **an** interesting **piece of news**.*
*They gave us **a** helpful **piece of advice**.*

c. Measurement words can be singular or plural.

*I bought **a pound of butter** and **three loaves of bread**.*

▶ Grammar Application

Exercise 3.1 Determiners and *Too* and *Enough*

A Complete the web article. Circle the correct words.

What Are Cookies? by Sue Wilder

(Many)/Much computer security experts are concerned about the use of cookies on the
(1)
Internet. A "cookie" is a piece of information stored in your computer. It contains information on all

the Internet sites that you look at. **A lot of/Much** websites send a cookie to your computer when
(2)
you visit them. Companies with websites can get **many/a lot of** information about consumers
(3)
with cookies. For example, an online store sends a cookie that gives the store **much/some**
(4)
details about who you are. The next time you visit the store, it remembers your details.

There is **a lot of/many** concern about cookies because they are a privacy issue. However,
(5)
some/much experts do not think that there are **some/any** problems to worry about. These
(6)   (7)
experts say cookies do not have **any/much** harmful effects on your computer; that is, they do not
(8)
contain **a few/any** viruses.
(9)
You can change a setting on your computer to block cookies. However, one study showed

that **not many/a few** computer users do this.
(10)

B Complete the comments on the article in A with *too much*, *too many*, or *enough*.

Comments (3)

Tom S., Canada: The writer spent <u>*too much*</u> time on cookies. She didn't spend
(1)
_____ time on social networking sites. _____ computer users
(2)   (3)
think those sites are private, but they're not.

Amy G., New York: I agree with Tom. Not _____ computer users understand
(4)
how social networking sites work. Some of those sites give out _____
(5)
information. There isn't _____ privacy!
(6)

Maria R., Houston: It's not the site's fault if you put up _____ silly pictures
(7)
of yourself! And you can set your profile to "private." It only takes a minute, so everyone has

_____ time to do that.
(8)

Exercise 3.2 Measurement Words

A Match the measurement words and the nouns.

1. a piece of ____*b*____   a. rice   5. a cup of _____   e. chocolate

2. a package of _____   b̶. cake   6. a bar of _____   f. paper

3. a glass of _____   c. pizza   7. a scoop of _____   g. coffee

4. a slice of _____   d. milk   8. a sheet of _____   h. ice cream

B 🔊 Complete the article about privacy issues and shopping. Use the correct form of the words in the box. Then listen and check your answers.

bar	box	carton	l̶o̶a̶f̶	pound
bottle	can	gallon	package	tube

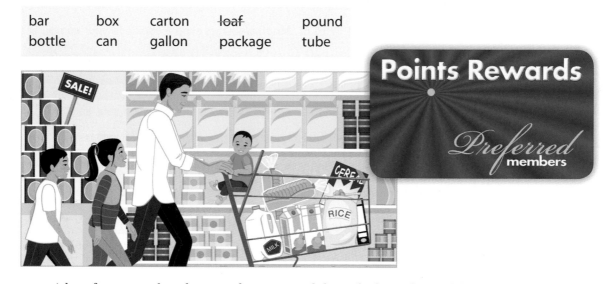

A lot of supermarket shoppers have store club cards these days. Club cards give you lower prices or points for shopping. To get the lower prices, you swipe your card every time you make a purchase. The card tells the store who you are and what you buy. Here is an example. Shopper 1 buys three ___*loaves*___ of bread, two
(1)
_____ of juice, a _____ of milk, a _____
(2)   (3)   (4)
of toothpaste, a _____ of rice, a _____ of soap, and two
(5)   (6)
_____ of cereal each week. What does that tell the store? It probably
(7)
tells the store that he has a big family, and he probably has children. Shopper 2 buys

seven _____ of water, seven _____ of tuna, and a
(8)   (9)
_____ of turkey each week. What does this tell the store? Shopper 2
(10)
is probably single, and she is probably dieting or is concerned with her health. How does the store use this information? It sends advertising to the shoppers with specific information about the products that they buy. This gets them back into the store to buy more products.

C *Pair Work* Ask and answer questions with a partner about the things that the shoppers in B bought or did not buy. Use *How much*, *How many*, *any*, and measurement words.

A *How many loaves of bread does Shopper 1 buy each week?*

B *Shopper 1 buys three loaves of bread. How much milk does Shopper 2 buy each week?*

A *Shopper 2 doesn't buy any milk.*

D *Group Work* What did you buy this week? Write three sentences on a piece of paper. Do not write your name! Read the papers in groups and try to guess who wrote them.

This person bought three loaves of bread and two tubes of toothpaste. It might be Nicki because she has a big family.

4 Avoid Common Mistakes ⚠

1. A singular count noun needs a determiner.

        a
I do not have ∧ card for this store.

2. Do not use *a / an* with a noncount noun.

You need a̶ permission to use my credit card.

3. Do not use a noncount noun in the plural.

        information
The supermarket has personal ~~informations~~ about shoppers.

4. Do not use *many* or *too many* with a noncount noun.

    a lot of
There was ~~many~~ Internet crime last year.

5. Do not use *much* with a noncount noun in affirmative statements.

    a lot of
She had ~~much~~ cash in her wallet when somebody stole it.

Editing Task

Find eight more mistakes in this article about Internet spyware.

        a
Spyware is ∧ type of computer software. Someone sends it to computer without your knowledges or permissions. It takes control of your computer. It can make your computer run slowly or even crash. Spyware often records an information about your computer use. It gives the information to advertisers or other people who want to collect informations on you. Many spyware sneaks into your computer when you are downloading and installing programs from

the Internet. One way to prevent a spyware is to put security settings on your Internet browser. Set your browser to a medium or higher setting. There is also much software you can buy that blocks spyware.

5 | Grammar for Writing

Using Count and Noncount Nouns with Determiners and Measurement Words

Writers use noncount nouns to refer to general ideas, which they then go on to give details about.

Remember:

- **Use noncount nouns to refer to a general idea.**

  An important issue today is <u>privacy</u>. Websites, stores, and other places all gather details about our habits and preferences.

- **Use *a little*, *too much*, and *not much* only with noncount nouns.**

- **Use *many* and *a few* only with count nouns.**

- **Use measurement words to describe amounts of noncount nouns.**

  I have a lot of <u>pieces of</u> paper in my wallet. I keep a small <u>bottle of</u> hand cleaner in my purse.

Pre-writing Task

Read the paragraph below. Underline the count nouns in **bold** and circle the noncount nouns in **bold**.

Passwords and Personal Identification Numbers

Protecting personal **information** is a major problem today, and it is especially important to protect **details** like passwords and PINs or personal identification numbers. Most people have a few PINs and a lot of different passwords. For example, they use one PIN to get **money** from the **bank** and another PIN to pay bills by

5 telephone. In addition, they use **passwords** to get onto websites and access their **e-mail**. One problem is that many people use the same password for all their accounts and websites. This is because it is easy to forget different passwords or PINs. However, this is a bad **idea**. Common **advice** these days is to have a few passwords and PINs and change them often. Do not use passwords that are easy to guess, such as "1234" or your

10 pet's name. Harder passwords make it more difficult for people to steal your **identity**.

Writing Task

1 *Write* Use the paragraph in the Pre-writing Task to help you write about how an idea or issue affects people. Use noncount nouns to refer to the general idea, and then give details about the idea. You can write about:

- online privacy
- protecting personal information
- traffic
- airport security
- safety where you live
- your own idea

2 *Self-Edit* Use the editing tips to improve your paragraph. Make any necessary changes.

1. Did you use noncount nouns to refer to a general idea and then go on to give details about the idea?
2. Did you use the correct determiner (*a little*, *too much*, *a few*, etc.) with count and noncount nouns?
3. Did you use measurement words to explain amounts of noncount nouns?
4. Did you avoid the mistakes in the Avoid Common Mistakes chart on page 91?

Articles

The Media

1 Grammar in the Real World

A Where do you get the news? Read the web article about how people get their news from a website. What are some ways that people get news online?

Getting the News

⟨●●●●⟩

How do you get **the** news? Do you get it from TV, **the** Internet, **the** radio, or **the** newspaper? For many people, this is changing.

Take Christina Jackson, **an** office manager in Dallas, for example. Each morning, she checks her phone for news headlines. Then she checks **a** social networking site and her
5 e-mail to see what news stories her friends are discussing. In other words, friends are becoming **the** new news editors.

A recent study analyzed how people get their news. It found that news is becoming **an** online social activity. Seventy-one percent of adults get their news online, and many of them leave comments for other people to read. They write their reactions to news
10 stories on social networking sites, and they e-mail their friends links to interesting stories on news sites.

The study also showed that people like to customize their news. For example, they go to **a** news site and list **the** type of stories they want to read. They tell **the** news site if they want pictures or video, and they also get news stories sent to them by e-mail. A lot of
15 people go to **a** wide range of sites to get their news. Fifty-seven percent visit between two and five different news sites each day. Some popular news subjects online are **the** weather, health, business, and international events.

Even though many people do not read **a** daily newspaper anymore, they still have more access to **the** news they want, thanks to **the** Internet.

B *Comprehension Check* Answer the questions.

1. How does Christina Jackson get the news?
2. What is changing about the way people get the news?

3. The article says news is becoming an online social activity. What are some examples of this?

4. What are some very popular news subjects on the Internet right now?

C *Notice* Read the sentences from the article and answer the questions.

1. "They go to **a** news site and list the type of stories they want to read. They tell **the** news site if they want pictures or video."

    In the first sentence, do we know which site this is? Is the site in the second sentence the same one?

2. "Many people do not read **a** daily newspaper anymore."

    Do we know which newspaper the writer is talking about?

3. "They still have more access to the news they want, thanks to **the** Internet."

    Do we know what the article refers to by "Internet"? Is this part of our general knowledge?

2 | Articles

▶ Grammar Presentation

Articles are used with nouns. The indefinite article is *a* or *an*. The definite article is *the*.	*A recent study analyzed how people get* ***the*** *news.* ***The*** *study found that news is becoming* ***an*** *online social activity.*

2.1 Using *A* and *An*

a. Use *a / an* with singular count nouns. It means "one."	*A study analyzed news trends.*
Use *a* with consonant sounds. Use *an* with vowel sounds.	*I went to a website.* *I wrote an e-mail.*
b. *A / An* can go before a noun or an adjective and a noun.	*It's a study.* *It's a new study.* *It's an interesting study.*
c. Do not use *a / an* with plural nouns or noncount nouns.	*I watch (some) TV news shows every day.* *I watch a̶ TV news shows every day.*
You can use no article or *some* with plural or noncount nouns instead.	*Wei gets (some) information from the Web.* *Wei gets a̶n̶ information from the Web.*
d. Use *a / an* with a person, place, or thing when you and your listener are not familiar with it or when the specific name of it is not important.	*I go to a news site each day.* (We do not know which news site it is.) *Raul bought a newspaper yesterday.* (We do not know which newspaper it is.)

2.2 Using *The*

a. Use *the* with singular nouns, plural nouns, and noncount nouns.

The study *showed Internet news habits.*
The news stories *were interesting.*
The information *was useful.*

b. *The* can go before a noun or an adjective + noun.

I read **the news** *online every morning.*
Did you hear **the big news**? *Tom got married!*

c. Use *the* with people, places, and things that are familiar to you and your listener. For example, when:

1. The noun is unique – there is only one (*the sun*, *the moon*, *the Internet*).

People walked on **the moon** *in 1969.*
(We know that there is only one moon.)

2. The noun is part of your and your listener's everyday world or general knowledge (*the dog*, *the newspaper*).

I read **the newspaper** *every day.*
(The newspaper is part of our everyday life.)

3. There is additional information that explains which noun you are talking about (*the building on the left*, *the computer in the lab*).

I watch **the news show** *that's on at 11:00 p.m.*
(It is a specific news show, the one that is on at 11:00 p.m.)

d. People often use *a / an* the first time they speak or write about a new noun, and then use *the* every time after that.

A recent study *analyzed how people get their news. (We do not know which study it is.)*
The study *found that not many people read newspapers. (Now we know that it is the study you just mentioned.)*

▶ # Grammar Application

Exercise 2.1 *A* or *An*?

Complete the sentences about people's media habits. Circle the correct words.

1. (A)/ **An** recent study showed **a / an** change in media habits.

2. Sara Cameron, a business student, used to read **a / an** newspaper every day, but now she visits **a / an** Internet news site several times a day.

3. Last night, her friend Rachel sent her **a / an** interesting news story from **a / an** business blog.

4. Rachel also put **a / an** link to **a / an** news video in **a / an** e-mail to all her friends.

5. Rachel used to write articles for **a / an** fashion magazine, but now she posts articles on **a / an** online fashion blog.

6. Last month, Sara bought **a / an** book at **a / an** used bookstore. Yesterday, she downloaded **a / an** electronic book instead.

7. When she misses **a / an** episode of her favorite TV show, she watches it on **a / an** TV website the next day.

Exercise 2.2 *A / An* or *The*?

Look at the pictures. What are the people saying? Circle the correct answer.

1. a. Did you see a movie?
   b. Did you see the movie?

2. a. My laptop's on a chair.
   b. My laptop's on the chair.

3. a. I want to buy a phone.
   b. I want to buy the phone.

4. a. Let's watch a news show.
   b. Let's watch the news show.

Exercise 2.3 *A / An*, *The*, or No Article?

A Read an excerpt from a report on jobs in new media. Write *a*, *an*, *the*, or Ø (no article).

Public relations (PR) firms create ____Ø____ publicity for companies. For example,
(1)
_____ PR person writes _____ interesting story about _____ company and
(2)   (3)   (4)
tries to get _____ story into a newspaper. PR firms also try to get people on TV or on
(5)
_____ radio to talk about the company. PR firms like to use these media. However,
(6)
today, they also get their stories into new media, for example, on _____ social
(7)
networking sites or in _____ blogs. PR firms often hire young people to help them
(8)
do this. For example, while Ali Lewis, a 25-year-old from Boston, was in college, he wrote
_____ popular blog about the media. _____ public relations firm read his blog
(9)   (10)
and asked him to come in for _____ job interview. Ali is _____ good writer, and
(11)   (12)
he understands how new media work, so they gave him _____ job. In his new job, Ali
(13)
helps companies work with social networking sites and blogs.

B ◀)) Now listen to the report and check your answers.

Exercise 2.4 *The*: Only One or General Knowledge

People often use *the* with these nouns. There is only one of these nouns (e.g., the *moon*), or it is clear which one is meant.

the government	the media	the past	the environment	the moon
the president	the Internet	the future	the weather	the sky
the public	~~the radio~~		the world	the sun
	the press		the Earth	

A Complete the blog and follow-up comments with a word from the word box above. Sometimes, more than one answer is possible.

The News Today

February 11 by Claire Sanchez

I'm so bored with the news these days! Everything in the media – including TV, the Internet, magazines, and newspapers, and even *the radio* – is about celebrities.
                                                                                (1)
It seems that the only stories that we see in the media are about celebrities and their personal problems! There are a lot of serious issues in _____ today,
                                                                                (2)
and we don't see much in _____ about them. What's your opinion?
                           (3)

---

3 Comments

Emily: I agree. For example, climate change is a serious issue. We need more stories about how global warming is affecting the environment. _____ is
                                                                                (4)
in danger, and the public isn't interested. I mean, it's great to see the blue sky and
_____ every day, but ice is melting in the Arctic! Why aren't people
          (5)
interested in this?

NewsBoy: I agree, too. There isn't enough news about education in my opinion. In
_____ , when I was a kid, schools had enough money and classes
          (6)
weren't crowded. Today, it's getting very hard to get into a class at the community college. _____ won't be better, unless we do something in the present.
                    (7)

Erkan: Actually, _____ was talking about education on TV last night,
(8)
NewsBoy. But even though the president thinks we need more money for education,
that doesn't mean that _____ is doing anything about it. I don't think
(9)
_____ really cares about education. I mean, think about the average
(10)
person – your neighbors, for example. Do they really care about crowded college classes?

B *Group Work* Discuss these questions in groups.

1. What's a recent news story that you were really interested in?
   Why did it interest you?
2. What kind of news stories do you hate reading? Why?
3. What do you think is the best (or worst) way to get the news?

3 | Generalizing: More About Articles

▶ Grammar Presentation

Generalizations are true statements about all or most members of a group.	*Teens usually get their news from the Internet.* (=Almost all teens do this; this is true in general.)

3.1 Using Articles in Generalizations and Definitions

a. To make generalizations, you can use:
  1. a plural noun with no article
  2. a noncount noun with no article
  3. *a/an* or *the* + a singular count noun

Young people don't read newspapers.
Information on new media habits is available.
A good journalist covers all sides of an issue.

b. Do not use *the* with a plural count noun or a noncount noun when you make generalizations.

   Society
~~The society~~ needs people with ~~the~~ good communication skills.

c. You can also use quantifiers like *most*, *a lot of*, and *some* in generalizations.

Most Internet users visit more than one news site each day.
A lot of teenagers get the news from the Internet.
Some people get the news on their phones.

d. You can use *a/an* with definitions to say what something is.

A PR firm creates publicity for companies.

▶ Grammar Application

Exercise 3.1 Generalizations

Complete the report on a survey. Circle the correct words.

The /(**Ø**) information on the media habits of young people is very useful to companies
(1)
that produce **the / Ø** movies, video games, and music, as well as to **the / Ø** advertising firms.
(2)   (3)
A recent study analyzed the media habits of American teens. The study showed that **the / Ø**
(4)
American teens are not giving up TV for new media. In fact, they are watching more TV than
before. For **the / Ø** TV viewers aged 13–20, the top show was *American Idol* in the year of
(5)
the survey. This was the same for **the / Ø** parents, too. The survey found that teens also play
(6)
the / Ø video games, and not always **the / Ø** violent games.
(7)   (8)

According to the study, **the / Ø** U.S. teens remember **the / Ø** TV advertisements well
(9)   (10)
and do not have a negative attitude toward them. **Most / The** young people also love the
(11)
Internet, but they spend less time on it than **the / Ø** adults. They download **the / Ø** music
(12)   (13)
and spend about two or three hours a day listening to it.

Most teens own **the / Ø** cell phones. **A / Ø** typical U.S. teen sends and receives about
(14)   (15)
1,500 text messages every month. However, **the / Ø** phone calls are not so popular; on
(16)
average, teens make about seven a day.

Exercise 3.2 Definitions

A Complete the definitions. Use *a*, *an*, or Ø (no article) and the correct form of the words
in the box.

adult	parent	senior	tween
minor	preteen	~~teenager~~	twenty-something

1. _A teenager_ is a young person between 13 and 19 years old.

2. _____ is a person over the age of 18.

3. According to the law, _____ is a person below the age of 18.

4. _____ are people with children.

5. _____ are people over the age of 65.

6. _____ is a person between the ages of 20 and 29.

7. _____ is like a preteen – a child aged 8 to 12 years old. It's a new
word in marketing.

8. _____ are young people under the age of 13.

B *Over to You*   What do you know about the media habits of the groups in A?
Make generalizations. Tell a partner.

I think seniors get their news from newspapers, not from the Internet.
The average twenty-something watches a lot of TV shows online.

Exercise 3.3 More Generalizations

A Survey three or more classmates. Ask the questions below, and write their answers in
the chart. Add one more question of your own.

Question	Student 1	Student 2	Student 3
How do you get the news?			
How often do you read or listen to the news?			
What is your favorite news topic?			

B *Over to You*   Write a short report about the news habits of your classmates.
Make generalizations.

The students in this class mostly get the news from the Internet. Some students also
listen to the radio.

4 | Avoid Common Mistakes ⚠

1. Use *a / an* the first time you mention a new idea.
　　　　　a
　Do you have ∧social networking site?

**2. Use *the* with a noun when there is only one or when the noun is part of your
and your listener's everyday world or general knowledge.**
　The
　∧Internet is a good source of news.

3. Use plural nouns without *the* in generalizations.
　　　Online
　~~The online~~ news consumers go to many different websites.

4. Use noncount nouns without *the* in generalizations.
　　　Communication
　~~The communication~~ is changing.

Editing Task

Find and correct 10 more mistakes in this article on microblogging.

> *a*
> Microblogging is ∧way of keeping in touch with other people. The people write
>
> microblogs for their friends and families. They use microblogging sites to publish
>
> information about their activities. It is an economical way to give a lot of information to a
>
> lot of people.
>
> 5   Microblogs are very useful method of communicating for companies, too. The
>
> companies advertise their products with microblogs. They send the information in short
>
> messages to customers.
>
>   In education, some teachers use microblogging with the students. Students write down
>
> all their study activities, and teachers send the advice. Some people use audio blogs in the
>
> 10 education. They record the spoken messages and upload them to a microblogging site.
>
>   People first started using microblogs in 2005. By 2007, there were 111 microblogging
>
> sites around world. The microblogs are becoming more and more popular.

5 | Grammar for Writing

Using Articles with Nouns

Writers use articles to give the reader extra information about nouns. The article lets you know if the topic is new or old for the reader. It can also let you know if the writer is not referring to a specific noun, but generalizing instead.
Remember:

- **Use *the* for count and noncount nouns that are familiar to the reader or are unique.**

  The local newspaper is not very good.

  The news article you are reading looks very interesting.

- **Use the indefinite article for singular count nouns that are not familiar or not specific.**

  A recent study showed that online news sites are becoming very popular.

- **You can use indefinite articles for definitions.**

  A blog is a journal you keep on the Internet.

- **Use indefinite articles, definite articles, and quantifiers for generalizations.**

  Most young people get their news online. The average college student reads the news online four times a week. A typical high school student visits a news site three times a week.

Pre-writing Task

1 Read the paragraph below. Underline the indefinite articles (*a, an*) and circle the definite articles (*the*). <u>Double underline</u> the nouns that do not have an article.

Changing TV Habits

These <u>days</u>, <u>television habits</u> are very different from (the) way they used to be. Many people watch TV shows on the Internet. Often, you can find a TV show on the Internet the day after it was on TV. There is an advertisement about every 10 minutes, but usually there is only one advertisement at a time. On TV, there are usually three or more advertisements during a commercial break. A commercial break on the Internet often lasts only 30 seconds. On TV, though, a commercial break lasts about three minutes. People used to rush home to turn on the television for a special show, but now they just watch the show online when they are ready. It is like personalized TV viewing.

2 Read the paragraph again. Look at the list below. Identify one article for each of the meanings below. Sometimes more than one answer is correct.

1. familiar count and noncount nouns (*the newspaper, the dog*)

2. unfamiliar singular count nouns or not specific ones (*a study, a website*)

3. definitions or explained nouns (*a 20-story building, a computer in the lab*)

4. generalizations (*The average teen sends 50 texts a day. A good journalist covers all sides of an issue.*)

5. unique nouns (*the sun, the moon, the Internet*)

Writing Task

1 *Write*   Use the paragraph in the Pre-writing Task to help you write about how people's news, TV, or other media habits have changed. You can write about these things or use your own ideas.

- reading, listening, or watching the news
- listening to music or buying music
- using textbooks
- reading habits

2 *Self-Edit*   Use the editing tips to improve your paragraph. Make any necessary changes.

1. Did you use the indefinite article with unfamiliar count nouns or not specific ones?
2. Did you use any definitions or generalizations in your paragraph?
3. Did you use the definite article with specific, familiar, or unique count and noncount nouns?
4. Did you avoid the mistakes in the Avoid Common Mistakes chart on page 101?

Pronouns;
Direct and Indirect Objects
Challenging Ourselves

1 | Grammar in the Real World

A What challenges do you face in your life? Read the web article about ways people challenge themselves. What are some reasons to challenge yourself every day?

Challenging Ourselves

We all face challenges in **our** lives. For example, people lose **their** jobs, or **they** deal with health problems. These challenges are difficult for all of us. However, if **you** challenge **yourself**, even when **your** life is going well, **you** can be ready to handle tough situations in the future. **You** will become more confident and more creative. **You**
5 will also improve **your** problem-solving skills.

Challenging **yourself** means trying new things. These things will help **you**, but **they** may also be difficult or scary. People have **their** own needs and goals, so other people's challenges may be different from **yours**. Here are some examples:

- Alison wants to be more fit. To challenge **herself, she**
10 works out an extra half hour each day.

- Dan wants to improve **his** performance at work. **He** challenges **himself** by volunteering to do difficult tasks that no one else wants to do.

- Mari is afraid to speak in public, so **she** challenges
15 **herself** by taking a public speaking class.

- Ken wants to improve **his** critical thinking skills. **He** now reads articles with opinions that are different from **his**.

Do you want to challenge **yourself**? Follow these three easy steps:

  1. Write down **your** goal. Give **your** plan a start and a finish date.
20 2. Tell people about **your** goal. This helps you stick to **your** plan.
  3. Go one step further than **you** originally planned. For example, do **you** want to save $25 a week to buy a car someday? Then save $30.

Take on small challenges every day. Small challenges give people strength. **They** help people handle life's *big* challenges when **they** happen.

B *Comprehension Check*   Answer the questions.

1. According to the text, what are some reasons to challenge yourself?
2. How does challenging yourself help you when you have *real* problems?
3. If you want to challenge yourself, what are some steps to follow?

C *Notice*   Read the sentences from the article and answer the questions.

1. "Mari is afraid to speak in public, so **she** challenges **herself** by taking a public speaking class."

   Who does *she* refer to? _____

   Who does *herself* refer to? _____

2. "Ken wants to improve **his** critical thinking skills."

   Who does *his* refer to in this sentence? _____

2 | Pronouns

▶ Grammar Presentation

Pronouns replace or refer to nouns.	(= MARI) (= MARI) ***Mari** is afraid to speak in public, so **she** challenges **herself** by taking a public speaking class.*

2.1 Pronouns

Subject	Object	Possessive Determiner + Noun	Possessive	Reflexive	Reciprocal
I	me	my + noun	mine	myself	
you	you	your + noun	yours	yourself	
he	him	his + noun	his	himself	
she	her	her + noun	hers	herself	each other
it	it	its + noun	—	itself	one another
we	us	our + noun	ours	ourselves	
they	them	their + noun	theirs	themselves	

2.2 Using Pronouns

a. Use subject pronouns to replace nouns in the subject position.	*Alison wants to be more fit. **She** is taking an exercise class.*
b. Use object pronouns to replace nouns in the object position.	*Sara loves **exercise classes**. She takes **them** three times a week.*
c. Use a possessive pronoun to replace a possessive determiner + singular or plural noun. The possessive pronoun agrees with the subject that it replaces.	***My exercise class** is at night. **Hers** is on the weekend. (hers = her exercise class)* ***Amy's classes** meet in the afternoon. **His** meet in the morning. (his = his classes)*
d. Use reflexive pronouns when the object of the sentence is the same as the subject. Use them in the object position.	*I taught **myself** to speak Japanese.* ***Ken** challenges **himself** by reading different opinions.* ***The students** didn't hurt **themselves** in the exercise class.*
e. Use *by* + a reflexive pronoun to mean "alone" or "without any help."	*My son can ride a bike **by himself**.* (He does not need any help.) *Lara works out **by herself**.* (She works out alone.)
f. Use reciprocal pronouns when two or more people give *and* receive the same action or have the same relationship.	*Mari and I have the same challenges. We help **each other**. (I help Mari, and Mari helps me.)* *Tom and his sisters e-mailed **one another** about the news. (Each person e-mailed the other people.)*
g. You can use *one* to replace a singular noun. Use *ones* to replace a plural noun.	*I need an **exercise class**. That **one** looks good.* A *The white **running shoes** are nice.* B *I like the black **ones**.*

 Each other is about four times more frequent than *one another*.

▶ Grammar Application

Exercise 2.1 Pronouns

A Complete the interview. Circle the correct pronouns.

▶ How Do You Challenge Yourself?

Town Talk asked people: What is difficult for you in life? How are you challenging yourself to improve?

Q How do you challenge **your** /(**yourself**)?
(1)

Al I never finish my work on time, so I'm challenging

mine / **myself** to use time better. I made a study schedule. I
(2)

did it all by **myself** / **me**. No one helped **it** / **me**! The schedule
(3)   (4)

is very tight, but I'm staying on **him** / **it**. My friends and my
(5)

teachers all say that I'm doing well!

Q People are telling us how they are improving **their** / **theirs**
(6)

lives. How are you improving **your** / **yours**?
(7)

Kay I'm afraid of flying, so travel is difficult. I got help from

a friend. She also was afraid of flying, and she got better

by **herself** / **her**. Now she's helping **I** / **me**. My first flight is
(8)   (9)

next week. I feel very good about **it** / **her**. I feel strong and
(10)

confident now.

Q We're asking people about their challenges in life. What's

your / **yours**?
(11)

Tim **Ours** / **Our** is saving money. Daniela and I want to buy
(12)

a house, so **our** / **we** challenge is not spending too much
(13)

money. **We** / **Us** are challenging **us** / **ourselves** to make a
(14)   (15)

budget and save money each week.

Daniela We remind **one another** / **us** to be careful about money.
(16)

We help **each other** / **ourselves** think about ways to spend
(17)

less money.

B *Pair Work*   Discuss these questions with a partner.

1. What is difficult for you?
2. What do you challenge yourself to do?

A *I'm afraid of public speaking. I'm challenging myself to speak in class whenever I can. How about you?*

B *I'm challenging myself . . .*

Exercise 2.2 *One* and *Ones*

Complete the conversations. Use *one* or *ones*.

1. *A*   Do you want the large box of cereal?

   B   No. I'm saving money. I want the small _one_ .

2. *A*   Which exercise class are you taking?

   B   The _____ at 3:00 p.m. looks good.

3. *A*   I'm making a budget. Can I borrow your calculator?

   B   Sorry, I don't have _____ .

4. *A*   Which sports do you like to do?

   B   I like the challenging _____ , like skiing and rock climbing.

5. *A*   Being a parent is challenging! I need some books to help me.

   B   Sure. The _____ on the shelf over there are very useful.

6. *A*   Do you want to return these running shoes?

   B   Yes. The _____ that I ordered were white.

7. *A*   Do you want to sign up for a credit card with our store?

   B   No. I don't want _____ . I'm challenging myself to get out of debt.

8. *A*   I need to go downtown. Which bus stop should I go to?

   B   The _____ on Oak Street.

Exercise 2.3 Prepositions with Reflexive Pronouns

Data from the Real World

Research shows that reflexive pronouns frequently follow these verbs with *for*, *to*, and *about*: *do* (something) *for*, *make* (something) *for* *talk to* + (someone) *talk about*, *think about*, *feel* + adjective + *about* (something / someone)	I **made** a schedule **for myself**. Sometimes I **talk to myself**. Tim never **thinks about himself**. She **feels good about herself**.

A Complete the article about controlling your nerves in an uncomfortable situation. Circle the correct preposition.

Do You Get "the Jitters"?

When people do challenging activities, they get nervous. Sometimes this is called "the jitters." Getting nervous is a normal reaction. Like an athlete before an event, maybe you get the jitters before a

5   class presentation or a test. Here are some tips from successful students to help you control the jitters when you have to take a test or speak in front of the class.

- Be well prepared. For example, for a test, make a study schedule **for**/**to** yourself
(1)
and stick to it. For a presentation, make an outline **about**/**for** yourself and
(2)
10   memorize it.

- Be positive. Think **to**/**about** yourself and how well prepared you are. Talk **for**/**to**
(3)   (4)
yourself before the event. Tell yourself that you are smart and well prepared.

- Focus on the task. If you are taking a test, focus on the test. If you are speaking, think about the topic of your talk. Don't think **about**/**for** yourself during the event.
(5)

15 - Reward yourself. After the event, feel good **for**/**about** yourself! You did
(6)
something very challenging! Now, do something nice **for**/**about** yourself.
(7)
Make a nice meal **for**/**to** yourself, or go out with friends and celebrate!
(8)

B *Pair Work* Discuss these questions with a partner.

1. How do you prepare for a challenging activity? What do you think about?
2. How do you reward yourself afterward?

I prepare by practicing a lot with my friends. I think about how much I practiced, and I try not to think about myself. I also make a schedule for myself. . . .

3 | Direct and Indirect Objects

▶ Grammar Presentation

Objects are nouns that receive the action of a verb. Some sentences have two objects after the verb: an indirect object (IO) and a direct object (DO).	IO DO *They gave **the winner an award**.*

3.1 Using Direct and Indirect Objects

a. The direct object is the person or thing that receives the action of the verb.

>   DO
> *The teacher gave the student **a test**.*
> (What did the teacher give? A test.)

b. The indirect object is the person or thing that receives the direct object.

>   IO   DO
> *The teacher gave **the student a test**.*
> (The student received the test.)

c. You can use indirect object + direct object.

>   IO   DO
> *The teacher gave **the student a test**.*

You can also use direct object + preposition + indirect object.
These sentences have the same meaning.

>   DO PREP   IO
> *The teacher gave **a test to the student**.*

Do not use *to* and *for* with indirect object + direct object.

> ~~*The teacher gave to the student a test.*~~

d. The pronouns for indirect objects are *me, you, him, her, it, us,* and *them*.

>   IO   DO
> *The teacher gave **her** a test.*
>   DO   IO
> *The teacher gave a test **to her**.*

You can replace both the direct and the indirect objects with pronouns when you use direct object + preposition + indirect object.

>   DO   IO
> *The teacher gave **it to her**.*
> (it = the test; her = the student)

Do not replace both the direct and the indirect objects with pronouns when you use indirect object + direct object.

>   IO DO
> *The teacher gave ~~her it~~.*

▶ Grammar Application

Exercise 3.1 Direct and Indirect Objects

A Read the text. For each numbered sentence, write *DO* above the direct object and *IO* above the indirect object. Then label the sentences *IO + DO* (indirect object + direct object) or *DO + PREP + IO* (direct object + preposition + indirect object).

Vu Tran wanted to go to college, but he did not have any money. However, Vu had a very helpful counselor in high school, Mrs. Ramirez.

              IO   *DO*

1. Mrs. Ramirez gave Vu some good advice.   *IO + DO*

2. Mrs. Ramirez gave Vu the names   _____

    of 10 scholarship organizations.

3. Vu and Mrs. Ramirez sent the   _____

    completed applications to the

    scholarship organizations.

4. A few months later, Vu told   _____

    Mrs. Ramirez the good news.

5. Five of the 10 organizations offered   _____

    a scholarship to Vu.

6. Vu chose one organization, and it sent   _____

    a check to his college.

Today, Vu is a successful computer technician. He overcame a great challenge with help from Mrs. Ramirez.

B Rewrite each sentence in A. Change the IO + DO sentences to DO + PREP + IO sentences. Then change the DO + PREP + IO sentences to IO + DO.

1. *Mrs. Ramirez gave some good advice to Vu.* _____

2. _____

3. _____

4. _____

5. _____

6. _____

Exercise 3.2 *To* and *For* with Direct Objects

Data from the Real World 🌐

Research shows that the following verbs and prepositions are frequently used together in sentences with the pattern: verb + direct object + preposition + indirect object.

verb + DO + *to* + IO *e-mail, give, lend, offer, owe, read, sell, send, show, teach, tell* *To* emphasizes the direction of the action.	I **e-mailed** pictures **to** you. The teacher **gave** a test **to** the student. (The test went from the teacher to the student.)
verb + DO + *for* + IO *bake, buy, cook, do, find, get, keep, leave, make, order, save* *For* means that the subject does the action to please or help the other person or thing.	I got tickets **for** my friends. The students baked a cake **for** the teacher. (The students baked a cake to please the teacher.)
verb + DO + *to* / *for* + IO *bring, take, write* These verbs use either *for* or *to*.	He took a schedule **for** his friend. (He took it to give to his friend as a favor.) He took a schedule **to** his friend. (He carried or gave it to his friend.)

A Complete the text with *to* or *for*.

Is it possible to change the way you think? Sometimes. Take Ken, for example. Ken had
very strong opinions about a lot of things. One day, Ken's teacher, Mrs. Green, gave an exam
<u>to</u> the class. When Mrs. Green showed the test results _____ Ken, he was shocked. The
₍₁₎   (2)
results showed that he didn't always base his ideas on correct information. Ken then decided
to challenge himself and Mrs. Green helped Ken. First, she found a website _____ Ken.
                                               (3)
It published articles on ideas that were different from Ken's. Ken discussed the articles with
Mrs. Green. Mrs. Green also made quizzes _____ Ken on the articles he read. In addition,
                                       (4)
Mrs. Green found a critical thinking skills class _____ Ken. He also e-mailed some
                                     (5)
reports on the class _____ Mrs. Green. Today, Ken has excellent critical thinking skills.
                 (6)

B 🔊 *Pair Work*   Listen to the text. There is additional information about Ken. Write
down three new things you hear. Then tell your partner.

1. _____
2. _____
3. _____

   A *Ken was a biology student at a community college.*
   B *Right. And the exam was about . . .*

Exercise 3.3 Object Pronouns

Complete the answers in the conversations with the correct indirect object pronoun for the underlined word. Then rewrite each answer using a different pattern.

1. *A* Where did <u>Ken</u> get that course schedule?

   B Mrs. Green gave the schedule to *him* . *Mrs. Green gave him the schedule.*

2. *A* What did Mrs. Green give <u>Ken</u>?

   B She gave _____ an exam. _____

3. *A* What did Mrs. Green find for <u>Ken</u>?

   B She found a critical thinking skills class for _____ . _____

4. *A* What did Mrs. Ramirez do for <u>Vu</u>?

   B She wrote _____ a letter of recommendation. _____

5. *A* Did Vu mail the applications to <u>the scholarship organizations</u>?

   B Yes, he e-mailed _____ the applications. _____

6. *A* Did the scholarship organization send some of the scholarship money <u>to Vu's parents</u>?

   B No, it didn't mail the money to _____ . _____

7. *A* Did your school give <u>you and your sister</u> scholarships?

   B No, our school gave _____ a loan. _____

8. *A* Can you give <u>me</u> $100 for books this semester?

   B No, but I can give _____ $50. _____

4 Avoid Common Mistakes ⚠

1. Do not confuse subject and object pronouns.

   She gave the schedule to Ken and ~~I~~. *(me)*

2. Do not use *to* or *for* in sentences with the pattern verb + indirect object + direct object.

   Tom gave ~~to~~ his brother a skateboard.   Tom bought ~~for~~ his brother a skateboard.

3. Some verbs take *to*. Some verbs take *for*.

   I e-mailed the assignment ~~for~~ you. Did you get my message? *(to)*

   I made a cake ~~to~~ you. *(for)*

4. In sentences with verb + indirect object + direct object, do not replace both the direct and the indirect objects with pronouns.

   The teacher gave ~~her it~~. *(her the test)*

Editing Task

Find and correct eight more mistakes in this story about a personal challenge.

        Lara was afraid of heights. The fear caused many problems for ~~she~~ *her*. Her life was very difficult. For example, her was very uncomfortable on airplanes. She also did not like to take elevators in tall buildings. Lara's husband gave to her some advice. He told to Lara a secret: If she deals with her fears, she can improve in all areas of her life. Then her husband found a skydiving class to her. He found a schedule online, and he gave her it. Then he gave Lara money to pay for the class. He also bought the equipment to her. Lara took the class. It was hard, but she challenged herself. After Lara finished the class, her husband gave a present for her. He baked for her a cake, and they celebrated together.

5 | Grammar for Writing ✏

Using Pronouns and Objects

    Writers use pronouns to replace or refer to nouns. This helps connect sentences and ideas. It also helps the writer avoid repeating the same noun over and over.
Remember:

- **Subjects are the "doers" of the action in a sentence. Objects are the "receivers." Subjects and objects can be nouns or pronouns.**

  Tom gave Marcia the car keys. After <u>he</u> gave <u>them</u> to <u>her</u>, <u>he</u> gave <u>her</u> some money.

- **Use reflexive pronouns when the object and the subject are the same.**

  Marcia gave <u>herself</u> plenty of time to get to work, but she still arrived late.

- **Use reciprocal pronouns when two or more people are the "doer" and the "receiver" of the same action.**

  Tim and Adam helped <u>each other</u> study for the test. Tim helped Adam, and Adam helped Tim.

Pre-writing Task

1 Read the paragraph below. Underline the subject pronouns and circle the object nouns and pronouns.

Improving a Relationship

        Brian and Theresa were happily married, but they never had enough time for each other. They were always working or taking care of their children. Theresa often worried about their relationship, but she never talked to her husband about it. One day, Theresa heard an interesting program on the radio. She told Brian about it. The program said that couples often forgot to have fun with each other. So they decided to challenge themselves to have more fun together. That weekend, they went to a local restaurant, and they did not talk about their problems. They had a great time. After that night, they made a promise to each other. They promised to do something special together every month.

2 Read the paragraph again. Which pronouns are reflexive? Which are reciprocal? Which words are possessive determiners + nouns?

Writing Task

1 *Write* Use the paragraph in the Pre-writing Task to help you write about a change you (or someone you know) made because of a personal challenge. Think about how and why you made this change. You can write about one of these topics or use your own ideas.

- deciding to take this English class
- finding time to spend on homework
- finding or changing a job
- getting over a fear

2 *Self-Edit* Use the editing tips to improve your paragraph. Make any necessary changes.

1. Did you use pronouns to focus attention on the actions instead of the nouns?
2. Did you use the subject and object pronouns to avoid repeating names and nouns?
3. Did you use reflexive pronouns when the object and the subject are the same?
4. Did you use reciprocal pronouns when two or more people give *and* receive the same action or have the same relationship?
5. Did you avoid the mistakes in the Avoid Common Mistakes chart on page 113?

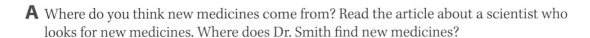

1 Grammar in the Real World

A Where do you think new medicines come from? Read the article about a scientist who looks for new medicines. Where does Dr. Smith find new medicines?

Interview with Jane Smith, Ph.D., Marine Biologist[1]

So, Dr. Smith, what exactly do you do?

We look for new medicines. We go to the ocean and discover chemicals in marine organisms – deep-sea animals and
5   plants. We use these chemicals to develop drugs to treat human diseases.

That's amazing. I didn't know medicines came from under the sea! Tell me more.

Over the years, scientists **have** also
10   **found** a lot of important drugs on land. For example, they **have developed** useful drugs from plants and animals in the Amazon rain forest in Brazil. Our work is similar. However, we look for medicines in
15   the ocean.

Where exactly do you find these chemicals?

We **have discovered** chemicals all around the world. Scientists **have found them** in warm water and in cold water, like in the Arctic Ocean. We**'ve found** them in shallow water and in very deep water, sometimes
20   tens of thousands of feet under the surface.

It sounds like you get to travel a lot for your work. Where have you been?

I**'ve been** around the world twice. My team **has led** underwater expeditions[2] in Africa, the Caribbean, the Pacific Ocean, off the coast

[1]**marine biologist:** someone who studies plants and animals that live in the ocean | [2]**expedition:** a long journey with a special purpose, e.g., to discover something

25 of South America, and in Asia. I**'ve been** very lucky with this job! I**'ve**
visited more than 50 countries for my work.

What are some of the most exciting things you have seen or done?

I**'ve made** hundreds of very deep dives and **had** some exciting adventures.
For example, about two years ago, we took a submarine³ inside an
underwater volcano. However, we didn't know it was a volcano. Suddenly,
30 the volcano erupted. The submarine shot up 200 feet a minute! That was
really exciting!

³**submarine:** a boat that travels underwater

B *Comprehension Check* Who went to these places? According to the article, did
they find medicines or chemicals there? Check (✔) the correct boxes. Sometimes more
than one answer is correct.

	Did Dr. Smith go there?	Did other scientists go there?	Did people find medicines or chemicals there?
1. the Amazon	☐	☐	☐
2. the Arctic Ocean	☐	☐	☐
3. Africa	☐	☐	☐
4. the Pacific Ocean	☐	☐	☐
5. an underwater volcano	☐	☐	☐

C *Notice* Find the sentences in the article and complete them.

1. We _____ chemicals all around the world.

2. I _____ around the world twice.

3. I _____ more than 50 countries for my work.

4. About two years ago, we _____ a submarine inside an
underwater volcano.

In which sentence do we know when the action happened? In which sentences is the
time indefinite?

2 Present Perfect

▶ Grammar Presentation

The present perfect describes past events that are important in the present, but the specific time that the events happened is not important or is unknown.	We **have found** chemicals all over the world. (We found them sometime in the past, and this is still important now.)

2.1 Statements

Subject	Have / Has (+ Not)	Past Participle		Contractions
I You We They	**have** **have not** **haven't**	**visited**	50 countries.	I have → I**'ve** You have → You**'ve** We have → We**'ve** They have → They**'ve**
He She It	**has** **has not** **hasn't**			He has → He**'s** She has → She**'s** It has → It**'s**

2.2 *Yes / No* Questions and Short Answers

Have / Has	Subject	Past Participle		Short Answers	
Have	I you we they	**found***	new medicines?	Yes, I **have.** Yes, you **have.** Yes, we **have.** Yes, they **have.**	No, I **haven't.** No, you **haven't.** No, we **haven't.** No, they **haven't.**
Has	he / she / it			Yes, he / she / it **has.**	No, he / she / it **hasn't.**

*Found is an irregular past participle. Irregular Verbs: See page A3.

2.3 Information Questions and Answers

Wh- Word	Have / Has	Subject	Past Participle		Answers
Where	**have**	I	**traveled**?		You **have traveled** around the world.
Why	**have**	you	**gone**	to the Amazon?	I **have gone** to look for medicines.
What	**have**	we	**discovered**?		We**'ve discovered** chemicals in plants.
How	**have**	they	**studied**	life under the sea?	They**'ve studied** it in submarines.
How often	**has**	he / she / it	**traveled**	in a submarine?	He**'s traveled** in a submarine many times.

Wh- Word	Has	Past Participle		Answer
Who	**has**	**been**	to Africa?	Dr. Smith **has been** to Africa.

2.4 Using Present Perfect

a. Use the present perfect to talk about past events that are still important now.

*People **have discovered** medicines in the Amazon.* (This began in the past and is important now.)

b. Use the present perfect to describe actions or events that happened once or repeatedly at indefinite times in the past.

*She **has traveled** to Mexico.*
*She **has traveled** around the world many times.* (We don't know exactly when she did these things.)

c. Use the present perfect to give the number of times something happened up to now.

*I**'ve been** to Africa twice.* (Before now, I went there two times.)

d. Use the present perfect to give lists of past experiences.

*I**'ve been** to France, Spain, and England.*

You can also use the present perfect with "been" to mean "go and come back again."

A *Where **have** you **been**?*
B *I**'ve** just **been** to the store.* (I went to the store and have come back again.)

e. Use *ever* in present perfect questions to ask if something happened at any time in the past.

A ***Have** you **ever traveled** to Africa?*
B *Yes, I have. / No, I haven't.*

A ***Have** you **ever been** inside a volcano?*
B *Yes, I have. / No, I haven't.*

Verbs that are often used with the present perfect in speaking and writing include *agree, be, do, experience, find, go, say, see, show, talk,* and *think*.	Scientists **have done** experiments in space. Researchers **have found** useful chemicals under the sea. Research **has shown** there is water on Mars. **Have** you **thought** about that?

▶ Grammar Application

Exercise 2.1 Statements

Complete the sentences about a biotech company, a company that develops medicines. Use the present perfect form of the verbs in parentheses.

A number of drug companies _have found_ (find)
(1)
medicines in the rain forest. In fact, over 120 medicines

_____ (come) from rain forest plants. Some
(2)
companies _____ (get) information about
(3)
these plants from the local people. In many cases, the people

_____ (live) there for hundreds of years, and they
(4)
know all about the plants. However, they _____
(5)
(not receive) money or other benefits for their help. Some drug companies

_____ (not think) about the rights of the local people who help them.
(6)
Also, some companies _____ (not take) care of the local environment.
(7)
    One drug company, Rain Forest Biotech, _____ (take) steps to
(8)
improve things. Rain Forest Biotech _____ (develop) a new way to
(9)
find drugs and respect the people and land at the same time. Rain Forest Biotech

also _____ (set) up programs to help the local people they work with.
(10)

Exercise 2.2 Questions and Answers

A ◄))) Complete the interview with the president of Rain Forest Biotech. Use the present perfect form of the verbs in parentheses. Then listen and check your answers.

Chris Green   My guest today is Dr. Marty Robles. Dr. Robles is the president of Rain

Forest Biotech. Rain Forest Biotech has made some exciting discoveries in

the rain forests of the Amazon. Dr. Robles, you have an exciting company, and

you _'ve had_ (have) an exciting life, too, I think. Tell us a
(1)
little bit about your life. How many times _____
(2)
you _____ (be) to the Amazon?
(2)

Dr. Robles   I _____ (make) 100 trips to the Amazon
(3)
region.

Chris Green   Who _____ (go) with you?
(4)

Dr. Robles   My team.

Chris Green   And who else _____ you _____ (work)
(5)   (5)
with there?

Dr. Robles   Well, I _____ (meet) many traditional healers on my trips.
(6)
These people _____ (teach) me how they use local plants to
(7)
cure diseases. I _____ (learn) a great deal about their lives and
(8)
about their land, too.

Chris Green   _____ you _____ (be) to Africa?
(9)   (9)

Dr. Robles   No, I _____ (not be) to Africa, but my team _____ _____
(10)   (11)
(visited) New Guinea, and I _ _____ (do) research in Australia.
(12)

B 🔊)) Listen again. What else do you learn about Dr. Robles? Circle the correct words.

1. Dr. Robles has traveled to rain forests in **Central America** / **Central Asia**.

2. His team has discovered medicines for **heart** / **brain** disease.

3. He's brought his children with him on **some** / **all** of his expeditions.

Exercise 2.3 More Questions

A Unscramble the words to make questions.

1. lived / have / How many / places / different / you / ?

    How many different places have you lived?

2. Chicago / you / in / lived / Have / ?

    _____

3. Where / traveled / you / have / ?

    _____

4. Have / New York City / visited / you / ever / ?

    _____

5. with / Who / you / traveled / have / ?

_____

6. your family / you / helped / has / How / ?

_____

7. Has / advice / you / your family / life / given / about / ?

_____

8. learned / have / this class / in / you / What / ?

_____

B *Pair Work* Ask and answer the questions in A with a partner. Give true answers about yourself. Ask follow-up questions and add extra information.

A How many different places have you lived?
B Two.
A Where have you lived?
B I've lived in El Salvador and the United States.
A Have you ever visited . . . ?

3 | Present Perfect or Simple Past?

▶ Grammar Presentation

The present perfect describes events that happened at an indefinite time in the past and may still be happening in the present. These events are still important or still have an effect in the present. The simple past is for finished events that happened at a specific time in the past.	She **has visited** the rain forest many times. She **went** there last year.

3.1 Present Perfect or Simple Past?

a. Use the present perfect for things that happened at an indefinite time (or times) in the past.	She **has been** to Costa Rica. Scientists **have discovered** medicines in the Amazon.
Use the simple past for things that happened at a specific time (or times) in the past.	She **went** to Costa Rica in 2010. Scientists **discovered** a new medicine in the Amazon last year.

3.1 Present Perfect or Simple Past? *(continued)*

b. Use the present perfect for things that have happened in an unfinished time period (e.g., *today, this morning, this year*).	He **has traveled** to Africa twice this year. (This year is not finished. He may travel there again.) I **have visited** three cities for my current job. (My job is not finished. I may visit more cities for it.)
Use the simple past for things that happened in a time period that is finished (e.g., *yesterday, last night, a year ago*).	He **traveled** to Indonesia twice last year. (Last year is finished. He cannot go to Indonesia again in that time period.) I **visited** three cities for my old job. (That job is finished. I can't travel for it again.)
c. Use the present perfect to introduce a topic, and then use the simple past to give the details.	We'**ve had** a lot of exciting experiences. For example, we **took** a submarine into an underwater volcano last year.

▶ Grammar Application

Exercise 3.1 Present Perfect or Simple Past?

A Complete the article about Amanda Lewis, an astronaut. Circle the correct verbs.

She **has wanted** / (**wanted**) to be an astronaut when she
⁽¹⁾
was a child. She **has grown up** / **grew up** in Texas and
⁽²⁾
has studied / **studied** biology and engineering at the University
⁽³⁾
of Texas. After college, she **has been** / **was** a pilot in the Navy.
⁽⁴⁾
She **has joined** / **joined** NASA in 1999 and **has become** / **became**
⁽⁵⁾   ⁽⁶⁾
an astronaut. Since then, she **has orbited** / **orbited** the Earth
⁽⁷⁾
230 times and **has gone** / **went** on three spacewalks in the last
⁽⁸⁾
mission. She also participates in science experiments as part
of her job, and she **has studied** / **studied** the effects of radiation on
⁽⁹⁾
plants for the past six months. The most exciting thing she
has seen / **saw** as a pilot is the Northern Lights. She **has seen** / **saw**
⁽¹⁰⁾   ⁽¹¹⁾
them on a mission last year.

B *Pair Work* Compare your answers with a partner. Discuss the time that the actions in each sentence happened. Decide if the time is definite or indefinite, finished or unfinished.

A In number 1, the time is definite. It's when she was a child.

B Right. That's why the verb is in the simple past. And in number 2, the time is in the past, but it's finished.

A Right. She isn't growing up anymore.

Exercise 3.2 More Present Perfect and Simple Past

A Complete the text with the present perfect or simple past form of the verbs in parentheses.

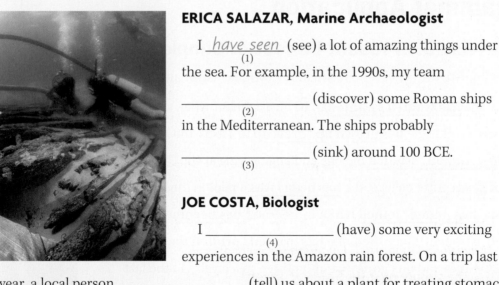

SCIENCE TALK

Three scientists answer the question, "What is the most interesting or exciting thing you have seen or done in your work?"

ERICA SALAZAR, Marine Archaeologist

I _have seen_ (see) a lot of amazing things under
  (1)
the sea. For example, in the 1990s, my team

_____ (discover) some Roman ships
         (2)
in the Mediterranean. The ships probably

_____ (sink) around 100 BCE.
       (3)

JOE COSTA, Biologist

I _____ (have) some very exciting
           (4)
experiences in the Amazon rain forest. On a trip last
year, a local person _____ (tell) us about a plant for treating stomach
                              (5)
problems. My stomach _____ (be) upset, and I _____
                                (6)   (7)
(try) a traditional healer's plant. I _____ (feel) better immediately!
                                                  (8)

JENNY LEE, Astronaut

We _____ (see) many wonderful sights
(9)
from the International Space Station. On our last

mission, we _____ (look) out a window
(10)
and _____ (see) a meteor shower.
(11)
Some of the meteors _____ (hit) the
(12)
station. It _____ (be) spectacular!
(13)

B *Over to You* What is one exciting or interesting thing you have seen or done in
your life? Tell your partner. Use the present perfect to begin, and give the details in
the simple past.

A *I've had a lot of exciting adventures. For example, last summer I climbed*
Mount Whitney.

B *The most interesting thing I've seen is an eclipse. I saw it when I was a child.*

4 Avoid Common Mistakes ⚠

1. Use the correct word order in present perfect information questions.
has he
Where ~~he has~~ gone?

2. Use the correct form of the past participle in the present perfect.
found
I have ~~finded~~ many useful plants in the Amazon.

3. Use the simple past for finished actions or events.
graduated
She ~~has graduated~~ from the University of Texas in 2011.

4. Use the simple past to say exactly when something happened.
went
They ~~have gone~~ on an expedition last year.

**5. Use the present perfect for actions or events in the indefinite past that are still
important now.**
have gone
I ~~went~~ to three different countries on my trip so far.

Editing Task

Find and correct nine more mistakes in this interview with a rain forest explorer.

Claire Smith	How did you decide to become a rain forest explorer?
Bettie Silva	I ~~have been~~ *was* interested in the rain forest when I was a child. I have grown up in Brazil, and I heard many stories about the rain forest regions in my country as a child.
5 *Claire Smith*	When did you go on your first expedition?
Bettie Silva	I have gone on my first expedition in the 1980s. I have seen a lot of amazing sights on that first trip.
Claire Smith	Where have you gone on your first trip?
Bettie Silva	I went to rain forests in the Amazon and in Asia.
10 *Claire Smith*	Who you have traveled with?
Bettie Silva	I've traveled with teams of scientists and other explorers at different times.
Claire Smith	Have you ever had any dangerous experiences in the rain forest?
Bettie Silva	Yes. Sadly, I have loosed team members. For example, last year, a poisonous snake has bitten one of my group members. But I had many wonderful
15	experiences on trips so far, too. I have helped scientists discover new medicines, and I have meeted many interesting local people.

5 | Grammar for Writing

Using Present Perfect and Simple Past Together

Writers often use the present perfect to introduce a topic about the past. Then they change to the simple past to talk about specific events and experiences.

The present perfect is used in writing about a person's experiences and accomplishments over a period of time.
Remember:

- **Use the present perfect when exact dates are not important or are unknown or for actions and events that have happened over time and up to now.**

  I have learned a lot of new vocabulary words this year.

- **Use the simple past when the action or event was completed at a definite time or times in the past, or the time of the action is important.**

  Marcela took five classes last semester. It was very stressful.

Pre-writing Task

1 Read the journal entry below. What are some things the writer has done recently?

My Trips to Nearby Places

I do not have time to take long trips, but my family and I have visited some interesting places this year. We have taken three trips to Rivertown. We went last weekend by car. My sister lives there. We went fishing and had a picnic. We have been to the aquarium twice. We went there two months ago by bus. We took a tour, and we learned a lot about the animals. My children loved the sea lions. We have been to the park many times. Last night there was a concert. We danced and sang. It was a lot of fun. I like to take small trips to nearby places with my family.

2 Read the paragraph again. Underline the verbs in the simple past and circle the verbs in the present perfect. What time expressions (*last weekend*, etc.) does the writer use with the simple past? What time expressions (*this year*, etc.) does the writer use with the present perfect?

Writing Task

1 *Write* Use the paragraph in the Pre-writing Task to help you write about places you have visited. Where have you been? What did you do there?

2 *Self-Edit* Use the editing tips to improve your paragraph. Make any necessary changes.

1. Did you use the present perfect when exact dates are not important or are unknown, or for actions that have happened over time and up to now?
2. Did you use the simple past when the action is finished or the time of the action is important?
3. Did you avoid the mistakes in the Avoid Common Mistakes chart on page 125?

UNIT 11

Adverbs with Present Perfect;
For and *Since*

Unsolved Mysteries

1 | Grammar in the Real World

A In your opinion, what has been the most important scientific discovery? Read the article from a science magazine. What are some mysteries that science has not yet solved?

Unsolved Mysteries

Humans have learned many things over the years. For example, we have discovered DNA, and we have cured many diseases. We have visited the moon and sent robots to Mars. However, scientists **still** have not solved these mysteries.

Bird migration[1] How do birds travel thousands
5 of miles over land and sea without getting lost? Scientists have **never** understood this. There are some theories. One idea is that birds have magnetic particles[2] in their brains to help them find their way. However, science has **never** proven this.

10 **Earthquake lights** Blue and white lights flash in the sky just before an earthquake occurs. People have reported this for hundreds of years. Photographs from the 1960s prove the lights exist, but researchers **still** have not found the cause. One explanation is that the lights are gas escaping from openings in the earth.

Disappearing bees Scientists have **recently** said that billions of bees have
15 died since the 1980s. Why? They have not figured out the cause **yet**. However, they have **already** given the problem a name: Colony Collapse Disorder.

Yawning Why do we yawn? Scientists **still** have not solved this
mystery. People yawn when they are tired, but they also yawn in other situations, such as during exercise. Another mystery is why
20 yawning is "contagious" – we yawn when other people yawn. In fact, you may have **just** yawned from reading this sentence!

These and other mysteries are a challenge for scientists. Although we have not **yet** solved them, we are making progress every day.

¹**migration:** movement from one place to another │ ²**particles:** a technical term for very small pieces

B *Comprehension Check* Answer the questions.

1. What is one theory about why birds do not get lost when they migrate?
2. How do we know earthquake lights exist?
3. How many bees have died since the 1980s?
4. What are some situations in which people yawn?

C *Notice* Read the sentences from the article and answer the questions.

1. "They have not figured out the cause **yet**."
   Did scientists figure out the cause? Does the writer think that they will figure it out in the future?

2. "They have **already** given the problem a name: Colony Collapse Disorder."
   Did scientists give the problem a name?

3. "Why do we yawn? Scientists **still** have not solved this mystery."
   Did scientists solve the mystery? Does the writer want them to solve it?

2 | Adverbs with Present Perfect

▶ Grammar Presentation

Adverbs *already*, *still*, and *yet* with the present perfect show how a past event relates to the present.	He has **already** given a name to the disease, but he has not discovered the cause **yet**. He **still** has not found a cure for it. (This is the situation right now, up to this point in time.)

2.1 Adverbs with Present Perfect

a. Use *already* when something happened sooner than expected.	Scientists have **already** given the disease a name. It is only 8:00 p.m., but they have **already** gone home.
Use *already* in affirmative statements and in questions. It usually comes before the past participle.	PAST PARTICIPLE Have they **already** solved the problem?
b. Use *yet* with things that have not happened. It often means you expected something to happen or expect something to happen soon.	There are many mysteries scientists have not figured out **yet**.
Use *yet* in negative statements and in questions. It usually comes at the end of the sentence.	Have they discovered the cause **yet**?

c. Use *still* with things that have not happened. It often means you want something to happen, but it has not.	*Scientists are **still** looking for an explanation.*
Use *still* in negative statements, but avoid it in questions. It usually comes before *have / has*.	*It is past midnight, and she **still** has not gone home.*
d. Use *never* and *not ever* to mean "not at any time" or "zero times." They usually come before the past participle.	PAST PARTICIPLE *Scientists have **never** understood the cause.* *They haven**'t ever** understood the cause.* (These sentences have the same meaning.)
You can use *ever* in *Yes / No* questions.	*Have you **ever** thought about these mysteries?*
e. Use *just*, *lately*, and *recently* when something happened a short time ago. *Just* usually comes before the past participle. *Lately* usually comes at the end of a sentence. *Recently* can go in either position.	PAST PARTICIPLE *We have **just** discovered a new type of fish.* *She has been sick **lately**.* *Scientists have **recently** studied the issue.* *Scientists have studied the issue **recently**.*

▶ Grammar Application

Exercise 2.1 *Already, Yet, and Still*

Complete the statements about earthquake prediction with the present perfect form of the verbs in parentheses. Then check the correct statement about the action.

	The action has happened.	The action has not happened.
1. People ___*have not been*___ (not be) able to predict earthquakes **yet**.	☐	☑
2. However, many people _____ **already** _____ (notice) that animals behave strangely before an earthquake.	☐	☐
3. The United States Geological Survey (USGS) _____ **already** _____ (do) a few studies on animal behavior and earthquakes.	☐	☐
4. However, the USGS _____ (not prove) that animals can predict earthquakes **yet**.	☐	☐
5. As a result, Western scientists **still** _____ (not be) able to develop a warning system for earthquakes.	☐	☐
6. However, Asian scientists _____ **already** _____ (determine) the connection between animal behavior and earthquakes.	☐	☐
7. In fact, Chinese researchers _____ **already** _____ (use) animal behavior to save many people during earthquakes.	☐	☐
8. Many people think that we **still** _____ (not do) enough animal studies in the West.	☐	☐

Exercise 2.2 More Adverbs

A Complete the article about cow behavior. Circle the correct adverb.

Have you ever noticed that groups of cows all face the same way? Scientists have **ever** /(**never**) been able to explain this. Satellite photos have ₍₁₎

recently / **yet** shown that cows around the world ₍₂₎ all face either north or south. Scientists have

already / **still** not learned why cows do this. ₍₃₎ One theory involves magnets. The Earth is like

a huge magnet, and magnets point to the north. Studies have **already** / **yet** shown that ₍₄₎ this helps some small animals, such as bats, find their way. In addition, researchers have

never / **already** found that fish and whales have tiny magnetic particles in their brains. ₍₅₎ Therefore, some researchers have **recently** / **yet** guessed that cows also have magnetic ₍₆₎

particles in their brains. However, they have not found any proof **already / yet**. They
(7)
still / lately have not done any tests to see if cows have magnetic particles in their brains.
(8)

B 🔊) Now listen and check your answers.

Exercise 2.3 Position of Adverbs

Put the adverb in parentheses into the correct place in these sentences about the
mystery of aging. Sometimes more than one answer is possible.

1. Medical researchers ₋have not discovered the causes of aging. (still)

2. We have seen that humans are living longer and longer. (already)

3. However, we have not seen many people live beyond the age of 100. (still)

4. So far, humans have not lived past the age of 130. (ever)

5. Researchers have begun to understand the processes that occur in the body as
   we age. (just)

6. Scientists have discovered chemicals in the body that tell it to start aging.
   (recently)

7. Many people wonder what we can do to extend our lives, but science has not
   found the answers. (yet)

8. Some say that eating a low-calorie diet can extend life, but science has not
   proven this. (still)

Exercise 2.4 Questions and Answers

A Unscramble the words to make questions. Use the present perfect form of the verbs and
add *have* or *has* where needed. Sometimes more than one answer is possible.

1. scientists / another planet like Earth / yet / find / ?

   Have scientists found another planet like Earth yet?

2. already / we / what planets / send spaceships to / ?

   _____

3. find / ever / people / a cure for the common cold / ?

   _____

4. what medicines / recently / discover / researchers / ?

   _____

5. people / already / where / look / for new medicines / ?

   _____

6. figure out why we dream / yet / anyone / ?

   _____

7. any scientists / recently / in the news / be / ?

_____

8. you / wonder about a scientific mystery / ever / ?

_____

B *Group Work* Discuss the questions in A. Try to give extra information and ask follow-up questions.

A *Have scientists found another planet like Earth yet?*

B *I don't know. If they've already found a planet like Earth, I want to visit it!*

C *I don't think they've found a planet like Earth yet. But one is probably out there somewhere.*

3 | Present Perfect with *For* and *Since*

▶ Grammar Presentation

For and *since* with the present perfect describe the length of time that an action or event from the past continues into the present.	*She has not exercised **for** more than 30 years.* *She has not exercised **since** 1982.*

3.1 *For* and *Since*

a. Use the present perfect with *for* and a period of time (*20 years, three days, an hour, a long time*) to show the length of time of an action or event.

*He has lived here **for 20 years**.*
*They have studied this problem **for a long time**.*

b. Use the present perfect with *since* and a point in time in the past (*2009, last year, May 15*) to show when an action or event started.

*Humans have kept bees **since 4000 BCE**.*
*We have known about Colony Collapse Disorder **since the 1990s**.*

c. You can also use *since* before a clause.

*I have eaten chocolate **since I was a child**.*

d. You can use *for* and *since* in negative sentences to show when something happened for the last time.

*We **have not gone** to the moon **since** the 1970s.*
(The last time we went there was the 1970s.)

*There **has not been** an eclipse **for** five years.*
(The last eclipse was five years ago.)

e. You can ask about periods of time with *How long . . . ?*

A ***How long** have you lived here?*
B *For four years.*
A ***How long** has this been a problem?*
B *Since the 1980s.*

In conversation, people often omit *for* with these verbs: *live*, *work*, *be*, *know* (a person), and *play*.	Say: *"She's lived here a long time."*
In conversation, people also often say *in* instead of *for* in negative statements.	Say: *"I haven't exercised **in** years."*
Always use *for* in writing.	Write: *She has lived here **for** a long time.* Write: *I have not exercised **for** years.*

▶ Grammar Application

Exercise 3.1 *For* or *Since*?

A Complete the paragraph from an article about another scientific mystery: people who have bad lifestyle habits but live very long lives. Circle the correct words.

Experts have agreed (**for**)/ **since** many years that exercise, a good diet, and other
(1)
healthy lifestyle habits lead to a long life. However, why do some people with bad lifestyle habits live long lives? Scientists do not know. Take Sarah Baines, for example. She is 99 years old, and she is in good health. However, Sarah has had unhealthy habits **for** / **since**
(2)
her entire life. For example, Sarah has not exercised **for** / **since** she was a child. She has
(3)
smoked **for** / **since** 75 years, **for** / **since** she was a young woman.
(4)   (5)

Sarah also loves to eat. She has not been on a diet **for** / **since** 1952. She does not like
(6)
vegetables, and she has not eaten any salads **for** / **since** the last 40 years. She also loves
(7)
fatty food. She has eaten high calorie meals such as steak, potatoes with butter, and ice cream almost every day **for** / **since** her entire life. In addition, Sarah does not get much
(8)
sleep. She has not gone to bed before midnight **for** / **since** she was 13 years old. This
(9)
lifestyle is incredibly unhealthy, and Sarah often does not feel well, but she is stubborn and will not change.

B *Pair Work* Compare your lifestyle habits with Sarah's. Try to use *for* and *since*. Tell a partner.

   A I've exercised three times a week since 1999. How about you?

   B I haven't exercised for many years, but I've eaten healthy food since I was a child.

Exercise 3.2 More *For* or *Since*?

A Complete the interview with Mel Green, who is 85 years old. Use the present perfect form of the verbs in parentheses. Write *for* or *since* before each time expression.

Andy Jones We're at the Corner Café, and I am speaking with the chef and owner, Mel Green. Mel is 85 years old today. He's in excellent health. He has a sharp mind, and he still works! Happy birthday, Mel!

So, tell us a little about your long life. Have you lived here a long time?

Mel Green Well, I <u>'ve lived</u> (live) in California _____ 50 years, and
     (1)   (2)

I _____ (be) here in San Miguel _____ 1972.
  (3)   (4)

Andy Jones How do you spend your days?

Mel Green I work! I _____ (work) as a chef _____ 1945.
       (5)   (6)

Andy Jones How long _____ you _____ (own) the
         (7)   (7)

Corner Café?

Mel Green I __ _____ (own) this restaurant _____ 1980.
     (8)   (9)

Andy Jones What else do you do?

Mel Green I love to learn languages. I _____ (learn) Spanish, and
          (10)

I speak a little Chinese, too.

Andy Jones Wow!

Mel Green Yeah. Now I can speak Spanish with some of my customers.

Andy Jones What _____ you _____ (do) to stay healthy
      (11)   (11)

_____ so many years?
  (12)

Mel Green I _____ (not do) anything special to stay healthy, but
    (13)

I _____ (not eat) sweets _____ I was in
  (14)   (15)

my twenties.

Andy Jones   What are some of your other lifestyle habits?

Mel Green   I get up early. I _____ (get) up at 5:00 a.m. every morning
                 (16)
            _____ about 30 years.
               (17)

Andy Jones   What about exercise?

Mel Green   I _____ (not exercise) _____ a long time, but
               (18)   (19)
   my work keeps me active. I'm on my feet all day.

Andy Jones   What are your recommendations for a long life?

Mel Green   Keep busy!

B Find one place in the interview in A where you can omit *for* and circle it. Then find one place where you replace *for* with *in* and write *in* above *for*.

C *Pair Work*   Ask about your partner's life and answer questions about your life. Use the questions in A or your own ideas. Use the present perfect and time expressions with *for* and *since*.

   A How long have you lived here?
   B I've lived here (for) a long time.

   A How do you spend your days?
   B I work. I've worked at a repair shop since last year.

   A How long have you been a student at this school?
   B I've been here since 2010. / (for) two years.

   A Do you work out at the gym?
   B Yes, but I haven't worked out in / for months.

4 | Avoid Common Mistakes ⚠️

1. Use *never* in affirmative statements, not negative statements.

         never
Science has ~~ever~~ been able to explain this.

2. Use *ever* in negative statements, not affirmative statements.

         ever
They have not ~~never~~ been able to explain this.

3. Use the correct word order with adverbs and present perfect.

He   *just*
~~Just he~~ has ∧returned from his trip.

4. Use *since* with a point in time in the past. Use *for* with a period of time.

           for   *since*
I have not exercised ~~since~~ three years. I have not exercised ~~for~~ last month.

5. Do not use *for* or *since* with the simple present or present progressive.

have studied   *have studied*
We ~~study~~ this problem for 30 years. We ~~are studying~~ this problem since the 1960s.

Editing Task

Find and correct eight more mistakes in this article about blushing.

     Max is a drama major. Today, he is presenting a scene from a play in one of his

                     has taken
classes. He ~~is taking~~ acting classes since he was a child. He is acting, in front of people

since many years, and he has been in the drama department since three years. He has ever

felt uncomfortable on the stage. However, for some reason, Max just has forgotten his

5 lines, and his face has become red. Max is blushing.

     Many people blush when they are embarrassed, but science has not never been able

to explain why we blush. Researchers know how we blush: The nervous system causes the

blood vessels in our face to dilate. This increases blood flow to the face, and this makes it

look red. Researchers know for many years that teenagers blush more than adults do, but

10 still there has not been much research on blushing.

5 | Grammar for Writing

Using Present Perfect with Adverbs and *For* and *Since*

Writers use the present perfect to describe past actions or events that are not finished or are important now. They use *for* with the present perfect to tell you how long something happened. *Since* and present perfect tells you when something began. Writers use adverbs such as *yet*, *already*, and *still* to give the reader information about their expectations.

Remember:

- **Use *for* before a period of time and *since* before a starting time or clause.**

  It has not snowed <u>for six years</u>.

  There have not been any earthquakes <u>since I moved here</u>.

- **Use *yet* and *still* in negative sentences to talk about things that you expect or want to happen.**

  They have not cured cancer <u>yet</u>.

  Kimi <u>still</u> hasn't graduated.

- **Use *already* in affirmative statements to show that something has been accomplished.**

  They have <u>already</u> found cures for many diseases.

- **Use *just*, *lately*, and *recently* to show that the event happened a short time ago.**

  They have <u>just</u> discovered a new planet.

Pre-writing Task

1 Read the paragraph from a student essay and underline the present perfect verbs.

Butterfly Migration Mystery

There is an area in the woods near my house with a lot of butterflies. Butterflies stop and rest there during their migration south every year. The county bought this land so no one could build houses on it. It has owned the land for about eight years. There have been fences around the area since 2005 because a lot of people come to see the butterflies.

The number of butterflies that stop at the migration area has decreased every year for the last few years. Scientists have not yet learned why. The county has recently decided that the butterflies need more protection. They are asking volunteers to stay there during the migration period. Many people have already signed up to help.

2 Read the paragraph again. Circle the adverbs and *for* or *since*. Which adverbs go with actions or events that have happened? Which go with actions or events that have not happened?

Writing Task

1 *Write* Use the paragraph in the Pre-writing Task to help you write explanations or reasons for one of the following topics, or use your own ideas.

- weather changes in your area or other recent changes in nature
- behavior changes in people because of use of cell phones or the Internet
- the increase in interest in reality TV shows
- the increase in childhood autism, obesity, or other diseases

2 *Self-Edit* Use the editing tips to improve your paragraph. Make any necessary changes.

1. Did you use adverbs with the present perfect to show your expectations?
2. Did you use *yet* and *still* in negative sentences to talk about things you expect or want to happen?
3. Did you use *already* in affirmative statements to show that something has been accomplished?
4. Did you use *just*, *lately*, and *recently* to show that an action or event happened a short time ago?
5. Did you avoid the mistakes in the Avoid Common Mistakes chart on page 137?

Present Perfect Progressive

Cities

1 | Grammar in the Real World

A What do you like about big cities? What *don't* you like? Read the web article about problems caused by the growth of cities. How is city life improving?

City Life

Half of the world's population now lives in cities – that is over 3 billion people. Cities are growing at a faster and faster rate because people around the world **have been leaving** the countryside in search of jobs and a better life in urban areas. Current estimates are that 180,000 people migrate to
5 cities each day.

This trend **has caused** problems in some countries. Cities are growing too fast. For example, the population of Mumbai, India, increases by 4.2 percent each year. Beihai,
10 China, **has been growing** by 10.6 percent every year. There often isn't enough housing for all of the new people. As a result, the number of people living in slums[1] **has risen** in many cities. Environmental problems **have**
15 **been getting worse**, too.

Luckily, architects and urban planners **have found** solutions to some of these problems. In many cities around the world, architects **have designed** "green" buildings.
20 They use solar power, and they use less water.

In addition, urban planners **have been creating** green belts in cities. Green belts are large pieces of natural land that offer fresh air and places for recreation for people in cities.
25 Planners **have reclaimed**[2] green belts, too. In Seoul, South Korea, for example, planners

¹**slum:** a poor and crowded area of a city | ²**reclaim:** take something back

uncovered a small river in the middle of the city that was under a highway and built a park on both sides of the river.

These ideas **have not solved** all of the problems of big cities. There is still
30 not enough housing, for example. Also, green buildings and green belts are too expensive for some cities. However, these ideas **have made** life better for many people around the world.

B *Comprehension Check*   Answer the questions.

1. Why do people migrate to cities?
2. What happens when cities grow too fast?
3. Who has found solutions to some of these problems? What are the solutions?
4. What examples of green buildings and green belts does the article mention?

C *Notice*   How does the writer express these ideas in the article? Write the sentences from the article.

1. Environmental problems are now worse than they were.

   _____

2. Urban planners started creating green belts in cities, and they are still doing this.

   _____

2 | Present Perfect Progressive

▶ Grammar Presentation

The present perfect progressive usually shows something that started in the past and continues into the present time.	*Environmental problems* ***have been getting worse***. (This started in the past and continues into the present time.)

2.1 Statements

Subject	Has / Have (+ Not)	Been	Verb + -ing		Contractions	
I You We They	have have not haven't	been	working migrating living	here.	I have → I**'ve** You have → You**'ve** We have → We**'ve** They have → They**'ve**	
He She It	has has not hasn't				He has → He**'s** She has → She**'s** It has → It**'s**	

2.2 *Yes / No* Questions and Short Answers

Has / Have	Subject	*Been*	Verb + *-ing*	Short Answers	
Have	I you we they	**been**	**working**?	Yes, I **have**. Yes, you **have**. Yes, we **have**. Yes, they **have**.	No, I **haven't**. No, you **haven't**. No, we **haven't**. No, they **haven't**.
Has	he / she / it			Yes, he / she / it **has**.	No, he / she / it **hasn't**.

2.3 Information Questions

Wh- Word	*Has / Have*	Subject	*Been*	Verb + *-ing*
Where **When** **Why** **How** **How long**	**have**	I you we they	**been**	**working**?
	has	he / she / it		

Wh- Word	*Has / Have*	*Been*	Verb + *-ing*	
What	**has**	**been**	**happening**?	
Who			**migrating**	to cities?

2.4 Using Present Perfect Progressive

a. Use the present perfect progressive for actions and events that started in the past and continue into the present time or for actions that have just stopped.

*Environmental problems **have been getting** worse.*

*We**'ve been talking** about these problems for years.*

b. Use the present perfect progressive with *for* and *since* to show the duration of an action or event. Remember: Use *for* + a length of time and *since* + a specific time.

*I**'ve been living** here for a year.*

*He **hasn't been working** since last May.*

c. Use the present perfect progressive for actions or events that are new, temporary, or changing.

*He**'s been staying** with a friend until he finds his own apartment.*

*We**'ve been talking** about the news all day.*

d. Use the present perfect progressive with time expressions and adverbs, such as *this week / month / year, these days, nowadays, recently*, and *lately*.

*The city planners have been working hard **this week**.*

*A lot of people have been coming into the cities **lately**.*

Do not use the present perfect progressive with time expressions that describe finished time periods, such as *last year* or *three days ago*.

*The city **built** a lot of new housing last year.*

The city ~~has been building~~ a lot of new housing last year.

▶ Grammar Application

Exercise 2.1 Statements

Complete the blog post on city improvements. Use the present perfect progressive form of the verbs in parentheses.

Jen's Bay City Blog

New Report Has Good News on City Improvements
May 25

If you're like most Bay City residents these days, you _have not been feeling_ (1) (not feel) happy about garbage pickup, safety, transportation, and the libraries for a long time. However, a new report from the city this week has some good news. According to the report, people _____ (notice) (2) a lot of improvements lately. Here are just a few:

- The garbage collection service _____ (pick) (3) up trash on time. In addition, the garbage collection service _____ (not leave) garbage around the (4) pickup areas. I haven't noticed this one on my block, but I'm glad some of you have.

- People _____ (feel) safer in the park at night. (5) This is because more police _____ (patrol) (6) the park after dark. This is one that I've definitely experienced. I walked through the park the other night, and it felt much better.

- Public transportation _____ (improve). People
(7)
_____ (not complain) about rude bus drivers
(8)
lately. I guess those lucky people aren't on *my* bus line!

- The libraries _____ (stay) open
(9)
on weeknights. As a result, more families and working people

_____ (use) them. I haven't
(10)
been to the library recently, but I want to check this out.

What do you think? Leave a comment below with your opinion!

Exercise 2.2 Questions and Answers

A Complete an interview with a city planner. Use the present perfect progressive form of the verbs in parentheses in the questions. Write *for* or *since* in the answers.

Bay City News Talks to . . . Lisa Daniel

By Pedro Martin

Lisa Daniel is the chairperson of the Bay City Planning Committee. *Bay City News* spoke to her about her job and the future of the city.

Q Lisa, how long <u>*have*</u> you <u>*been working*</u> (work) as a city planner?
(1)　　　　　　　(1)

A I've been doing this <u>*since*</u> 2003.
(2)

Q And _____ you _____ (work) on the city's
(3)　　　　　　　　　(3)
planning committee for Bay City long?

A Not really. I've been working as a Bay City planner _____ three years.
(4)

Q What _____ the planning committee _____
(5)　　　　　　　　　　　(5)
(focus) on lately?

A Well, we've been looking at environmentally friendly design _____
(6)
last year.

Q That sounds interesting. _____ the planning committee
(7)
_____ (develop) new green belts in our city?
(7)

A Yes. We've been increasing green belts around the city _____ 2005.
(8)
For example, we've been tearing down old, unused warehouses and turning the
land into parks.

Q _____ you _____ (address) some of the
(9)   (9)
environmental issues that all cities are facing?

A Yes. We've been traveling to other cities _____ the past two years
(10)
and studying environmental projects.

Q Where are there some interesting environmental projects these days?

A Well, Berlin, for example.

Q What _____ (happen) there?
(11)

A Berlin has been doing some very interesting work adding trees and plants to the
tops of buildings in the last few years.

Q Is Bay City growing like other big cities?

A Absolutely. Bay City's population has been increasing _____
(12)
1990. It has caused some problems, but we have been keeping housing costs low
_____ the city passed the new rent laws.
(13)

B *Pair Work* Make a list of some of the problems in your town or city. Then, with a
partner, write five questions about the problems to ask a member of your town or city
planning committee.

- *high housing costs*
- *crowded public transportation*
- *pollution*

Has the city been growing a lot recently?
What improvements have you been talking about?

3 Present Perfect Progressive or Present Perfect?

▶ Grammar Presentation

The present perfect progressive focuses on an ongoing action or event, which may or may not be finished. The present perfect often suggests that the action or event is complete.	*Planners **have been reclaiming** green belts all over the city. (They may still be doing this.)* *Planners **have reclaimed** green belts all over the city. (They are not doing this anymore.)*

3.1 Present Perfect Progressive or Present Perfect?

a. Use the present perfect progressive for an action or event that started in the past and may or may not be finished yet.	*Urban planners **have been creating** green belts in cities.* (They aren't finished. They may still be doing this.)
You can use the present perfect for an action or event that is finished.	*Urban planners **have created** green belts in cities.* (They have finished. The green belts are done.)
b. Use the present perfect progressive to focus more on the *activity* of the action or event.	***I've been writing** a paper on city planning.* (focus on the activity of writing)
Use the present perfect to focus on the *results* of the action or event.	***I've written** a paper on city planning.* (focus on the completed paper)
c. Use the present perfect progressive for situations that are new or temporary (only for a short time).	*It takes time to find housing in the city, so I**'ve been staying** with my aunt and uncle.* (I am doing this for a short time only.)
Use the present perfect for situations that are permanent (last for a long time).	*He**'s lived** in the same house for 30 years.* (This is a permanent situation.)
d. Use the present perfect, not progressive, when you say how much or how many times something has happened.	*The planners **have visited** Berlin three times.* *They **have built** three green apartments in Brooklyn.*
e. With *get, go, increase, live, study,* and *work*, you can often use either form. The progressive suggests the action or event is new or temporary.	*We **have lived** here for 20 years.* *We **have been living** here for two months.*

3.1 Present Perfect Progressive or Present Perfect? *(continued)*

f. Do not use the progressive form with stative verbs such as *be, believe, hate, know, like,* and *understand.*	They **have known** about the problem for many years. They have ~~been knowing~~ about the problem for many years.

Data from the Real World

The present perfect is much more common than the present perfect progressive, especially in writing. When you have a choice of forms in writing, use the present perfect if you need to sound more formal.

Less formal: *I've been living* here since 2008.
More formal: *I have lived* here since 2008.

▶ Grammar Application

Exercise 3.1 Present Perfect Progressive or Present Perfect?

A Check (✓) the sentences that you can rewrite in the present perfect progressive. Then do B with a partner.

1. Environmental problems in our city have increased. ☑

   _____

2. For example, air pollution has been a big problem. ☐

   _____

3. We have known about the causes of air pollution for many years. ☐

   _____

4. Studies have shown that green belts reduce air pollution. ☐

   _____

5. Planners have talked about creating more green belts in our city. ☐

   _____

6. They have studied the effects of green belts in other cities for the past year. ☐

   _____

7. For example, planners have reclaimed two green belts in New York City. ☐

   _____

8. As a result, air quality has improved by 10 percent. ☐

   _____

B *Pair Work* Compare your answers in A with a partner. Discuss the reason for each of your answers. Then rewrite the sentences you checked. Use the present perfect progressive.

> A *You can rewrite number 1 in the present perfect progressive.*
> *"The environmental problems have been increasing."*
>
> B *Right. But you can't rewrite number 2 because be is . . .*

Exercise 3.2 Present Perfect, Present Perfect Progressive, or Both?

A Complete the paragraphs about a student's description of her neighborhood. Write the form of the verbs in parentheses – either the present perfect or the present perfect progressive.

There have been a lot of changes in my neighborhood in the last year. Some changes _have been_ (be) good. For example, four
(1)
new restaurants _____ (open).
(2)
The city _____ (build) a new
(3)
children's playground, and it should be ready next month. They _____ also
(4)
_____ (build) some green
(4)
apartments – they finished them six months ago. A lot of new people _____ (move) in already.
(5)

Unfortunately, some things _____ (get) worse. About six stores
(6)
_____ (close) down, just on my street. Two of my favorite stores
(7)
_____ (go) out of business. Also, crime _____ (increase).
(8)   (9)
Thieves_____ (break) into the deli on my street twice in the last six months. I
(10)
guess both good and bad things can happen at the same time.

B 🔊 Now listen and check your answers. You can use both present perfect progressive and the present perfect for two of the verbs in A. Which ones?

C *Pair Work* Compare your neighborhood with the one in A. Talk with a partner about the good changes and the bad ones. Use the present perfect or the present perfect progressive.

> A *We've had some good changes in my neighborhood. For example, the city has built a new park. How about you?*
>
> B *The city has started a farmers' market right in my neighborhood. We've been getting great fresh fruit and vegetables straight from the farm right down the street.*

4 Avoid Common Mistakes ⚠

1. **Use *have* when forming the present perfect progressive.**

   have
   They ‸ been creating green belts in cities.

2. **Use *has* with singular third-person subjects (*he, she, it*). Use *have* with other subjects.**

   has
   This city ~~have~~ been getting more expensive in the last few years.

3. **Use the present perfect with stative verbs. Do not use the present perfect progressive.**

   known
   Experts have ~~been knowing~~ about the problem for many years.

4. **Use the present perfect progressive, not the present progressive, with *for* and *since*.**

   have been
   Environmental problems ~~are~~ getting worse here for many years.

Editing Task

Find and correct eight more mistakes in this interview with a green architect.

have
Kyle Jones Urban planners and architects ‸ been remodeling city buildings to
make them more energy efficient. This been making life in our city
kinder to the environment. It have also been making life healthier for
city residents. Today, we are asking the architect Vinh Hu about his

5 work. Mr. Hu, how long you been designing green buildings?

Vinh Hu Oh, a long time. We're designing these buildings for almost 20 years.
We've been believing for a long time that green buildings are an
important way to improve city life. We've also been knowing for a long
time that most people prefer green apartments. In the future, no one

10 will want to live in a building that isn't environmentally friendly.

Kyle Jones What you been working on lately?

Vinh Hu We've been building two new apartments on Murray Street.

Kyle Jones Yes, I am watching those apartments go up for a while. What makes
them green?

15 **Vinh Hu** They use solar energy for heat.

Kyle Jones Very interesting! Thank you, Mr. Hu.

5 | Grammar for Writing ✏

Using Present Perfect Progressive and Present Perfect Together

Writers often use the present perfect to talk about changes that have already happened. They use the present perfect progressive to talk about changes that are continuing to happen.

The present perfect progressive is common in newspaper and magazine articles. It is less common in academic writing.
Remember:

- **Use the present perfect progressive to talk about new or temporary changes that are still happening now.**

  The city's population has been growing rapidly for several years.

- **Use the present perfect when an action or event is finished or to talk about how many times something has happened in the past.**

  Housing in the city has improved. The city has built more than 10 new apartment buildings.

Pre-writing Task

1 Read the paragraph from a student essay. What has caused the recent changes in this neighborhood?

Good and Bad Neighborhood Changes

There have been many changes in our neighborhood recently. Home developers have built about 10 new houses in the last two years. This has caused a lot more traffic on our street, and some of our new neighbors have been driving too fast through our neighborhood. We have been trying to slow them down with signs. We have also been telling our children not to play soccer and basketball in the street the way they used to. One good thing about this is that the home developer has started construction on a new park nearby. They have been working on it for about a month. They have already put in a playground, and there are plans for a skateboard park as well. We are all looking forward to using it.

2 Read the paragraph again. Underline the present perfect verbs and circle the present perfect progressive verbs. Which present perfect sentence talks about how many times something happened? Which describes an action or event that is finished? Which uses a stative verb?

Writing Task

1 *Write* Use the paragraph in the Pre-writing Task to help you write about some recent changes you know about. You can write about one of these topics or use your own ideas.

- your neighborhood
- your town or city
- your state or country
- your family or group of friends
- the environment
- your workplace

2 *Self-Edit* Use the editing tips to improve your paragraph. Make any necessary changes.

1. Did you use the present perfect progressive to talk about changes that are continuing to happen?
2. Did you use the present perfect progressive for new or temporary changes?
3. Did you use the present perfect when an action or event is finished or you want to say how many times an action or event happened?
4. Did you avoid the mistakes in the Avoid Common Mistakes chart on page 149?

Adjectives
A Good Workplace

1 | Grammar in the Real World

A What makes a good workplace? Read the poster about workplace rights. What are some rights that workers have?

Know Your Rights on the Job

In the United States, you have **legal** rights to **fair** treatment in the workplace. You also have rights to **safe** conditions at work. **Ethical**[1] employers follow the laws, but some employers do not, so you should know what your rights are on the job.

Fairness

You have a right to **fair** treatment on the job. Women, men, **young** people, and **old**
5 people all have **equal** rights. Discrimination is **illegal**. For example, women and men have the right to **equal** pay for the **same** job.

You also have a right to a workplace that is not **hostile**.[2] If your co-workers treat you badly because of your race or the place you come from, this is **illegal**. You have the right not to feel **embarrassed** or **humiliated**[3] at work.

10 Report **hostile** behavior at work to the Equal Employment Opportunity Commission (EEOC). It is your **legal** right.

Safety

Workers have the right to a **safe** workplace. These are some examples of **unsafe** or **unhealthy** conditions.

- working near **toxic**[4] chemicals
15 - working with **dangerous** machines
- **slippery** floors
- **sharp** objects
- **loud** noise

You have the right to **free training** courses on the
20 **safety** issues in your workplace. For example, you have the right to get training on how to use **dangerous** machines.

If you see **dangerous** or **unsafe** conditions at work, report them to your supervisor or the Occupational
25 Safety and Health Administration (OSHA). Your company cannot fire you for reporting problems. Everyone has the right to a **safe**, **fair** workplace.

[1]**ethical:** good, correct, moral | [2]**hostile:** unfriendly, showing strong dislike | [3]**humiliate:** make you feel ashamed, lose respect for yourself | [4]**toxic:** poisonous

B *Comprehension Check* Answer the questions.

1. Why is it important to know your rights on the job?
2. What are two fair treatment rights that workers have?
3. What are two safety rights that workers have?
4. Who do you report unsafe conditions to?

C *Notice* Find the sentences in the poster and complete them.

1. _____ employers follow the laws.

2. You have a right to _____ treatment on the job.

3. You also have a right to a workplace that is not _____ .

4. You have the right not to feel _____ or _____
   at work.

Look at the words you wrote. Which words do they describe?

2 | Adjectives

▶ Grammar Presentation

<table>
<tr>
<td>Adjectives describe nouns – people, places, things, and ideas.</td>
<td>**Ethical** employers follow the laws.
(*Ethical* describes *employers*.)
Discrimination is **illegal**.
(*Illegal* describes *discrimination*.)</td>
</tr>
</table>

2.1 Using Adjectives

<table>
<tr>
<td>**a.** Adjectives usually go before nouns, not after.</td>
<td>*Women and men have the right to* **equal** *pay.*
Women and men have the right to ~~pay equal~~.
Workers have **legal** *rights to* **fair** *treatment.*
Workers have ~~rights legal~~ *to* ~~treatment fair~~.</td>
</tr>
<tr>
<td>**b.** However, adjectives can go after *be* or after linking verbs like *become, look, feel, sound, smell, taste, seem,* and *appear*.</td>
<td>*My company* **is** *an* **ethical** *employer.*
That job **looks safe**.
The boss **seems nice**.</td>
</tr>
<tr>
<td>**c.** Adjectives do not have plural forms. Do not add -*s*.</td>
<td>*This is your* **legal** *right. These are your* **legal** *rights.*
These are your ~~legals~~ *rights.*
Ethical *employers create an* **ethical** *workplace.*
~~Ethicals~~ *employers create an ethical workplace.*</td>
</tr>
</table>

2.1 Using Adjectives (continued)

d. Use *an* (not *a*) before an adjective that starts with a vowel sound with a singular count noun.	***An e**thical employer means **an e**thical workplace.* *~~A~~ ethical employer means . . .* *Don't use **an u**nsafe machine without training.* *Don't use ~~a~~ unsafe machine . . .*

2.2 Using Nouns as Adjectives

a. You can use some nouns as adjectives before other nouns. Do not make these plural.	*Workers have **safety** rights. They also have **health** rights.* *They also have ~~healths rights~~.*
b. To describe the age or duration of a noun, you can use expressions like *15-year-old* or *six-month* as adjectives before the noun. Notice that the age and time nouns (e.g., *year*) are always singular, never plural.	***Fifteen-year-old** teenagers work in some restaurants.* *~~Fifteen years old~~ teenagers work in some restaurants.* *I want to take a **six-month** course in green office design.* *I want to take a ~~six months course~~.*

2.3 Using More Than One Adjective

Opinion	Size	Quality	Age	Shape	Color	Origin	Material	Type
beautiful nice	big long	free safe	old young	round square	blue red	Canadian Thai	cotton leather	evening training

When you use two or more adjectives before a noun, use the order in the chart above, from left to right.	AGE ORIGIN NOUN
	She drives an **old** **Japanese** **car** *to work.*
	
	          COLOR MATERIAL NOUN
	He wears **black** **leather** **boots** *to work.*
	
	          OPINION AGE TYPE NOUN
	There's an **interesting** **new** **safety** *course* *at work.*

Adjectives: Order Before Nouns: See page A9.

▶ # Grammar Application

Exercise 2.1 Word Order

A Rewrite these sentences. Use *be* + adjective.

1. Some factories have unhappy workers.   Some workers ___*are unhappy*___ .

2. They earn low wages.   Their wages _____ .

3. They have bad working conditions.   Their working conditions _____ .

4. They work long hours.   Their hours _____ .

B Rewrite these sentences. Put the adjective before the noun. Use *a* or *an* where needed.

1. The workers' pay at this company is equal.   At this company, the workers get _equal pay_ .

2. The bosses are ethical.   They are _____ .

3. The training courses are free.   They are _____ .

4. Our work day is eight hours.   We have _____ .

Exercise 2.2 Using Adjectives

A 🔊 Listen to Annie telling Nick about her new job. Then complete the conversation with the words in the box.

beige	cotton	great	leather	~~new~~	sport
black	fantastic	interesting	long	running	ugly

Nick I hear you have a __new__ job.
(1)

Annie Yes. I'm a technician at PC Emporium.

Nick That's great. What are your hours?

Annie We work 40 hours a week.

Nick And do you get a vacation?

Annie Yes. Even new employees get a _____
(2)
vacation – two weeks.

Nick That sounds _____ ! Do they
(3)
train you?

Annie Sure. I'm taking an _____ training
(4)
course right now. It goes for three days.

Nick Everything sounds _____ !
(5)

Annie Not everything. We have to wear an _____ uniform. I wear
(6)
_____ pants and a _____ shirt. The pants
(7)   (8)
are _____ and the shirt is _____ . Oh, and
(9)   (10)
black shoes.

Nick _____ shoes?
(11)

Annie No! _____ shoes.
(12)

B 🔊 Listen again and complete the paragraph about the conversation. Sometimes, more than one answer is possible.

Annie has a <u>40-hour</u> work week. She gets a _____ vacation
(1)   (2)

each year. Right now, she's taking a _____ training course. She wears
(3)

_____ _____ pants, a _____ _____
(4)   (4)   (5)   (5)

shirt, and _____ _____ shoes to work.
(6)   (6)

Exercise 2.3 Adjective Endings

Data from the Real World 🌐

Here are some common adjective endings with the most common adjectives that use them.

-able	-ful	-ial	-ic	-ical	-ive	-ous
comfortable	wonderful	social	public	medical	expensive	serious
available	beautiful	special	basic	political	positive	ridiculous
reasonable	awful	financial	economic	physical	active	dangerous

A Write the correct adjective endings in the opinion column about working conditions.

On average, American workers get only two weeks of paid vacation. I think that is ridicul<u>ous</u> . There are many beauti_____ places
(1)   (2)

in the United States, but no one has time to see them. Vacation time is more reason_____ in a lot of
(3)

other countries. For example, the French get about 37 paid vacation days, and the Koreans get about

25. American companies give short vacations for econom_____ reasons. It is
(4)

expens_____ for the company to pay workers for time off, but short vacations don't
(5)

help give employees a posit_____ attitude about their workplaces.
(6)

The working hours in the United States are another problem. Some Americans have

a 50-hour work week. Some say they do not have time for a soc_____ life. A long work
(7)

week can also be danger_____ . If you work all the time, you can have med_____ problems.
(8)   (9)

This is a seri_____ issue.
(10)

B *Pair Work* Imagine you are working in your ideal job. Tell your partner about:

- what you can wear
- how much vacation you have
- the hours you work
- what your co-workers are like

In my ideal job, I don't wear a uniform. I wear casual clothes, like my favorite black running shoes and a sweatshirt. I have a 40-hour work week with no overtime, and I get a four-week vacation every year.

3 | More About Adjectives

▶ Grammar Presentation

3.1 Adjectives Ending in *-ed* and *-ing*

a. Use *-ed* adjectives to describe how a person feels.	*I'm **interested** in workers' rights.* *I get **bored** when I work by myself.*
b. Use *-ing* adjectives to say what something or someone is like.	*My new job is **interesting**.* *Working in an office is **boring**.*

3.2 Adjective Patterns

a. You usually need a noun or pronoun after an adjective.	*I have a black shirt and a beige **shirt** / a beige **one**.* *I have a black shirt ~~and a beige~~.* *I wear nice clothes to work, but I don't wear expensive **clothes** / expensive **ones**.* *~~I don't wear expensive.~~*
b. Adjectives follow a measurement noun (*years*, *feet*, etc.).	*There are **eighteen-year-old** workers in some of the factories.* *That ladder is over ten **feet high**.*
c. Adjectives can follow the pronouns *something, anything,* and *nothing*.	*I want to wear **something special** for my first day at work.* *Are you doing **anything interesting** this weekend?*
d. Adjectives can follow the verb *make* + an object.	OBJECT ADJECTIVE *My boss **makes me nervous**.* OBJECT ADJECTIVE *Chemicals **make some people sick**.*
e. Do not use these adjectives before a noun: *afraid, alike, alive, alone, asleep, awake, aware*. They usually come after the verb *be*.	*The workers were all still **alive** after the factory explosion.* *He's not **asleep**. He's **awake**.* *I'm **afraid** of heights.*

▶ Grammar Application

Exercise 3.1 *-ed* or *-ing*?

A Complete the conversations. Choose the correct word.

1. *A* Have you ever felt (**embarrassed**)/ **embarrassing** by a joke that someone told at work or at school?

   B Yes, I have. Someone joked about my accent. That was **annoyed** / **annoying**.

2. *A* Are you **interested** / **interesting** in workers' rights? Or do you think it's a **bored** / **boring** issue?

   B No, it's a **fascinated** / **fascinating** subject. I'm not **bored** / **boring** by it at all.

3. *A* Are you **annoyed** / **annoying** by different kinds of discrimination at work?

   B Yes, of course. I'm **surprised** / **surprising** that it still happens. It's a **depressed** / **depressing** situation.

4. *A* Is your job ever **relaxed** / **relaxing**?

   B No, but I don't think work is supposed to be **relaxed** / **relaxing**. My job is sometimes **excited** / **exciting**, and I like that.

5. *A* Did you ever wear an **embarrassing** / **embarrassed** uniform to school or to work?

   B No. I wore a uniform, but it wasn't **embarrassed** / **embarrassing** because I liked it.

B *Pair Work* Practice the conversations with a partner. Then practice them again. This time, give your own answers.

Exercise 3.2 Adjective Patterns

Complete the conversations with *one / ones* and the words in parentheses.

1. *A* Which pants should I wear, the blue pants or the _brown ones_ ?

(brown)
   B The brown pants look better.

2. *A* How's your job?
   B It's OK. There are some nice co-workers and some _____ .

(less friendly)

3. *A* Joe has such an interesting job! He always has funny stories to tell.
   B That's true. We only have _____ .

(boring)

4. *A* Who goes to your restaurant?
   B Most of the customers are young professionals, but there are _____ , too.

(older)

5. *A* I work for an ethical employer.
   B You're lucky. I work for an _____ .

(unfair)

Exercise 3.3 Adjective Patterns

A Correct the mistakes in these sentences. You may need to add or change words.

1. Many ~~aware~~ people are ᴀ*aware* of gender, race, and ethnic discrimination in the workplace.

2. However, many aware people are not of size and age discrimination in the workplace.

3. For example, if a thin woman and an overweight woman apply for the same job, the thin often gets the job.

4. If a tall man and a short man try to get a promotion, the tall often gets the promotion.

5. A recent survey showed that the average Chief Executive Officer (CEO) in the United States is 6 tall feet.

6. Another survey showed that only 3 percent of CEOs in the United States are less than tall 5 feet, 7 inches.

7. Many older afraid workers are of age discrimination.

8. An older employee with a lot of experience can make nervous a young boss.

9. Some laws make illegal age discrimination.

10. For example, after you are 40 years, a law called the Age Discrimination Employment Act protects you.

B *Pair Work* Have you heard about someone who experienced discrimination? Tell a partner about it.

Exercise 3.4 Adjectives After Pronouns

A Add adjectives to the questions below.

1. Do you want a job where you do something _____ every day?

2. In your job, do you ever do anything _____ ?

3. Have you met anyone _____ at work recently?

4. Did anything _____ happen at your job recently?

B *Group Work* Ask and answer your questions in A. Give extra information in your answer.

A *Do you want a job where you do something exciting every day?*

B *No, actually, I don't. I don't have the energy for that. I want a quiet job where I don't do anything exciting or dangerous.*

Exercise 3.5 Using *Make* + Object + Adjective

A Answer the questions about work or school. Use the words in the box or your own ideas to help you answer the questions.

chemicals	early mornings	interesting work	long vacations
dangerous machines	an ethical boss	late nights	loud noise
discrimination	friendly co-workers	long hours	uncomfortable chairs

1. What makes you happy in the workplace?

   _____

2. What things about your job make you unhappy?

   _____

3. What workplace situations make you worried?

   _____

4. Has anything in your workplace ever made you sick?

   _____

B *Pair Work* Discuss your ideas in A with a partner.

A *Friendly co-workers make me happy in the workplace. What about you?*

B *Long vacations make me happy.*

4 Avoid Common Mistakes

1. **Notice the correct spelling of adjectives ending in -ful (not -full).**

   stressful
   She has a ~~stressfull~~ job.

2. **Don't confuse these common verbs and adjectives: interest ≠ interested, relax ≠ relaxed, stress ≠ stressed, worry ≠ worried.**

   worried
   I'm ~~worry~~ about my job.

3. **Be careful with adjectives that describe ages and length of time before a noun.**

   Fifteen-year-old
   ~~Fifteen-years-old~~ teenagers work in some restaurants.

4. **Remember to put opinion adjectives before others in a list before a noun.**

   wonderful little
   We work at a ~~little wonderful~~ shop on the weekends.

Editing Task

Find and correct eight more mistakes in this blog on work–life balance.

Balancing Work Life and Personal Life

interested
I have a very busy life. I have a fun job, and I am ~~interest~~ in my work. My

boss is fair, and I work for an ethical company. I have friends. My life sounds

perfect, right? However, I work a 60-hours week. I can't get all my work done

during the day, so I take it home. I do not spend much time with my husband

5 and our little beautiful four-years-old daughter. I also do not see my wonderfull

friends. This makes me feel very stress. I am never relax. I know my friends and

family are worry about me.

   I think I have a problem. I need some balance between my work life and my

personal life. I know there are usefull articles with tips for balancing your life. The

10 problem is, I do not have the time to read them!

---

5 | Grammar for Writing

Using Adjectives to Describe People, Places, Things, and Ideas

Writers use adjectives to give readers a more detailed picture of what they are writing about. Adjectives appear in almost every kind of text and are useful in descriptive writing about experiences, ideas, and opinions.

Remember:

- **Adjectives usually go before the nouns they describe. You can use many nouns as adjectives.**

  My friend has a <u>terrific job</u>. She works for a <u>computer company</u>.

- **Adjectives can also go after *make* + object, or after linking verbs such as *be*, *look*, *feel*, and *seem*.**

  My co-workers <u>make me happy</u>. It <u>feels great</u> to be in a positive work environment.

Pre-writing Task

1 Read the paragraph below. What did the writer like about the job? What did the writer not like?

My Fast-Food Job

I used to work in a fast-food restaurant. There were some enjoyable things about the job, but there were also some annoying things about it. We had a terrible boss, but all the workers were very friendly. We were mostly 17-year-old high school students, so we had a lot of good times together. We used to tell each other funny or silly jokes all the time. The boss was the main problem at that job. He often yelled at us, and that made us all nervous. It made the customers uncomfortable, too. Also, the pay was low. After a while, the fried food began to smell awful to us. I was very happy when I left that job.

2 Read the paragraph again. Underline the adjectives. Which ones come before nouns? Which are nouns used as adjectives? Which follow *make* + object or a linking verb?

Writing Task

1 *Write* Use the paragraph in the Pre-writing Task to help you write about a job you or someone you know has had. What was good about the job? What was bad about the job? Use adjectives to describe the workplace.

2 *Self-Edit* Use the editing tips below to improve your paragraph. Make any necessary changes.

1. Did you use adjectives to give a detailed "picture" of the topic?
2. Did you put the adjective before the noun? Did you correctly use nouns as adjectives?
3. Did you put the adjective after *make* + object or after linking verbs?
4. Did you avoid the mistakes in the Avoid Common Mistakes chart on page 161?

Adverbs of Manner and Degree
Learn Quickly!

1 | Grammar in the Real World

A Is language learning easy or hard for you? Read the web article about language learning strategies. What are some ways to learn a language, both inside and outside the classroom?

Learn to Learn a Language

Everyone has his or her own style[1] of learning a new language. Some students listen **quietly** in class. Others ask lots of questions. Some students study **alone**, and others study
5 in groups. However, one thing is true for all learners. You can become a better language learner by using learning strategies. Language learning strategies are techniques[2] that help you learn. There are strategies that help you
10 do **well** in your class, and there are strategies that help you use the language with others.

There are many study strategies for your classes. For example, in class, listen **carefully** and take notes. The first time you read something, skim it. This means you read the material **quickly** and only look for
15 the main points. Then read again and take notes on your reading. Make a list of new words and study the list **regularly**. Do not study for a test at the last minute. Also, do not stay up **late** the night before a test. Instead, get lots of sleep. A good night's sleep helps you think **clearly**.

Strategies also help you communicate with people in a new language. Talking
20 to people is a good way to improve listening and speaking. However, some people speak very **quickly**, and they do not speak **clearly**. **Politely** ask a person to speak **slowly** and **clearly**. This is a useful strategy. It is also a good idea to ask the person to repeat things. If you do not understand a word or phrase, **politely** ask the person to explain.

25 Learning strategies are good both for your classes and for communication outside of class. They help you to learn a new language **quickly** and **easily**.

[1]**style:** way of doing something that is typical of a person, group, place, or time | [2]**technique:** a specific way of doing a skillful activity

B *Comprehension Check* Answer the questions.

1. What is a learning strategy?
2. What are two strategies that help you do well in class?
3. Why is it a good idea to get a good night's sleep before a test?
4. What are two strategies that help you communicate?

C *Notice* Find the sentences in the article and complete them.

1. In class, listen _____ and take notes.

2. Make a list of new words and study the list _____ .

3. Also, do not stay up _____ the night before a test.

4. If you do not understand a word or phrase, _____ ask the person to explain.

Do the words in your answers describe people, or do they describe how an action happens?

2 | Adverbs of Manner

▶ Grammar Presentation

Adverbs of manner describe how an action happens.	*I read* **quietly** *in the library.* *The teacher says the answers* **quickly**.

2.1 Forming Adverbs of Manner

a. Add *-ly* to most adjectives to form adverbs of manner.	*quick* → *quickly* *She* **quickly** *memorized the words.* *careful* → *carefully* *Nick read the chapter* **carefully**.
b. Some adverbs have the same form as adjectives: *alone, early, fast, hard, high, late, low, right, wrong.*	*He studied* **alone**. *(adverb; describes how he studied)* *The boy is* **alone**. *(adjective; describes the boy)*
These adverbs usually go after the verb.	*He* ~~alone~~ *studied. He studied* **alone**.
c. The adverb form of *good* is *well*.	*Tom did* **well** *on the test.* *Tom did* ~~good~~ *on the test.* *She speaks English* **well**. *She speaks English* ~~good~~.
Well only goes after the verb.	*We communicate* **well**. *We* ~~well~~ *communicate.*

2.1 Forming Adverbs of Manner *(continued)*

d. Some adjectives end in *-ly*. They are not adverbs. Examples: *friendly, lively, lovely, silly, ugly*.	*Sara is **friendly**.* (adjective; describes *Sara*) *She makes **silly** faces in class.* (adjective; describes *faces*)

2.2 Using Adverbs of Manner

a. Most adverbs of manner come after the verb or after the verb + the object. Do not put an adverb between a verb and the object.	*He spells **terribly**.* *She always writes her essays very **carefully**.* *They take ~~carefully~~ tests.*
b. Many adverbs of manner can also come before the verb for emphasis.	*She **nervously** looked at the test.*
c. Adverbs of manner usually come between the auxiliary verb (*be, have*) or modal verb (*can, should*) and the main verb.	*They are **quietly** waiting for the test results.* *He has **suddenly** left the room.* *You can **politely** ask a question.*
d. Do not use adverbs after *be* or linking verbs (*appear, look, feel, sound, seem, smell, taste*). Use an adjective instead.	*The test **sounds** easy.* *The test sounds ~~easily~~.*

▶ Grammar Application

Exercise 2.1 Forming Adverbs

Complete the sentences with the correct adverb forms.

The Learners' Blog

What learning strategies do YOU use? Here's what our readers are using!

Marc J. I have a lot of reading assignments. I read _quickly_ (quick) through a
(1)
whole chapter. Then I read it _____ (careful) a second time.
(2)

Lisa L. I'm studying Chinese. I make flash cards for new words, and I study them

_____ (regular). It works! I always do _____
(3)   (4)
(good) on tests.

Roberto R. I don't like to study _____ (alone), so I joined a study group.
(5)
We study _____ (hard), but we have a good time, too!
(6)

Danielle F. I always go to bed _____ (early) before a big test.
(7)
The next day, I think _____ (clear) and do
(8)
_____ (good).
(9)

Nick B. When I read a textbook chapter, I skim the headings and

_____ (quick) read the first sentence of each paragraph.
(10)

Jin P. There are a lot of hard words in textbooks! If I don't know a word, I read

the sentence _____ (slow) and try to figure out the meaning.
(11)

Exercise 2.2 Adverb or Adjective?

Read a student's blog entry about memory tricks. Decide if each word in **bold** is
an adverb or an adjective. Circle the adverbs. Underline the adjectives.

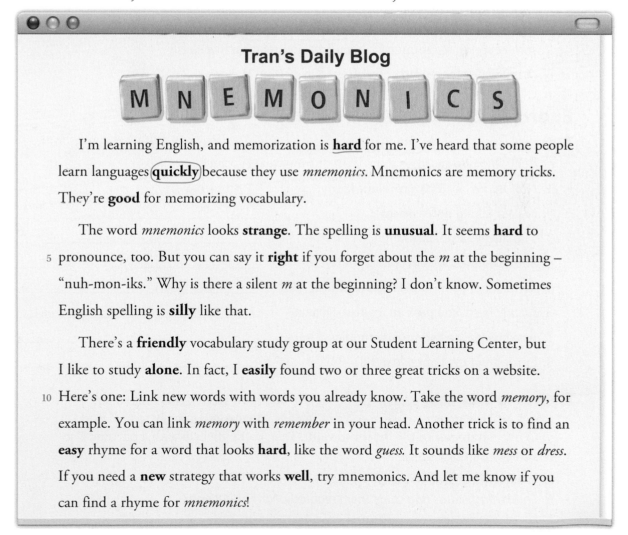

Tran's Daily Blog

M N E M O N I C S

I'm learning English, and memorization is <u>hard</u> for me. I've heard that some people
learn languages (quickly) because they use *mnemonics*. Mnemonics are memory tricks.
They're **good** for memorizing vocabulary.

The word *mnemonics* looks **strange**. The spelling is **unusual**. It seems **hard** to

5 pronounce, too. But you can say it **right** if you forget about the *m* at the beginning –
"nuh-mon-iks." Why is there a silent *m* at the beginning? I don't know. Sometimes
English spelling is **silly** like that.

There's a **friendly** vocabulary study group at our Student Learning Center, but
I like to study **alone**. In fact, I **easily** found two or three great tricks on a website.

10 Here's one: Link new words with words you already know. Take the word *memory*, for
example. You can link *memory* with *remember* in your head. Another trick is to find an
easy rhyme for a word that looks **hard**, like the word *guess*. It sounds like *mess* or *dress*.
If you need a **new** strategy that works **well**, try mnemonics. And let me know if you
can find a rhyme for *mnemonics*!

Exercise 2.3 Adverbs and Adjectives

Complete the sentences about preparing for tests.
Circle the correct words.

1. Studies show that students who do not sleep
   well / **good** do **poor** / **poorly** on tests.

2. Try to get a **good** / **well** night's sleep before a test.

3. Do not stay up **late** / **lately** the night before a test.

4. It is common to feel **nervously** / **nervous** the night
   before a big test, so try to relax.

5. Review everything **carefully** / **careful** two nights
   before a test; that way, you will sleep **sound** / **soundly**
   the night before the test.

6. The evening before a test, spend your time
   peaceful / **peacefully**: listen to music or take
   a warm bath.

7. On the morning of the test, eat **proper** / **properly**. For example,
   some experts recommend a high-protein breakfast like eggs.

8. Drink water **frequently** / **frequent** throughout the day.

Exercise 2.4 Word Order

A Rewrite the sentences. Change the adjectives into adverbs, and put them in the
correct place. Sometimes more than one answer is correct.

1. I got up for my 8:00 a.m. class. (early)   *I got up early for my 8:00 a.m. class.*

2. Max is taking notes. (neat)   _____

3. Tim always studies. (alone)   _____

4. She asks questions in class. (polite)   _____

5. My teacher pronounces new words. (clear)   _____

6. I study hard, so I pass all my tests! (easy)   _____

7. Ana has learned some mnemonics. (quick)   _____

8. I proofread my paper. (careful)   _____

B *Over to You*   Make a list of the strategies you have seen in this unit so far.
Check (✔) the ones you use now and the ones you are going to try to use. Add
your own strategies to the list if you want. Then compare lists with a partner. Use
adverbs of manner.

  A *What strategies do you use?*

  B *I make flash cards and study them regularly. How about you?*

3 Adverbs of Degree

▶ Grammar Presentation

Adverbs of degree make other adverbs or adjectives stronger or weaker.	*The reading was **quite** confusing.* *The teacher speaks **kind of** softly.*

3.1 Adverbs of Degree

more formal	quite extremely very	rather fairly	somewhat	
stronger	⟵		⟶	**weaker**
less formal	really so	pretty	kind of sort of	

3.2 Using Adverbs of Degree

a. Adverbs of degree can be used with adjectives or adverbs to make them stronger or weaker.

>   ADVERB   ADVERR
> *The teacher speaks **extremely softly**.*
>   ADVERB   ADJECTIVE
> *The reading was **extremely difficult**.*
>   ADVERB   ADJECTIVE
> *I had a **really wonderful** day!*

b. Do not use the weaker adverbs of degree in negative statements.

> *Tim did **not** study **very** hard for the test.*
> *Tim did not study ~~fairly~~ hard for the test.*
> *Ana did not ask ~~somewhat~~ politely.*

c. Use these adverbs of degree with adjectives or adverbs to give opinions: *amazingly, dangerously, horribly, incredibly, seriously, terribly, wonderfully.*

> *She did **amazingly well** on the test.*
> *We worked **incredibly hard** on our class project.*
> *Your paper is **wonderfully creative**.*

d. Use *enough* after an adverb or an adjective to show whether an amount is acceptable.

> *I studied hard **enough**.*
> (an acceptable amount)
>
> *Your essay seems long **enough**.*
> (an acceptable amount)
>
> *I did not study hard **enough**.*
> (an unacceptable amount)
>
> *Your essay doesn't seem long **enough**.*
> (an unacceptable amount)

3.2 Using Adverbs of Degree *(continued)*

e. Use *too* before an adverb or an adjective to show whether an amount is more than necessary.	We studied **too** hard! (more than necessary) Your essay is **too** long. (more than necessary) We did not study **too** hard. (not more than necessary) Your essay is not **too** long. (not more than necessary)

▶ Grammar Application

Exercise 3.1 Adverbs of Degree

A Complete the sentences. Circle the adverb of degree that matches the type in parentheses: either weak, strong, or in the middle.

1. My English class is **sort of** / **pretty** fun. (weak)

2. The teacher is **really** / **pretty** nice. (strong)

3. My teacher speaks **very** / **kind of** quickly. (weak)

4. I listen **really** / **pretty** hard, but I don't understand everything. (in the middle)

5. My math class is **extremely** / **somewhat** difficult. (weak)

6. I do the assignments **pretty** / **very** carefully. (strong)

7. We have a **very** / **rather** difficult quiz every Friday. (strong)

8. I study **so** / **fairly** hard every night. (strong)

9. I get **fairly** / **quite** nervous before every quiz. (in the middle)

10. I'm **pretty** / **really** sure I'm going to get a good grade. (in the middle)

B *Over to You* Write six sentences about your teachers, your classes, and your schoolwork. Then discuss your sentences with a partner. Use adverbs of degree that are weak, strong, and in the middle.

A I'm pretty sure I'm going to get a good grade in English.
B Why?
A I study very hard before every test.

Exercise 3.2 Using *Too* and *Enough*

A Match the statement on the left with the correct response on the right. Complete the responses with *too* or *enough* and the adjectives or adverbs in parentheses.

1. I didn't do as well as I expected on

   the test. ___f___

2. I have to rewrite my essay. _____

3. I have a big test tomorrow. _____

4. Is my homework OK? It's due soon. _____

5. The group meets at 8:00 a.m.

   Can you come? _____

6. We have only two days to write

   a paper. _____

7. The teacher didn't hear my

   questions. __ _

8. We've studied all day. I'm tired! _____

a. Yes, we've studied _____ .
   (long)
   Let's go to bed.

b. Two days doesn't seem _____ !
   (long)

c. Sure. That's not _____ for me.
   (early)

d. Then don't stay up _____
   (late)
   tonight!

e. Maybe you didn't speak _____ .
   (loudly)

f. Maybe you didn't study __*hard enough*__ .
   (hard)

g. Maybe it was _____ .
   (short)

h. Sure. It looks _____ . You
   (good)
   can turn it in.

B *Pair Work* Practice the statements and responses in A with a partner.

Exercise 3.3 Formal Adverbs of Degree

Data from the Real World	
Research shows that the formal adverbs of degree are more common in class papers, presentations, and other formal situations.	*The questions were **extremely** difficult.* (more formal)
Use the less formal adverbs of degree in conversations with friends, in e-mails, and in other informal situations.	*The questions were **really** difficult.* (less formal)

Read a formal letter that a student wrote to a professor. Choose the correct adverbs of degree.

Dear Dr. Green,

   I am in your Math 101 class. I am **really**/**quite** worried about my
(1)
grades for this class. I am **pretty**/**fairly** sure that I am not doing **very**/**so** well.
(2)   (3)
The work for this class is **so**/**extremely** difficult for me. I do the assignments
(4)
pretty/**rather** carefully, but I do not understand everything. I study **quite**/**so**
(5)   (6)
hard for every test. However, I did not study **extremely**/**sort of** hard for the last
(7)
test, and I know I did not do **so**/**very** well.
(8)
   Can you give me some advice? I am **very**/**really** eager to improve in
(9)
your class.

Thank you.

Sincerely,

Matthew Yee

Exercise 3.4 Listening for Adverbs of Degree

A ◀)) Listen to a group of students. They are working on a flier about study skills.
Complete their conversation with the adverbs of degree that you hear. Then
compare your answers with a partner.

Alison So, what are some tips for studying and

          getting good grades?

Dinh   Well, it's important to study

          really hard.
          (1)

Alison Right. It's also _____
                              (2)
          important to do all of your homework.

          What do you think, Carlos?

Carlos Um, my vocabulary notebook is

          _____ helpful to me!
                  (3)

Alison How does that help?

Carlos   When I want to use a new word, my notebook has sentences to help me

remember how to use it.

Dinh   Hmm, I don't know . . .

Carlos   Oh, it works _____ well, in my opinion.
(4)

Dinh   OK. So, a vocabulary notebook is a _____ good idea.
(5)

Alison   Yes. So we have three tips. Study, do your homework, and keep a vocabulary

notebook. What else?

Dinh   Asking questions. Ask questions in class. That's _____
(6)

important.

Carlos   Here's another one: I think it's a _____ good idea to have a
(7)

study group. It's _____ important to have people to study
(8)

with and to talk about class with, in my opinion.

Dinh   I agree. Studying together is _____ helpful!
(9)

B *Group Work*   Brainstorm ideas for a group about study skills. Use the ideas
from the conversation and your own ideas. Then make a flier on a piece of paper.
Use formal adverbs in your flier, not the informal ones that the students used.

4 Avoid Common Mistakes ⚠️

1. Use an adverb, not an adjective, to describe how something happened.

carefully
She studied very ~~careful~~.

2. *Well* is the adverb for *good*.

well
He did ~~good~~ on the test.

3. Do not put an adverb between the verb and the object.

the questions loudly
They answered ~~loudly the questions~~.

4. In negative statements, only use strong adverbs.

very
They did not study ~~fairly~~ hard.

5. Remember that some adverbs have the same form as adjectives.

hard
He is working ~~hardly~~ at his new job.

Editing Task

Find and correct seven more mistakes in this conversation about studying.

   Marisa I didn't do ~~good~~ *well* on the test today!

     Sam Did you study hardly last night?

   Marisa I tried, but it was so loud in the library. How about you?

     Sam I didn't do good, either. I studied, but I didn't sleep pretty well.

5 *Marisa* And the test seemed easy.

     Sam But it wasn't. It was too hard!

   Marisa Well, what happened? We took carefully notes.

     Sam And we listened good in class.

   Marisa Maybe we didn't study careful enough.

10   *Sam* I'm suddenly getting nervous!

   Marisa Why?

     Sam Well, we don't have a pretty long time before the next test!

5 | Grammar for Writing

Using Adverbs of Manner and Degree

Writers use adverbs to describe verbs, adjectives, and other adverbs. Like adjectives, they add detail. Adverbs of degree can also make adjectives and other adverbs stronger or weaker.

The adverb *very* is often overused. Try not to use it too much. You can use another word instead. Instead of *I felt very tired*, write *I felt extremely tired*, or *I felt exhausted*. Remember:

- **Do not use adverbs between a verb and its object.**

    slowly
    She read ~~slowly~~ each study question. She read ~~carefully~~ her notes. *carefully*

- **Use adverbs of degree to further explain adverbs of manner or adjectives.**

    "How <u>carefully</u> did you read each question?"   *"I read each question <u>extremely</u> carefully."*

Pre-writing Task

1 Read the paragraph below. What does the writer's language learning trick help the writer to learn?

My Personal Language Learning Trick

It is extremely hard to learn new words. My roommates and I have a vocabulary learning trick that works very well for us. First, when we hear or see a new word, we quickly write it down in our vocabulary notebooks. Then, each night, we meet briefly to tell each other our new words. One person carefully chooses one of the words for us. Then, the next day, we all try hard to use that word appropriately as many times as possible. By the end of the day, we usually know the word pretty well. Each night, we compare the number of times we used the word. Then the winner chooses the word for the next day. This way, we easily learn about seven new words each week. This trick works well for me, and I recommend it to everyone.

2 Read the paragraph again. Underline the adverbs of manner. Circle the adverbs of degree.

Writing Task

1 *Write* Use the paragraph in the Pre-writing Task to help you write about a study skill or learning strategy you use or have heard about. Use adverbs of manner and degree to help you explain the learning strategy.

2 *Self-Edit* Use the editing tips below to improve your paragraph. Make any necessary changes.

1. Did you use adverbs to explain *how* an action or event happens?
2. Did you put the adverbs in the correct position?
3. Did you use any adverbs of degree to add more meaning to your adjectives and adverbs?
4. Did you avoid the mistakes in the Avoid Common Mistakes chart on page 173?

1 Grammar in the Real World

A Where did the food you ate today come from? Read the article about how food is produced and sometimes wasted. Where are three places that food goes before it reaches our plates?

From Plow to Plate
(and Sometimes to the Trash)

In 2008, more than 17 million households **in** the United States could not afford to eat every day. **In** the same year, businesses threw away 48 billion dollars' worth of food. In addition, families threw away around 25 percent of the food they bought. Most of this food is perfectly good and safe to eat. Why do we waste this food? How
5 can we waste less of it?

Our food has often traveled hundreds of miles **from** farms **to** our plates. **At** every step of this journey, people throw away food. **On** farms, farmers throw away food that is the wrong size, shape, or color. **From** the farm, food usually goes **to** a processing[1] plant. **At** the processing plant, workers clean it, package it, and sometimes cook it or
10 add chemicals. They also throw away food they cannot transport or sell. Then food leaves the plant. Trucks take it **across** the country to warehouses, distribution centers,[2] and supermarkets. All of these places throw away food that people do not buy.

After this long process, we buy the food and store it **in** our refrigerators. Sometimes we forget it, or we buy too much. Then we throw it away,
15 too. Restaurants also throw away food that we do not order or eat.

We can waste less food. Supermarkets and restaurants can give unused food to food banks – groups that distribute food to poor and hungry people. **At** the supermarket, we can ask ourselves, "Do I really need to buy this? Will I use this food right away?" We can also buy
20 food **from** local farmers. This food does not go **through** processing plants, so there is less waste.

[1]**processing:** the preparation, change, or treatment of food with chemicals to make it last longer
[2]**warehouse, distribution center:** large building used for storing goods

B *Comprehension Check* Answer the questions.

1. How much food did businesses and families throw away in 2008?
   Is this food safe to eat?
2. According to the article, why do farmers throw away food?
3. Why do processing plants throw away food?
4. What are food banks?
5. Why is it better to buy food from local farmers?

C *Notice* Find the sentences in the article and complete them.

1. _____ 2008, more than 17 million households _____ the United States could not afford to eat every day.

2. Our food has often traveled hundreds of miles _____ farms _____ our plates.

3. _____ the farm, food usually goes _____ a processing plant.

4. Trucks take it _____ the country to warehouses, distribution centers, and supermarkets.

Look at the words you wrote in the blanks. Which words show time? Which show place? Which show movement?

2 | Prepositions of Place and Time

▶ Grammar Presentation

Prepositions can show place and time.	*People often have too much food **on** the table.* ***In** 2008, U.S. families threw away around 25 percent of the food they bought.*

2.1 Prepositions of Place

Use prepositions of place to show where people and things are.

a. *in*		***in** my room* ***in** the city* ***in** Canada* *People store food **in** the refrigerator.*
b. *on*		***on** the table* *things **on** my desk* ***on** the floor* *People often have too much food **on** the table.*
c. *at*		***at** home* ***at** work* ***at** school* *sitting **at** my desk* *They process the food **at** a food processing plant.*

2.1 Prepositions of Place (continued)

d. under

things **under** my desk   **under** the bridge
She always has a box of cookies **under** her desk!

e. behind

sit **behind** someone in class   **behind** the door
The store must keep the bags **behind** the counter.

f. near

near the city   **near** my house
The farm is **near** the processing plant, so the journey is short.

2.2 Prepositions of Time

a. Use prepositions of time to say when events happen.

Use *at* for clock times and with *night*.	The trucks arrive **at** noon every day with fresh food. We often go out **at** night.
Use *in* for parts of the day (except *night*), months, seasons, and years.	**In** the spring, the farmers plant new crops. The trucks arrive at the plant **in** the morning.
Use *on* for dates and special days.	People often have barbecues and picnics **on** July 4.

b. In sentences that include two different times . . .

use *before* to refer to the earlier time.	I need to go grocery shopping **before** dinner. (First is grocery shopping, then dinner.)
use *after* to refer to the later time.	**After** breakfast, we do the dishes. (First is breakfast, then the dishes.)

c. Use *during* to refer to the time that something is in progress.

The food loses freshness **during** its journey to supermarkets.

food loses freshness

X

journey

d. Use *for* to say how long something takes or lasts.

The food stays at the distribution center **for** three days.

Day 1   Day 2   Day 3

Use *since* to refer to the time from a point in the past up to now.	**Since** June, the farm has sold 120 tons of fruit. X June now

2.3 Prepositional Phrases

A prepositional phrase is a preposition followed by an object of a preposition. The object must be a noun phrase or a verb in the *-ing* form.

PREP.   OBJECT OF PREP.
*They put the food **in the refrigerator**.*

PREP.   OBJECT OF PREP.
*The fruit is **on the counter**.*

PREP.   OBJECT OF PREP.
*We need fresh water **for drinking**.*

▶ # Grammar Application

Exercise 2.1 Prepositions of Place and Time

A Complete the magazine article. Circle the correct prepositions.

The Long Journey of a Tomato

On / **At** Monday, July 13, Jeff Green picked the tomatoes at his farm in Florida. The
(1)
next day, a truck arrived. It took the tomatoes to a processing plant **near** / **in** Jeff's
(2)
farm. The plant was about five miles away. The tomatoes were there for three days.

At / **During** that time, workers checked them, washed them, and put them **at** / **in**
(3)   (4)
plastic containers. **In** / **On** July 17, the tomatoes went on trucks. The trucks took them
(5)
to a distribution center 300 miles away. **After** / **Before** that, the tomatoes went to a
(6)
supermarket in New Jersey. Ana Luz bought them, took them home, and put them in
her refrigerator. **After** / **Before** that, the tomatoes sat **in** / **on** the supermarket shelf
(7)   (8)
for / **since** two days. It was Friday, July 24. Ana did not know that her "fresh" tomatoes
(9)
were 11 days old.

B *Pair Work* Write answers to the questions below. Use prepositions. Then ask and answer the questions with a partner.

1. *A* When did Jeff Green pick tomatoes on his farm?

   B _On Monday, July 13._

2. *A* Where did a truck take the tomatoes?

   B _____

3. *A* Where was the processing plant?

   B _____

4. *A* How long were the tomatoes at the processing plant?

   B _____

5. *A* Where did the processing plant workers put the tomatoes?

   B _____

6. *A* Where did the tomatoes sit for two days?

   B _____

Exercise 2.2 Prepositions of Place

A Look at the picture and complete the answers. Use the prepositions in the box.
You will use some prepositions more than once.

at	behind	in	on	under

1. *A* Where is the box of oranges?   *B* It's _on_ the floor.

2. *A* Where are the plastic bags?   *B* They're _____ the checkout stand.

3. *A* Where are the cartons of milk?   *B* They're _____ the checkout stand.

4. *A* Where are the cartons of juice?   *B* They're _____ the refrigerator case.

5. *A* Where are the bananas?   *B* They're _____ the melons.

6. *A* Where is the cashier standing?   *B* She's _____ the checkout stand.

7. *A* Where is the water?   *B* It's _____ the shelf _____ the refrigerator case.

8. *A* Where are the tomatoes?   *B* They're _____ a box _____ the floor.

9. *A* Where are the apples?   *B* They're _____ the bananas.

B *Over to You* Answer these questions in complete sentences. Use a preposition from the box in A. Then compare your answers with a partner.

1. Where are you right now?

_____

2. Who is sitting behind you right now?

_____

3. Who is sitting near you?

_____

4. What is on your desk?

_____

3 | Prepositions of Direction and Manner

▶ Grammar Presentation

Prepositions can show direction and manner (a way of doing something).	The food goes **from** the processing plant **to** the supermarket. (direction: from X ➝ Y) She prepares the food **with** fresh ingredients. (manner: how she prepares the food)

3.1 Prepositions of Direction and Movement

Use these prepositions to show how people and things move.

from to	The food goes **from** the distribution center **to** the supermarket.	through	The food passes **through** two factories before it gets to the stores.
into	They throw old food **into** the trash.	over	Farmers fly **over** their crops to spray them.
across	Trucks transport the food **across** the United States.	around	Food often travels **around** the world before it gets to our homes.

3.2 Prepositions of Manner and Logical Relationships

a. *With* shows what people use to do something.	*They treat the food **with** chemicals.*
b. *For* shows the purpose, intention, or goal of something.	*They create meals **for** vegetarians.*
c. *About* refers to the topic of something.	*The report is **about** food waste in the United States.*
d. *As* refers to the role or job of a person or thing.	*He works **as** a truck driver for a food processing company.*
e. *Of* shows a close relationship, such as possession, identity, or being a part of something.	*Families in the United States waste about a pound **of** food per day.* *Most **of** this food is perfectly good to eat.*
f. *Between* refers to the space that separates two people, things, or numbers.	*Families waste **between** 25 percent and 33 percent of the food that they buy.*

3.3 Using Prepositions with Noun Phrases and Pronouns

a. You can use prepositions before noun phrases and pronouns. Use the object form of personal pronouns (*me, him, us*).	***On** <u>my birthday</u>, I had a special meal.* *Some friends cooked it **for** <u>me</u>.*
b. You can use prepositions with *Wh-* questions (questions that start with *who, what, which*, etc.).	*<u>Who</u> do I send this fruit basket **to**?*

Data from the Real World

Research shows that the 20 most common prepositions in writing and speaking are:

about	around	at	between	during	from	into	on	since	to
after	as	before	by	for	in	of	over	through	with

▶ # Grammar Application

Exercise 3.1 Prepositions of Direction and Movement

A teacher is taking a group of students on a tour of a local supermarket. Complete the conversation. Use the prepositions in the box.

across	around	from	into	over	through	~~to~~	to

Ms. Ross OK, everyone, let's go <u>*to*</u> the fruit and vegetable section. Now, can
(1)

anyone tell me: Where do these peaches come _____ ?
(2)

Claire Let's see. Georgia.

Ms. Ross Right. And we're in Oregon. They came a long way.

They traveled right _____ the United

(3)

States, from the South to the Northwest.

Rob But peaches from Georgia are the best. I flew

_____ Georgia once and saw some

(4)

fruit farms from the air. Do you think these peaches

came _____ Oregon by air?

(5)

Ms. Ross They probably came by truck. Workers put them

_____ boxes and put the boxes into

(6)

refrigerated trucks. Then they probably passed _____ a couple of

(7)

factories and warehouses, too. Now, let's look at these beans. Where are they from?

Julia Kenya.

Ms. Ross Correct. A lot of these fruits and vegetables probably traveled

_____ the world before they got here.

(8)

Exercise 3.2 🔊 Pronunciation Focus

Some common prepositions have two pronunciations: a strong form and a weak form.		**Strong Form**	**Weak Form**
	at	/æt/	/ət/
	for	/fɔːr/	/fər/
	from	/frʌm/ (or /frɑm/)	/frəm/
	of	/ʌv/ (or /ɑv/)	/əv/
	to	/tuː/	/tə/

Use the weak form in informal conversation, when you speak quickly and naturally.	*Let's go **to** the supermarket.* *These tomatoes are **from** Florida.*
Use the strong form: • when you speak formally, slowly, and carefully • when you need to stress the preposition • when the preposition is at the end of the sentence • with *to* when the next sound is a vowel sound	*Welcome **to** this presentation of my work.* *I was driving **to** the store, not **from** the store.* *Where do these peaches come **from**?* *Let's go **to a** farmers' market.*

A 🔊 Listen to the questions and answers and repeat them.

1. *A* Are they from California?   *B* No.
2. *A* So, where are they from?   *B* From Georgia.
3. *A* Is that a box of apples?   *B* No, it's a box of tomatoes.
4. *A* I'll see you at the restaurant.   *B* No, let's go to the cafeteria.
5. *A* Who is this peach for?   *B* It's for you. Enjoy!
6. *A* Are you going to the supermarket today? *B* No, we're going to a farmers' market.

B *Pair Work* Now practice asking and answering the questions in A with a partner.

Exercise 3.3 Prepositions of Place, Manner, and Logical Relationships

A 🔊 Listen to the presentation and complete it with the prepositions that you hear.

Good morning. My talk today is __*about*__ merchandising. Supermarkets
                                    (1)
position items carefully. They place things _____ refrigerator cases,
                                                      (2)
_____ shelves, and even _____ the checkout stand.
       (3)   (4)
This is called *merchandising*.

Merchandising helps supermarkets sell more items
to people in the store. For example, they put candy
_____ other food items, so children
       (5)
ask for the candy when their parents are buying other
things. Supermarkets also place certain items near the
floor. They put them _____ a place that
                            (6)
children can see easily. For example, they put items
children want _____ the lower shelves. And have you ever noticed kitchen
                    (7)
gadgets _____ the food items on the shelves? This is another example of
              (8)
merchandising.

Supermarkets also place items like magazines at the checkout stands. People
see them when they are waiting in line and put them _____ their carts.
                                                              (9)
In addition, research shows that people buy more cold items, for example juice or
cheese, when the refrigerated shelves are open. That's because they can see what is
_____ them.
       (10)

So, next time you're waiting in line _____ the checkout stand, ask
                                         (11)
yourself, "Why did I buy this? Was it because I needed it, or just because I saw it?"

Even _____ careful shoppers, we all sometimes put things we don't need
         (12)
in our carts.

B 🔊)) Listen again and check your answers.

C *Pair Work*   When you go to a supermarket, what do you notice?
Discuss your ideas with a partner. Talk about these things:

- the prices of things
- information about ingredients, or what is in things
- information about where food comes from
- any other things that you notice or look for

A *The first things I notice are the products at the ends of the aisles.
What about you?*
B *I usually look for what's on sale.*

4 | Phrasal Prepositions and Prepositions After Adjectives

▶ Grammar Presentation

Some prepositions consist of more than one word. These are called *phrasal prepositions*. Many adjectives have particular prepositions that follow them.	*Wei was standing **in front of** me at the checkout stand.* *Are you **good at** shopping for the best prices?*

4.1 Using Phrasal Prepositions

You can use phrasal prepositions just like one-word prepositions, before noun phrases and pronouns. Use the object form of personal pronouns (*me, him, us*).	*The organic food store is **next to** the bank on Ginsberg Street.* *My teacher was standing **in front of** me at the supermarket checkout yesterday.*

Data from the Real World 🌐

Research shows that these are the most common phrasal prepositions in speaking and writing.

Phrasal Prepositions	Meaning	
as well as	means "and" or "also"	Restaurants, **as well as** supermarkets, throw away tons of food every year.
because of	tells you the reason	The food loses its freshness **because of** the long journey from the plow to the plate.
close to	means "near"	I live **close to** a small store.
in front of		At the checkout stand, do you look at what the person **in front of** you is buying?
instead of	means "A, not B"	Nowadays, I shop at a farmers' market **instead of** a big supermarket. (I shop at farmers' markets, not big supermarkets.)
next to		The tea is **next to** the coffee on the supermarket shelf.
out of		When the food comes **out of** the processing plant, it goes to a distribution center.
outside of		Do you buy food that is produced **outside of** the United States?
such as	means "for example"	The supermarket places products **such as** candy and toys on the lower shelves.
up to		Take the elevator **up to** the second floor, and you will see the books about food and nutrition.

4.2 Using Adjectives with Prepositions

a. You can use adjectives with prepositions before nouns, noun phrases, and pronouns. Use the object form of personal pronouns (*me, him, us*).

*The cafeteria was **full of** students.*
*Junk food is **bad for** people's health.*
*I was **surprised by** the article about wasted food.*
*Frozen food is **separate from** the fresh fruit in the supermarket.*
*I'm **worried about** the chemicals used in food.*
*Fresh vegetables are **good for** us.*
*He looks sick. Is anything **wrong with** him?*

b. You can use adjectives with prepositions without a noun or pronoun in sentences with a *Wh-* word (*who, what, which*, etc.).

*What are the high food prices **due to**?*
*Which games are the kids **excited about**?*
*Who is the supermarket manager **responsible for**?*

Data from the Real World 🌐

These are the most common adjectives used with prepositions.

Adjectives	Preposition	
aware full	of	*Many people are not **aware of** the cost of transporting food.* *Farmers' markets are **full of** fresh, local produce.*
different separate	from	*The tomatoes from my friend's garden were **different from** the supermarket tomatoes.* *Restaurants keep produce **separate from** meat and poultry.*
due similar	to	*High food prices this year are **due to** bad weather.* *The price of local fruit is sometimes **similar to** the price of imported fruit.*
familiar wrong	with	*Are you **familiar with** this type of merchandising?* *There's something **wrong with** these peaches. They're hard and dry.*
good surprised	at	*Are you **good at** math? Can you add up these prices?* *I was **surprised at** the amount of food we waste.*
interested	in	*I'm not **interested in** the quality of the food. I just want to eat.*
responsible good	for	*Who is **responsible for** the quality of food in the student cafeteria?* *Cooking at home is **good for** you.*
worried excited	about	*I'm **worried about** all the chemicals that they use to treat food.* *We're **excited about** the new restaurant in town.*

▶ Grammar Application

Exercise 4.1 Phrasal Prepositions

Complete the sentences. Use the words in the box.

because	instead	~~outside~~	such	well
close	instead	outside	well	

1. Many types of food come from places _outside_ of our own country or region.

2. Items _____ as exotic fruits often travel across continents to supermarkets.

3. Transportation costs, as _____ as production costs, are very high.

4. Buying food from farms _____ of our own country or region means food travels farther.

5. _____ of these factors, food prices are high.

6. Nowadays, many people prefer to buy local food _____ of food from other countries.

7. They prefer to buy food from farms that are in or _____ to their own region or state.

8. If you go to a local store or market _____ of a store that is a long way from your home, you are saving gas, as _____ as helping your neighborhood economy.

Exercise 4.2 More Phrasal Prepositions

Look at the pictures. Complete the statements. Use the words in the box.

| as well as | close to | ~~next to~~ | out of |
| because of | in front of | next to | outside of |

1. In picture 1, Lisa is sitting _next to_ Diego.

2. Ali is sitting _____ Blanca.

3. Chelsea is sitting _____ Anne.

4. Anne isn't sitting _____ Blanca.

5. In picture 2, the traffic is going slowly _____ the snow.

6. There are trucks _____ cars on the highway.

7. The traffic is going _____ the city.

8. The highway is _____ the city.

Exercise 4.3 Phrasal Prepositions and Adjectives with Prepositions

A Complete the questionnaire about shopping. Write the missing prepositions.

1. When you are in a supermarket, are you aware ___of___ different package sizes? Are you more likely to buy a larger package than a smaller package of something?

2. At a supermarket, what do you get excited _____ ?

3. Are you ever surprised _____ how much your grocery bill is at the checkout?

4. Do you only buy things that are good _____ you?

5. Is your supermarket cart often full _____ things you don't really need?

6. Do you buy books, clothes, and food all in one store, or do you prefer bookstores and clothing stores that are separate _____ supermarkets?

7. When you spend too much at the supermarket, do you think it is due _____ your choices, or is it the fault of the supermarket?

8. Do you think there is anything wrong _____ the way people shop in supermarkets? If yes, what?

B *Pair Work* Make your own questionnaire about shopping behavior. Choose the five best questions to ask about shopping from the questions in A. Then work with a partner. Take turns asking and answering your questions. Then compare your answers with the class.

A Is your supermarket cart often full of things you don't really need?
B No. I only buy things on my shopping list.

5 | Avoid Common Mistakes ⚠

1. Use *in*, not *at*, with large areas such as cities, states, and countries.

There are thousands of farmers' markets ~~at~~ ᵢₙ the United States.

2. Use *on*, not *at* or *in*, for days and dates.

I always do my grocery shopping ~~in~~ ᵒⁿ Saturdays.

3. Use *for*, not *during* or *since*, to refer to how long something takes or lasts.

The food stays at the processing plant ~~since~~ ᶠᵒʳ two or three days.

4. Use the correct preposition after an adjective.

I am interested ~~on~~ ⁱⁿ ways to save money on food.

Editing Task

Find and correct six more mistakes in this article about the problem of wasting food.

              in

Meg Handford lives ~~at~~ a small town in Oregon. She read about food processing and

distribution. She was worried on the amount of gas people use to transport food from

farms to supermarkets and from supermarkets to homes. She thought it was bad to the

environment, so she decided to do something about it.

5   Meg wanted to make things better. She thought, "Maybe people can share shopping

trips." So in July 2007, Meg set up Food Pool.

      Food Pool is like a car pool. In a car pool, neighbors and colleagues travel to

work together in one car instead of two or three. With Food Pool, neighbors go to the

supermarket or a farmers' market together. They do this in Saturdays or other free days.

10   Meg started a website. She was surprised at the number of interested people. Soon

her inbox was full in e-mails. Now there are more than 50 families at her area that share

the trip to the supermarket. Food Pool has been running since five years and is growing

every year.

6 | Grammar for Writing

Using Prepositions and Phrasal Prepositions

Writers use prepositions and phrasal prepositions to explain a process or a way of doing something.

Prepositions are common in all kinds of writing, including instructions, recipes, and directions.

Pre-writing Task

1 Read the paragraph below. What does the writer recommend to avoid food waste?

How to Avoid Food Waste

Food waste is a problem for many people. Here are some suggestions to help you

waste less food, save money, and become more responsible for your environment. First,

plan your shopping. Make sure you are aware of the food in your refrigerator. Examine

your refrigerator carefully. There may be food behind the milk or in the vegetable

5 drawer, so be sure you see everything on the shelves. Next, make a shopping list and

become familiar with it. When you are at the supermarket, only buy food on your list. The shelves in front of you may be full of items on sale, but only buy sale items if you really need them. Finally, check each item on your list during your shopping trip. When you are done, go directly to the cash register. If you follow these suggestions, you will be

10　surprised at the benefits. You will save money, you won't need to go to the supermarket as often, and extra food in your refrigerator will not go bad.

2 Read the paragraph again. Underline the prepositions. Find one preposition from the paragraph that shows a place, one that shows a time, and one that shows a direction.

Writing Task

1 *Write*　Use the paragraph in the Pre-writing Task and the sentence starters below to help you write about waste in your household. When do you throw away food? How can you be less wasteful?

- We usually buy food _____ . (*Where? When? From who?*)
- We store food _____ . (*Where? For how long?*)
- We throw away food _____ . (*When? Where? Why?*)

2 *Self-Edit*　Use the editing tips below to improve your paragraph. Make any necessary changes.

1. Did you use prepositions to describe a process or how you did something?
2. Did you use the correct prepositions to explain where things are, when things happen, and the movement of things?
3. Did you avoid the mistakes in the Avoid Common Mistakes chart on page 189?

Future (1)

Life Lists

1 | Grammar in the Real World

A What exciting things do you want to do someday? Read the blog about a "life list."
What does the writer hope to do someday?

My Life List

September 23
posted by: Lisa Sanchez

   Welcome to a new feature of my blog – my life list.
What is a life list? It's a list of things that you **are going
to do** before you die, if you can. Here are some things
on my life list:

5 • I**'m going to ride** in a hot-air balloon.
   • I**'m going to live** in Spain.
   • I**'m going to write** a poem.
   • I**'m going to travel** to all 50 states in the
     United States.

10   Psychologists[1] agree that life lists are motivating. They encourage people to try new
things. However, to achieve the goals on your list, you need to be realistic[2] and have
a plan. For example, I**'m not visiting** all 50 states this year. I don't have the money!
First, I**'m going to make** a plan to save money for each trip, and I**'m going to do**
research on the places I want to visit. That is the point of a life list. It motivates you to
15 work toward your goals. I**'m going to have** to work to accomplish my life list!

   Are you **going to create** a life list, too? Here are some tips:

1. Make a list that reflects the direction you want for your life. For example,
   I want to understand more about the world, so travel is a big part of my
   life list.

20 2. Understand that it **is going to take** time to accomplish the things on your list –
   maybe a lifetime!

   If you follow these simple steps, you **aren't going to be** disappointed. Your life **is
going to be** full of new adventures and new accomplishments.

[1]psychologist: someone who studies the mind and emotions and their relationship to behavior | **[2]realistic:** showing an
understanding of how things really are

B *Comprehension Check* Answer the questions.

1. What is a life list?
2. What is one reason to create a life list?
3. What are two tips to help you create a life list?

C *Notice* Find the sentences in the article and complete them.

1. I _____ ride in a hot-air balloon.

2. I _____ travel to all 50 states in the United States.

3. _____ you _____ create a life list, too?

4. Understand that it _____ take time to accomplish the things on your list.

Are the sentences about the present or the future?

2 *Be Going To*, Present Progressive, and Simple Present for Future Events

▶ Grammar Presentation

Be going to describes future plans, predictions, and expectations. The present progressive and the simple present can also refer to the future.	I**'m going to ride** in a hot-air balloon. I**'m moving** to Spain next month. My flight **leaves** at 7:00 tomorrow morning.

2.1 *Be Going To*: Statements

STATEMENTS				
Subject	*Be*	*(Not) going to*	Base Form of Verb	
I	am			
You We They	are	**(not) going to**	live	in Spain.
He She It	is			

CONTRACTIONS		
Affirmative	Negative	
I**'m**	I**'m not**	
You**'re** We**'re** They**'re**	You**'re not** We**'re not** They**'re not**	You **aren't** We **aren't** They **aren't**
He**'s** She**'s** It**'s**	He**'s not** She**'s not** It**'s not**	He **isn't** She **isn't** It **isn't**

2.2 *Be Going To*: *Yes / No* Questions and Short Answers

Be	Subject	*Going to*	Base Form of Verb	Short Answers			
Am	I	**going to**	visit Spain?		Yes, I **am.**	No, I**'m not.**	
Are	you we they				Yes, you **are.** Yes, we **are.** Yes, they **are.**	No, you **aren't.** No, we **aren't.** No, they **aren't.**	
Is	he / she / it				Yes, he / she / it **is.**	No, he / she / it **isn't.**	

2.3 *Be Going To*: Information Questions

Wh- Word	*Be*	Subject	*Going to*	Base Form of Verb
What	am	I	**going to**	see?
Where **When**	are	you we they		go?
	is	he / she / it		

Wh- Word	*Be*	*Going to*	Base Form of Verb
Who **What**	is	**going to**	visit Spain? happen?

2.4 Using *Be Going To*, Present Progressive, and Simple Present

a. Use *be going to* when future plans are *not* specific or definite.

I**'m going to visit** *Spain someday.*
(I don't know when exactly.)
I**'m going to have** *a baby before I'm 35.*
(This is my plan, but I'm not pregnant yet.)

b. Use the present progressive when future plans are specific or definite.

I**'m visiting** *Spain next week.*
(I have plane tickets and my plan is definite.)
I**'m having** *a baby in June.*
(I'm pregnant and I know when the baby will be born.)

c. Use *be going to* to talk about predictions, expectations, or guesses.

You**'re going to have** *fun in Miami next week.*

d. Use *be going to* when a future event is certain to happen because there is evidence for it. Do not use the present progressive.

*Look at those clouds. It***'s going to rain** *soon.*
Look at those clouds. It ~~is raining~~ *soon.*

2.4 Using *Be Going To*, Present Progressive, and Simple Present (continued)

e. Use the simple present, not *be going to*, for scheduled events in the future, such as class schedules, timetables, and itineraries. Some common verbs for this meaning are *arrive*, *be*, *begin*, *finish*, and *leave*.

*My flight **is** tomorrow.*
*I **leave** at 7:00 a.m.*

▶ Grammar Application

Exercise 2.1 *Be Going To*: Statements

Complete the sentences with the correct form of *be going to* and the verbs in parentheses.

1. Lisa's blog _is going to motivate_ (motivate) people to create life lists.

2. Jessica _____ (create) a life list on her blog. Here are two of the goals she wants to put on her list.

3. She _____ (not miss) the family reunion this year.

4. Jessica and her twin sister Kelly _____ _____ (attend) a twins convention someday.

5. Sam _____ (not achieve) any of his goals this year, but someday he will.

6. Here are some things that I _____ (do) someday.

7. I _____ (take) a trip to New York.

8. I _____ (learn) martial arts someday.

9. My mother and I _____ (ride) in a hot-air balloon for her birthday.

10. Remember, you _____ (not do) everything in one year!

Exercise 2.2 *Be Going To*: Questions

A Complete the conversation with the correct form of *be going to* and the verbs in parentheses.

Marco Hey, Julio. What _are_ you _going to do_ (do) now?
   (1)   (1)

Julio I'm going to start a new job.

Marco Where _____ you _____ (work)?
       (2)   (2)

Julio At the Central Café.

Marco Nice! What _____ you _____ (do) there?
(3)   (3)

Julio I'm going to cook! I always wanted to be a chef – it's number 10 on my life list.

Marco That's great! _____ you _____ (get) some training?
(4)   (4)

Julio Yes. I'm going to learn a lot on the job! And I'm also going to take a class at

Briteway Community College.

Marco What _____ you _____ (take)?
(5)   (5)

Julio I'm going to take a class on food safety.

Marco That's great. _____ it _____ (be) hard?
(6)   (6)

Julio No, I don't think so.

Marco What _____ (happen) with the rest of your life list?
(7)

Julio Oh, the trip to China?

Marco Yes. When _____ that _____ (happen)?
(8)   (8)

Julio Well, first I'm going to earn a good salary at the Central Café. I'm going to

save a lot of money, and then I'm going to go to China.

Marco That sounds like a plan!

B Write questions about Julio for the answers below. Use *be going to*.

1. _What is he going to do?_____
   He's going to start a new job.

2. _____
   He's going to work at the Central Café.

3. _____
   He's going to cook.

4. _____
   Yes, he's going to learn a lot on the job.

5. _____
   Yes, he's going to take a class at the community
   college.

6. _____
   He's going to take a class on food safety.

7. _____
   No, he doesn't think the class is going to be hard.

8. _____
   He's not going to visit China very soon.

Exercise 2.3 *Be Going To*, Present Progressive, or Simple Present?

A 🔊) Listen and complete the conversation with the form of the verbs that you hear: *be going to*, present progressive, or simple present.

Anne So, Jin, what _are_ you _going to do_ (do) this weekend?
       (1)   (1)

Jin I'm finally _____ (accomplish) one of my big goals:
                         (2)
       I _____ (ride) in a hot-air balloon.
                (3)

Anne Wow! Did you already make a reservation?

Jin Yes. I _____ (take) the flight that goes over
                      (4)
       the ocean.

Anne The ocean! You _____ (have) a great time.
                            (5)

Jin Yeah, and I heard the weather report. It _____ (be)
                                                      (6)
       great this weekend. Do you want to come?

Anne When _____ you _____ (go)?
               (7)   (7)

Jin We _____ (meet) in the park at noon on Sunday,
                 (8)
       and the flight _____ _____ (leave) at 1:00 p.m.
                             (9)

Anne I'd love to come, but I have other plans.

Jin What _____ _____ you _____ (do)?
              (10)   (10)

Anne I _____ (go) to the airport on Sunday
               (11)
       afternoon. I _____ (pick up) an old friend. She
                          (12)
       _____ (stay) with me for a week, and her flight
             (13)
       _____ (arrive) right at noon.
             (14)

Jin Well, it sounds like you _____ (have) a good
                                       (15)
       time, too!

B 🔊) Listen again and check your answers.

Exercise 2.4 More *Be Going To*, Present Progressive, or Simple Present?

A Complete another entry from Lisa's blog. Use *be going to*, the present progressive, or the simple present and the verb in parentheses. Use contractions where possible.

Achieving #7 on My Life List

January 15
posted by: Lisa Sanchez

Finally! I *'m going to achieve* (achieve) goal
                   (1)
number 7 on my life list! I've bought my ticket, so it's

definite now. I _____ (move) to Spain! I
                        (2)
_____ (leave) on Friday, February 3rd. I
       (3)
got a job, too! I _____ (work) as a tour
                          (4)
guide for a hotel in Barcelona. I _____
                                          (5)
(start) on March 3rd, so I planned a little trip. I _____ (travel)
                                                              (6)
around the country for three weeks. I already bought a rail pass. I've checked the

weather, too. It _____ (be) great. It _____
                        (7)   (8)
(be) nice the entire time. Any advice?

_____

2 Responses   leave one

Robert: Lisa, you _____ (have) a fantastic time! But watch out –
                              (9)
I've been to Spain many times in the winter. It _____
                                                         (10)
(rain). You _____ (need) an umbrella.
                   (11)

Amy: Hey Lisa, I _____ (travel) in Spain at the same time!
                            (12)
I bought a rail pass, too! I _____ (arrive) in Catalonia
                                    (13)
on February 11th. I _____ (stay) at the youth hostel.
                            (14)
I made a reservation for three days. There's a big festival in Catalonia in

February. I've heard a lot about it. It _____ (be) fun.
                                               (15)
Do you want to meet up?

B *Pair Work*   Compare your answers with a partner. For each answer, explain the reason for the verb form you chose.

Exercise 2.5 Statements and Questions

A Think of six things to write on your life list. Begin with *I'm going to. . . .*

I'm going to ride a horse on the beach.

1. _____
2. _____
3. _____
4. _____
5. _____
6. _____

B *Pair Work*   Compare life lists with a partner. Ask as many *going to* questions as you can about your partner's list. Then write down the six things your partner wants to do.

A *What are you going to do?*
B *I'm going to ride a horse on the beach.*
A *Where are you going to do that?*
B *I'm going to do that in Australia.*

1. _____
2. _____
3. _____
4. _____
5. _____
6. _____

3 | Avoid Common Mistakes ⚠

1. Use *be* with *going to* to describe future plans.

      is
She ˄ going to write a poem someday.

2. Use the correct form of *be* with *going to*.

        are
Jared and Jason is going to go to a twins convention next year.

3. Use *be* before the subject in *Wh-* questions with *be going to*.

     are you
What you are going to do?

Editing Task

Find and correct eight more mistakes in this web interview about life lists.

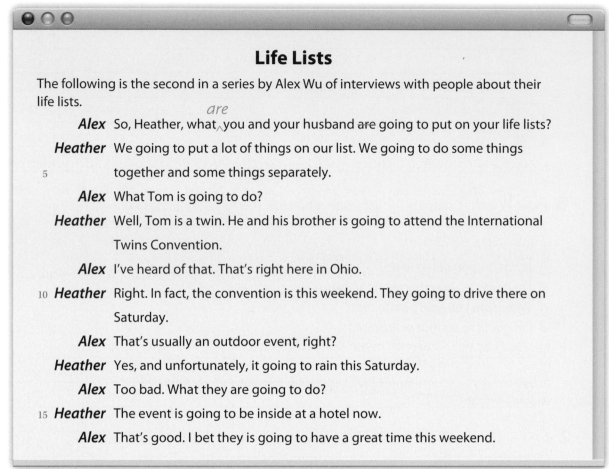

Life Lists

The following is the second in a series by Alex Wu of interviews with people about their life lists.

Alex So, Heather, what ∧ you and your husband ~~are~~ going to put on your life lists?
are

Heather We going to put a lot of things on our list. We going to do some things
5   together and some things separately.

Alex What Tom is going to do?

Heather Well, Tom is a twin. He and his brother is going to attend the International
         Twins Convention.

Alex I've heard of that. That's right here in Ohio.

10 **Heather** Right. In fact, the convention is this weekend. They going to drive there on
         Saturday.

Alex That's usually an outdoor event, right?

Heather Yes, and unfortunately, it going to rain this Saturday.

Alex Too bad. What they are going to do?

15 **Heather** The event is going to be inside at a hotel now.

Alex That's good. I bet they is going to have a great time this weekend.

4 Grammar for Writing ✎

Using *Be Going To* and Present Progressive Together

When you talk about goals, you can use *be going to* and the present progressive in the same paragraph. Using both of the forms tells your reader which goals are things you hope to do (use *be going to*) and which goals are definite plans (use present progressive). You can also use *be going to* for definite plans, but the present progressive is more common with plans for the very near future.

Remember:

- **Use *be going to* when you hope to do something, but you don't have definite plans.**
  <u>I'm going to have</u> a big family in the future.

- **Use the present progressive when you have a definite or specific plan.**
  <u>I'm getting</u> my degree next May.

Pre-writing Task

1 Read the paragraph below. What are a lot of married couples not doing immediately? What things are they doing?

Planning for the Future

Today, more and more couples who want to get married are not starting families right after the wedding. There are many reasons for this. Some couples are graduating from school before they have children. They know they are going to be busy when they have children, so they want to finish school first. Then, after they finish school, many couples are planning to look for jobs and work for a year or two to save money. Other couples are going to travel before they settle down. If they are not having children right away, they are going to have interesting stories to tell their families later on!

2 Read the paragraph again. Underline *going to* + verb. Circle the present progressive verbs. Which describe definite plans, and which describe plans that are not definite?

Writing Task

1 *Write* Use the paragraph in the Pre-writing Task to help you write about your plans for the future. What do you hope to do a year from now? What are you going to do many years from now? Include things you don't have definite plans for as well as at least one definite plan.

2 *Self-Edit* Use the editing tips below to improve your paragraph. Make any necessary changes.

1. Did you use *be going to* and the present progressive to talk about things you hope to do in the future?
2. Did you use *be going to* for plans that are not definite?
3. Did you use the present progressive for plans that are definite or specific?
4. Did you avoid the mistakes in the Avoid Common Mistakes chart on page 199?

Future (2)

Getting Older

1 | Grammar in the Real World

A What do you think it's like to be 100 years old? Read the magazine article about centenarians. What are some of the effects of people living longer?

Centenarians[1]

In 1980, there were 15,000 people over the age of 100 in the United States. In 2000, there were 50,000. This number **will** grow, and as a result, many more people **will** live
5 to see their 100th birthday. In fact, there **will** be several million centenarians in the United States by the end of the twenty-first century. This is according to the U.S. Census Bureau. What changes **will** we see with so many
10 people over 100?

The United States **will** see many changes because of this. For example, more people **will** have illnesses such as cancer and heart conditions. According to a study by the University of Albany in New York, we **will** probably not have enough doctors to take care of them. In addition, these changes **will** affect government services. This means that there **will** be
15 less money for programs such as Social Security[2] and Medicare.[3] Many older people **will** possibly not have enough money to support themselves for a longer period of time. As a result, many **will** need to work in their 70s and even in their 80s.

On the other hand, there are some very positive aspects of aging. One is increased happiness. A study by Stanford University in California found that older people tend to be
20 happier than younger people. Why? As people age, they change their goals. They know they have less time ahead of them, and as a result, they focus on the present. They spend more time on their relationships and know themselves better. This leads to increased happiness.

As people live longer, there **will** be more of us in the world. With more people who are happier, though, perhaps the world **will** be a happier place.

---

[1]**centenarians:** people aged 100 or older | [2]**Social Security:** a U.S. government program that gives financial help to people who are old, people whose husbands or wives have died, and people who cannot work | [3]**Medicare:** a U.S. government program that pays part of the medical expenses of people 65 or older

B Comprehension Check Answer the questions.

1. What will happen to the population by the end of the twenty-first century, according to the U.S. Census Bureau?
2. What are two negative effects of a large number of centenarians?
3. What is one positive effect of aging?
4. Why do older people tend to be happier?

C Notice Find the sentences in the article and complete them.

1. There _____ be several million centenarians in the United States by the end of the twenty-first century.

2. What changes _____ we see with so many people over 100?

3. For example, more people _____ have illnesses such as cancer and heart conditions.

4. Many older people _____ possibly not have enough money to support themselves for a longer period of time.

Do we use *will* to talk about the future, the present, or the past?

2 | Future with *Will*

▶ Grammar Presentation

Will describes events that take place in the future.	*There **will** be several million centenarians in the United States by the end of the twenty-first century.*

2.1 Statements

Subject	Will (Not)	Base Form of Verb
I You He / She / It We They	**will** **will not** **won't**	help people.

2.2 *Yes / No* Questions and Short Answers

Will	Subject	Base Form of Verb	Short Answers	
Will	I you he / she / it we they	help?	Yes, I **will**. Yes, you **will**. Yes, he / she / it **will**. Yes, we **will**. Yes, they **will**.	No, I **won't**. No, you **won't**. No, he / she / it **won't**. No, we **won't**. No, they **won't**.

2.3 Information Questions

Wh- Word	Will	Subject	Base Form of Verb	Wh- Word	Will	Base Form of Verb
How Where When	will	we they	solve the problem?	What	will	happen?

2.4 Using *Will*

a. Use *will* to make predictions. Predictions are things that people believe about the future.

Many people **will** *live to 110.*
There **will** *be several million centenarians by the end of the twenty-first century.*

b. You can use *likely, possibly, probably, certainly, definitely,* and *undoubtedly* after *will* and before the main verb to show different degrees of certainty. In negative statements, these adverbs can usually go between *will* and *not* or before *won't*.

Humans **will possibly** *live to 200 in the distant future.*
Technology **will undoubtedly** *change the world.*
They **will probably not** *do much physical work.*
They **definitely won't** *do much physical work.*

Maybe and *perhaps* start a sentence.

less certain		more certain
maybe		certainly
possibly	likely	definitely
perhaps	probably	undoubtedly

Maybe *older people will not have enough money.*
Perhaps *the world will be a happier place.*

c. Use the full forms (*will, will not*) in formal writing.

Increased population **will** *lead to crowding.*
People **will not** *need to work so hard in the future.*

Use the contracted forms (*'ll, won't*) in informal situations.

*I'***ll** *live in a little house near the ocean.*
We **won't** *have to work very hard.*

Data from the Real World

Research shows that the normal position for adverbs of certainty is after *will*.	*Many older people* **will possibly** *not have enough money to support themselves.*
You can also put the adverb before *will* to add emphasis, but this is less common.	*My parents didn't have to work in their 70s, but I* **probably will**.

▶ Grammar Application

Exercise 2.1 *Will*: Statements

Complete the statements with *will*. Use the verbs in parentheses.

1. People _will live_ (live) longer in the future.

2. In fact, many people _____ (see) their 100th birthday.

3. This means that there _____ (be) a lot more healthy older people.

4. These healthy older people _____ (need) something productive to do.

5. Therefore, many people _____ (not retire) at the age of 60 or 65.

6. They _____ (work) in their 70s.

7. However, they _____ (not do) as much physical work.

8. This _____ (help) the economy, as it _____ (not cause) problems for government programs such as Social Security and Medicare.

Exercise 2.2 *Will*: Questions and Adverbs

A Complete the questions in an online interview with an expert on aging. Use *will* and the correct form of the words in parentheses.

Chris Zurawski's Future Blog

I recently interviewed Dr. Sam Young. Dr. Young is an expert on aging and how it will change the government and the economy. Following is our discussion.

Q Dr. Young, _will people live_ (people/live) longer in the future?
     (1)

A Yes. People will live longer. Life expectancy will increase in most countries.

Q _____ (why/people/have) longer lives?
     (2)

A Well, they'll have better medical care, and that will mean a healthier life.

Q _____ (people/live) longer everywhere in the world?
     (3)

A I think so. A lot of countries will have more centenarians.

There will be millions in countries such as the United

States and Japan.

Q So, _____ (everyone/be) healthy?
     (4)

A Well, no, not everyone. People will live longer, but

they'll have more long-term illnesses such as cancer

and diabetes.

Q I'm only 24. I'm worried about Social Security.

_____ (what/happen) to Social
     (5)

Security?

In the future, people will live longer – and work longer.

A Social Security will begin to have serious problems in the future. Something will need to change.

Q But let's say it doesn't change. _____ (what / happen)?
                                              (6)

A In that case, Social Security payments will be very low, or they won't be available at all.

Q So, _____ (how / people like me / support) ourselves?
                              (7)

A Even today, Social Security provides only about one-third of the average person's income. So, just like now, most people will need other sources of income as they age.

Q _____ (what other sources of income / people / have)?
                              (8)

A A lot of people your age will work longer. You'll keep your jobs. Some will work part-time, but many will continue to work full-time for many years.

B Add adverbs to some of Dr. Young's statements. Use the cues in parentheses to choose an adverb with the appropriate degree of certainty. Sometimes more than one answer is correct.

certainly	likely	perhaps	probably
definitely	maybe	possibly	undoubtedly

1. Life expectancy will *probably* increase in most countries. (in the middle)

2. Better medical care will mean a healthier life. (more certain)

3. A lot of countries will have more centenarians. (in the middle)

4. People will have more long-term illnesses such as cancer and diabetes. (less certain)

5. Social Security will begin to have serious problems in the future. (in the middle)

6. Social Security payments will be very low. (in the middle)

7. Most people will need other sources of income as they age. (more certain)

8. A lot of people your age will work longer. (less certain)

9. Many will continue to work full-time for many years. (more certain)

Exercise 2.3 *Will*: Questions, Answers, and Adverbs

A 🔊 Listen to an informal conversation about the future. Complete the summary of Sara's ideas. Circle the correct words.

Sara thinks she probably **will** / **will not** live to be 100. She thinks
                                         (1)
she **will probably** / **will probably not** have problems with money in old age.
              (2)

B 🔊 Listen again. Circle the correct adverb.

1. Sara will **probably** / **certainly** live to be about 85 or 90.

2. Sara will **perhaps** / **undoubtedly** work in her 80s.

3. At 80, Sara will **probably** / **definitely** have the same job she has now.

4. After retirement, Sara will **possibly** / **definitely** travel or garden.

5. Sara will **perhaps** / **very likely** not have enough money to travel.

6. Sara thinks she **possibly** / **certainly** won't get Social Security.

7. Sara thinks the government will **probably** / **undoubtedly** not have any money left in the future.

Listen again and check your answers.

C *Group Work* Use *will* and adverbs of certainty to talk about your future. Discuss these questions and give your own ideas.

- How long do you think you'll live? Why do you think that?

- How long will you work? What kind of job will you have at age _____ ?

- What will you do after you retire? If you get sick, who will help you?

- Will you have enough money after you retire? Will you get Social Security? Why or why not?

A *How long do you think you'll live?*
B *I'll probably live to be about 100.*
C *Perhaps I'll live to be 90. I hope so.*

3 | Future with *Will, Be Going To,* and Present Progressive

▶ Grammar Presentation

Will, be going to, and the present progressive can describe future events.	Life expectancy **will** increase. I**'m going to** look for a new job. She**'s starting** a retirement account next week.

3.1 Using *Will*, *Be Going To*, and Present Progressive for the Future

a. Use *will* or *be going to* to talk about plans in the future. Use the present progressive for arranged events.	I**'ll open** a retirement account soon. I**'m going to open** a retirement account soon. (This is my intention, what I want to do.) I**'m opening** a retirement account next week. (I have an appointment at the bank at a specific time next week. It's scheduled.)
b. Use *will* or *be going to* to make predictions, expectations, or guesses about the future.	More people **will live** longer in the future. More people **are going to live** longer in the future.
c. Use *be going to* when a future event is certain to happen because there is evidence for it.	Look at those dark clouds. It**'s going to rain**. We have a lot of work to do. We **are not going to finish** until 6:30.
d. Use *will* for immediate decisions.	I have to go. I**'ll call** you later. (= I just decided to call you.) I have to go. I'm going to call you later. I have to go. I'm calling you later.
e. Use *be going to* for intentions: things you hope or intend to do in the future.	I am healthy. I**'m going to live** to be 100 years old! I**'m not going to retire** and sit at home.
Do not use *will* or the present progressive with intentions.	I am healthy. I will live to be 100 years old! I am healthy. I'm living to be 100 years old!
f. Use *will* and *be going to* with adverbs to show different degrees of certainty about future events. You can use *likely*, *possibly*, *probably*, *certainly*, *definitely*, and *undoubtedly* after *be* and before *going to* when you want to show different degrees of certainty. For negative statements, put the adverb immediately after *be*.	He **definitely won't retire this year**. He hasn't studied. He **is probably going to fail** the exam. People **are certainly going to work** longer in the future. They **are probably not going to take** any English courses next year.
Maybe and *perhaps* can start sentences with *be going to*.	**Perhaps** the government **is going to fix** Social Security.

less certain		more certain
maybe		certainly
possibly	likely	definitely
perhaps	probably	undoubtedly

Data from the Real World 🌐

Research shows that *will* is 20 times more common in academic writing than *be going to*.	**Academic writing** will ▬▬▬▬▬▬▬▬ be going to ▪ Write: *People **will be** happier in the future.*
Research shows that *be going to* is three times more common in speaking than *will*.	**Speaking** will ▬▬▬ be going to ▬▬▬▬▬▬▬▬ Say: *"Everyone**'s going to work** to age 70 in the future."*

▶ Grammar Application

Exercise 3.1 *Will* or Present Progressive?

Complete this university press release. Circle *will* or the present progressive.
If both are possible, circle both.

> **FOR IMMEDIATE RELEASE**
> **New Program at Bay City University for Senior Citizens**
>
> *Bay City, September 5* – Life expectancy **is increasing /(will increase)** in the future.
> (1)
> This means that the population of Bay City **will grow / is growing** as well, and the
> (2)
> number of Bay City students over the age of 60 **will increase / is increasing** someday.
> (3)
> Already, the number of people over 60 who want to study is growing, and it
> **is probably doubling / will probably double** in the next 20 years. As a result, Bay
> (4)
> University **is needing / will need** more programs and more courses for older students.
> (5)
> Therefore, Bay City University **will announce / is announcing** later this week plans
> (6)
> for a new department for students over 60 called Lifelong Learning. The department
> **will open / is opening** officially next year. However,
> (7)
> Lifelong Learning **is holding / will hold** an orientation
> (8)
> event this Friday afternoon to introduce the
> department. Interested students can talk to
> instructors from the department about the courses
> they **are teaching / will teach** next year.
> (9)

Exercise 3.2 *Will* or *Be Going To?*

A Complete the conversation with *will* or *be going to* and the words in parentheses. Sometimes, both are correct.

Lisa What _are you going to do_ (do) in your old age?
(1)

Zack Well, I've thought about this. I _____ (not retire) early.
(2)

Maybe I'll retire in my 70s, but not before. Anyway, after retirement,

I _____ (travel).
(3)

Lisa That's expensive. You aren't rich. You _____ (not have) the
(4)

money for travel.

Zack You know, you're right. I _____ (start) a savings account right
(5)

away. How about you? What _____ you _____ (do) in your old age?
(6)   (6)

Lisa Well, I _____ (go) back to school.
(7)

Zack I'm surprised. You don't like school now. You _____ (not like)
(8)

it later.

Lisa I _____ (change) my attitude. In fact, I _____ (change)
(9)   (10)

it right now! Let's go to the library and study.

Zack That's a great idea! I _____ (drive).
(11)

B *Pair Work* Compare your answers with a partner. Discuss the reason for
your choices. Which statements and questions are about immediate decisions?
Which are about intentions? Which are about future events that are certain
due to evidence?

Exercise 3.3 Adverbs

A What will life be like when you are old? Read some predictions about the future.
Add an adverb that matches the degree of certainty in parentheses.

maybe	~~likely~~	definitely
possibly	probably	undoubtedly
perhaps	certainly	

likely
1. Robots will∧do all of our housework. (in the middle)

2. Computers won't have keyboards. (in the middle)

We are going to use our voices to communicate

with them. (less certain)

3. There will be no ice in the Arctic. (more certain)

4. People are not going to drive their own cars. (less certain)

   Satellites or computers will control them. (less certain)

5. Space flight is going to be available to anyone. (more certain)

   People will take vacations in space. (more certain)

B *Pair Work* Discuss the predictions with a partner. Do you agree or disagree with these predictions? Make statements with *will* and adverbs that are true for you. Give reasons for your answers.

A I agree with number 1. Robots will definitely do all of our housework in the future.

B Why do you think that?

A We already have this type of robot today. People use robots to build cars, so they will certainly use them for housework in the future.

C *Over to You* Make predictions about your life in the future. Use *will*, *be going to*, and adverbs. Compare your predictions with a partner.

A What will your life be like in the future?

B I'm going to make a lot of money. I'm definitely going to retire early. How about you?

4 Avoid Common Mistakes ⚠

1. Use *will* before the main verb in statements about the future.

In the future, people ∧*will* live to 110.

2. Use *will* for predictions, not *would*.

Perhaps, a few years from now, I ~~would~~ *will* have a job with a good salary.

3. Use *be* with *going to* for the future.

I take good care of myself. I ∧*am* going to live to be 100 years old!

4. Use the base form of the verb after *will*.

People will ~~to~~ live longer in the future. He will ~~lives~~ *live* longer.

Editing Task

Find and correct eight more mistakes in this interview with an actor.

> **Pablo Percy** A lot of women actors quit around the age of 40 or 50. They say there
> aren't good parts for older women. What ~~would~~ *will* you do in your later years?
>
> **Melanie Hinton** Well, I won't retire and sit at home. I work until I'm 90!
>
> **Pablo Percy** But there aren't many good parts for older women. How would you find work?
>
> 5 **Melanie Hinton** The entertainment business is changing. In the future, there be a lot
> more older people making movies *and* watching movies. That means
> there would definitely be more parts for older people, including older
> women, in the future.
>
> **Pablo Percy** Are you sure?
>
> 10 **Melanie Hinton** Absolutely. In fact, I wouldn't wait for these
> parts. I will to write my own scripts. I going
> to have a script ready next year.
>
> **Pablo Percy** What is it going to be about?
>
> **Melanie Hinton** I going to write a love story about two
> 15 80-year-olds.
>
> **Pablo Percy** Sounds wonderful!

5 | Grammar for Writing

Using *Will* and *Be Going To* for Predictions

Writers use *will* and *be going to* to make predictions about how things will be in the future. They are similar in meaning. However, in writing, it is much more common to use *will*. Predictions can be positive or negative, and adverbs of certainty, such as *definitely* and *possibly*, can make them weaker or stronger.

Remember:

- **In positive statements, adverbs of certainty go after *will* and before the main verb.**
  They will <u>probably</u> see their children and grandchildren a lot more than they do now.

- **In negative statements, the adverbs can go between *will* and *not* or before *won't*.**
  They <u>definitely</u> won't run out of things to do when they retire.

> • **Use *be going to* when you are certain that something is going to happen because you have evidence for it. Don't use *will* for predictions based on evidence.**
> *My parents <u>are going to retire</u> soon to travel. They already have plane tickets.*

Pre-writing Task

1 Read the paragraph below. What two things do this writer's parents want to do after they retire?

When My Parents Retire

My parents are going to retire next year. When they retire, their lives will be very different. Of course they will have a lot more free time. Luckily, they will also have enough money to support themselves and try new things. My mother loves reading books, so she will probably take some literature classes. My father will possibly learn to cook. They both love to travel, so I think they are going to spend a lot of time traveling and visiting new places. They will probably see their children and grandchildren a lot more than they do now. They definitely won't run out of things to do when they retire.

2 Read the paragraph again. Underline the verbs with *will*. Circle *be going to* + verb. Which verbs make predictions based on evidence?

Writing Task

1 *Write* Use the paragraph in the Pre-writing Task and the sentence starters below to help you write about your retirement. When will you (or someone you know) retire? What are you going to do? Make some predictions and talk about some plans.

1. When I am 65, I will probably _____ .

2. I will spend a lot of time _____ .

3. I am going to / not going to live in / visit / study _____

_____ .

2 *Self-Edit* Use the editing tips below to improve your paragraph. Make any necessary changes.

1. Did you use *will* or *be going to* to predict how things will be in the future?
2. Did you use *will* or *be going to* to talk about future plans?
3. Did you use *be going to* when you have evidence for a prediction about the future?
4. Did you avoid the mistakes in the Avoid Common Mistakes chart on page 211?

Future Time Clauses and Future Conditionals

Learning to Communicate

1 Grammar in the Real World

A What do you know about learning a language? Read the passage from a textbook. How do humans learn to communicate?

Children and Language Learning

Jake is two years old, and he is a typical American child. He plays, laughs, and cries. He also talks. He can understand about 200 English words. He uses fixed phrases. For example, he says "all gone" when
5 he finishes his food. **Until he is about four or five, Jake will talk** mostly about things around him – where he is and what he is doing at the moment. **When he is five years old, he will understand** thousands of words and will speak normally.
10 **Before he is six, he will learn** to form correct grammatical sentences.

When he starts school, he will begin to read and write. **After he starts to read, he will learn** to speak about things that are not happening right around
15 him – the past, the future, and faraway people and places. **Once he is literate,[1] Jake will learn** about a thousand words every year. **When he is 18, he will be** ready for college. He will have all the language and world knowledge he needs for his classes. Then, for the rest of his life, he will continue to learn.

20   Was Jake born with the ability to learn to speak, read, and write? Many experts say *yes*. Animals often live close to human beings, but they do not learn human language. Therefore, Jake must have a natural ability to learn his language. However, he speaks English only because his parents and the people around him use English.

25   Learning how to communicate is a combination of natural, genetic features[2] and our social environment. We need both things to be "human."

[1]literate: able to read and write | **[2]genetic feature:** a characteristic of living things passed on from parents to children

B *Comprehension Check* Answer the questions.

1. According to the textbook excerpt, how many words does a typical two-year-old child know?
2. What do children talk about before ages four or five?
3. What happens after children learn to read?
4. Two things make it possible for humans to learn language. What are they?

C *Notice* Find the sentences in the textbook passage and complete them.

1. _____ he is six, he _____ learn to form correct
   (a)   (b)
   grammatical sentences.

2. _____ he starts school, he _____ begin to read
   (a)   (b)
   and write.

3. _____ he starts to read, he _____ learn to
   (a)   (b)
   speak about things that are not happening right around him.

4. _____ he is literate, Jake _____ learn about
   (a)   (b)
   a thousand words every year.

Do the words in the *a* blanks refer to place or time?
Do the verbs in the *b* blanks talk about the present or the future?

2 | Future Time Clauses

▶ Grammar Presentation

Future time clauses show the time and order (first or second) of a future event.

FIRST EVENT   SECOND EVENT
***Once he is literate**, he will learn about a thousand words every year.*

FIRST EVENT   SECOND EVENT
***After he starts to read**, he will learn to speak about things that are not happening around him.*

2.1 Future Time Clauses

FUTURE TIME CLAUSE				MAIN CLAUSE			
Time Word	Subject	Simple Present		Subject	*Will*	Base Form of Verb	
Before **After** **When**	he	starts	school,	he	will	learn	to read.

MAIN CLAUSE				FUTURE TIME CLAUSE			
Subject	*Will*	Base Form of Verb		Time Word	Subject	Simple Present	
He	will	learn	to read	**before after when**	he	starts	school.

2.2 Using Future Time Clauses

a. Use future time clauses to say when the event in the main clause happens.

Use *after* when the event in the time clause happens first.

learns to read

✕

starts school

FIRST EVENT   SECOND EVENT

After she starts school, she will learn to read.

Use *when* when two events happen at or around the same time.

When he graduates from high school, he will go to college.

Use *as soon as* or *once* when the event in the main clause happens immediately after the event in the time clause.

✕   ✕

leaves college   gets a job

FIRST EVENT   SECOND EVENT

As soon as he leaves college, he will get a job.

Once he is literate, he will learn thousands of new words.

Use *before* when the event in the main clause happens first.

SECOND EVENT   FIRST EVENT

Before Anne starts school, she will learn hundreds of words.

Use *until* to show when the event in the main clause will stop or change.

talks about immediate environment

✕

four or five years old

Until he is about four or five, Jake will talk mostly about his immediate environment.

(Jake will stop doing this when he is four or five.)

b. The time clause can come before or after the main clause. Remember to use a comma when the time clause comes first.

As soon as he leaves college, he will get a job.

He will get a job *as soon as he leaves college.*

c. Even though the verb in the time clause is in the simple present, it refers to a future event.

*He will learn more English **before he visits** California **next year**.*

*I will stay in school **until I graduate two years from now**.*

▶ Grammar Application

Exercise 2.1 Future Time Clauses

Circle the correct verb.

1. Larisa is a typical three-year-old Russian girl. Before she
   will start / starts school at age 5, she **learns / will learn**
   to print her name in the Cyrillic alphabet: Лариса.

2. Her parents **will teach / teach** her to read simple words
   like *cat* (Кот) before she **will start / starts** school, too.

3. When she **goes / will go** to kindergarten, Larisa
   starts / will start to learn to read and write more
   simple words.

4. She **will learn / learns** even more words as soon as she
   starts / will start primary school.

5. Once Larisa **gets / will get** to the first grade, she
   learns / will learn to use handwriting instead of
   printing.

А	Б	В	Г	Д	Е	Ё
Ж	З	И	Й	К	Л	М
Н	О	П	Р	С	Т	У
Ф	Х	Ц	Ч	Ш	Щ	Ъ
Ы	Ь	Э	Ю	Я		

6. When she **is / will be** about nine years old, she **will recognize / recognizes**
   thousands of words.

7. She **reads / will read** some of her textbooks in English when she **goes / will go**
   to college.

8. After she **will finish / finishes** college, she **knows / will know** tens of
   thousands of words.

Exercise 2.2 Time Words

Complete the description of a class in American Sign Language (ASL). Circle the correct time word.

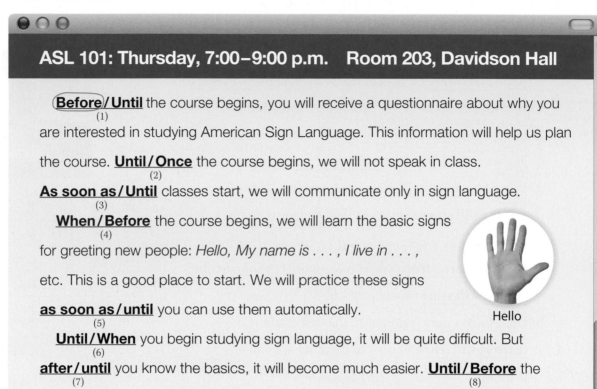

ASL 101: Thursday, 7:00–9:00 p.m.   Room 203, Davidson Hall

(Before)/**Until** the course begins, you will receive a questionnaire about why you
(1)
are interested in studying American Sign Language. This information will help us plan

the course. **Until/Once** the course begins, we will not speak in class.
(2)
As soon as/Until classes start, we will communicate only in sign language.
(3)
When/Before the course begins, we will learn the basic signs
(4)
for greeting new people: *Hello, My name is . . . , I live in . . . ,*

etc. This is a good place to start. We will practice these signs

as soon as/until you can use them automatically.
(5)

Hello

Until/When you begin studying sign language, it will be quite difficult. But
(6)
after/until you know the basics, it will become much easier. **Until/Before** the
(7)   (8)
course ends, you will learn to use a lot of sign language and have a lot of fun!

Exercise 2.3 More Future Time Clauses

A Dave is going to take all four levels of Spanish at Bay City College. Read the information about how many words a typical student in the program knows at each level. Complete the statements about Dave. Use the verbs in parentheses and the numbers in the chart.

	Starting Vocabulary	Ending Vocabulary
Level 1 student	about 500 words	about 1,500 words
Level 2 student	about 1,500 words	about 2,500 words
Level 3 student	about 2,500 words	about 3,500 words
Level 4 student	about 3,500 words	about 5,000 words

1. When he starts Level 1, Dave __*will know*__ (know) about __*500*__ words.

2. When he finishes Level 1, Dave _____ (know) about
   _____ words.

3. Dave will try to learn 1,000 more words before he _____ (finish) Level 2.

4. Dave will not start Level 3 until he _____ (know) about _____ words.

5. Once he _____ (reach) Level 4, Dave _____ (know) more than _____ words.

6. Once Dave _____ (read) and _____ (write) Spanish fluently, he _____ (apply) for a job in Spain.

B *Pair Work*   Complete each sentence in a way that is true for you. Then discuss your answers with a partner.

1. I *will continue* (continue) to study English until I *speak the language well* .

2. When I _____ (finish) this English course, I _____ .

3. I _____ (get) a job as soon as I _____ .

4. Before I _____ (complete) this course, I _____ .

A *I'll continue to study English until I speak it well. How about you?*
B *I'll continue to study English until I read and write it well.*

A *I'll get a job as soon as I finish all the classes in this program. How about you?*
B *I'll get a job as soon as I finish my job training course.*

C *Group Work*   Tell a group member about your partner's answers in B. Compare your answers.

A *Mei will get a job as soon as she finishes all the courses in this program.*
B *Rob will get a job as soon as he finishes the program, too.*

3 | Future Conditionals; Questions with Time Clauses and Conditional Clauses

▶ Grammar Presentation

Future conditional sentences describe possible situations in the future.	***If I pass all my exams,*** I will go to college. ***If Dave learns to read and write Spanish well, will he get*** a job in Spain?

3.1 Future Conditionals: Statements

FUTURE CONDITION				MAIN CLAUSE			
If	Subject	Simple Present		Subject	*Will*	Base Form of Verb	
If	he	passes	his exams,	he	will	go	to college.

MAIN CLAUSE				FUTURE CONDITION			
Subject	*Will*	Base Form of Verb		*If*	Subject	Simple Present	
He	will	go	to college	**if**	he	passes	his exams.

3.2 *Yes / No* Questions

FUTURE CONDITION OR FUTURE TIME CLAUSE				MAIN CLAUSE			
If / Time Word	Subject	Simple Present		*Will*	Subject	Base Form of Verb	
If **After** **When**	she	learns	Spanish,	will	she	get	a job in Spain?

MAIN CLAUSE				FUTURE CONDITION OR FUTURE TIME CLAUSE			
Will	Subject	Base Form of Verb		*If* / Time Word	Subject	Simple Present	
Will	she	get	a job in Spain	**if** **after** **when**	she	learns	Spanish?

3.3 Information Questions

FUTURE CONDITION OR FUTURE TIME CLAUSE				MAIN CLAUSE			
If / Time Word	Subject	Simple Present		*Wh-* Word	*Will*	Subject	Base Form of Verb
If **After** **When**	you	finish	this class,	what	will	you	do?

MAIN CLAUSE				FUTURE CONDITION OR FUTURE TIME CLAUSE			
Wh- Word	*Will*	Subject	Base Form of Verb	*If* / Time Word	Subject	Simple Present	
What	will	you	do	**if** **after** **when**	you	finish	this class?

3.4 Using Future Conditional Clauses and Future Time Clauses

a. Use *if* to refer to a situation that is possible in the future but that we cannot be certain about.	*If he finishes the program, he will get a job.* (We don't know if he will finish the program.)
b. Use *when* to refer to a situation at a point in the future that is expected or likely to happen.	***When** he finishes the program, he will get a job.* (We expect him to finish the program.)
c. Use a main verb in the simple present in the conditional clause.	*If she **gets** a better job, she will be very happy.* *If she ~~will get~~ a better job, she will be very happy.*
d. Use a comma in writing when the conditional clause or time clause comes first.	***If she arrives late,** she will miss the lecture.* ***When they finish their work,** they will leave.*

Data from the Real World

Research shows that in conversation, people often use time clauses and conditional clauses alone in answers.

A When will you start Level 3 of your course?
B As soon as I finish Level 2.

A Will you take another English course next year?
B Yes, if I have time.

▶ Grammar Application

Exercise 3.1 Future Conditionals

🔊 Listen to an interview with a scientist about Edna the ape. After you listen, write the verbs in the correct form.

Bob Diaz   Edna is a mature female ape. Researchers are going to try to find out if

they can teach Edna to communicate. We asked Dr. Sheila Viss, one of the

researchers, about the study. Dr. Viss, if you _teach_ (teach) Edna, _will_
                                                    (1)   (2)

she _learn_ (learn) human language?
      (2)

Dr. Viss   That is what we hope to find out. First, if we _____ (use)
                                                                      (3)

American Sign Language, Edna _____ (learn) the meaning of
                                         (4)

some signs. For example, we think Edna _____ (use) the sign
                                                   (5)

for "more" if she _____ (want) more food.
                        (6)

Bob Diaz   If Edna _____ (learn)
(7)
a sign that works in one situation,

_____ she _____ (use)
(8)   (8)
the same sign in a different situation?

Dr. Viss   Yes. For example, we think Edna

_____ (make) the sign
(9)
for a toy when she _____
(10)
(want) a different toy.

Bob Diaz   So, if she _____ (want) something special, _____ she
(11)   (12)
_____ (combine) the signs?
(12)

Dr. Viss   We think she will. If she _____ (do) this, Edna
(13)
_____ (make) simple sentences. For example, when she
(14)
_____ (want) food quickly, she _____ (make)
(15)   (16)
the signs for "give-food-hurry."

Bob Diaz   When she _____ (learn) to communicate, _____ she
(17)   (18)
_____ (learn) quickly?
(18)

Dr. Viss   Well, probably not. Edna will learn slowly compared to a human child.

Exercise 3.2 More Future Conditionals

A *Pair Work*   New words and expressions come into English every day. Match these new
words with their definitions. They appear in most new dictionaries. Discuss with
a partner how you think these expressions became popular.

1. blowback (noun) _____

2. to friend (verb) _____

3. a screenager (noun) _____

a. a young person who spends a lot of time
in front of a computer

b. a bad result of a political action

c. to add someone to your list of friends
on a social networking site

e

f

g

friend² /ˈfrend/ **verb** to connect with someone on
a social website so that you can share information,
pictures, etc.: *A lot of people from my old job have
friended me.*

B Read the sentences about how a new word or expression enters the language. Combine the sentences to make future conditional sentences. If the conditional clause is first, use a comma.

1. People use new words and expressions every day. The new words survive.

    If people use new words and expressions every day, the new words will survive.

2. You have a new development in technology. You get a new word that describes it.

    _____

3. New words also enter the language. There is a big world event such as a war.

    _____

4. Someone uses the new word on the Internet. People copy it.

    _____

5. For example, you use the word. Your social networking friends use it, too.

    _____

6. A new word or expression becomes popular. A lot of people use it.

    _____

7. A person on a TV news show says the new word. It sounds important.

    _____

8. A new word appears in the dictionary. A lot of people use it in speaking and in writing.

    _____

9. People stop using the new word or expression. It dies.

    _____

C *Pair Work* Ask and answer conditional questions about the information in B.

 A *If people use a new word or expression every day, will it survive?*
 B *Yes, it will.*

Exercise 3.3 Time Clauses and Future Conditionals

A 🔊 Listen to a campus radio interview with Jawad, a student. Complete the sentences about his plans.

1. Jawad will be successful if he _____ .

2. Jawad will get a good job if he _____ .

3. If he does well in his English classes, Jawad _____

   _____ .

4. Jawad will apply for a job when _____ .

5. When he graduates and gets his certificate, Jawad _____ .

B *Pair Work* Discuss your plans with a partner. Ask questions like the ones in the interview. Use time clauses and future conditional clauses where appropriate.

- Why are you here at [your school]?
- What are your plans?
- After you finish the program, what will you do?
- How will you feel when . . . ?

    A Why are you here at the community college?

    B Well, I'm here for my career. If my English improves, I'll probably find a better job.

4 Avoid Common Mistakes ⚠️

1. **Use the simple present in the conditional clause, not *will*.**

   If I ~~will~~ get good grades, I will go to college next year.

2. **Use *will* in the main clause, not the simple present.**

                          will know

   If she learns 1,000 words every year, she ₍ₐ₎ ~~knows~~ 3,000 words in three years.

3. **Use the simple present in the time clause, not *will*.**

         finishes

   When he ~~will finish~~ this course, he will take a vacation.

4. **Use *if* for something that is possible. Use *when* for something that you are certain will happen.**

     If

   ~~When~~ I become rich, I will help poor people.

Editing Task

Find and correct nine more mistakes in this web article about how birds can learn.

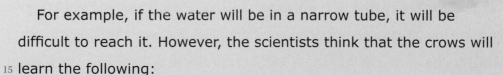

Intelligent Crows

A team of scientists is doing experiments with crows to test their intelligence. This is what the scientists think will happen:

5 • When the crows ~~will be~~ *are* thirsty, they will look for water.

• As soon as they will find water, they drink it.

• If there is no water, the crows
10 search for it.

• If they don't get the water easily, the crows think of ways to get it.

For example, if the water will be in a narrow tube, it will be difficult to reach it. However, the scientists think that the crows will
15 learn the following:

• If they will drop a stone into the tube, the water level will rise.

• If they will drop more stones, the level will rise more.

• The crows drop stones into the tube until the crows reach the water.

20 • When the experiment is successful, the scientists will prove that crows are intelligent birds.

5 | Grammar for Writing ✎

Using Future Time Clauses and Conditional Clauses

Writers use future time clauses to show the order of events in a future plan or process. Future time clauses help to connect ideas in writing about a process and show how different steps fit together.

Remember:

- **Use future time clauses when you know when something will happen.**
  As soon as Elaine gets home, she will do her homework.

- **Use *if* clauses when you aren't sure if something is going to happen.**
  If Elaine is not late, she will have enough time to do all her homework.

Pre-writing Task

1 Read the paragraphs below. What is Marie's goal? What steps does she need to take to reach the goal?

Study Goals

Marie is studying English at a community college because she wants to get a better job. She is currently working at a restaurant. She likes it, but she wants to be a nurse one day.

Last week, Marie met with a career counselor at school, and they developed a plan
5 of action. First, before she begins a nursing program, she will need to complete all four levels of her English program. Once she accomplishes this, Marie will begin taking science classes at the community college. If she does well in these classes, she will apply to nursing school. If the school accepts her, she will earn a nursing degree in two or three years. Once she earns her degree, she will look for a job at a hospital. If she
10 completes all of these steps, she will accomplish her goal of becoming a nurse.

2 Read the paragraphs again. Underline the future time clauses. Circle the *if* clauses. Which things is Marie less sure of?

Writing Task

1 *Write* Use the paragraphs in the Pre-writing Task to help you write about something you want to accomplish in the future. What will you need to do to accomplish this goal? You can write about:

- a job you want
- something you want to buy
- a place you want to visit or move to
- a person you want to meet
- something you want to study
- your own idea

2 *Self-Edit* Use the editing tips below to improve your paragraph. Make any necessary changes.

1. Did you use future time clauses to show the order of events in a future plan or process?
2. Did you use future time clauses to show when events happen?
3. Did you use *if* clauses to show that you aren't sure that something will happen?
4. Did you avoid the mistakes in the Avoid Common Mistakes chart on page 224?

1 | Grammar in the Real World

A Can you think of three recent medical inventions? Read the article from a science magazine. Which invention do you think is the most interesting?

Medical Breakthroughs

Some medical problems need engineers, not doctors. Technology **can** often solve problems when doctors alone **can't** help. Here are some examples of medical
5 breakthroughs[1] from the world of engineering.

The "ishoe"

Often when astronauts return from space, they **are not able to** balance.[2] MIT student Erez Lieberman invented the
10 "ishoe" to deal with this problem. The ishoe is a pad that goes inside a shoe and uses sensors[3] to send information about balance to a computer or cell phone. NASA scientists use this information to help the astronauts recover their balance. Lieberman **could**   15 see that his invention had other uses, for example, diagnosing[4] balance problems in elderly people.

The Autonomous Wheelchair

In the future, people **will be able to** tell their wheelchairs where they want to go.   20 The Autonomous Wheelchair **can** learn to recognize its environment by listening to its user's instructions. In addition, it uses Wi-Fi[5] to build a map of the person's home.

The Smart Pill

The doctor **can't** always be sure if some   25 people are taking their medication. Now a "smart" pill **can** tell a doctor when a patient last took his or her medication and report on the state of the person's health at the time.

[1]**breakthrough:** an important discovery or development that helps to solve a problem | [2]**balance:** have weight equally divided so something or someone can stay in one position | [3]**sensor:** a device that discovers and reacts to changes in things such as movement, heat, and light | [4]**diagnose:** recognize the exact disease or condition a person has | [5]**Wi-Fi:** a method of connecting to the Internet without using wires

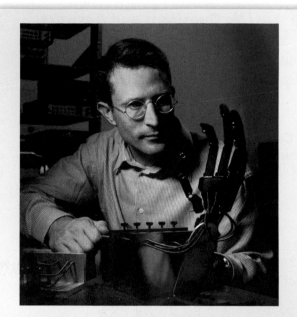

The Rocket-Powered Arm

Another invention from space research is the Rocket-Powered Arm. Until recently, people with artificial arms **were not able to** lift heavy objects. Now there is a new kind of power for artificial arms – rocket fuel. With rocket-powered arms, people **will be able to** lift objects up to 20 pounds.

These are just some of the amazing technological advances that will help improve people's lives. Who knows what other inventions they will come up with?

30

35

40

B *Comprehension Check* Match the technology with what it does.

1. The "ishoe" __b__
2. The Rocket-Powered Arm _____
3. The Autonomous Wheelchair _____
4. The Smart Pill _____

a. understands the human voice.
b. tells NASA scientists if you have problems with balance.
c. helps you pick things up.
d. gives doctors information about their patients' health.

C *Notice* Look at the verbs in **bold** in the article. Underline the verbs that are about the past. Circle the verbs that are about the future.

2 | Ability with *Can* and *Could*

▶ Grammar Presentation

Can and *could* describe ability and possibility.	Technology **can** often solve problems when doctors alone **can't** help. Lieberman **could** see that his invention had other uses.

2.1 Statements

Subject	Modal Verb	Base Form of Verb
I You He / She / It We They	**can** **can't** **cannot** **could** **couldn't** **could not**	help people.

2.2 *Yes / No* Questions and Answers

Modal Verb	Subject	Base Form of Verb	Short Answers		
Can **Could**	I you he / she / it we they	help?	Yes, No,	I you he / she / it we they	**can.** **can't.** **could.** **couldn't.**

2.3 Information Questions

Wh- Word	Modal Verb	Subject	Base Form of Verb	
How **Where** **When**	**can** **could** **can**	we they you	solve	the problem?

Wh- Word	Modal Verb	Base Form of Verb
What **Who**	**can** **could**	help?

Modal Verbs and Modal-like Expressions: See page A7.

2.4 Using *Can* and *Could*

a. You can use *can / can't* to talk about general ability and what people know how to do.	*My grandfather **can** swim, but he **can't** walk very well.* *Engineers **can** solve problems when doctors **can't**.*
b. You can use *can / can't* to talk about people's senses and mental abilities.	***Can** you **see** that tall building on the left?* *Some patients **can't remember** if they took their medication.*
c. You can use *can / can't* to talk about what is or is not possible and about known facts.	*Elderly people **can** have serious health problems after a fall.* *Technology **can't** solve every problem.*
d. Use *could / couldn't* for the past.	*Lieberman **could** see other uses for his product.* *In the past, people with artificial arms **couldn't** lift heavy objects.*

▶ Grammar Application

Exercise 2.1 *Can* and *Can't*: Statements

Complete the article about how a computer is helping a man. Use *can* or *can't* and the verbs in the box.

breathe ~~move~~ move move send speak talk use

Connecting with ERICA

When he was younger, Steve Nichols was very fit. However, in 1994 he learned he had ALS, a disease that causes loss of muscle control. Now Nichols _can't move_ (1) most of his body. For example, he _____ (2) his tongue. Because of this, he _____ (3). He also has trouble breathing. He _____ (4) without a machine.

However, Nichols _____ (5) _____ (5) his eyes. His computer, ERICA, has software that changes text to speech, so he _____ (6) to his wife and family. When Nichols looks at a letter on the keyboard on his computer screen, the computer types that letter. With ERICA, he _____ (7) e-mails. In addition, he _____ (8) the Internet. ERICA keeps Nichols connected to the rest of the world.

Exercise 2.2 *Can* and *Can't*: Questions and Answers

A Engineers in Japan have created nurse robots to help care for patients. Unscramble the words to write questions about these robots. Use *can*.

1. what / do / these robots / ?

   What can these robots do?

2. speak / they / ?

   _____

3. understand / how many languages / they / ?

   _____

4. they / patients / lift / ?

   _____

5. one robot / how much weight / lift / ?

   _____

6. a robot / recognize / people / ?

   _____

7. they / give medicine / to people / ?

   _____

8. make / what kinds of decisions / they / ?

   _____

B 🔊 Listen to an expert answer the questions in A. Write the answers.
Write things the nurse robots *can* do.

1. *They can do a lot of things.*   5. _____

2. _____   6. _____

3. _____   7. _____

4. _____   8. _____

C 🔊 Listen again. Write three things nurse robots *can't* do.

1. _____

2. _____

3. _____

Exercise 2.3 *Can, Can't, Could, or Couldn't?*

A Complete the paragraphs with *can*, *can't*, *could*, or *couldn't*.

Do You Use This Technology?

The Cell Phone

   Before the invention of cell phones, you _couldn't_ easily contact people away from
                                              (1)
their homes or offices. Now you _____ talk to friends and family at any time
                                        (2)
and in any place. With text messaging, you _____ also communicate silently.
                                                   (3)
How fast _____ you type a message?
              (4)

The Digital Music Player

   These days most people have a digital music player and _____ listen
                                                                  (5)
to their favorite music anywhere. _____ you remember life before portable
                                          (6)
music devices? Years ago you _____ only listen to your favorite music at
                                     (7)
home, in your car, or in a record store.

The GPS Navigator

_____ (8) you read maps? If you _____ (9) read a map very well, a GPS (global positioning system) can be very helpful.

You _____ (10) just put an address into your GPS and follow the instructions. Then you _____ (11) go anywhere you want.

B *Group Work* Make your own list of four important inventions in everyday life. Then compare your lists in a group and discuss the questions. Use inventions in these areas or your own ideas.

Inventions in . . .
- medicine
- travel
- communication
- home appliances
- entertainment

1. Can you remember (or imagine) life without these inventions? What was it like?
2. What can people do now that they couldn't do before these inventions?
3. As a group, choose the three most important inventions. What are they? Why are they the most important?

3 Be Able To

▶ Grammar Presentation

You can use *be able to* to talk about ability and possibility.	*Some astronauts **are not able to** balance after a space flight.* *People **will be able to** talk to their wheelchairs.*

3.1 Statements About the Present, Past, and Future

PRESENT AND PAST

Subject	Be	(Not) Able To	Base Form of Verb	
I	am/'m was			
You We They	are/'re were	(not) able to	use	a computer.
He/She/It	is/'s was			

3.1 Statements About the Present, Past, and Future *(continued)*

FUTURE				
Subject	*Will (Not)*	*Be Able To*	Base Form of Verb	
I You We They He / She / It	**will / 'll** **will not** **won't**	**be able to**	use	a computer.

3.2 *Yes / No* Questions and Short Answers About the Present and Past

Be	Subject	*Able To*	Base Form of Verb		Short Answers			
Are	you	**able to**	lift	heavy objects?	Yes, I **am**.	No, I**'m not**.
Were					Yes, I **was**.	No, I **wasn't**.

3.3 *Yes / No* Questions and Short Answers About the Future

Will	Subject	*Be + Able To*	Base Form of Verb		Short Answers	
Will	you	**be able to**	lift	heavy objects?	Yes, I **will**.	No, I **won't**.

3.4 Information Questions About the Present, Past, and Future

PRESENT AND PAST				
Wh- Word	*Be*	Subject	*Able To*	Base Form of Verb
When **How** **How often**	**are** **were**	you	**able to**	go?

Wh- Word	*Be*	*Able To*	Base Form of Verb
Who	**is / 's** **was**	**able to**	go?

FUTURE				
Wh- Word	*Will*	Subject	*Be + Able To*	Base Form of Verb
When **How** **How often**	**will**	you	**be able to**	go?

Wh- Word	*Will*	*Be + Able To*	Base Form of Verb
Who	**will / 'll**	**be able to**	go?

3.5 Using *Be Able To*

a. You can use *be able to* to talk and write about ability in the present, past, or future.	Sometimes astronauts **are not able to** balance after a space flight. In the past, artificial arms **weren't able to** lift heavy objects. In the future, people **will be able to** tell their wheelchairs where to go.
b. You can use *be able to* to talk and write about possibility.	People **will be able to** talk to their wheelchairs in the future.
c. In affirmative statements, you can use *was / were able to* for a specific event or a specific action that someone completed successfully in the past. Do not use *could*.	Lieberman **was able to** design a special shoe a few years ago. Lieberman ~~could design~~ a special shoe a few years ago.
Both forms are correct in negative statements.	In the past, they **weren't able to** lift heavy objects. In the past, they **couldn't** lift heavy objects.
d. You can use *be able to* after *going to*, *want to*, *would like to*, *need to*, and *have to*.	In the future, people **are going to be able to** use these inventions. Many people **would like to be able to** use these inventions now.
Do not use *can* (*can't*) or *could* (*couldn't*) after these verbs.	Scientists want to **be able to** invent new technologies. ~~Scientists want to can invent new technologies.~~
Can and *could* are more common than *be able to* in everyday conversation, especially in present time. Use *be able to* if you need to sound more formal.	**Can** your phone send e-mails? The most advanced robots **are** now **able to** make facial expressions.

Data from the Real World

People sometimes use *be unable to* instead of *be not able to*. This is more common in formal writing or speaking.	Formal: *When many astronauts return from space, they* **are unable to** *balance.* Informal: *When many astronauts return from space, they* **are not able to** *balance.*

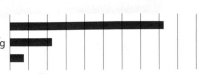

Be Unable To
in formal writing
in formal speaking
in conversation

▶ Grammar Application

Exercise 3.1 Questions and Answers

A Complete the article from a magazine. Use a form of *be able to* and the verbs in parentheses. Then, on a separate piece of paper, write what numbers can use *could* instead of *was able to*.

Seeing Through You

___Are___ brain scanners ___able to see___ (see)
　(1)　　　　　　　　　　　　(1)
your thoughts? _____
　　　　　　　　　　(2)
they _____ (read) your mind?
　　　　(2)
_____ they _____
　　(3)　　　　　　　　　　　(3)
(see) your memories? Yes, according to some

scientists. At a conference in 2009, researchers

_____ (prove) this. One
　　　　　(4)
researcher watched a movie, and the brain scanning software

_____ (show) the basic pictures that he was looking at.
　　(5)

　　　How _____ scientists _____ (use) this technology
　　　　　　　　(6)　　　　　　　　　　　　(6)
in the future? Some scientists say they are already using brain scan technology.

They say that brain scans _____ (tell) if someone is lying.
　　　　　　　　　　　　　　　(7)
　　　Scientists are not the only ones who plan to use technology like this

in the future. Some companies think they _____
　　　　　　　　　　　　　　　　　　　　(8)
(use) brain scanners for advertising as well. Advertisers hope they

_____ (see) the way people respond to their products.
　　　(9)
　　　What do you think? How _____ we _____ (use)
　　　　　　　　　　　　　　(10)　　　　　　　　　(10)
these technologies in the future?

B *Pair Work* What do you think about the article? Are brain scanners a good thing or a bad thing? Discuss with a partner.

　　A I think brain scanners are good because police will be able to tell if someone is lying.
　　B Perhaps the police will be able to catch more criminals with brain scanners.

Exercise 3.2 *Be Able To* After Other Verbs

Data from the Real World

The simple past forms (*was / were able to*) are more frequent than the simple present forms (*am / is / are able to*). However, *be able to* is most common after modal verbs like *will* and *should* and after verbs like *going to* and *want to*.

Be Able To

am / is / are able to

was / were able to

modal verb / verb + *be able to*

A *Over to You* Write five sentences about yourself. Write about work, school, technology, free time, or other ideas. For each sentence, choose one expression from Column A and one from Column B. Add *be able to*.

A	B
When I wake up in the morning, When I am in class, Someday, One day, Next year, In a few years, When I finish school,	would like to need to be going to want to have to will

Someday, I want to be able to buy a house.
When I finish school, I'm going to be able to get a better job.

B *Group Work* Compare your sentences. Give more information. Who has similar experiences and dreams?

4 | Avoid Common Mistakes ⚠

1. *Cannot* **is one word.**

cannot
This technology ~~can not~~ do everything, but it can help.

2. Don't forget the *be* **or** *to* **in** *be able to***.**

wasn't   to
I ~~not~~ ∧able∧ understand the instructions for my new phone.

3. In an affirmative sentence, use *was / were able to* **for a specific action that someone completed successfully in the past. Do not use** *could***.**

was able to
My grandmother fell yesterday, but she ~~could~~ get up.

Editing Task

Find and correct 11 more mistakes in this online review of an electronic translator.
Some sentences have more than one mistake.

TECHNOLOGY TUESDAY REVIEW:
The Instant Interpreter

         be

Will people really need to ⌃able to speak other languages in the future? That is a

question language students ask after they hear about the Instant Interpreter. This little

machine translates for you when you visit a foreign country. It listens to what you say

and is able translate your speech into eight world languages. It is also easy to use. If you

5 are able use a smart phone, you will able to use this.

     I tried the Instant Interpreter last week and I liked it. I able to order a cup of coffee

in a restaurant. When the server asked me a question, the Interpreter gave me the

translation, and I was able to answer. In the end, we were able to have a simple

conversation. However, we not able understand everything we said to each other.

10   One problem with this machine is that it can not work quickly when your

conversation becomes more complex. It needs time to able to learn your voice, too. I

could solve the problem by talking to it a lot, so it learned my voice.

    If you need to be able get around in a foreign city, this is a good buy. You can not

find a better translating machine on the market today.

5 | Grammar for Writing ✐

Using *Can*, *Cannot*, and *Be Able To* in the Present and Future

Writers use *can*, *cannot*, and *am / is / are able to* to talk about what is possible now.
They use *will be able to* to talk about abilities and possibilities in the future.
Remember:

- **Use *can*, *cannot*, and *am / is / are able to* to talk about the present.**
  Today, we <u>are able to use</u> cell phones almost everywhere, but we often <u>cannot</u> use them in elevators or subway trains in some cities.

- **Use *will be able to* to talk about the future.**
  If companies build better cell phone networks, we <u>will be able to</u> make calls underground.

Pre-writing Task

1 Read the paragraphs below. How does the writer think people will be able to listen to music in the future?

Music Now and in the Future

Today people can listen to music everywhere they go. When you walk down the street, you can see old and young people using ear buds. Digital music players are essential devices for many people these days, and I think they will become even more convenient in the future.

5   When I was young, I had a portable CD player. I could take my CD player everywhere, but I had to carry disks and buy batteries. I did not care. I loved my CD player.

Now I have a digital music player. It is much better than my old CD player. I can take it everywhere, and I can download many different kinds of music. In the future, I think digital music players will continue to get better. They will be very thin, and they will stick

10 to the skin. People will be able to walk around and not worry about the devices. Also, we will not have to worry about batteries. The energy from our bodies will charge the batteries.

2 Read the paragraphs again. Underline *can* + verb. Circle *be able to* + verb. Which verbs talk about the present? Which talk about the future?

Writing Task

1 *Write* Use the paragraphs in the Pre-writing Task and the sentence starters below to help you write about something you would like to invent or a problem you would like to solve. How will this help people?

1. I am going to invent a _____ . It will be able to _____ .

2. People will be able to _____ with this invention.

3. Currently, we can _____ , but we still cannot _____ .

4. My invention will not be able to _____ , but it will be able

   to _____ .

2 *Self-Edit* Use the editing tips below to improve your paragraph. Make any necessary changes.

1. Did you use *can, cannot,* and *will be able to* to talk about abilities or possibilities?
2. Did you use *can, cannot,* and *am / is / are able to* to talk about the present?
3. Did you use *will be able to* to talk about the future?
4. Did you avoid the mistakes in the Avoid Common Mistakes chart on page 237?

Requests and Offers
Good Causes

1 Grammar in the Real World

A What kinds of volunteer work are common in your city or town? Read Lisa's e-mail about a volunteer project. What is she trying to do?

From: Lisa Chen
To: Bay City Community College Student Volunteer Group
Date: November 20
Subject: Volunteer Work Assignments for Thanksgiving

5 Hi Everyone!

   Here are the volunteer work assignments for the Thanksgiving dinner at the Bay City Homeless Shelter. Please contact me if you have any questions.

   Professor Rodriguez, **could** you please pick up the turkey on Wednesday evening? Then, **could** you take it to Ana's apartment?

10   Wei, **would** you make the pumpkin pies on Wednesday? That way, Ana can use the oven for the turkey.

   Ana, **can** Eun give you a hand?¹

   Lara, **will** you do the vegetables? **Do you mind if** I help out? I make great sweet potatoes.

   Marcus, you said you had plates and silverware. **Can** you please bring them? Let me 15 know if you cannot.

   Mohammed has offered to take all the food in his van. Mohammed, **can** you go by Ana's around 11:00 on Thursday morning and pick everything up? **Can** I go with you? Then, Ana, **can** we go to the shelter together? **Do you mind if** we take your car?

   I think that's everything. Let's all meet at the shelter 20 and start serving at 1:00 p.m. Oh, wait! We really need a few more people to help with serving. Professor Rodriguez, **may** I please contact your sister? Mohammed, **can** I get in touch with² your roommate?

   Finally, would you like to get together at my apartment 25 on Friday for a "thank-you" pizza party?

   See you soon, and thanks! Enjoy the attached photo!

Lisa

¹**give you a hand:** help with doing something | ²**get in touch with:** communicate with

B *Comprehension Check* Match the person with his / her work assignment.

1. Professor Rodriguez __d__   a. is going to bring plates.
2. Wei _____   b. will do the vegetables.
3. Lara _____   c. will pick up all the food.
4. Marcus _____   d. is going to pick up the turkey.
5. Mohammed _____   e. will make pumpkin pies.

C *Notice* Find the questions in the e-mail and complete them.

1. Professor Rodriguez, _____ please pick up the turkey on Wednesday evening?

2. Wei, _____ make the pumpkin pies on Wednesday?

3. Professor Rodriguez, _____ please contact your sister?

4. Mohammed, _____ get in touch with your roommate?

Which sentences ask permission to do something? Which sentences ask someone else to do something?

2 | Permission

▶ Grammar Presentation

You can use *can, could, may,* and *do you mind if* to ask permission to do something.	*"**Could** I go with you to Ana's?"* *"Sure. No problem."* *"**Do you mind if** we take your car?"* *"No, not at all."*

2.1 *Can, Could, May*: Yes / No Questions and Responses

Modal Verb	Subject	Base Form of Verb		Responses	
Can				Yes, you **can**.	No, you **can't**.
Could **May**	I	go	in your car?	Yes, (of course).	No, (I'm afraid not).

2.2 *Do You Mind If*: Yes / No Questions and Responses

Do you mind if	Subject	Verb	Responses	
Do you mind if	I	**drive**?	No, I don't. Not at all. Sure. No problem.	Well, actually, I prefer to drive.

2.3 Asking for Permission

a. Less formal	can	*Can* is very common in conversation and informal writing. Use *can* in most situations.	***Can** I get in touch with your roommate?*
	could	*Could* is more formal and more polite than *can*.	***Could** we ride to the shelter with you, please?*
More formal	may	*May* is very formal and polite.	***May** I please contact your sister, Professor Rodriguez?*

b. Use the base form of the verb after modal verbs, including *can*, *could*, and *may*. Do not use other forms of the verb.	***Can** I be part of your volunteer group?* *Can I ~~am~~ part of your volunteer group?* *Can I ~~being~~ part of your volunteer group?*
c. Use *Do you mind if . . .* to be polite or when you think the request is inconvenient for the other person.	***Do you mind if** we take your car?*
With *Do you mind if . . . ?*, the verb agrees with the subject.	***Do you mind if Eun gives** you a hand?*
You can also use *Do you mind?* alone.	*Can we go to the shelter together?* ***Do you mind?***
d. You can say *please* with requests for permission, especially in formal situations. Use it at the end of the sentence or after the subject.	*Could I drive your car, **please**?* *May I **please** drive your car?*

2.4 Answering Requests for Permission

a. Use *can* and *may* in short answers to requests for permission. Do not use *could*.	*"Can I come with you in your car?"* *"Yes, you **can**."*
	                                          "Yes, you ~~could~~."
	
	"Could I call you later?" *"Yes."* / *"Yes, you **can**."*
	                                  "Yes, you ~~could~~."

May is more formal.	*"May I sit here, please?"* *"Yes, you **may**."*
b. In conversation, you can use other expressions such as *Sure, no problem.* / *Certainly.* / *Of course.*	*"Could I use your cell phone?"* ***"Sure, no problem."***
Use *Certainly* and *Of course* in formal situations.	*"May I contact your sister?"* ***"Of course."*** / ***"Certainly."***

c. You can soften negative responses with an apology and / or a reason.	*"Can I ride in your car?"* ***"Sorry**, I don't have room."***
	                               "I'm afraid** I don't have room."
	                               "~~I don't have room~~."

2.4 Answering Requests for Permission *(continued)*

Be careful with negative responses.
No, you can't and other direct negative
responses often sound rude.

d. Say *No* or *No, not at all* to agree with requests with *Do you mind if*.	***"Do you mind if** I borrow your cell phone?"* ***"No, not at all.** Here you are." / "**Sure, no problem**."* (*Yes* = Yes, I do mind. You can't use it.)
No means "No, I don't mind." You can also say *Sure* or *Sure, no problem*.	***"Do you mind if** I call you this evening?"* ***"No, not at all."*** (*No* = It's OK to call.)
Notice: *No* in response to *Do you mind if* means the opposite of *No* in response to *can, could,* and *may*.	***"Can** I call you this evening?"* *"No, I'm afraid I'm busy."* (*No* = It's not OK to call.)

Data from the Real World

Research shows that most requests for permission use *I*, but it is possible to ask permission for other people.	***Can Eun** give you a hand?*

▶ # Grammar Application

Exercise 2.1 Asking and Answering Requests for Permission

Lisa's volunteers reply to her e-mail, and their plans change. Correct the mistake in each request.

1. Dear Lisa: Yes, I can make the pies on Wednesday. Could I ~~to~~ borrow a pie pan from you? Thanks, Wei

2. Hi, Lisa: Do you mind if I picks up the turkey on Wednesday morning? Thank you, Professor Rodriguez

3. Dear Lara: Ana's oven is not working. Do you mind if she cook the turkey at your house? Thanks! Lisa

4. Hello, Lisa: Can my roommate calls you about volunteering? Do you mind if I give him your number? Mohammed

5. Dear Ana: May please I call you early on Wednesday morning to arrange a time? Professor Rodriguez

6. Dear Lisa: Yes, I can bring plates. Can you helping me carry them? Thanks! Marcus

7. Dear Professor Rodriguez: Yes, may you call on Wednesday morning. I'm available after 8:00 a.m. Ana

8. Hi, Ana: My car is not working. Could I please to ride to the shelter with you? Eun

Exercise 2.2 Formal Requests for Permission

A 🔊 Listen to a student asking a teacher for permission. Complete his requests in the chart below.

B 🔊 Listen again. Does the teacher agree to the student's requests? Check (✔) *Yes* or *No*.

		Yes	No
1. _Could I ask you_	a question, please?	☑	☐
2. _____	class early on Wednesday?	☐	☐
3. _____	the computer room?	☐	☐
4. _____	your CD player?	☐	☐
5. _____	our homework on Friday, not Thursday?	☐	☐

C *Pair Work* Now compare your answers with a partner.

Exercise 2.3 Asking for Permission

A Write two requests for permission to each person. Use the ideas in the box or your own ideas.

You want to:

ask a question about . . .	discuss an idea for . . .	get help with . . .	take a day off
borrow something	get a ride somewhere	sit down	talk after class about . . .

Your Teacher	A Friend	A Stranger in the Cafeteria	Your Boss
1. *Could I please talk to you after class about my paper?*	3.	5.	7.
2.	4.	6.	8.

B *Pair Work* Choose three of your requests. Read them to a partner. Do not identify the person you wrote the request to. Can your partner guess?

A *May I take a break now?*
B *Are you asking your boss?*

C *Pair Work* Take turns. Practice conversations. Use the situations from A. Make requests and respond.

(To a stranger in the cafeteria)
A *Do you mind if I sit down here?*
B *No, not at all.*

3 | Requests and Offers

▶ Grammar Presentation

You can use *can*, *could*, *will*, and *would* to ask people to do things. You can use *can*, *could*, *may*, and *will* to make offers.	*"**Could** you give me a hand?"* *"Yes, of course."* *"I'**ll** help you with that."* *"Thank you."*

3.1 Requests and Responses with *Can*, *Could*, *Will*, and *Would*

Modal Verb	Subject	Base Form of Verb	Responses	
Can **Could** **Will** **Would**	you	help?	Yes, I **can**. / Sure. No problem. Of course. / All right. / OK. Yes, I **will**. Yes, I'd be happy to. / I'd love to.	Sorry, I **can't**. I'm afraid I **can't**.

3.2 Asking People to Do Things with *Can*, *Could*, *Will*, and *Would*

a. Less formal	can / will	***Can*** you stop by Ana's around noon?
		Will you help me make the vegetables?
		Could you take the turkey to Ana's apartment?
More formal	could / would	***Would*** you make the pies, please?

Could and *would* are more polite and less direct.

b. You can say *please* to ask people to do things, especially in formal situations. Use it at the end of the sentence or after the subject.	*Would you help prepare the dinner, **please**?* *Can you **please** arrive at the shelter by noon?*
c. You can use *will* and *would* to ask if someone is willing to do something. *Would* is more polite than *will*. Use *would* in formal situations, and use *will* only with people you know well.	***Will*** *you buy the vegetables?* ***Would*** *you help us, Professor Rodriguez?*

3.3 Answering Requests to Do Things

a. Use *can* and *will* in short answers. Do not use *could* or *would*.	*"Could you drive me there?"* *"Yes, I **can**."* *"Yes, I ~~could~~."* *"Would you help?"* *"Yes, I **will**."* *"Yes, I ~~would~~."*
b. In conversation, you can use other expressions, such as *Sure, no problem. / Certainly. / Of course.*	*"Will you clean up after dinner, please?"* *"Sure, no problem."*
Certainly and *Of course* show emphasis. They can also sound more formal.	*"Would you please help me with this?"* *"Certainly."*
c. You can soften negative responses with an apology and / or a reason.	*"Can you help?"* *"**I'm sorry**, I don't have time this week."*
Be careful with negative responses. *No, I won't* and other direct negative responses often sound rude.	~~No, I won't,~~ I don't have time this week.

3.4 Making Offers with *Can*, *Could*, *May*, and *Will*

a. You can use questions with *can*, *could*, and *may* to make offers.

Less formal	can	***Can*** I help you with dinner?
	could	***Could*** I help you clean up after dinner?
More formal	may	***May*** I help you with that?

3.4 Making Offers with *Can*, *Could*, *May*, and *Will* (continued)

b. You can also use statements with *I'll*, *We'll*, *I can*, and *We can* to make offers.	***I'll cook*** the turkey this year. ***We'll make*** dinner tonight. ***I can drive*** you to the shelter. ***We can prepare*** the vegetables.

3.5 Responding to Offers

a. You can say *Thank you* or *No, thank you* to respond to an offer. *Thanks* and *No, thanks* are less formal.	"I can give you a ride." **"Thank you."** / **"Thanks."** "Could I help you with that?" **"No, thank you."**
You can also respond with *That would be great* or *OK*.	"I'll cook the turkey this year." **"That would be great."** / **"OK, thank you."**
b. You can respond *Yes, please* or *That would be great* to an offer that is a question.	"Can I make the vegetables?" **"Yes, please."**

▶ Grammar Application

Exercise 3.1 *Can*, *Could*, *Will*, and *Would*: Requests and Answers

A You need your co-workers' help to plan a charity raffle (an event where everyone who donates to the charity has a chance to win a prize). Use the words to write requests with *please*.

1. could / buy snacks and drinks   *Could you please buy snacks and drinks? /*
   Could you buy snacks and drinks, please?

2. would / set up tables _____

   _____

3. can / sell raffle tickets _____

_____

4. will / buy prizes for the raffle _____

_____

5. would / decorate the room _____

_____

6. could / serve snacks and drinks _____

_____

7. will / give a speech about the charity _____

_____

8. would / everyone / help clean up after the party _____

_____

B *Pair Work* Take turns asking and answering the requests in A.

A *Could you please buy snacks and drinks?*

B *Yes, of course. / I'm sorry. I don't have time to do that, but I can . . .*

Exercise 3.2 Formal and Informal Offers and Responses

A ◀)) It is the evening of the charity raffle. Listen. Complete the offers. Listen again. Complete the responses.

1. **A** Hi, Tony. *I'll drive* to the raffle tonight. OK?

   B Oh, that would be great. Thanks.

2. **A** Sarah, _____ carry those bags.

   B _____ . They're really heavy.

3. **A** _____ move those tables, Mr. Lee?

   B _____ . I just finished.

4. **A** _____ the snacks and drinks out now?

   B _____

5. **A** Jordy, _____ you take tickets.

   B _____

6. *A* Ms. Moncur, _____ with the decorations?

   B _____

7. *A* Oh, no!

   B _____

   A _____

8. *A* _____ that for you, Paula?

   B _____

B Which two conversations are the most formal?

_____ _____

Exercise 3.3 Requests and Offers

Data from the Real World

Research shows people also use *Do you want to* to make requests. These requests sound less direct.	*Do you want to help me with the dishes?* *Do you want to drive now?*

A *Pair Work* You and a partner are organizing a project for a good cause. Choose one of the projects below or use your own idea. Make a list of six to eight things you need to do.

- clean up a local park
- organize a party at a children's hospital
- organize a party at a senior center
- raise money for charity

Clean Up Green Park
1. *Put up fliers for volunteers: Tina, Cho, and Luis*
2. *Organize volunteer groups: Victoria*
3. *Plan jobs for each group: Tomás and Sophie*

B *Pair Work*   Take turns. Offer to do jobs on your list from A. Write your name or your partner's name under the jobs you each offer to do.

C *Group Work*   Work with another pair. Take turns making and responding to requests for help with your project. Ask questions with *can*, *could*, and *Do you want to . . . ?*

> A *Could you help me with a party at the children's hospital?*
> B *Yes, I can. What can I do?*
> A *Do you want to make a cake?*
> B *Oh, I'm not good at baking. Could I do something else?*

4 Avoid Common Mistakes ⚠

1. Use the base form of the verb after *can*, *could*, *may*, *will*, or *would*.

Could Lin ~~to~~ ride with you tomorrow?

2. Use *please* in a request at the end of the sentence or after the subject.

please

Can ~~please~~ I ride with you to the party?

or

party, please

Can ~~please~~ I ride with you to the ~~party~~?

3. Don't use *could* in short answers to requests for permission.

can

"Could I use your phone, please?"   "Yes, you ~~could~~."

4. Don't use *could* or *would* to respond to requests to do things.

will

"Would you carry this bag for me?"   "Yes, I ~~would~~."

Editing Task

Find and correct six more mistakes in the e-mail messages.

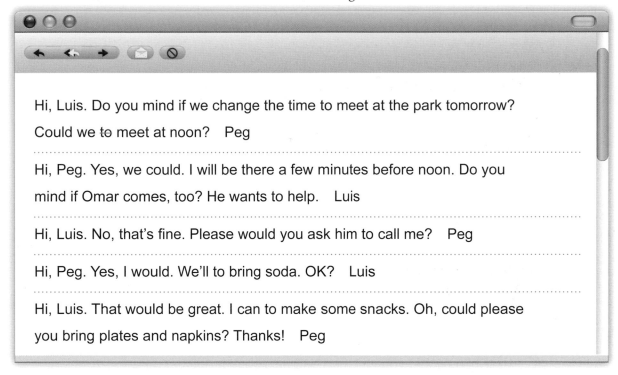

Hi, Luis. Do you mind if we change the time to meet at the park tomorrow? Could we ~~to~~ meet at noon?   Peg

Hi, Peg. Yes, we could. I will be there a few minutes before noon. Do you mind if Omar comes, too? He wants to help.   Luis

Hi, Luis. No, that's fine. Please would you ask him to call me?   Peg

Hi, Peg. Yes, I would. We'll to bring soda. OK?   Luis

Hi, Luis. That would be great. I can to make some snacks. Oh, could please you bring plates and napkins? Thanks!   Peg

5 | Grammar for Writing

Permission, Requests, and Offers in Writing

Writers use modals for permission, requests, and offers in e-mails and letters to plan events with other people.

These modals are common in e-mails, memos, and letters to friends and colleagues. Remember:

- **Use *may* and *could* to ask permission in more formal situations.**
  Mr. Smith, <u>could</u> we borrow your laptop for the meeting tomorrow?

- **Use *can, could, will*, and *would* to request things from other people.**
  Use *Do you mind if* . . . for difficult or inconvenient requests.

  Tom, <u>would</u> you take notes at the meeting? Also, <u>do you mind if</u> we change the time to 8:00 a.m.? Sorry it is so early.

- **Use *can, could*, and *will* to offer assistance.**
  I <u>can</u> bring coffee and breakfast food for the meeting.

Pre-writing Task

1 Read the e-mail about a volunteer project. What does Alicia offer to do? What does she need other people to do?

Dear Yan and Kobe,

We need to work on our group project tomorrow. Do you mind if I ask you both to help me with some things? Thanks. Here are the things we need to do.

5 • Could we all meet at 1:00 tomorrow to work on the project? The only problem is, my roommate is having a study group at the apartment at that time. Kobe, do you mind if we meet at your house instead of my apartment?

• If we meet at Kobe's house, I could bring some sandwiches. Yan,
10 would you be able to bring some dessert? Kobe, could you provide soda or juice?

• Yan, could you get the information on the soup kitchen before we meet?

• Kobe, would you call the homeless shelter and set up an
15 appointment for us to talk to the director?

• Kobe, could you let me know if you want me to bring my laptop?

See you both tomorrow!

Alicia

◀ Reply | → Forward | ▼

2 Read the e-mail again. Underline the requests and circle the offers.

Writing Task

1 *Write* Use the e-mail in the Pre-writing Task to help you write an e-mail requesting help to plan something. Use the words you underlined and circled in the paragraph to ask people to do things and to make offers. You can write about one of these events or your own idea.

• a car wash to raise money for charity

• a group cleanup of a neighborhood in need

• a yard sale to raise money for an organization

• a fund-raiser for an animal shelter

2 *Self-Edit* Use the editing tips below to improve your sentences. Make any
necessary changes.

1. Did you use words like *can, could, may, will, would,* and *Do you mind if . . . ?*
   to plan an event?
2. Did you use *may* and *could* to ask for permission in more formal situations?
3. Did you use *Do you mind if . . . ?* for difficult or inconvenient requests?
4. Did you use *can, could,* or *will* to offer assistance?
5. Did you avoid the mistakes in the Avoid Common Mistakes chart on page 250?

Advice and Suggestions
The Right Job

1 | Grammar in the Real World

A What are some important things to think about when you plan your career or look for a job? Read the article on advice for people looking for jobs. Which suggestion do you think is the most useful?

The Right Job for You

What are some important considerations¹ when you look for a new job? According to experts, you **ought to** think about these things:

First, know yourself! You **should** ask yourself exactly
5 what you want from a job. Is it money, interesting work, nice co-workers, or something else? Different people want different things from a job. Assess² yourself. Where³ are you now, and where do you want to be?

You also **might want to** think about your personal relationships. Consider which
10 relationships are going well, which ones are not, and, most importantly, why. This will help you understand how you relate to people you work with.

Make changes! If you had problems in another job (maybe you were always late, or you did not finish projects), then you **should** make changes *before* you take a new job. It is too late when you are in the job.

15 Decide what you *don't* want! If you just want a nine-to-five⁴ job, you **had better not** work for a company that expects you to be on call 24-7.⁵

If you have an interview, prepare! You **should** find out about an employer's business before your interview. Study the company's website. You **could** also call the company. Ask to speak with someone about the job.

20 Of course, many of these ideas are common sense,⁶ but a lot of people just don't think about them. As a result, they are very unhappy in their jobs.

¹**consideration:** something to think about when making decisions │ ²**assess:** judge or decide about │ ³**where:** in what situation │ ⁴**nine-to-five:** 9:00 a.m. to 5:00 p.m., a typical workday │ ⁵**24-7:** twenty-four hours a day, seven days a week, all the time │ ⁶**common sense:** the ability to use good judgment in making decisions and to live in a safe way

B *Comprehension Check* Circle the correct words.

1. Everyone wants **the same things / different things** from a job.

2. Looking at your personal relationships **can / cannot** help you learn more about how you relate to co-workers.

3. It is **easy / difficult** to make changes after you have started a new job.

4. **Everyone / Not everyone** uses common sense when they look for a job.

C *Notice* Find the sentences in the article and complete them.

1. According to experts, you _____ think about these things.

2. You _____ ask yourself exactly what you want from a job.

3. You _____ also call the company.

In these sentences, do *ought to* and *should* show advice or show ability? Does *could* show ability or make a suggestion?

2 | Advice

▶ Grammar Presentation

| *Should, ought to,* and *had better* are often used to give advice. | You **should** ask yourself exactly what you want from a job.
You **had better** make changes before you take a new job. |

2.1 Statements

Subject	Modal Verb / *Had Better (Not)*	Base Form	of Verb
I You He / She / It We They	**should** **shouldn't / should not** **ought to** **ought not to** **had better (not)** **'d better (not)**	make	changes.

2.2 *Yes / No* Questions and Responses

Should	Subject	Base Form of Verb		Responses	
Should	I you he / she / it we they	take	a different job?	Yes, you **should**. Yes, she **should**.	No, you **shouldn't**. No, she **shouldn't**.

2.3 Information Questions

Wh- Word	*Should*	Subject	Base Form of Verb	
When **Who**	**should**	I you he / she / it we they	call?	

Wh- Word	*Should*	Base Form of Verb	
What **Who**	**should**	come	next?

2.4 Using *Should, Ought to,* and *Had Better* for Advice

a. Use *should* and *ought to* for general advice.	You **should** *assess yourself before you look for a job.* *She* **ought to** *look for a new job.*
b. Use *had better (not)* only for very strong advice and warnings. *Had better (not)* is much stronger than *should* or *ought to*. It suggests that something negative will happen if you don't take the advice. We usually only use it in speaking.	You **had better** *finish this project, or you might lose your job!*
c. Use *should* in questions. *Ought to* and *had better* are not common in questions.	**Should** *I ask about the salary at the interview?*
d. Use *maybe, perhaps,* or *I think* to soften advice. These expressions usually go at the beginning of the sentence.	**Maybe** *you should be more careful when you write your résumé.* **I think** *he ought to look for a different job.*
e. You can also use *probably* to soften advice. It can go before or after *should*. It goes before *ought to*.	*She* **probably** *should take the job. / She should* **probably** *take the job.* *She* **probably** *ought to take the job.* *She* ~~ought to probably~~ *take the job.*

 Should not is much more common than *ought not to*. You can use *should not* in both speaking and writing.

Data from the Real World

Research shows that people often make advice stronger by adding *really*.

Really can go before or after *should/shouldn't*. When *really* goes before *should/shouldn't*, it is stronger.	You should **really** get advice from a career advisor. You **really** shouldn't quit your job before you've found another one.
Really goes before *ought to* and *had better*.	You **really** had better try to keep your current job. You **really** ought to update your résumé. You ~~ought to~~ **really** update your résumé.

▶ Grammar Application

Exercise 2.1 Statements

Unscramble the words and add *you* to write sentences that give advice. Sometimes more than one answer is possible.

1. decide what you want from a job / should / really / .

   You really should decide what you want from a job. / You should really decide what you want from a job.

2. had better / think about the hours you prefer / really / .

   _____

3. ought to / decide if you want to be on call 24-7 / perhaps / .

   _____

4. maybe / look for job advertisements online / should / .

   _____

5. tell your family about your plans / ought to / probably / .

   _____

6. really / shouldn't / get discouraged / .

   _____

7. should / ask for advice from a career counselor / I think / .

   _____

8. really / take a job you don't like / had better not / !

   _____

Exercise 2.2 Asking for and Giving Advice

A Complete the requests for job advice from an online forum. Add *should*. Sometimes you also need to add a *Wh-* word.

1. I've been offered my dream job. However, it is far from my family and friends. _Should_ I take the job?

   – Arthur, New York, NY

2. I need help to make plans for my career.

   _____ I talk to?

   – Ari, Toledo, OH

3. I've been looking for a job for several months. I finally have an offer, but it's not the perfect job for me. However, I really need money.

   _____ I take the job?

   – Camilla, San Francisco, CA

4. I absolutely hate my job! I want to look for another one, but I have lots of student loans. _____ I do?

   – Samuel, Miami, FL

5. I would like to change careers, but I don't have experience in the career I like. My friend told me to do volunteer work to get experience.

   _____ I do this?

   – Eleni, Austin, TX

6. I'm almost finished with school and I don't know what kind of job I want.

   _____ I do?

   – Katya, Denver, CO

7. My parents think money is the most important thing in a job. I want to look for a job that makes me happy. _____ I listen to my parents?

   – Helen, Seattle, WA

B *Pair Work* Discuss the situations in A with a partner. What do you think each person should do? Compare your answers.

> A *I think Arthur ought to talk to his family about his decision.*
> B *I think he should just take the job. It's his dream job.*

C 🔊 Listen to a career counselor give advice for each situation. Write the advice you hear.

1. Arthur *had better not take* the job and move.
2. Ari _____ to a career counselor.
3. _____ Camilla _____ the job.
4. _____ Samuel _____ for another job.
5. Yes, Eleni _____ some volunteer work.
6. Katya _____ talking to people.
7. _____ Terry _____ looking for another job. It doesn't sound good, but he _____ to his boss, too.
8. Helen _____ what makes her happy.

Exercise 2.3 More Asking for and Giving Advice

A Write two to four questions asking for advice about jobs / work or school.

B *Pair Work* Exchange your questions from A with a partner. Write responses to your partner's requests for advice. Then read and compare the advice. Do you agree with the advice? Why or why not?

> A *I need to find a part-time job. Where should I look?*
> B *I think you should ask at the school cafeteria. They often need help there.*

3 | Suggestions

▶ Grammar Presentation

Might (want to), could, why don't / doesn't, and *why not* are often used to make suggestions. Suggestions are not as strong as advice.	You **might want to** schedule your interview in the afternoon. **Why don't** you prepare questions for the interview?

3.1 Suggestions with *Might Want To* and *Could*

Subject	Modal Verb	Base Form of Verb	
I You He / She / It We They	**might want to** **might not want to** **could**	call	the company.

3.2 Suggestions with *Why Don't / Doesn't . . . ?*

Why Don't / Doesn't	Subject	Base Form of Verb
Why don't	I you we they	ask?
Why doesn't	he / she / it	

3.3 Suggestions with *Why Not . . . ?*

Why Not	Base Form of Verb	
Why not	buy	a new suit for the interview?

3.4 Making Suggestions

a. Use *might (want to)* and *could* to make suggestions. They often express a choice of possible actions.	You **might** schedule your interview in the morning, or you **could** wait until the afternoon.
Might is often used with *want to*.	You **might want to** think about volunteer work. You **might not want to** ask that question in an interview.
Do not use *could not* in negative suggestions. Use *might not want to*.	You ~~could not~~ ask that question in an interview.
b. *Why not* and *Why don't / doesn't* are both question forms and end with a question mark.	**Why don't you** prepare questions for your interview? **Why not** prepare questions for your interview?
Why don't / doesn't and *Why not* are very common in conversation. Do not use them in academic writing.	Say: "**Why don't** you practice for your interview?" Write: Interviewees **might want to** practice for their interviews.

▶ Grammar Application

Exercise 3.1 Making Suggestions

Complete the conversations. Circle the correct words.

1. **A** I sent my résumé in for a job a few weeks ago, but I haven't had any response.

   B (**You could**) / **Why don't you** call the company.

2. **A** I have an interview next week, and I'm worried about getting there on time. Traffic is so bad.

   B **You might** / **Why not** schedule the interview for the middle of the day, when traffic isn't as bad?

3. **A** I can't find a job in my field. I really need some work, any work!

   B You **why not** / **might want to** look for temporary work. That's often easier to find.

4. **A** I have an interview tomorrow, but I don't know a lot about the company.

   B **You might want to** / **Why don't you** do some research online. I'll help you.

5. **A** I'm nervous about my interview on Monday. I don't know what they'll ask me.

   B Well, **we could** / **why not** practice together. I can ask you questions.

6. **A** I'm going to dress casually for my interview tomorrow. It's a very informal company.

   B You **could not** / **might not want to** dress too casually. It's still a job interview.

7. **A** I have to drive to my interview tomorrow, and I always get lost when I drive.

   B **You might want to** / **Why don't you** print out directions or use a GPS.

8. **A** I just had a good interview, and I'm really interested in the job.

   B **Why don't** / **Why not** you follow up with a thank-you note? It's always a good idea.

Exercise 3.2 More Suggestions

A *Pair Work*   Read about Alex. He has a job interview in a few days. Write three more suggestions for him. Then compare answers with a partner.

> I always stay up late and wake up late in the morning.

> My suit is pretty old.

> I don't know what questions they'll ask me at the interview.

> I don't have directions to the interview location.

> I haven't had a haircut in a long time.

> I talk too much when I'm nervous.

1. *You could go to bed early.* _____
2. _____
3. _____
4. _____

B *Pair Work*   Tell a partner what you worry about in job interviews. Give each other suggestions.

   A I worry about the questions they might ask.

   B You might want to research the job and the company. Maybe that will help you.

4 | Avoid Common Mistakes ⚠

1. **Do not forget *had* or *'d* when you write *had better*.**

   You ˄ *had* better start looking for another job.

2. **Use *had better (not)* only for very strong advice and warnings.**

   At an interview, you ~~had better~~ *should* speak clearly and look interested in the questions.

3. **Do not use *could not* in negative suggestions. Use *might not want to*.**

   You ~~could not~~ *might not want to* wear jeans for the interview.

4. **Do not use an *-ing* form or a *to-* infinitive after *Why not*.**

   Why not ~~going~~ *go* to a career advisor?

   Why not ~~to~~ leave at 6:00 a.m.?

Editing Task

Find and correct five more mistakes in the conversation.

Jordan   There are a lot of changes happening at my company.

          I'm worried I might lose my job.

Isabela   Well, you *had* better probably start looking for something else.

Jordan   I guess so.

5 Isabela At the same time, you better try to keep your current job. They say

          it's a lot harder to find a new job when you're unemployed.

Jordan   Is there anything I can do?

Isabela   Yes, there's a lot you can do. First, why not to talk to your boss? You get along

          well, right? Why not asking for feedback on your work? Then, you probably ought

10   to tell your boss you're working on those things. You might want to keep in touch

          with her by e-mail.

Jordan   OK. What else?

Isabela   Well, do extra work. You ought to take on extra tasks whenever you can. And you

          could not complain about anything.

15 Jordan That makes sense. Thanks, Isabela. I'd better ask you for advice more often!

5 | Grammar for Writing ✏

Giving Advice and Suggestions

Writers use *should, ought to, had better,* and *might (want to)* to describe ways to solve problems, offer solutions, and say why the solutions are good.

These modals are common in magazine articles, advice columns, personal e-mails, and other texts that give people advice.

Remember:

- **Use *had better* only to give strong advice or warnings.**
  You <u>had better</u> apologize to the boss. If you do not, you will probably lose your job.

- **You can make advice stronger with *really* before or after *should*. When *really* goes before *should*, it is even stronger.**
  They <u>really</u> should leave soon. You should <u>really</u> check the traffic report.

- **You can soften advice with *maybe, perhaps,* and *I think* at the beginning of sentences.**
  <u>*Perhaps*</u> *he shouldn't wear those pants to the interview.*

Pre-writing Task

1 Read the advice column below. What is the question about? Which suggestion in the reply do you think is best?

Problems? Ask Aunt Advice!

Dear Aunt Advice,

I have my first job interview next week. I am nervous. Please help.
– Nervous in New York

Dear Nervous,

5   Here is some general job-interview advice. Good interviewers ask you questions, but they also want you to ask questions. You should come to the interview with interesting questions. This will help you to feel well prepared. Also, you should be ready to write down some questions during the interview, so you should bring a small notebook. This shows that you are very interested in what the interviewer is saying. You
10   might want to ask the interviewer if it is all right to take notes first, though. Interviewers often ask about your weaknesses. You really should make a list of them in advance. I think you should be honest about your weaknesses, but only the weaknesses that will not cause problems on the job. Also, you had better be ready to talk about your plans to

overcome these weaknesses. This shows that you want to learn and grow in your job. In
15 addition, you really ought to practice an interview in advance. Perhaps you could ask a
friend to help you. However, you had better do that a few days in advance so you have
time to fix any problems.

If you follow this advice, you show the interviewer that you are serious about the
job and the company, and that helps you feel less nervous.
20 Good luck,
Aunt Advice

2 Read the text again. Underline the sentences that give advice. Which sentences
offer strong advice? What words make the advice strong?

Writing Task

1 *Write* Use the advice column in the Pre-writing Task to help you write a letter
about a problem and a reply letter that gives advice. You can ask for advice about:

- asking a boss for more money or time off
- getting along with a difficult co-worker
- finding a job
- your own idea

2 *Self-Edit* Use the editing tips below to improve your paragraph. Make any
necessary changes.

1. Did you use *should, ought to, had better*, and *might (want to)* to describe ways
   to solve a problem?
2. Did you use *had better* for strong advice or warnings?
3. Did you use *really* to make advice stronger?
4. Did you avoid the mistakes in the Avoid Common Mistakes chart on page 262?

1 Grammar in the Real World

A What are three different kinds of advertising you see every day? Read the article about advertising companies. What are two difficulties for advertisers?

The Challenges[1] of Advertising[2]

Advertising is not a new idea. Long ago, sellers called out to people on the street. They tried to persuade[3] people to buy their products. Now advertising is everywhere. It is on the street, on the Web, in magazines, and on phones.

Although there are now many ways to advertise, it is not an easy business. There are
5 many challenges. Companies **need to** appeal[4] to consumers so they buy their products. This can be quite difficult because people have so many choices these days. Each advertiser **must** make its choice seem better than all the others.

Advertising is also very expensive. Companies **would rather** not spend a lot of money on it. They **would prefer** to save their money. However, to sell their products, companies
10 often **need to** spend large amounts of money on ads. Consumers see or hear up to 3,000 advertising messages each day. Each one **has to** be clever.[5] This means companies **have to** pay to show the ads on TV, online, or in other places, and they also **need to** pay creative people to make them.

There is another challenge for companies when they advertise. Today, there are
15 numerous rules they **must** follow. For example, they **must not** lie. Companies also **need to** be careful when they try to sell products to children.

Advertisers **must** do a number of different things at once. This is not easy, but it is also a big business with big rewards. Just one good advertisement can convince millions of people to buy a product.

---

[1]**challenge:** something that needs great mental or physical effort to be done well | [2]**advertising:** making something known generally in public, especially in order to sell it | [3]**persuade:** cause someone to do or believe something, especially by explaining why they should | [4]**appeal (to):** be attractive or interesting | [5]**clever:** showing quick intelligence in doing something

B *Comprehension Check* Answer the questions.

1. How did people advertise in the past?
2. Why is it difficult for advertisers to appeal to consumers?
3. How many advertisements do people see or hear each day?
4. What must advertisers not do?

C *Notice* Find the sentences in the article and complete them.

1. Companies _____ appeal to consumers so they buy their products.

2. Companies _____ not spend a lot of money on it.

3. They _____ to save their money.

4. Each one _____ be clever.

Which of these sentences talk about something that is necessary? Which talk about something that is preferred?

2 | Necessity and Prohibition

▶ Grammar Presentation

Have to, have got to, need to, and *must (not)* are used to say what is necessary, not necessary, or prohibited.	An ad **has to** appeal to consumers. (necessary) They **do not need to** advertise abroad. (not necessary) Companies **must** follow rules when they create ads. (necessary) They **must not** lie in their advertising. (prohibited)

2.1 *Have To, Have Got To,* and *Need To*: Statements

Subject	*Have To / Have Got To / Need To*	Base Form of Verb	
I You We They	**have to / do not have to** **have got to** **need to / do not need to**	be buy	clever. advertising.
He / She / It	**has to / doesn't have to** **has got to** **needs to / doesn't need to**		

2.2 *Must*: Statements

Subject	Modal Verb	Base Form of Verb	
I You He / She / It We They	**must** **must not / mustn't**	be buy	clever. advertising.

2.3 *Have To* and *Need To*: Yes / No Questions

Do / Does	Subject	Have To / Need To	Base Form of Verb
Do	you	**have to**	advertise?
Does	he / she / it	**need to**	

2.4 *Have To* and *Need To*: Information Questions

Wh- Word	Do / Does	Subject	Have To / Need To	Base Form of Verb
When **Why** **Where**	do	you	**have to**	advertise?
	does	he / she / it	**need to**	

Wh- Word	Have To / Need To	Base Form of Verb
Who	**has to** **needs to**	advertise?

2.5 Expressing Necessity and Prohibition

a. Use *have to* and *need to* to say something is necessary.	*Advertisers* **have to** *think about consumers.*
Have to is twice as common as *need to*.	*The company* **needs to** *be more creative.*
b. You can also use *have got to* in affirmative statements. It is usually less formal. The contraction for *has* is *'s*.	*The ad* **has got to** *appeal to a lot of people. It***'s got to** *be interesting.*
Have got to is not usually used in negative sentences.	*The ad* ~~**hasn't got to**~~ *appeal to children.*
c. *Must* is very strong and sounds formal or official. It is often used in writing to state rules or laws and is rare in speaking.	*Advertising companies* **must** *follow these rules.* *He* **must** *report this immediately.*
d. You can use *don't have to* and *don't need to* to say something is not necessary.	*She* **doesn't need to** *finish that.*
However, use *must not / mustn't* to express strong prohibition or to forbid something.	*Companies* **must not** *lie in their advertising.*
Be careful: *have to* and *must* have a similar meaning in the affirmative, but they are very different in negative sentences.	*You* **must / have to** *use a pen.* (A pen is necessary.) *You* **don't have to** *use a pen.* (A pen is not necessary. You have a choice.) *You* **must not** *use a pen.* (A pen is prohibited. You have no choice.)

2.5 Expressing Necessity and Prohibition (continued)

e. Use *have to* and *need to* to ask about necessity. Use a form of *do* in the question and answer.	*"**Do** we **have to** follow this rule?"* *"Yes, we **do**."* *"**Does** this ad **need to** appeal to kids?"* *"No, it **doesn't**."*
We often use *can't* instead of *must not* to express prohibition, especially in spoken English.	Say: *"You **can't** do that. It's against the rules."* Write: *Drivers **must not** exceed the speed limit.*

🔊 Pronunciation Focus: *Have To, Has To, Have Got To*

In informal conversation:	*have to* is often pronounced "hafta." *has to* is often pronounced "hasta." *got to* is often pronounced "gotta."

▶ Grammar Application

Exercise 2.1 Statements

A 🔊 Listen to an advertising manager discuss plans with his employees. Complete the sentences with the verbs you hear.

1. We *'ve got to* do this quickly, so we really _*have to*_ work together.

2. Each team _____ choose a leader.

3. The leader _____ organize the team.

4. Then, you'll all _____ work together to make a plan for the project.

5. I absolutely _____ have all plans by the end of the week.

6. You really _____ e-mail a report of your progress to me at the end of each week.

7. The report _____ be long, but it _____ explain your progress clearly.

8. You _____ forget this because I _____ report to the president every week.

9. We _____ create some really interesting ads.

10. But remember, we _____ be honest in all of the ads.

B Which sentence says that something is not necessary? Which sentence says that something is prohibited?

Exercise 2.2 Questions and Answers

Complete the e-mail messages with the correct form of the verbs in parentheses.

Hi team,   October 21, 10:00 a.m.

Remember, we are meeting tomorrow to discuss our plan. I _need to_ (need to)
                                                                    (1)
get your ideas on it. I _____ (have to) hand the plan in on Friday. Let
                              (2)
me know if you have questions.   – Nick

Nick,   October 21, 10:15 a.m.

_____ we _____ (have to) bring specific ideas for ads
        (3)   (3)
to the meeting?   – Blanca

Hi Blanca,   October 21, 10:30 a.m.

No, you _____ (not need to) have specific ideas. But, we
                  (4)
_____ (must) start brainstorming soon. I _____ (have to)
        (5)   (6)
give Mr. Gomez an update on our ideas next week.   – Nick

Dear Nick,   October 21, 10:45 a.m.

I have specific ideas. Is it OK if I start to work on them?   – Jason

---

Hi Jason,   October 21, 11:00 a.m.

It's better to wait. Mr. Gomez _____ (have to) approve our
                                        (7)
ideas before we begin work on them. He _____ (need to) put
                                                (8)
them all together. Bring them tomorrow, and we can discuss them.   – Nick

---

Hi Nick,   October 21, 11:15 a.m.

When _____ Mr. Gomez _____ (need to) have the
          (9)   (9)
ideas? I will be on vacation for a few days next week. _____ I
                                                               (10)
_____ (have to) finish them before I leave?   – Claire
        (10)

Dear Claire,   October 21, 11:30 a.m.

Yes, I'm afraid so. We _____ (have got to) do them quickly. He
                               (11)
_____ (need to) have them sometime next week.   – Nick
        (12)

Exercise 2.3 More Questions and Answers

A *Over to You* Write answers to the questions.

1. What is one thing you have to do every day?

   _____

2. What is something you need to do but haven't done yet?

   _____

3. What is something you do at work or school that you don't have to do?

   _____

4. What is something that you must do at work or school?

   _____

5. What is something that you must not do at work or school?

   _____

B *Pair Work* Ask and answer the questions in A with a partner. Try to add extra information.

   A *What is one thing you have to do every day?*
   B *I have to take my children to school every day. Their school starts at 7:30, so I have to get up at 6:15.*

C *Group Work* Tell the class about your partner.

   Raul has to take his children to school every day. Their school starts at 7:30, so he has to get up at 6:15.

3 | Preference

▶ Grammar Presentation

Would rather, would like to, and *would prefer* are used to express preferences.	I **would rather not watch** those commercials. They **would like to see** some new and interesting ads. I**'d prefer to turn** the TV off.

3.1 *Would Rather*: Statements

Subject	*Would Rather (Not)*	Base Form of Verb
I You He / She / It We They	**would rather (not)**	advertise.

3.2 *Would Like* and *Would Prefer*: Statements

Subject	Would (Not) Like / Would Prefer (Not)	Infinitive
I You He / She / It We They	**would (not) like** **would prefer (not)**	to advertise.

3.3 *Yes / No* Questions

Would	Subject		Infinitive
Would	you	**like** **prefer**	to advertise?

Would	Subject		Base Form of Verb
Would	you	**rather**	advertise?

3.4 Information Questions

Wh- Word	Would	Subject		Infinitive
What	would	you	**like** **prefer**	to advertise?

Wh- Word	Would		Infinitive
Who	would	**like** **prefer**	to buy this product?

Wh- Word	Would	Subject	Base Form of Verb
What	would	you	**rather** advertise?

Wh- Word	Would	Base Form of Verb
Who	would	**rather** buy this product?

3.5 Expressing Preferences

a. You can use *would rather, would like,* and *would prefer* to express preference. *Would prefer* is more formal.	I **would rather** *spend a little money on advertising.* I **would prefer** *to listen to the radio.*
Use *would rather* with a base form of the verb. Use *would like* and *would prefer* with an infinitive. The contraction of *would* is *'d.*	I **would rather** *see more interesting advertising.* I **would like** / **would prefer** *to see more interesting advertising.* I**'d like** *to see more interesting advertising.*
b. In negative sentences, *not* goes between *would* and *like.* It goes after *would prefer* and *would rather.*	He **wouldn't like** *to work at that advertising company.* He **would prefer not** *to work at that advertising company.* We**'d rather not** *watch all the commercials.*

3.5 Expressing Preferences *(continued)*

c. You can use the verb *prefer* without *would*. When used without *would*, *prefer* takes *-s* with *he / she / it*.	*She* **would prefer to** *watch shorter commercials.* *She* **prefers** *to watch shorter commercials.* *She* ~~prefer~~ *to watch shorter commercials.*
d. *Would prefer* and *prefer* can be followed by a noun, an infinitive, or a verb + *-ing*.	*He prefers / would prefer* **a TV channel** *without ads.* *He prefers / would prefer* **to watch** *TV without commercials.* *He prefers / would prefer* **watching** *TV without commercials.*
e. Use *or* in questions about preference to offer a choice. The verb after *or* is usually in the base form.	*Would you like to go out* **or** *(to) stay home?* *Would you rather go out* **or** *stay home?*
f. You can use *I'd rather not* to respond to suggestions or requests.	*A We could go out tonight.* *B* **I'd rather not.** *I'm tired.*
g. You can make a comparison with *would rather* and *than*. If there is a verb after *than*, it is also in the base form.	**I'd rather see** *one long ad* **than** *a few short ones.* **I'd rather see** *ads on the Internet* **than watch** *them on TV.*

▶ # Grammar Application

Exercise 3.1 Questions and Answers

Complete the conversation between two colleagues at an advertising agency. Use the correct form and the correct order of the words in parentheses. Add words if necessary.

A Let's discuss the ad for the new music player. What do you think? What

<u>   would   </u> consumers <u> like to see </u> (would like / see)?
     (1)   (1)

B Well, we need to give some detail about the size, weight, memory – things like that.

Not too much, though. People _____ (not / would rather / get)
                           (2)

all the details in an ad. I think a consumer usually _____ (prefer / get)
                                        (3)

a general idea and then research it more if they're interested.

A OK, good point. _____ they _____ (would rather / see)
                 (4)   (4)

an ad that's more informative or one that's more fun?

B Well, I _____ (not / would like / see) an ad that's just informative.
                 (5)

I _____ (would rather / see) one that's really fun than one that's
        (6)

really informative. That seems a little boring.

A OK, but I think we need to do both – entertain and inform.

B True. Now, what do you think? _____ (7) people _____ (would prefer / see) (7) a man or a woman in the ad?

A Let's include both.

B I _____ (not / would rather). It (8) costs a lot to hire two actors.

A Both men and women buy music players.

I _____ (would prefer / hire) both. I think it's worth the cost. (9)

B Let's think about that. This is a good start. We can discuss all of this tomorrow.

Exercise 3.2 More Questions and Answers

Unscramble the words to make questions.

1. see a lot of ads on TV / would / rather / not / you / ?
   Would you rather not see a lot of ads on TV?

2. prefer / e-mail ads / you / advertising by mail / do / or / ?
   _____

3. a lot of ads before you buy things / to see / like / would / you / ?
   _____

4. you / to watch TV / prefer / without commercials / would / ?
   _____

5. not / have advertising / would / you / online / rather / ?
   _____

6. ads on the radio / you / ads on TV / do / prefer / or / ?
   _____

7. more informative ads or more funny ads / you / like / to see / would / ?
   _____

8. not / rather / would / any advertising at all / you / have / ?
   _____

4 Avoid Common Mistakes ⚠️

1. Use *don't have to* or *don't need to* to say something is not necessary, not *must not*.

   don't need to
   You ~~must not~~ take notes. I'll give you a copy at the end of the meeting.

2. Do not use an infinitive with *would rather*. Use an infinitive with *would like* and *(would) prefer*.

   We would rather ~~to~~ use this idea for the ad.

3. Use *would* before *rather*.

   would
   I ᵥrather not start work at 7 o'clock.

Editing Task

Find and correct seven more mistakes in the e-mail messages.

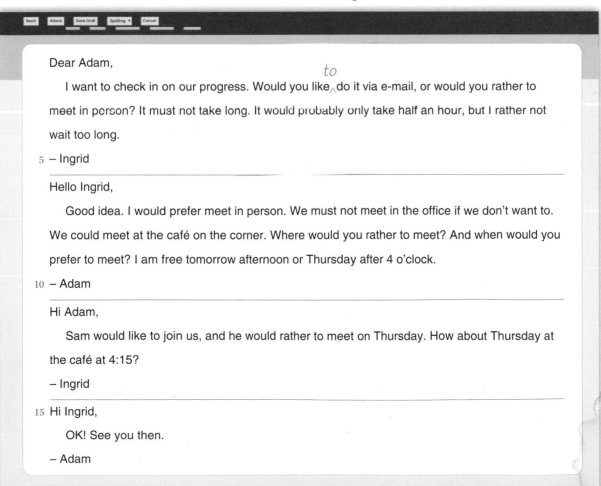

Dear Adam,

   I want to check in on our progress. Would you like ᵥ do it via e-mail, or would you rather to
meet in person? It must not take long. It would probably only take half an hour, but I rather not
wait too long.

5 – Ingrid

Hello Ingrid,

   Good idea. I would prefer meet in person. We must not meet in the office if we don't want to.
We could meet at the café on the corner. Where would you rather to meet? And when would you
prefer to meet? I am free tomorrow afternoon or Thursday after 4 o'clock.

10 – Adam

Hi Adam,

   Sam would like to join us, and he would rather to meet on Thursday. How about Thursday at
the café at 4:15?

   – Ingrid

15 Hi Ingrid,

   OK! See you then.

   – Adam

5 | Grammar for Writing

Writing About Necessities and Expressing Preferences

Writers use *have to, need to, must, would rather, would like,* and *would prefer* to talk about problems or situations that they want to change or improve.

Have to, need to, must, would rather, would like, and *would prefer* are common in articles, newspaper editorials, and other texts that give personal opinions. Remember:

- ***Have to*** and ***need to*** describe things that are necessary. *Must* is very strong.
  The government <u>must</u> do something about ads on highways. People <u>need to</u> pay attention when they are driving, not look at ads.

- Use ***would rather, would like, would prefer,*** or ***prefer*** to talk about preferences.
  I <u>would like</u> to know about good deals near me, but I <u>would rather not</u> receive advertisements for them on my phone.

Pre-writing Task

1 Read the paragraph below. Why does the writer think the advertisements are a problem? How does the writer want to improve the situation?

Too Many E-mail Advertisements

There are too many e-mail advertisements. These e-mails advertise cheap watches, medicine, diet pills, online classes, and other things. Most people do not need to buy these things. They would prefer not to see ads for them. They often have to delete 20 or 30 of these e-mails every day. This takes too much time. Many people would like to use

5 an e-mail service that automatically deletes them. Some people would rather not receive these e-mails, so they send reply e-mails to the ads to unsubscribe them. This does not usually help. In addition, many of these e-mails are from criminals who would like to steal from you. For example, the e-mail offers a great price on jewelry, but you need to enter your credit card number. The thieves use your credit card to buy things for themselves. Of

10 course, the law says they must not do this, but it is very common. The government needs to do more to stop these criminals.

2 Read the paragraph again. Underline the sentences with necessities and requirements. Circle the sentences with preferences.

Writing Task

1 *Write* Use the paragraph in the Pre-writing Task to help you write a paragraph complaining about something and insisting on some changes. You can write about:

- ads on TV
- ads on the radio
- ads in text messages
- ads on roads
- ads on websites
- your own idea

2 *Self-Edit* Use the editing tips below to improve your paragraph. Make any necessary changes.

1. Did you use *have to, need to, must, would rather, would like,* and *would prefer* to talk about something you want to change or improve?
2. Did you use *have to* and *need to* when something is necessary? Did you use *must* only for very strong meanings?
3. Did you use *would rather, would like, would prefer,* or *prefer* to express preferences?
4. Did you avoid the mistakes in the Avoid Common Mistakes chart on page 275?

UNIT
23

Present and Future Probability
Life Today, Life Tomorrow

1 | Grammar in the Real World 🌐

A What is one way you think society will be different in the future? Read the article about trends in the United States. What is happening in the United States now? What might happen in the future?

The United States of Tomorrow

Now

30 years from now

Which current trends¹ are likely to affect us most? Which trends **might** be important for society in the future? One trend that **could** be important in the United States is a decline² in the yearly birthrate.³ The birthrate has been going down for several years. Why is this happening? According to experts, there **may** be more
5 than one reason for this change. Women **might** be choosing to have fewer children because more women now have careers. The economy **might** also affect birthrates. Today, it costs more than $300,000 to raise a child from birth to age 17. Even small changes in the economy **could** increase this cost. As a result, couples **may** worry about having children during unsure economic times.
10 How **could** a lower birthrate today affect U.S. society in the future? This is not completely clear. Some effects **could** be positive. For example, cities **could** become less crowded, and there **may** be less pollution. However, other effects **could** be negative. There **might** be fewer people in the workforce. This **could** cause economic

¹**trend:** direction of changes or developments | ²**decline:** a decrease in amount or quality | ³**yearly birthrate:** a measure of how many children are born each year

278

difficulties. In addition, as people age, there **could** be fewer doctors and other
15 health professionals to care for them. This **could** cause a decline in the general
health of the population.

No one can predict[4] exactly what society will be like in the future. However,
when experts study trends like the yearly birthrate, they can learn important facts
to help us plan for a better tomorrow.

[4]**predict:** say that an event will happen in the future

B *Comprehension Check* Answer the questions.

1. What are two possible reasons for the decline in the yearly birthrate?
2. How much does it cost to raise a child in the United States?
3. What is one possible positive result of the change in the birthrate?
4. What is one possible negative result of this change?

C *Notice* Find the sentences in the article and complete them.

1. The economy _____ also affect birthrates.

2. Even small changes in the economy _____ increase this cost.

3. For example, cities _____ become less crowded.

4. There _____ be fewer people in the workforce.

Do these sentences describe something that is certain or uncertain? Are *could* and
might used to talk about the present, the future, or both?

2 Present Probability

▶ Grammar Presentation

The modals *can't, cannot, could (not), may (not), might (not), must (not),* and *should (not)* talk about probability in the present. These modals express how certain you are that something is true.	This **could** be because more women now have careers. The economy **might** also affect birthrates.

2.1 Affirmative Statements

Subject	Modal Verb	Base Form of Verb	
I You He / She / It We They	**must** **should** **may** **might** **could**	be	important.

2.2 Negative Statements

Subject	Modal Verb		Base Form of Verb
I You He / She / It We They	**must not / mustn't could not / couldn't cannot / can't should not / shouldn't may not might not**	be	important.

2.3 Expressing Present Probability

Certain	**a.** When you are **certain** that something is true in the present, you do not need a modal. Use a present form.	*The birthrate this year **is** not the same as last year.* *The birthrate **is declining**.*
Almost Certain	**b.** Use *must (not)* to draw a conclusion about the present, often because you have evidence. You are **almost certain** about your conclusion.	*She **must not live** nearby. She never walks to work.*
	Do not use the contraction *mustn't* in this case.	*She ~~mustn't~~ live nearby. She never walks to work.*
	c. Use *could not*, *couldn't*, *cannot*, or *can't* when you are **almost certain** that something is impossible. These modals usually express strong disbelief or surprise. We usually use *can't* or *couldn't*.	*The birthrate statistics **can't be** right. They look completely wrong.* *They **couldn't be** at home. They left for vacation yesterday.*
Fairly Certain	**d.** Use *should*, *should not*, or *shouldn't* when you are **fairly certain** that something is true, often because you have evidence. We often use *shouldn't*.	*They **should be** at work. They usually are at this time of the day.* *They **shouldn't be** at work. It's Saturday.*
Not Certain	**e.** Use *may (not)*, *might (not)*, or *could* when you are **not certain** that something is true. You are uncertain, but you are making an "educated guess."	*The economy **may (not) be** the reason for the declining birthrate. Experts are not sure.*
	Do not use *mightn't*. It is very rare.	*The economy **might not be** the reason for the declining birthrate.* *The economy ~~mightn't~~ be the reason for the declining birthrate. Experts are not sure.*
	f. *Can* is not usually used for present probability. Use *may*, *might*, or *could*.	*They ~~can be~~ related. They look similar.* *They **might be** related. They look similar.*

2.4 Answers to Questions About the Present

a. You can use modals of present probability to answer questions about the present. Use them when you are not 100 percent sure about your answer.

"Where are they?"
*"They **might be** at home."*

"What does this information mean?"
*"It **could mean** society is changing."*

b. In short answers to *Yes / No* questions, you can use the modal alone.

"Do they know about this?"
*"They **must**."*

c. If *be* is the main verb in *Yes / No* questions, use the modal + *be* in short answers.

"Are they correct?"
*"They **must be**."*

▶ # Grammar Application

Exercise 2.1 Present Probability

A ◀») Listen to the conversation about a trend for young adults. Complete the sentences you hear.

1. The economy _*must*_ be part of the reason.

2. It _____ be easy if you have a lot of debt and college loans.

3. And it _____ be hard for young people to find a good job these days.

4. Yes, but there _____ be other reasons, too.

5. They _____ be able to afford an apartment.

6. It _____ be better financially for them to live at home.

7. It _____ always be easy for them.

8. Maybe, but it _____ be nice, too.

9. Some parents _____ like to have their children around as they get older.

10. I guess it _____ depend on the family.

11. Of course. It _____ .

B 🔊 Listen again. How certain are the speakers about each statement? Check (✓) the correct box.

	Not Certain	Almost Certain
1. The economy is part of the reason young adults move back home.	☐	✓
2. It isn't easy if you have a lot of debt and college loans.	☐	☐
3. It is hard for young people to find a good job these days.	☐	☐
4. There are other reasons students move home.	☐	☐
5. Students can't afford apartments.	☐	☐
6. It is better financially for them to live at home.	☐	☐
7. It isn't always easy for parents.	☐	☐
8. It is nice when children return home, too.	☐	☐
9. Some parents like to have their children around as they get older.	☐	☐
10. It depends on the family. (female speaker)	☐	☐
11. It depends on the family. (male speaker)	☐	☐

Exercise 2.2 Questions and Answers About Present Probability

Circle the correct words. Add *be* where necessary.

1. *A* Is this information correct?

   B It (must)/ could ___be___ . We checked it very carefully.

2. *A* Is the birthrate changing?

   B It **must not / may** _____ . We'll know when we have all the statistics.

3. *A* Does he have children?

   B He **shouldn't / must** _____ . I see him walking with a little boy every morning.

4. *A* Does she know him?

   B She **should / can't** _____ . They work in the same office.

5. *A* Do they know about this?

   B They **couldn't / might not** _____ . I'm not sure if anyone has discussed it.

6. *A* Is she away on vacation?

   B She **might not / can't** _____ . I just saw her a few minutes ago.

7. *A* Does he live far away?

   B He **might / can't** _____ . He's sometimes late for work.

8. *A* Does the birthrate affect society?

   B It **may / must** _____ . It's hard to know.

Exercise 2.3 Using Modals of Present Probability

A *Over to You*   Write possible reasons for these trends. Use modals of present probability.

1. More people are going to college.   *This might be because there are fewer jobs.*

2. More young adults live with their parents.   _____

3. People have more credit card debt.   _____

4. Fewer people have phones at home.   _____

5. People are getting married later.   _____

6. Couples are having children later.   _____

B *Pair Work*   Compare your reasons with a partner. Are they similar or different?

3 | Modals of Future Probability

▶ Grammar Presentation

Cannot, could (not), may (not), might (not), and *should (not)* talk about future probability.	Society **might change** a lot in the future. It **shouldn't be** difficult to see how things change.

3.1 Affirmative Statements

Subject	Modal Verb	Base Form of Verb	
I You He / She / It We They	**will** **should** **may** **might** **could**	be	different in the future.

3.2 Negative Statements

Subject	Modal Verb	Base Form of Verb	
I You He / She / It We They	**will not / won't could not / couldn't cannot / can't should not / shouldn't may not might not**	be	different in the future.

3.3 Expressing Future Probability

Certain	**a.** Use a future form (*will* or *be going to*) when you are **certain** about the future.	*More people* **will live** *in cities in the future.* *A lot of cities* **are going to be** *bigger in the future.*
Almost Certain	**b.** Use *cannot* or *can't* when you are **almost certain** that something is impossible in the future. They usually express strong disbelief or surprise. We usually use *can't*.	*The economy* **can't** *get any worse!*
Fairly Certain	**c.** Use *should (not)* or *shouldn't* when you are **fairly certain** about the future, often because you have evidence. In the negative, we usually use *shouldn't*.	*The changes in society* **should be** *clear.* *It* **shouldn't be** *difficult to see the changes.*
Not Certain	**d.** Use *may (not)*, *might (not)*, or *could* when you are **not certain** about the future. You are uncertain, but you are making an "educated guess."	*More people* **may live** *with their families in the future.* *It* **could be** *more difficult to find affordable housing.*
	Do not contract **may not**. **Mayn't** is rare.	*There* **may not** *be any changes in the statistics next year.* *There* ~~mayn't~~ *be any changes in the statistics next year.*
	e. *Must*, *can*, and *couldn't* are not usually used for future probability.	*They* ~~must~~ *be tired tomorrow.* *They* ~~can~~ *be tired tomorrow.* *They* ~~couldn't~~ *be tired tomorrow.*

3.4 Questions and Answers About Future Probability

a. *Should*, *may*, *might*, and *could* are not usually used to ask questions about the future. Use a future form instead. You can use modals of future probability to answer questions about the future.	*"***Are** *you* **going to** *go to the lecture?"* *"Yes, but I* **might be** *late."* *"When* **is** *the lecture* **going to** *start?"* *"It* **should start** *in a few minutes."* *"How long* **will** *the economy have problems?"* *"It* **could be** *a long time."*

3.4 **Questions and Answers About Future Probability** (continued)

b. In short answers to *Yes / No* questions, you can use the modal alone.	*"Will society change?"* *"It **should**."*
c. If *be* is the main verb in *Yes / No* questions, you can use the modal + *be* in short answers.	*"Is the economy going to be different?"* *"It **should be**.*

▶ Grammar Application

Exercise 3.1 Future Probability

A 🔊 Listen to an interview about what schools and education might be like in the future. Complete the sentences with the words you hear.

1. Schools and education *will* be quite different.

2. There _____ be small changes.

3. There _____ be larger ones.

4. Technology _____ be the most important thing.

5. It _____ be necessary to have physical schools in the future.

6. For example, parents and schools _____ organize social activities in new places.

7. In some ways, we _____ need libraries.

8. There _____ always be some people who want to read real books.

B 🔊 Listen again. How certain is Professor Li about each idea? Check (✔) the correct box.

	Not Certain	Certain
1. Schools and education will be quite different.	☐	☑
2. There will be small changes.	☐	☐
3. There will be larger changes.	☐	☐
4. Technology will be the most important thing.	☐	☐
5. There will not be physical schools in the future.	☐	☐
6. There will be new places to learn social skills.	☐	☐
7. There will not be libraries in the future.	☐	☐
8. Some people will want books in the future.	☐	☐

Exercise 3.2 Practicing Future Probability

Complete the online postings about future family trends. Circle the correct words.

```
● ● ○
```

Family Life in the Future: What Do You Think It Might Be Like?

Family life in the future will be more like it was in the past. Grandparents will live

with their children and grandchildren. This **may / must** be for economic reasons, or it
                                          (1)

may not / might just be easier. Grandparents could help raise the grandchildren. Also, it
(2)

might / should not be nice for grandparents to have young people in the same house.
(3)

– Miriam H.

Couples are having children later, when they are older. This **can't / may** cause problems.
                                                                        (4)

Older parents **could / might not** find it difficult to deal with children, especially during their
              (5)

children's teenage years.

– Jake P.

Technology **couldn't / might** affect families in the future. We're all busy texting,
          (6)

talking on cell phones, or using computers. We don't have time to just talk anymore.

It shouldn't surprise us if families communicate less in the future. This **could / can't**
                                                                         (7)

change family life a lot.

– Pete N.

Young adults are going to live at home longer. It **could / should not** be more difficult for
                                                  (8)

them to find jobs in the future, so they **should / may** need to live with their parents. This is
                                         (9)

not necessarily a bad thing. It **may / may not** make families stronger over time.
                               (10)

– Darla B.

Exercise 3.3 Using Modals of Future Probability

A *Over to You* Write three predictions about the future. Use these topics or your own ideas.

- family life
- transportation
- jobs and the workplace
- living situations
- technology
- schools

I think family life could change a lot. More people may live in one house together.
We might have better public transportation in the future.

1. _____

2. _____

3. _____

B *Group Work*   Compare your predictions as a class or group. How similar or different are your ideas?

4 Avoid Common Mistakes ⚠

1. Do not use *can* for present or future probability.

could
It's after 5 o'clock, but they ~~can~~ still be at work.

2. Do not confuse *maybe* with *may be*.

may be   *Maybe*
The situation ~~maybe~~ different in the future. ~~May be~~ things will change.

3. Do not use *couldn't* when you aren't certain. Use *may not*, *might not*, or *shouldn't*.

may not
She ~~couldn't~~ be in a meeting right now. I'll check and see.

4. Do not use *must* or *must not* to talk about probability in the future.

will
The situation ~~must~~ be different next year. It always changes.

5. Use the modal alone in short answers to *Yes / No* questions. Use the modal + *be* in short answers when *be* is the main verb in a *Yes / No* question.

"Do they work together?"   "They might ~~work~~."

be
"Is the meeting starting at 11:00 a.m.?"   "It may ∧."

Editing Task

Find and correct 11 more mistakes in the discussion about a class presentation.

Jim   OK. The trend we're going to discuss in our presentation is the increase in the number of people going to college. Let's start by discussing reasons.

Lucy   Well, it ~~can~~ *might* be because a lot of people are unemployed. They can be getting a degree because they don't have work. They stay busy at school.

5 **Alex**   Yes, I think that maybe the most important reason.

Jim   But is that the only reason?

Lucy   No, it can't.

Alex   May be students are also preparing for a better job.

Lucy   Yes, that can be another reason.

10 **Jim**   OK, good. May be we'll add more reasons later. What about the future effects of this trend, though? Will they be good or bad?

Alex   There must be a lot of good effects in the future, I'm sure. It must be good to have more educated people in the workplace in the future.

15

Lucy   Yes, but there can be some problems in the future, too. People could have a lot of debt when they finish school.

Jim   Hmm. Good point. I think it couldn't be difficult to think of several more

20   effects. We're doing very well so far. Let's summarize our ideas and see if we need any more information. We couldn't have enough, or we might have just what we need.

5 Grammar for Writing

Writing About Probability in the Present and Future

Writers often use modals like *cannot*, *could (not)*, *may (not)*, *might (not)*, *must (not)*, and *should (not)* to talk about changes in the present that will affect things in the future.

These modals are common in newspaper reports, magazine articles, and academic writing about trends and future predictions.

Remember:

- **People do not usually use *must (not)*, *can*, or *couldn't* to talk about future probability. Instead, use *cannot*, *should (not)*, *may (not)*, *might (not)*, or *could*.**

  We do not know for sure, but we think more people <u>may</u> take courses online in the future.

- **Use *should (not)* when you are fairly certain because you have evidence.**

  More children are studying Chinese today, so there <u>should</u> be more fluent Chinese speakers in the future.

Pre-writing Task

1 Read the paragraph below. What trend is the writer writing about?

A New Trend in Education

More students are going to community colleges these days. Many of these students are planning to transfer to universities after two years. This trend could be because universities are getting more expensive. They are also becoming more competitive. This could be because more young people want to go to college than

5 before. This must be making the universities harder to get into. It should also make

community colleges more competitive in the future. In addition, class sizes might get

bigger. Students may not be able to register for the classes they want. It could take

longer than two years for a full-time student to finish. The average age of university

juniors and seniors could start to rise. However, community colleges are also getting

10 more tuition money. As a result, they should be able to avoid these problems by hiring

more teachers in the future.

2 Read the paragraph again. Underline the modal verbs. Which express present
probability? Which express future probability? When is the writer certain about
the future because he or she has evidence?

Writing Task

1 *Write* Use the paragraph in the Pre-writing Task to help you write a paragraph
about a current trend. Why do you think this trend is happening? How will it
affect the future? You can write about:

- the cost of housing
- the availability of jobs
- popular subjects to study
- clothing changes
- the use of plastic bags
- your own idea

2 *Self-Edit* Use the editing tips below to improve your paragraph. Make any
necessary changes.

1. Did you use modals like *cannot, could (not), may (not), might (not), must (not)*,
   and *should (not)* to write about changes in the present that will affect things
   in the future?
2. Did you use the correct modals to express future probability?
3. Did you use *should (not)* to express future probability when you have evidence?
4. Did you avoid the mistakes in the Avoid Common Mistakes chart on page 287?

Transitive and Intransitive Verbs; Verbs and Prepositions

Getting Along at Work

1 | Grammar in the Real World

A How often do you read advice columns? Where do you read them: in newspapers, in magazines, or online? Read the advice column about problems in the workplace. What do you think is the best advice for getting along at work?

Ask the Expert

Welcome to our advice column, where you can **ask an expert for** advice on all your workplace problems. Here are this week's questions and our expert's answers.

5   *Dear Expert: A new employee **arrived** yesterday. She **wears too much perfume**, and it **distracts**¹ **the other employees**. I'm her boss. What should I do? – Rosa M.*

Dear Rosa: You should **discuss this with** your employee. You can tell her that most
10 offices ask employees not to **use perfume** because some people are allergic² to it.

*Dear Expert: Something terrible **happened** last week! I **told a joke** at work, and now a co-worker from China is angry with me. I think I **offended him**. – Jorge P.*

Dear Jorge: **Apologize for** your behavior. Humor is very different in different cultures, so you probably shouldn't **tell jokes** to people you don't know well. It's
15 also not a good idea to **talk about** politics, religion, or how much money a person has.

*Dear Expert: I have a very difficult boss. She constantly **makes outrageous**³ **demands**. For example, she asked me to **get her suit** from the dry cleaners the other day. This is a personal task, not a work-related task, and she shouldn't ask me to do this. How can I handle this? – Mei Lee W.*

20 Dear Mei Lee: This is a difficult situation to **deal with**. It might help to **make a list** of things you are working on for your boss. When she asks you to run an errand,⁴ **show the list** to her. Then she will know how busy you already are.

¹**distract:** take someone's attention away from what the person is doing | ²**allergic:** having an illness from eating, touching, or breathing something specific | ³**outrageous:** shocking and unacceptable | ⁴**run an errand:** make a short trip to do something, such as buy groceries

B *Comprehension Check*   Answer the questions.

1. According to the advice column, why is it a bad idea to wear perfume in the workplace?
2. Why does Jorge think his co-worker is angry?
3. According to the advice column, why should people avoid telling jokes to people they don't know well?
4. Why does Mei Lee have a problem with her boss?

C *Notice*   Find the sentences in the advice column and complete them.

1. A new employee _____ yesterday.

2. Something terrible _____ last week!

3. I _____ a joke at work.

4. I think I _____ him.

Which verbs are followed by a noun or pronoun?

2 | Transitive and Intransitive Verbs

▶ Grammar Presentation

A transitive verb needs an object. The object completes the meaning of the verb. An intransitive verb does not need an object.	VERB OBJECT The new employee ***wears perfume***. (transitive) VERB The new employee ***arrived***. (intransitive)

2.1 Transitive Verbs

Subject	Verb	Object
I You We They	wear	perfume.
He / She / It	wears	

2.2 Intransitive Verbs

Subject	Verb
I You We They	arrived.
He / She / It	arrived.

2.3 Using Transitive and Intransitive Verbs

a. The object after a transitive verb is often a noun or an object pronoun.	*She wears* **perfume**. *My boss doesn't like* **me**.
b. An intransitive verb does not have an object. However, it is often followed by an expression of time, place, or manner.	*The flight arrived* **at 5:30 p.m.** *How many people work* **at your office**? *She resigned* **unexpectedly**.
c. Some verbs can be transitive or intransitive. Sometimes the meaning of the verb is the same.	TRANSITIVE *He* **drives a truck**. INTRANSITIVE *He* **drives** *badly*.
Sometimes the meaning of the verb is different.	TRANSITIVE *She* **runs a company** *in Phoenix.* (manages) INTRANSITIVE *She can* **run** *fast*.

Data from the Real World

Most English verbs are transitive. The most common intransitive verbs in speaking and writing are *come, die, fall, go, happen, live, remain, rise, stay,* and *work*.	*He* **died** *in 1998.* *Gas prices* **are rising**.
The most common verbs that can be transitive or intransitive are *begin, call, change, leave, move, open, run, start, stop,* and *study*.	OBJECT *Could you* **move** *your car, please?* (transitive) *We all sat very still. No one* **moved**. (intransitive)

▶ Grammar Application

Exercise 2.1 Transitive or Intransitive?

Read the e-mail. Label each underlined verb *T* (transitive) or *I* (intransitive) according to how it is used in the e-mail. Circle each object.

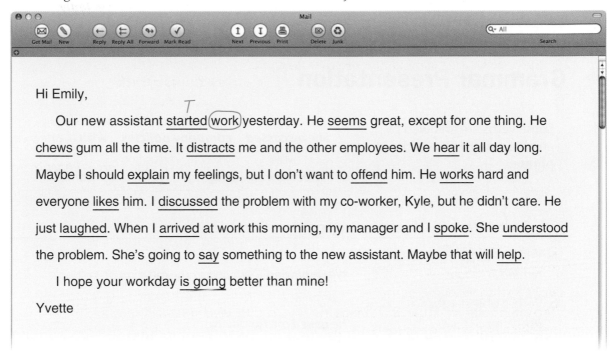

Hi Emily,

Our new assistant started work yesterday. He seems great, except for one thing. He chews gum all the time. It distracts me and the other employees. We hear it all day long. Maybe I should explain my feelings, but I don't want to offend him. He works hard and everyone likes him. I discussed the problem with my co-worker, Kyle, but he didn't care. He just laughed. When I arrived at work this morning, my manager and I spoke. She understood the problem. She's going to say something to the new assistant. Maybe that will help.

I hope your workday is going better than mine!

Yvette

Exercise 2.2 Questions and Answers

A Underline all of the transitive verbs in the questions. Circle all of the intransitive verbs.

1. What distracts you most when you are studying?
2. How often do you stay late at work (or school)?
3. What time do you usually leave for work (or school)?
4. What has changed in your work (or school) life recently?
5. What time do you usually begin your workday (or school day)?
6. What time does your workday (or school day) usually end?

B *Pair Work* Ask and answer the questions in A with a partner. Are your answers similar or different?

> A *What distracts you most when you are studying?*
>
> B *Nice weather really distracts me. I always want to go outdoors.*

3 | Verb + Object + Preposition Combinations

▶ Grammar Presentation

Some verbs are followed by an object and a prepositional phrase.	VERB OBJECT PREPOSITION *She **discussed** **company policies** **with** the new employees.* VERB OBJECT PREPOSITION *He **borrowed** **a laptop** **from** his co-worker.*

3.1 Some Verb + Object + Preposition Combinations

a. Verb + object + *about* *remind . . . about*	*We **reminded** them **about** the meeting at 3 o'clock.*

b. Verb + object + *for*
    ask . . . for
    thank . . . for
	*He **asked** me **for** advice.*
	 *I **thanked** him **for** his help.*

c. Verb + object + *from*
    borrow . . . from
    get . . . from
    learn . . . from
    take . . . from
	*She **borrowed** the book **from** me.*
	 *We **got** some good feedback **from** our manager.*
	 *Have you **learned** a lot **from** her?*
	 *They **took** the information **from** the new employees.*

d. Verb + object + *to* *explain . . . to*	*She **explained** the problem **to** her boss.*

e. Verb + object + *with*
    discuss . . . with
    help . . . with
    spend . . . with
	*I **discussed** the project **with** my manager.*
	 *He **helps** her **with** the mail.*
	 *Does she **spend** a lot of time **with** him?*

▶ Grammar Application

Exercise 3.1 Verb + Object + Preposition Combinations

🔊 Listen to the conversation about a woman's day at work. Complete the sentences with the verbs and prepositions you hear.

1. I _explained_ company policies _to_ them.

2. I _____ some time _____ them after the meeting.

3. I _____ everything _____ them one more time.

4. I couldn't fix them, so I _____ a laptop _____ the technology department.

5. I _____ Robert _____ some information.

6. I had to wait and _____ it _____ Carrie.

7. Carrie _____ me _____ a department meeting at 11:30.

8. Robert and Carrie both had time to _____ me _____ it then.

9. I _____ Carrie and Robert _____ their help.

Exercise 3.2 More Verb + Object + Preposition Combinations

A *Over to You* Write three sentences about things you have to do or have recently done at work or school. Choose from these topics.

- discuss something with someone
- explain something to someone
- get something from someone
- remind someone about something
- borrow something from someone
- help someone with something

I had to discuss a problem at work with my boss yesterday.
_____
_____
_____

B *Pair Work* Read a partner's sentences. Tell the class about your partner.

Nuria borrowed some books from her teacher, and then she lost them. She doesn't know what to do about this.

4 | Verb + Preposition Combinations

▶ Grammar Presentation

Some verbs are often followed by specific prepositions.	*I always **listen to** my co-workers during meetings.* *Don't **worry about** the project. I'll help you.*

4.1 Some Verb + Preposition Combinations

a. Verb + *about*

ask about	*The new employees **asked about** company policies.*
talk about	*We **talked about** the problem at our meeting.*
think about	*I **thought about** it, and I don't think it's a good idea.*
worry about	*Do you **worry about** work problems?*

b. Verb + *at*

laugh at	*She is **laughing at** us.*
look at	*Could you **look at** this report and tell me what you think?*

c. Verb + *for*

apologize for	*I **apologize for** my behavior.*
ask for	*Did she **ask for** a raise?*
look for	*I'm **looking for** my boss. I have a question for him.*
wait for	*We've been **waiting for** you.*

d. Verb + *on*

count on	*You can **count on** me in a crisis.*
depend on	*A company's success **depends on** every employee's hard work.*
rely on	*He **relies on** me for help.*

e. Verb + *to*

belong to	*Does this **belong to** you?*
happen to	*What **happened to** Tom's boss? I haven't seen her lately.*
listen to	*We **listened to** the discussion.*
talk to	*Our boss **talked to** all the employees on Monday.*

f. Verb + *with*

agree with	*No one **agrees with** him.*
argue with	*It's not a good idea to **argue with** your co-workers.*
deal with	*I can't **deal with** her.*

▸▸◂ Verb and Preposition Combinations: See page A5.

4.2 Using Verb + Preposition Combinations

a. Verb + preposition combinations often include verbs for communication and verbs for thinking and feeling.	You should **ask about** the new job. (communication) Don't **worry about** it. (thinking and feeling)
b. The preposition can come at the end of an information question.	*"What did you talk **about**?" "We talked about work."* *"Who does this bag belong **to**?" "It belongs to me."*
c. Some verbs can combine with more than one preposition. The meaning may be different.	*I **talked to** him yesterday. (had a conversation with)* *We **talked about** our new project. (discussed)*

▶ Grammar Application

Exercise 4.1 Verb + Preposition Combination in Statements

Complete the text about company policies with the correct form
of the verbs in parentheses and the correct preposition from the box.

about	about	for	~~to~~	to	with
about	at	to	to	with	

Yesterday, our boss __*talked to*__ (talk) the new
(1)
employees on their first day. She _____
(2)
(talk) company policies. The employees

_____ (listen) her attentively. She said
(3)
everyone should _____ (think) the policies.
(4)
She told them to _____ (ask) anything that
(5)
was unclear.

One employee asked if it was acceptable to speak

his first language at work. The boss said, "We prefer everyone to speak English, but we think

it's important to _____ (look) each situation. Sometimes it's acceptable to use
(6)
your first language, for example, if you're _____ (talk) a customer who speaks
(7)
your language."

At the end of the meeting, she said, "We all _____ (belong) the
(8)
same organization and have the same goals. If you need help, please don't hesitate to

_____ (ask) it." It seemed like everyone _____ (agree) the
(9)   (10)
boss's views. Nobody _____ (argue) her.
(11)

Exercise 4.2 Verb + Preposition Combinations in Questions

A Use the words to write questions. Add the correct preposition.

1. Who / you / talk / most at work (or school) / ? *Who do you talk to most at work?*

2. What / you / usually talk / at work (or school) / ? _____

   _____

3. What / you / worry / at work (or school) / ? _____

   _____

4. Who / you / depend / for help / ? _____

5. Whose advice / you / listen / most / ? _____

   _____

6. Who / you / sometimes argue / ? _____

7. Who / you / usually agree / ? _____

8. What / clubs or professional organizations / you / belong / ? _____

   _____

B *Pair Work*   Ask and answer the questions in A with a partner.

A *Who do you talk to most at work?*
B *I talk to my co-worker, Sandra.*

5 | Avoid Common Mistakes ⚠

1. A transitive verb needs an object. Don't forget the object.

   I went to see the movie, but I didn't like_∧. *(it)*

2. Some verbs need a preposition. Don't forget the preposition.

   My co-workers often don't listen_∧me. *(to)*

3. Use the correct preposition with verbs that need them.

   Don't worry ~~on~~ the presentation. I'll help you finish it. *(about)*

4. Don't use a preposition with verbs that don't need them.

   Let's discuss ~~about~~ the problem.

Editing Task

Find and correct eight more mistakes in this magazine article.

《《《《《《 **Not Appreciated at Work?** 》》》》》》

Do these problems sound familiar to you? If so, you are not alone. These are the common problems our readers sent to us in our recent survey. Try our solutions! They could help you change your work life forever!

› Problem: Some people do not appreciate me, or even like.
                                                        me

5   Solution: Maybe you should talk your boss about the problem.

› Problem: My co-workers often argue me. I don't like it.

Solution: You could talk with the problem with your co-workers.

› Problem: Nobody listens me when I have a new idea.

Solution: Maybe you need to explain your ideas more clearly to them.

10 › Problem: I always thank my co-workers for their help, but they never thank.

Solution: You could discuss about the problem with them, but this may not change.

› Problem: My co-worker always asks me help. I don't mind helping him, but then I don't finish my own work.

Solution: Discuss this him. Tell him you want to help, but you must also do

15   your work. I think he'll understand.

6 Grammar for Writing 🖊

Using Transitive and Intransitive Verbs

Writers often use transitive and intransitive verbs to show how people interact with each other.

Remember:

- **Transitive verbs need an object to complete the sentence.**

  John <u>received his boss's e-mail</u> yesterday.

- **You can use verb + preposition combinations to talk about communicating, thinking, and feeling.**

  A good boss <u>listens to</u> her employees.   She is <u>thinking about</u> her employees.

Pre-writing Task

1 Read the paragraph from a magazine article. What are two suggestions in the article?

Getting a Raise

If you are like most people, you work hard at your job and you believe you are good at it. You also probably believe that you deserve more money. The problem is, how do you ask your boss for a raise? Here are a few suggestions. First, choose the right time to ask your boss. Some managers believe their
5 employees should not ask for them. Other bosses are happy to discuss salary with their employees, but only when they are in a good mood and are not too busy. Second, before you ask your boss, be prepared. Think about things you do to help the company. What do people depend on you for? Do you look for ways to save money? Make a list of these things so you can remind
10 your boss about them. Finally, when you ask your boss, be confident. Don't apologize for your desire to make more money. At the same time, you should also be polite. Explain your opinion to your boss gently, with a smile. Also, don't forget to thank your boss for his or her time.

2 Read the paragraph again. Underline the verb + object + preposition combinations and circle the verb + preposition combinations.

Writing Task

1 *Write* Use the paragraph in the Pre-writing Task to help you write some suggestions for improving things at work or at school. Use verb + preposition and verb + object + preposition combinations from the unit. You can write about:

- getting a raise
- getting along with a difficult co-worker
- finding a new job
- asking a teacher for extra help
- looking more professional at work or school
- your own idea

2 *Self-Edit* Use the editing tips below to improve your paragraph. Make any necessary changes.

1. Did you use verbs with the correct prepositions to show how people interact with each other?
2. Did you use objects after transitive verbs to complete the meaning of the sentence?
3. Did you use verb + preposition combinations to describe communicating, thinking, and feeling?
4. Did you avoid the mistakes in the Avoid Common Mistakes chart on page 298?

Phrasal Verbs

Money, Money, Money

1 | Grammar in the Real World

A What are some good habits for managing money? What are some bad habits? Read the article about managing money. What two steps does the author's plan include?

Does your money usually **run out** before the end of the month? Do you spend more money than you earn? Are you starting to **build up** credit card debt? Have you **taken out** a loan and can't **pay** it **off**? If this describes you, you might want to **sort out**[1] your finances now, before bad habits **set in**.[2]

5 Do not **put** it **off** until tomorrow. Here is a plan to help you get control of your money.

Step 1: **Figure out** your income and your spending habits. **Sit down** with a notebook and **write down** how much you make every month. Then **find out** where your money goes. Over the next month, **write down** all your

10 monthly expenses and **add** them **up**. Include everything you buy or spend money on. The purpose of this exercise is to get a clear picture of your usual spending habits. Do you **eat out** too much? What do you need to **give up**?

Step 2: **Set up** a budget. Use your notebook to **work out** what you can

15 spend. Then, prioritize[3] your expenses. Rent, food, electricity, and gas are the most important. These are high-priority[4] expenses. Movies and dinners out are not. You can allow yourself some treats, but remember to **put** money **away** for unexpected expenses, such as repairs when your car **breaks down**.

Once you are in control of your finances, you can set a goal like **paying**

20 **off** your credit card or saving for a large purchase. You can also relax, enjoy life more, and worry less.

[1]**sort out:** organize something or solve a problem | [2]**set in:** begin and continue for a long time |
[3]**prioritize:** put things in order of importance | [4]**high-priority:** important

B *Comprehension Check* Answer the questions.

1. Why should you write down your expenses?
2. According to the article, which expenses are the most important ones?
3. According to the article, what are some expenses that are not important?
4. What are two financial goals that the article mentions?

C *Notice* Find the sentences in the article and complete them with the missing verbs.

1. If this describes you, you might want to _____ your finances now, before bad habits _____ .

2. _____ with a notebook.

3. Over the next month, _____ all your monthly expenses.

How many words are there in each blank, one or two? Which words are followed by an object (transitive)? Which words are not followed by an object (intransitive)?

2 | Intransitive Phrasal Verbs

▶ Grammar Presentation

Phrasal verbs are two-word verbs. They include a verb and a particle. A particle is a small word like *up, down, back, out, on, off,* or *in.*

VERB PARTICLE
Does your money usually **run out** *before the end of the month?*

VERB PARTICLE
Sit down *with a notebook.*

2.1 Intransitive Phrasal Verbs

Subject	Verb	Particle
I You We They	sit sat	down.
He/She/It	sits sat	

2.2 Using Intransitive Phrasal Verbs

a.	Intransitive phrasal verbs do not need an object to complete their meaning.	***Sit down*** *with a notebook.* *Do you **eat out** too much?*
b.	The particle comes after the verb.	*They **came back** from vacation today.*
	Note: Do not put a word or phrase between the verb and the particle of an intransitive phrasal verb.	*They came ~~from vacation~~ back today.*
c.	The meaning of some phrasal verbs is easy to understand.	*I **go out** every night.* *Can you **stand up** for a moment?* *She **went away** for a month and then **came back**.*
d.	Some intransitive phrasal verbs have more than one meaning. The meaning of some phrasal verbs is not easy to understand.	*She walked into the room and then **ran out**.* (left) *Does your money **run out**?* (be completely used) *Her plane **takes off** at 12:00.* (leaves) *Debt counseling has **taken off**.* (grown; been successful) *My car **broke down** last week.* (stopped working) *He **broke down** in tears.* (started to cry) *We **work out** at a gym.* (exercise) *My job **didn't work out**.* (didn't go as planned)
e.	Many everyday spoken commands use intransitive phrasal verbs.	*Hold on. / Hang on.* (Wait.) *Go ahead!* (Do it!) *Come on.* (Hurry. Let's go.) *Go on.* (Continue.) *Look out! / Watch out!* (Be careful!) *Sit down.* (Sit.)

2.3 Some Intransitive Phrasal Verbs

break down (1. stop working 2. lose control)
come back (return)
come on (1. hurry 2. start)
eat out (eat in a restaurant)
get along (have a good relationship)
give up (stop)
go ahead (start or continue)
go away (leave; go to another place)
go on (continue)
go out (not stay home)
go up (rise; go higher)
grow up (become an adult)
hang on (1. wait 2. keep going)

hold on (1. wait 2. persist)
look out (be careful)
move in (1. take your things to a new home 2. begin living somewhere)
run out (1. leave 2. be completely used)
set in (begin and continue for a long time)
sit down (sit; take a seat)
stand up (stand; rise)
take off (1. leave on an airplane 2. grow; be successful)
watch out (be careful)
work out (1. exercise 2. go as planned)

▸◂ Phrasal Verbs: Transitive and Intransitive: See page A10.

Data from the Real World

In general, phrasal verbs are less common in academic writing, but writers often use these verbs: *grow up, go on, go back, turn out, break down, come up, work out.*

Talks between the two countries have **broken down**.
One question **came up** *in the discussion.*

▶ Grammar Application

Exercise 2.1 Intransitive Phrasal Verbs

Underline the phrasal verbs in the conversations. Circle the particles.

1. *A* Come(on)! We're going to be late.

   B Hold on. I'm coming.

2. *A* It's Friday night. Let's eat out somewhere.

   B I can't. My money's already run out, and I don't get paid until next week.

3. *A* I have some new neighbors. They moved in last week.

   B Are they nice? Do you think you'll get along?

4. *A* I want to go out now. Do you want to come?

   B No, go ahead. I'm tired. I'm going to stay home.

Exercise 2.2 Using Phrasal Verbs

A Complete the story. Use the particles from the boxes.

along	away	back	in	~~up~~

Peter and Carlos grew _up_ in the same neighborhood.
(1)
They were good friends and got _____ really well.
(2)
Carlos went _____ to college when he was 18, but they
(3)
kept in touch. When Carlos came _____ , they decided
(4)
to share an apartment. Peter found an apartment, and they
moved _____ .
(5)

on	out	out	out	up

It all worked _____ well for a while. They shared the bills. They went _____ for
(6)   (7)
pizza or to see a movie after work. Then Carlos got a great job in a bank and wanted to eat

_____ more often and in more expensive restaurants.
(8)
Peter couldn't afford it, but he used his credit card and tried

not to worry. Life went _____ as normal, but Peter's
(9)
spending was going _____ every day.
(10)

down	down	on

One morning Peter sat _____ to have coffee and pay some bills online while
(11)
Carlos was at work. He saw his high credit card bill and broke _____ . "I can't go
(12)
_____ like this," he said. He called Carlos's voice mail and left a message. He said . . .
(13)

B *Pair Work* Study the story for two minutes. Tell it to your partner using the
phrasal verbs.

Two boys grew up together. They were good friends and . . .

C *Group Work* What do you think Peter said in his voice mail to Carlos? What
do you think Carlos said to Peter in his response? Discuss in a group.

*I think Peter said, "Hi Carlos, it's Peter calling. I read my credit card bill this morning.
It's very high. I can't go on like this. . . ."*

Exercise 2.3 Questions and Answers

A Complete the questions with the correct particle. Use Chart 2.3 on page 304 to
help you.

1. Do you go _out_ on weekends very often?

2. Do you eat _____ for lunch, or do you bring your own lunch?

3. Do you exercise at home or work _____ at a gym?

4. Has your computer or car broken _____ lately and needed
   expensive repairs?

5. Have prices for anything been going _____ lately? If so, what has been
   getting more expensive?

6. After this course, would you like to go _____ and study more? If so, what
   would you study?

7. Do you make a budget? If so, does it usually work _____ ?

B *Pair Work* Ask and answer the questions with a partner. How similar or
different are your answers?

3 | Transitive Phrasal Verbs

▶ Grammar Presentation

Transitive phrasal verbs need an object.	VERB PARTICLE OBJECT *Have you* **taken** **out** *a* **loan**? VERB OBJECT PARTICLE *Can you* **pay** **it** **back**?

3.1 Transitive Phrasal Verbs

Subject	Verb	Particle	Object (Noun)
I You We They	**figure** **figured**	**out**	the budget.
He / She / It	**figures** **figured**		

Subject	Verb	Object (Noun or Pronoun)	Particle
I You We They	**figure** **figured**	the budget it	**out**.
He / She / It	**figures** **figured**		

3.2 Using Transitive Phrasal Verbs

a. Some phrasal verbs are transitive. They need an object to complete their meaning.

> *He paid back* **the money he owed**.
> *She added up* **her expenses**.

b. Most transitive phrasal verbs are "separable." This means that noun objects can come **before** or **after** the particle.

> VERB   PARTICLE   OBJECT
> *Write* **down** *your expenses*.
> VERB   OBJECT   PARTICLE
> *Write* *your expenses* **down**.

Object pronouns come **before** the particle.

> *Write* **them** *down*.

Do not put an object pronoun after the particle.

> *Write down* ~~them~~.

3.2 Using Transitive Phrasal Verbs *(continued)*

c. Indefinite pronoun objects (e.g., *something, nothing, someone, no one, everyone*) can come before or after the particle.	She **throws away** everything. She **throws** everything **away**.
d. Longer objects usually go after the particle.	Is he **setting up** a new financial management company? Is he **setting** ~~a new financial management company~~ **up**?
e. Some transitive phrasal verbs have more than one meaning.	They are **bringing up** three children. (raising a child) I'd like to **bring up** the subject of money. (introduce a topic) Please **turn down** the radio. It's too loud. (lower the volume) I **turned down** the invitation to the party because I had to work. (rejected)
f. Some phrasal verbs have one meaning when they are transitive. They have a different meaning when they are intransitive.	I **worked out** a budget. (transitive; solved or calculated something) I **work out** at a gym every day. (intransitive; exercise)

3.3 Some Transitive Phrasal Verbs

add up (add together; combine)
bring up (1. raise a child 2. introduce a topic)
build up (accumulate)
figure out (find an answer; understand)
find out (discover information; learn)
give up (quit)
pay back (repay money)
pay off (repay completely)
put away (1. save for the future
2. put in the correct place)

put off (delay, postpone)
set up (1. arrange 2. plan 3. build)
sort out (1. organize 2. solve)
take out (1. remove
2. obtain something officially)
throw away (get rid of something; discard)
turn down (1. lower the volume 2. reject)
work out (solve; calculate)
write down (write on paper)

▶◀ Phrasal Verbs: Transitive and Intransitive: See page A10.

Data from the Real World

Research shows that the following transitive phrasal verbs are common in academic writing:

break off	*cut off*	*point out*	*sum up*
carry out	*find out*	*set up*	

▶ Grammar Application

Exercise 3.1 Transitive and Intransitive Phrasal Verbs

Label the phrasal verbs *T* (transitive) or *I* (intransitive) according to their use in the sentences. Circle the objects.

1. Experts say you should work on your money problems now. Don't **put** (them) **off.** ___T___

2. Most experts say it's a good idea to **write down** all your expenses. _____

3. For example, Mariah S., from Chicago, **adds up** everything she's spent at the end of the month. _____

4. After Mariah **worked out** a budget, she changed some of her spending habits. _____

5. She used to pay for an expensive gym membership, but now she **works out** at home. _____

6. She also decided to **give up** expensive dinners in order to save money. _____

7. Mariah didn't **give up** and eventually saved enough money to start a business. _____

8. She also **paid back** some money her family had loaned her. _____

Exercise 3.2 Transitive Phrasal Verbs

🔊 Listen to the expert give advice about money. Complete the list of advice. Use phrasal verbs.

Dana's Money Advice

1. _Put away_ a little money each month.

2. Even a small amount will _____ over time.

3. You need to _____ a budget.

4. _____ your expenses.

5. Don't _____ receipts.

6. Don't _____ a lot of debt.

7. _____ your credit card every month.

8. You need to _____ the topic _____ and discuss it.

9. Don't _____ money matters.

Exercise 3.3 More Transitive Phrasal Verbs

A Complete the conversations. Unscramble the words in A's questions. Use the verb given and an object pronoun in B's answers.

1. *A* Do you usually _write your expenses down / write down your expenses_ (your expenses / write down)?

   B No, I don't. I _don't add them up_____ (not add up) every month, either.

2. *A* Do you _____ (your receipts / throw away), or do you keep them?

   B I usually _____ (throw away).

3. *A* Do you ever _____ (things / put off), like doing your finances?

   B I do. I know I should _____ (sort out).

4. *A* Do you think it's a good idea to _____ (a loan / take out)?

   B Yes, but only if you can _____ (pay off) quickly.

5. *A* Do you think it's difficult to _____ (a budget / work out)?

   B I don't think so. You just need to _____ (figure out).

B *Pair Work* Ask and answer the questions in A with a partner. Answer with your own opinion or information.

   A Do you usually write down your expenses?

   B Yes, I do. I write everything down. Then I add it up at the end of the month.

4 | Avoid Common Mistakes ⚠️

1. **Don't forget a particle when you need one. Be especially careful with these verbs:** *pick up*, *break down*, **and** *point out*.

   He's picked $\overset{up}{\wedge}$ bad spending habits, like eating out every night.

2. **Don't use a particle when you don't need one. Be especially careful with these verbs:** *fall, rise, go, find*.

   Gas prices fell ~~down~~, then rose ~~up~~.

   Things are going ~~on~~ well for me.

3. **Don't confuse** *grow up* **and** *grow*. *Grow up* **means to grow from a child to an adult.** *Grow* **means get bigger.**

   Before the children grew $\overset{up}{\wedge}$, we didn't have any savings.

   Now our savings have grown up.

4. **Do not put object pronouns after particles. They go before particles.**

   She summed $\overset{it\ up}{\text{~~up it~~}}$.

Editing Task

Find and correct eight more mistakes on this website.

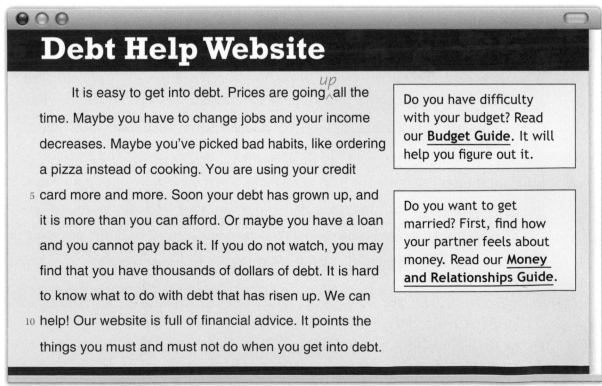

Debt Help Website

It is easy to get into debt. Prices are going $\overset{up}{\wedge}$ all the time. Maybe you have to change jobs and your income decreases. Maybe you've picked bad habits, like ordering a pizza instead of cooking. You are using your credit

5 card more and more. Soon your debt has grown up, and it is more than you can afford. Or maybe you have a loan and you cannot pay back it. If you do not watch, you may find that you have thousands of dollars of debt. It is hard to know what to do with debt that has risen up. We can

10 help! Our website is full of financial advice. It points the things you must and must not do when you get into debt.

Do you have difficulty with your budget? Read our **Budget Guide**. It will help you figure out it.

Do you want to get married? First, find how your partner feels about money. Read our **Money and Relationships Guide**.

5 | Grammar for Writing ✏

Using Transitive and Intransitive Phrasal Verbs

Writers often use transitive and intransitive phrasal verbs to give instructions.

Phrasal verbs appear in almost every kind of text and are very common in informal texts that give advice or instructions.

Remember:

- **The meaning of verbs often changes when they are paired with particles.**

  Work out a plan for your retirement early. Then you know how long you will have to work.

- **The object can appear before or after the particle in most transitive phrasal verbs.**

  They added up their expenses.   They added their expenses up.

Pre-writing Task

1 Read the paragraph from a magazine article about money. What is the writer's suggestion for teaching teens about money?

Teens and Money

Teenagers have a lot of problems with money. They can easily spend money, but they often do not know how to save it. Teaching teenagers about money is important. One way to do this is to loan your teen money. Imagine your teenage son wants a new cell phone, but he
5 does not have enough money. You can loan him the money and then, each month, your teen can pay you back a percentage of the loan. Do not forget to write the loan agreement down on a piece of paper or in a notebook. In addition, make sure your teen pays back all the money and does not give up. This is a good way for your teen to find out the value of
10 money and possessions. This is a lesson that will last a lifetime.

2 Read the paragraph again. Underline the phrasal verbs. Which are intransitive? Which are transitive? What are the objects of the transitive phrasal verbs?

Writing Task

1 *Write* Use the paragraph in the Pre-writing Task to help you write a paragraph that gives people instructions on managing money. What tips do you know for managing money? How can they help people?

2 *Self-Edit* Use the editing tips below to improve your paragraph. Make any necessary changes.

1. Did you use phrasal verbs to give instructions?
2. Did you choose the correct particle to express the correct meaning of the verb?
3. Did you use an object with the transitive phrasal verbs?
4. Did you avoid the mistakes in the Avoid Common Mistakes chart on page 311?

Comparatives
We Are All Different

1 | Grammar in the Real World

A Think of a family you know with more than one child. How similar or different are the children's personalities? Read the web article about birth order and personality. Do you agree with the results of the research it describes?

Does Birth Order¹ Affect Personality?

Some researchers believe that birth order affects people's personalities. According to Dr. Frank Sulloway, professor of psychology, birth order differences are **as strong as** gender differences.²

First-born children, he says, are often **more responsible** and **more conservative**.
5 They are also **more likely** to be successful, and many first-born children are presidents and CEOs. Because first-born children are usually **bigger** and **stronger** than their **younger** siblings,³ they can try to dominate⁴ them.

As a result, says Sulloway, **younger** children can be rebellious and **less likely** to obey rules. Younger children are often **more adventurous** and **more creative**
10 **than older** children. They are also **more independent**. They may **try harder** to get attention from their parents, and parents often do not discipline **younger** children **as strictly as** their **older** siblings.

Not all researchers agree with these ideas, but most do agree that middle children can have a very difficult time. They are **more likely** to have to repeat a
15 grade in school. Middle children often worry that they are **not** loved **as much as** their siblings. However, middle children are often the peacemakers in the family and are **more easygoing** as a result.

Parents are often **less strict** with the "baby,"
20 or last-born child of the family. Last-born children are **more often** spoiled. Parents are usually **more relaxed** with them, and they often seem to have an easy time. However, if you are from a large family, that may be
25 something you already know!

¹**birth order:** order in which children were born | ²**gender difference:** difference between men and women |
³**sibling:** brother or sister | ⁴**dominate:** control

B *Comprehension Check* Match the child with the description.

1. The first-born child _____   a. can be good at resolving conflicts.

2. The younger child _____   b. often has an easy time.

3. The middle child _____   c. often wants to be a leader.

4. The last-born child _____   d. can often be creative and break rules.

C *Notice* Find the sentences in the article and complete them.

1. Because first-born children are usually _____ and

   _____ _____ their younger siblings,

   they can try to dominate them.

2. Younger children are often _____ _____ and

   _____ _____ _____ older children.

Look at the adjectives and other words you wrote. The sentences show two ways to make comparisons. How are the two ways similar? How are they different?

2 | Comparative Adjectives and Adverbs

▶ Grammar Presentation

Comparative adjectives and adverbs show how two things or ideas are different.	COMPARATIVE ADJECTIVE *First-born children are usually **bigger than** their siblings.* COMPARATIVE ADVERB *Younger children try **harder** to get their parents' attention.*

2.1 Comparative Adjectives

Subject	Verb	Comparative Adjective	*Than*	
First-born children	are	**stronger** **more responsible** **less easygoing**	**than**	their siblings.

2.2 Comparative Adverbs

Subject	Verb (+ Object)	Comparative Adverb	*Than*	
First-born children	do things obey rules get spoiled	**better** and **more easily** **more often** **less often**	**than**	their siblings.

2.3 The Spelling of Comparative Adjectives and Adverbs

a. Add -er to one-syllable adjectives and adverbs.	fast → fast**er** hard → hard**er** strong → strong**er**
For one-syllable adjectives that end in a vowel + consonant, double the consonant. Do not double the consonant w.	big → big**ger** hot → hot**ter** low → low**er**
b. Remove the -y and add -ier to two-syllable adjectives ending in -y.	early → earl**ier** funny → funn**ier** heavy → heav**ier**
c. Use *more* with most adjectives and adverbs that have two or more syllables.	hardworking → **more** hardworking intelligent → **more** intelligent quickly → **more** quickly often → **more** often

d. Some comparative adjectives and adverbs are irregular.

Adjectives		**Adverbs**	
good → better		well → better	
bad → worse		badly → worse	

▸◂ Adjectives and Adverbs: Comparative and Superlative Forms. See page A12.

2.4 Using Comparative Adjectives and Adverbs

a. You can use comparative adjectives to describe how two nouns are different.	NOUN ADJECTIVE NOUN *First-born children are sometimes **taller than** their siblings.*
You can use comparative adverbs to compare the way two people do the same action.	VERB ADVERB VERB *My son **works harder** in school **than** my daughter works.*
b. *Less* is the opposite of *more*.	*Julia is **more independent than** her brother Lucas.* *Lucas is **less independent than** Julia.* *He plays **more quietly than** his sister does.* *His sister plays **less quietly**.*
Less is not usually used with one-syllable adjectives or adverbs, except *clear*, *safe*, and *sure*.	*My daughter is **younger than** my son.* *My daughter is ~~less old~~ than my son.*
c. You can use a pronoun after *than* instead of repeating the noun. In academic writing, use a subject pronoun + verb.	*Tim's sister is more creative than **he is**.*

2.4 Using Comparative Adjectives and Adverbs (continued)

When both verbs are the same, you do not need to repeat the verb after *than*.	*She works harder than* **Tim**.
You can also use an auxiliary verb.	*Tim's sister works harder than* **he does**. *She did better in college than* **he did**. *She's gone further in her career than* **he has**.
d. You do not need *than* plus the second part of the comparison when the meaning is clear.	*Older children* **are** *often* **more conservative**. *(than younger children)*
e. You can also use a comparative adjective without *than* before a noun when the comparison is clear.	*Parents are strict with* **older** *children.* *(older than other children)*
f. In speaking, you can use an object pronoun after *than*. In formal speaking or academic writing, use a noun or subject pronoun and a verb or auxiliary verb.	*Say:* "*Tim's sister works harder than* **him**." *Write: Tim's sister works harder than* **Tim / he does**.

Data from the Real World

Some two-syllable adjectives have two comparative forms. However, one form is usually more frequent, especially in writing.	
Use *-er* to form these comparative adjectives: *easier, narrower, quieter, simpler*	*Mateo is* **quieter** *than his sister.*
Use *more* to form these comparative adjectives: *more likely, more friendly*	*Do you think she is* **more friendly** *than her brother?*

▶ Grammar Application

Exercise 2.1 Comparative Forms

◀)) Listen to the news report about birth order and intelligence. Fill in the blanks with the words you hear.

A Norwegian study says that there may be differences in intelligence between brothers. The study showed that older siblings are <u>*more intelligent than*</u> their younger

(1)

siblings. The researchers gave intelligence tests to 60,000 pairs of brothers. They found

that the older siblings did _____ their brothers on the tests. The

(2)

_____ boys' scores were definitely _____ ,

(3)   (4)

although not by very much.

Researchers say one reason for this may be that older siblings have

_____ language skills. Their language may develop
(5)

_____ because they have been in an adult environment
(6)

_____ . It is possible that younger siblings are
(7)

_____ in other ways, for example, in emotional intelligence.
(8)

The Norwegian study did not look at age differences. However,

_____ research suggests that when the age difference
(9)

between two brothers is _____ , the difference in
(10)

intelligence is _____ .
(11)

Exercise 2.2 More Comparative Forms

A Complete the sentences with the correct comparative forms. Use the information in the chart.

	Tom Mason	Dave Mason
Age	32	28
Height	6 feet, 3 inches tall	5 feet, 11 inches tall
Weight	200 pounds	152 pounds
Work style	hardworking	doesn't work hard
Personality	very conservative, serious, not very friendly	a little conservative, easygoing, funny, friendly
Hobbies and skills	good at sports, especially tennis; not good at guitar	plays tennis but not very athletic; plays guitar well

1. Dave is _younger than_ (young) Tom.

2. Tom is Dave's _____ (old) brother.

3. Tom is _____ (tall) Dave.

4. Tom is _____ (heavy) Dave.

5. Dave is _____ (hardworking) Tom.

6. Tom works _____ (hard).

7. Tom is a _____ (conservative) person.

8. Tom is _____ (athletic) Dave.

9. Tom is _____ (friendly) Dave.

10. Dave plays the guitar _____ (good) Tom.

B Write three more sentences about Tom and Dave. Use comparatives.

Dave is shorter than Tom.
Tom is better at sports than Dave.

_____

_____

_____

Exercise 2.3 Comparatives with *Be* and *Do*

A Rewrite the sentences about Sarah and Louisa, two sisters who go to the same college. Use comparatives with the correct form of *be* or *do*.

1. In Biology 101, Sarah works really hard, but Louisa doesn't.

   Sarah works harder than Louisa does.

2. Louisa is very creative. Sarah isn't.

   _____

3. Sarah lives very far from school. Louisa doesn't.

   _____

4. Louisa is good at writing. Sarah isn't.

   _____

5. Sarah learns quickly. Louisa doesn't.

   _____

6. Louisa is very quiet. Sarah isn't.

   _____

B What happens when you cross out *be* or *do*? Is the meaning still clear?

C *Pair Work*   Rewrite the sentences in A so they are true for you and your partner. Give reasons. Tell the class about your partner.

Virginia works harder than I do. She has three jobs!

Exercise 2.4 More Comparative Practice

A How have you changed? Answer the questions. Use comparatives and try to give extra information.

1. Are you more or less shy than you used to be?

   I'm less shy than I used to be. Now I enjoy parties because I'm more confident.

2. Do you work or study harder than you did when you were younger?

   _____

   _____

3. What can you do more easily now than last year?

   _____

   _____

4. What do you do on weekends more often than you used to?

   _____

   _____

5. What has been more difficult about studying English than you thought?
   What has been easier?

   _____

   _____

B *Group Work* Discuss your answers in a group. Have you changed in similar or in different ways?

I am less shy than I used to be, but Leona is more shy. She doesn't like speaking in front of the class. We've changed in different ways.

3 | Comparisons with *As . . . As*

▶ Grammar Presentation

You can use *as . . . as* to say that two ideas are the same or similar. *Not as . . . as* means "less."	*Birth order differences are **as strong as** gender differences.* *Older children are sometimes **not as creative as** younger children.* (= Older children are less creative.)

3.1 *As ... As* with Adjectives

Subject	Verb	*As*	Adjective	*As*	
Younger children	are are not aren't	**as**	**smart creative good**	**as**	older children.

3.2 *As ... As* with Adverbs

Subject	Verb	*As*	Adverb	*As*	
The younger boys	learned didn't learn	**as**	**easily quickly well**	**as**	their older brothers.

3.3 Using (*Not*) *As ... As*

a. You can use *as* + adjective + *as* to show that two nouns are similar or the same.	*Max is **as intelligent as** his brother.*
You can use *as* + adverb + *as* to show that the way two people do things is the same or the way that two events happen is the same.	*Max **works as hard as** his brother.* (How Max works = how his brother works.)
b. *Not as ... as* shows that two ideas are not similar. It means "less than."	*Andreas is **not as ambitious as** his brother.* (= Andreas is less ambitious than his brother.)
Use *not as ... as* instead of *less* with short adjectives and adverbs, such as *bad, easy, high, great,* and *big.*	*My brother's test score **was not as high as** my score.* (= My brother's score was lower than my score.)
c. *As ... as* can be followed by a noun or a subject pronoun + a verb or auxiliary verb.	*Kate's brother is as intelligent as **Kate/she is**.* *Kate's brother did as well in college as **she did**.* *He works as hard as **she does**.* *He's gone as far in his career as **she has**.*
d. You do not need to use *as* + the second part of the comparison when the meaning is clear.	*Middle children feel their parents **don't love them as much** (as the other children).*
e. In speaking informally, you can use an object pronoun after *as ... as.*	Say: "*Kate's brother isn't as creative as **her**.*"
In formal speaking or academic writing, use a noun or subject pronoun and a verb or auxiliary verb.	Write: "*Kate's brother is not as creative as **Kate/she is**.*"

Data from the Real World

Research shows that these are some of the most common adjectives and adverbs with (*not*) *as . . . as* in speaking and writing:

adjectives: *bad, big, easy, good, great, hard, high, important, popular, simple, strong*
adverbs: *easily, fast, hard, much, often, quickly, well*

▶ Grammar Application

Exercise 3.1 Forming (*Not*) As . . . As Sentences

A Rewrite the sentences in the article with (*not*) *as . . . as.* Keep the same meaning.

How Much Gender Difference Is There?

The following statements are common beliefs about gender differences:

1. Boys are better than girls at math.

Girls *are not as good as* boys at math.

2. Women are better than men at communication.

Men _____ women at communication.

3. Teenage boys are more confident than teenage girls.

Teenage girls _____ teenage boys.

4. Men solve problems more easily than women.

Women _____ men.

A study by psychologist Janet Shibley Hyde (2007) showed that these beliefs may not all be true. According to her study:

5. People think the differences between boys and girls are big, but they aren't.

The differences _____ people think.

6. Young girls and boys do equally well in math.

Young girls _____ boys in math.

7. Communication is equally hard for men and women.

Communication for women _____ _____ it is for men.

8. Girls and boys are equally likely to have low confidence.

Boys _____ girls to have low confidence.

Hyde found that in 78 percent of tests, men and women were about the same. She did find some differences.

9. Boys are more aggressive than girls.	Girls _____ _____ .
10. Men get angry more quickly than women.	Women _____ _____ .
11. Men can throw objects further than women.	Women _____ _____ .

Hyde's study shows that most differences are in our beliefs, and not really in our gender. She hopes these beliefs will change.

B *Pair Work* Discuss the information with a partner. What did you know? What surprised you?

A *I didn't know that girls do as well as boys in math.*
B *I know. That surprised me, too.*

Exercise 3.2 Using As . . . As

A *Pair Work* Answer the questions. Then ask and answer the questions with a partner.

What is something . . .

1. you do as often as possible? Why?

   I play soccer as often as I can because it is my favorite sport.

   _____

2. you can't do as often as you'd like? Why?

   _____

3. you do as quickly as you can each day? Why?

   _____

Who is . . .

4. as creative as you? Why do you think so?

   _____

5. as adventurous as you? Why do you think so?

   _____

B *Group Work* Tell the class about your partner.

A *Agnes plays soccer as often as possible. It's her favorite sport.*
B *Boris visits his parents as often as he can because he misses them.*

Exercise 3.3 Using (*Not*) As . . . As

A *Over to You* Think of a person you know who fits each description below. Write a sentence about each person using (*not*) *as . . . as* + a subject pronoun + verb.

1. works as hard as you   *My sister works as hard as I do.*

2. doesn't talk as much as you   _____

3. did as well as you in school   _____

4. isn't as old as you   _____

5. hasn't lived here as long as you   _____

6. can speak English as well as you   _____

7. doesn't drive as carefully as you   _____

8. has studied as much as you   _____

B *Pair Work* Discuss the people you know with a partner. Are your friends, relatives, and teachers similar or different?

A *My sister works as hard as I do.*
B *What does she do?*
A *She's a nurse. We're both nurses.*

4 Avoid Common Mistakes ⚠️

1. Do not use a comparative when you are not comparing two ideas.

   young
I have two very ~~younger~~ sons.

2. Use *than*, not *that*, after a comparative.

   than
I am more patient now ~~that~~ I was.

3. Do not use *more* and *-er* together.

My work is ~~more~~ better than it used to be.

I work ~~more~~ harder now than I used to.

4. Do not forget the second *as* in *as . . . as* comparisons.

   as
I do not see my family now as much ∧ I did last year.

Editing Task

Find and correct 12 more mistakes in this student's personal essay.

How I Have Changed

I think I have changed in three important ways since high school. First, I have a ~~more~~ kinder personality now. I used to be less patient that I am now, especially with my grandparents. I have spent a lot of time with my grandparents in the last three years, and I have learned to be more patient

5 with them and to understand them more better. I can see that getting old can be more difficult, so I try to help my grandparents as often I can.

Second, I did not use to be as serious I am now about my education. I now realize that I need to study as much possible so I can get a diploma in engineering. Five years ago, I was very younger and did not study a lot. Now

10 I'm studying more harder than I did then, and I do not skip classes as much I did in high school.

Finally, I worry less that I did because I have goals now. I know what I want and where I am going. In general, I have grown up and become more clearer about who I am and what I want out of life. I believe I am a better

15 person that I used to be.

5 | Grammar for Writing ✏️

Using Comparatives with Adjectives and Adverbs

Writers often use adjectives and adverbs to compare people when writing about family or friends.

Comparatives are common in reviews, academic writing, and personal essays that compare products, things, ideas, and people.

Remember:

- **Use adjectives to compare people's appearance and their personalities.**

  Younger siblings often aren't <u>as serious as</u> their older siblings, but I am much <u>funnier</u> than my younger siblings.

- **Use adverbs to compare the way people do things.**

  My mother speaks English <u>more fluently</u> than my father, but <u>not as well as</u> my sister.

Pre-writing Task

1 Read the paragraph about types of parents. How are the writer's parents different from other parents?

Different Ways to Be a Parent

Everyone has strong ideas about the right and wrong ways to take care of children. Some parents watch their children more closely than others – some are stricter, while others are more lenient. My parents always gave my brother and me a lot of freedom. They were not as strict as our friends' parents. They wanted us to learn to make
5 our own decisions about things. Most of my friends' parents were stricter with their children, and the parents made the decisions for them. Our friends were not allowed to stay out as late as we were, for example. Also, when our friends' grades were not as good as they could be, they were punished. When our grades were not good, our parents talked to us about how to do better in school. In my opinion, this was more effective. I
10 think my brother and I matured faster than some of our friends. I also think some of our friends are less confident about themselves and their decisions than we are. There are many different ways to take care of children, and I feel lucky that my parents raised us the way they did.

2 Read the paragraph again. Underline the comparative adjectives and circle the comparative adverbs. What verbs are the adverbs comparing? What nouns are the adjectives comparing?

Writing Task

1 *Write* Use the paragraph in the Pre-writing Task to help you write a paragraph comparing families or family members. Use adjective and adverb comparisons from the unit. You can write about:

- parents
- siblings
- grandparents

- aunts and/or uncles
- cousins
- your own idea

2 *Self-Edit* Use the editing tips below to improve your paragraph. Make any necessary changes.

1. Did you use adjectives and adverbs to compare family members?
2. Did you use comparative adjectives to compare people's appearance or personalities?
3. Did you use comparative adverbs to compare the way people do things?
4. Did you avoid the mistakes in the Avoid Common Mistakes chart on page 324?

Superlative Adjectives and Adverbs

The Best and the Worst

1 | Grammar in the Real World

A What are some ways we can help people during disasters? Read the web article about technology and disaster relief. What is one way people use technology for disaster relief?

The Technology of Relief

Natural disasters¹ can strike at any time and with no warning. However, **today's newest** technologies can help disaster victims in new and amazing ways. Here are a few examples.

5 When Hurricane Katrina hit the southern United States in 2005, it was a terrible disaster. The city of New Orleans was hit **the hardest**. TV, newspapers, and radio all covered the storm, but **one of the best** sources of news about the disaster was Craigslist, an online network 10 for free advertising. Soon after the storm hit, Craigslist dedicated part of its site to disaster relief.² People used it to post³ reports of missing persons and to share news and stories. This seemed to be **the quickest** and **the most efficient** way to give and get information. The news on the 15 radio and TV was often not **the most current**.⁴

Social networking sites have also become important during disasters. **One of their most important** roles is to help raise money.⁵ Soon after the major earthquake in Haiti in 2010, the Red Cross and other organizations that help people in disasters were very popular topics on social networking sites. The Red Cross raised more than $8 million in fewer than 48 hours 20 through these sites. This was **the fastest** worldwide money-raising event in history.

Unfortunately, disasters will continue to happen. Hopefully, however, new technologies will continue to develop as well. They can help people to get and to give disaster relief in **the best** ways possible.

¹**natural disaster:** a natural event (e.g., hurricane) that causes great damage | ²**relief:** help | ³**post:** announce; put something on the Internet | ⁴**current:** up-to-date, present | ⁵**raise money:** convince people to give money, usually for a charity

B *Comprehension Check* Answer the questions.

1. When did Hurricane Katrina happen?
2. Which city was hit hardest by the hurricane?
3. What is Craigslist?
4. What is one way people used Craigslist after the hurricane?
5. How did the Red Cross use social networking sites after the 2010 earthquake in Haiti?

C *Notice* Read the sentences from the article and answer the questions.

1. "The city of New Orleans was hit the hardest."
   Was another city hit harder?

2. "This (Craigslist) seemed to be the quickest and the most efficient way to give and get information."
   Did there seem to be a quicker and more efficient way to get and give information?

3. "This was the fastest worldwide money-raising event in history."
   Was there a faster worldwide money-raising event?

2 | Superlative Adjectives and Adverbs

▶ Grammar Presentation

Superlative adjectives and adverbs compare one idea to other ideas. They mean "more / less than all of the others."	SUPERLATIVE ADJECTIVE *Social networking sites are **the newest** way to communicate after a disaster.* SUPERLATIVE ADVERB *The city of New Orleans was hit **the hardest**.*

2.1 Superlative Adjectives

Subject	Verb	*The*	Superlative Adjective	
The hurricane	was is	**the**	**biggest** **most expensive** **least damaging**	storm of the season.

2.2 Superlative Adverbs

Subject	Verb	(*The*)	Superlative Adverb	
Rescuers	worked	(**the**)	**hardest** **most quickly** **least efficiently**	right after the disaster.

2.3 Forming Superlative Adjectives and Adverbs

a.	Add *the* and *-est* to one-syllable adjectives and adverbs.	*fast* ➞ **the** *fast***est** *hard* ➞ **the** *hard***est** *strong* ➞ **the** *strong***est**
b.	For adjectives that end in a vowel + consonant, double the consonant.	*big* ➞ the *bi***gg***est* *hot* ➞ the *ho***tt***est*
c.	Remove the *-y* and add *-iest* to two-syllable adjectives ending in *-y*.	*busy* ➞ the *bus***iest** *early* ➞ the *earl***iest** *heavy* ➞ the *heav***iest**
d.	Use *the most* with almost all adjectives that have two or more syllables and with adverbs ending in *-ly*.	*expensive* ➞ **the most** *expensive* *frequently* ➞ **the most** *frequently*
e.	Some superlative adjectives and adverbs are irregular.	**Adjectives** **Adverbs** *good* ➞ the best *well* ➞ the best *bad* ➞ the worst *badly* ➞ the worst

▸▮ Adjectives and Adverbs: Comparative and Superlative Forms: See page A12.

2.4 Using Superlatives

a.	Superlative adjectives show that a noun has the most or least of a certain quality. They compare one noun to the other nouns in a group.	*It was **the biggest** forest fire in the state.* (Compares one forest fire to all others in the state.)
b.	Superlative adverbs show that a verb happens in the most or least of a certain way. They compare one action or situation to others in a group.	*That group worked **most effectively** after the disaster.* (Compares the way that group worked to the way all other groups worked.)
c.	*The least* + adjective or adverb is the opposite of *the most* + adjective or adverb.	*This storm was **the least dangerous** one of the season. There wasn't much damage from it.*
	The least is not usually used with one-syllable adjectives or adverbs.	*My daughter is **the youngest** of my children.* *My daughter is the ~~least old~~ of my children.*
d.	You do not need to repeat words after the superlative when the meaning is clear.	*That disaster was **the biggest** (disaster).* *Of all the technologies we use, this is **the easiest** (technology).*

2.4 Using Superlatives *(continued)*

e. You can identify the group being compared with:
- a prepositional phrase (*in* and *of* are the most common prepositions).

*It was **the worst** storm **in** years.*

- a possessive form, like a possessive pronoun or noun. You do not need *the* before the superlative when you use possessives.

***Today's newest** technologies help us during disasters.*
***Our biggest** problem was raising relief money.*

f. You can use *one of the* or *some of the* before a superlative adjective.

*It is **one of the** best ways to communicate quickly.*

Use a plural noun or a noncount noun with these expressions.

*These are **some of the** most interesting new technologies.*

Data from the Real World

The five most common superlative adjectives with *-est* in writing are *best, biggest, greatest, highest,* and *largest*.	*They are **the best** workers to have during a disaster.* *The disaster struck **the largest** city in the country.*
The five most common superlative adjectives with *most* in writing are *most common, most effective, most famous, most important,* and *most popular*.	*It's **the most popular** site for social networking.* *What is **the most common** problem after a disaster?*
Research shows that *the* is rarely used before superlative adverbs, except in formal speaking and writing.	*Rescue workers worked **fastest** in the first days after the event.*

▶ Grammar Application

Exercise 2.1 Superlative Forms

Complete the sentences with the superlative form of the adjectives or adverbs in parentheses. Use *most* or *-est* with ↑. Use *least* with ↓. Some forms are irregular.

1. The flood was _the largest_ (↑ large) disaster of the past 10 years.

2. Rescue workers worked _____ (↑ hard) during the first few days.

3. It was one of _____ (↑ big) earthquakes in history.

4. This is _____ (↓ useful) way to help during a disaster.

5. This disaster was the state's _____ (↑ bad) storm.

6. People donated money _____ (↑ quickly) using websites.

7. It was the area's _____ (↓ damaging) hurricane of the year.

8. Medical staff worked _____ (↓ effectively) during the night.

Exercise 2.2 More Superlative Forms

A 🔊 Write the superlative form of each of the words below. Then listen to the lecture about the eruption of Mount Vesuvius and the Great Chicago Fire. Listen for the superlative forms of the words in the chart, and check (✓) which event they describe.

		Eruption of Mount Vesuvius	Great Chicago Fire
1. bad	*the worst*	☐	☐
2. big		☐	☐
3. famous		☑	☐
4. fast		☐	☐
5. good		☐	☐
6. helpful		☐	☐
7. important		☐	☐
8. interesting		☐	☐
9. popular		☐	☐

B 🔊 Listen again. Complete the sentences with the words you hear.

1. The eruption of Mount Vesuvius is _____ _____ natural disasters in history.

2. It is also probably _____ disaster in history.

3. However, it has also been _____ events in history for archeologists.

4. It was _____ fire and _____ disaster in the history of the city.

5. _____ story is that a cow kicked over a lantern in a barn and started the fire.

6. The way people worked together after the fire was _____ result.

7. I think that has to be _____ building projects in history.

8. This also shows how people often work together _____ when they are helping one another.

Mount Vesuvius

The Great Chicago Fire

Exercise 2.3 More Superlative Practice

A Look at the information in the chart about three forest fires. Write eight more sentences about the information. Use superlative adjectives and adverbs from the box. Use some words more than once.

| ~~big~~ | damaging | expensive | long | quickly | short | small |

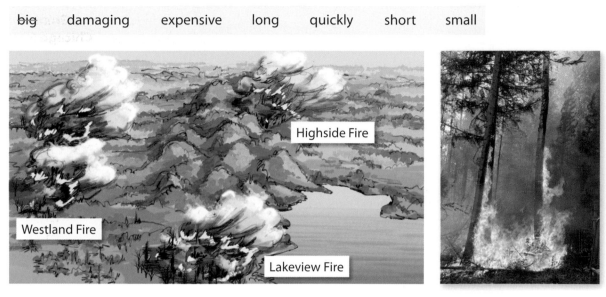

Highside Fire

Westland Fire

Lakeview Fire

	Westland Fire	**Highside Fire**	**Lakeview Fire**
1. Size of fire	100 acres	25 acres	50 acres
2. How long the fire lasted	10 days	3½ days	4 days
3. Damage from the fire (+ = 20 cabins destroyed)	++++	++	+++
4. Cost of fighting the fire	$$$$$	$$	$$$
5. How quickly the firefighters arrived to fight the fire	5 minutes	7 minutes	8 minutes

The Westland fire was the biggest fire. The Highside fire was the smallest.

1. _____

2. _____

3. _____

4. _____

5. _____

6. _____

7. _____

8. _____

B *Pair Work* Check your partner's sentences. Are they similar or different from yours?

Exercise 2.4 Using Superlatives

A *Over to You*   Write three superlative sentences about yourself or people you know. In each sentence, use one word or expression from each column.

Expressions	Adjectives	Nouns
one of the some of the my friend's / brother's / family's . . . my / our / your	good bad interesting exciting difficult useful funny enjoyable unusual	job family story classes hometown technology life pet hobby

This has been one of the least exciting years of my life.
My brother's most unusual pet was a spider.

B *Over to You*   Write three more superlative sentences about yourself or people you know. In each sentence, use one word or expression from each column.

Verbs	Adverbs	Expressions
study work play learn walk run speak English cook drive	well badly carefully quickly slowly easily fast quietly creatively	I know of anyone I know of my life of the year in my life in my family in the world

My friend Lisa cooks the best of anyone I know.
In my family, my mother drives the most carefully.

C *Pair Work*   Compare your sentences with a partner.

D *Group Work*   Tell the class something interesting about your partner and the people he or she knows.

This has been the most exciting year of Natalia's life. First, she came to the United States and started studying English. Then she met her fiancé.

3 | Avoid Common Mistakes ⚠️

1. Use *the most* with long adjectives. Do not use *-est*.

They were the ~~helpfulest~~ *most helpful* workers after the hurricane.

2. *Good* and *bad* have irregular superlative adjective and adverb forms.

It was the ~~baddest~~ *worst* fire of the year.   Everyone worked ~~wellest~~ *best* early in the morning.

3. Use a possessive pronoun before a superlative. Do not use an object pronoun.

Cleaning up after the storm was ~~him~~ *his* biggest problem.

4. Do not put a superlative adverb between the verb and the object.

They helped ~~the fastest~~ those people ∧ *the fastest* after the storm.

Editing Task

Find and correct nine more mistakes in the e-mail.

Hi Miko,

We had a terrible storm last week. It was the ~~baddest~~ *worst* storm of the decade. It was

probably the terrifyingest experience of my life. The children were home with me. All three

of them were scared, but Alexis behaved the wellest. She was the helpfulest. She kept the

5 other children calm. The dog was probably the difficultest! He barked and barked.

After the storm, we went outside. The damage to our house is the baddest. Me biggest

problem is getting someone to help us fix it. There were some people injured, so rescue

workers helped the fastest those people. After that, they started cleaning up the most

quickly our neighborhood. A tree fell on our garage and is still there, so that's us biggest

10 problem right now. We hope someone will move it tomorrow.

Pat

4 | Grammar for Writing ✏

Using Superlative Adjectives and Adverbs

Writers often use superlative adjectives and adverbs when writing about disasters and other extreme events.

Superlatives are common in news articles, academic writing, and other texts about important events in the news or in history.

Remember:

- **Use superlative adjectives and adverbs to focus on only one thing or situation and to show how it is the best, worst, least, or most of all the others.**

  The latest oil leak disaster was in the Gulf.

  One of the scariest days of my life was during Hurricane Andrew.

- **Put *the* in front of superlatives unless the superlative immediately follows a possessive.**

  The fire burned down many houses in the richest part of town. It was one of this year's worst fires.

Pre-writing Task

1 Read the paragraph below. What extreme event did the writer write about, and why was it so extreme?

The Worst Wildfire

There have been a lot of wildfires since we moved to California, but last year's fire was the worst because it was the biggest and it came the closest to our neighborhood. It was very hard to put out, and it lasted the longest of all the fires in the last few years. We watched the fire begin in the hills behind our neighborhood. At first, it was

5 very small, but it spread quickly. A lot of ash fell on us for days. The thickest ash fell during the first few days of the fire. It looked like thick, white snow. The air was also the smokiest on those days because the winds were blowing the hardest then. Those were my family's scariest days and nights. Many people think that lightning is the most common cause of wildfires, but this is not true. People are the biggest cause of wildfires.

10 In fact, the fire behind our neighborhood was caused by people camping in the woods.

2 Read the paragraph again. Underline the superlative adjectives and circle the superlative adverbs. <u>Double underline</u> the possessive + superlative combination.

Writing Task

1 *Write* Use the paragraph in the Pre-writing Task to help you write about an extreme event that you or someone you know experienced. Use superlative adjectives and adverbs to describe the event. You can write about events such as:

- a hurricane or very heavy rainstorm
- snow, hail, or a thunderstorm
- a very hot or very cold period
- a flood
- a tornado
- your own idea

2 *Self-Edit* Use the editing tips below to improve your paragraph. Make any necessary changes.

1. Did you use superlative adjectives and adverbs to write about an extreme event?
2. Did you use superlatives to focus on a single thing that was the worst or most compared to all the others?
3. Did you use *the* with superlatives unless you used a possessive?
4. Did you avoid the mistakes in the Avoid Common Mistakes chart on page 335?

Gerunds and Infinitives (1)
Managing Time

1 | Grammar in the Real World

A Think of a time when someone made you wait. How did you feel? Read the web article about how different cultures think about time. What are some different ways that people see time?

Views of Time

Joe is a new manager at his company. He is leading his first team meeting today, and he is feeling frustrated. He **remembered to e-mail** everyone about the meeting, but one person is missing. Did she **forget to come**? Also, Joe **needs to leave** soon, but the group has not discussed everything on the agenda.[1] He **remembers arranging** a

5 two-hour meeting, and he has **tried to keep** the discussion moving forward. However, he has not succeeded. What is the problem? Many of Joe's team members are from different cultures, and different cultures see time very differently.

For people in some cultures, like Joe's, time is linear.[2] Events happen one after the other, along a time line, and each one has a beginning and an end point. People in

10 these cultures **like to control** their time. For example, Joe **enjoys keeping** a schedule, and he **likes being** punctual.[3]

However, people from other cultures, like some of Joe's team members, see time

15 as a cycle.[4] In this view, events do not have specific beginning and end points – they occur and then reoccur. People from these cultures do not **expect to control** time, so they often do not **like to make** schedules.

20 Instead, they **prefer to be** flexible.

[1]**agenda:** list of points to discuss | [2]**linear:** following a straight line; continuing in a clear way from one part to the next | [3]**punctual:** on time | [4]**cycle:** a process that repeats

How can Joe **avoid experiencing** problems with multicultural meetings? Here are some tips: Get other people on the team to help plan the meeting. If they help create the agenda, it will be more realistic for them. Also, **try to be** flexible. Understand the reasons behind different ideas about time. **Try following** these tips, and you will

25 have more productive meetings.

B *Comprehension Check* Answer the questions.

1. Why does Joe feel frustrated?
2. If people like to control time, which view do they have?
3. If people don't expect to control time, which view do they have?
4. What are two tips for avoiding time problems with multicultural groups?

C *Notice* Underline the first verb (main verb) in the sentences below. Circle the second verb.

1. Joe needs to leave soon.

2. People from these cultures do not expect to control time.

3. Joe enjoys keeping a schedule.

4. How can Joe avoid experiencing problems with multicultural meetings?

Look at the second verb in the sentences. How are the second verbs in sentences 1 and 2 different from the ones in sentences 3 and 4?

2 | Verbs Followed by Gerunds or Infinitives

▶ Grammar Presentation

A gerund is the *-ing* form of a verb, used as a noun. An infinitive is *to* + the base form of a verb.	VERB GERUND *I **kept looking** at the clock during the meeting.* VERB INFINITIVE *We **expected to finish** by 4:00 p.m.*

2.1 Using Verbs with Gerunds and Infinitives

a. Some verbs can be followed by a gerund, but not by an infinitive.	*I **kept looking** at the clock during the meeting.* *I kept ~~to look~~ at the clock during the meeting.*
b. Some verbs can be followed by an infinitive, but not by a gerund.	*We **expected to finish** by 4:00 p.m.* *We expected ~~finishing~~ by 4:00 p.m.*

2.1 Using Verbs with Gerunds and Infinitives *(continued)*

c. Some verbs can be followed by an infinitive or by an object + an infinitive. These verbs include *expect*, *need*, and *want*.

	VERB	INFINITIVE	
Roberto	expects	to go	soon.

	VERB	OBJECT	INFINITIVE	
Roberto	expects	**us**	to go	soon.

d. When a verb is followed by an infinitive or gerund, use *not* before the infinitive or gerund to form a negative statement.

*Jim suggested **not leaving** early today.*
*We agreed **not to work** after 5 o'clock.*

e. You can use *and* or *or* to connect two infinitives or two gerunds. When you connect infinitives, you don't usually repeat *to*, especially when the sentence is short.

*We **suggested waiting and going** another day.*
*I **need to stop and think** about this for a minute.*

▶▶ Spelling Rules for Verbs Ending in *-ing*: See page A4.

2.2 Verbs Followed by a Gerund Only

avoid	involve
consider	keep (continue)
deny	mind (object to)
enjoy	recall (remember)
finish	suggest

2.3 Verbs Followed by an Infinitive Only

agree	plan
decide	refuse
expect	seem
hope	tend (be likely)
need	want

▶▶ Verbs + Gerunds and Infinitives: See page A5.

Data from the Real World

Research shows that these are the most common verbs followed by a gerund in speaking and writing:			These are the most common verbs followed by an infinitive in speaking and writing:		
avoid	finish	miss	agree	hope	seem
consider	involve	practice	decide	need	tend
deny	keep	risk	expect	plan	want
enjoy	mind	suggest	fail	refuse	

▶ Grammar Application

Exercise 2.1 Listening for Gerunds and Infinitives

🔊 Listen to a podcast about how people think about time. Complete the sentences with the gerund or infinitive you hear.

Most people feel that time speeds up as they get older. At the end of each day, adults often ask themselves: Why haven't I done the things that I planned _to do_ (do) today?
(1)

When you are a child, time seems _____ (go) very slowly. As you get
(2)
older, time tends _____ (pass) more quickly. Why do adults and children
(3)
see time differently?

According to psychologists, one theory is that children tend _____ (look) forward. On a car trip, for example, children always
(4)
want _____ (arrive). They ask, "Are we there yet?" Children
(5)
look forward, so time seems _____ (last) longer. Adults, on the
(6)
other hand, enjoy _____ (look) back and _____ (think)
(7)   (8)
about their memories.

In addition, adults tend _____ (be) busy, so time
(9)
often passes more quickly for them. Also, most adults will keep
_____ (look) at their watch throughout the day, and as a
(10)
result, be more aware of time.

Finally, children have a lot of new experiences to process, but as people get older, they do not tend _____ (have) so many new experiences.
(11)
This also speeds time up. Maybe experiencing new adventures as we get older can help us feel as if we can regain a little bit of that childhood sense of time.

Exercise 2.2 Gerund or Infinitive?

Complete the e-mail about problems with time in multicultural business settings.
Circle the correct answer.

To: Production Team
From: jj@cambridge.org
Date: Wednesday, July 13
Subject: Time Management Issues

Dear Team,

As you all know, yesterday morning we had an important meeting. I hoped
(to finish)/finishing at noon. However, the meeting did not end until 1:30 p.m. In
(1)
addition, we did not finish **to discuss/discussing** everything on the agenda. I do
(2)
not mind **to end/ending** late. However, we need **to cover/covering** everything on
(3)   (4)
the agenda.

At the end of the meeting, some of you suggested **to continue/continuing**
(5)
our discussions over lunch. I usually avoid **to combine/combining** work with
(6)
meals, so I suggested **not to do/not doing** that. We also considered
(7)
to stop/stopping and **to continue/continuing** another day. In the end, we decided
(8)   (9)
to arrange/arranging another meeting for next week.
(10)
I want **to feel/you to feel** good about coming to meetings when I ask you to
(11)
come. For this reason, I need **to help/the team to help** me plan meetings from now
(12)
on. Can we agree **to write/writing** the agenda for next week's meeting together?
(13)
Can I expect **to participate/everyone to participate** with me in this?
(14)
Good time management involves **to agree/agreeing** on an agenda and then
(15)
follow/following it. I hope you all agree.
(16)
Sincerely,

Joe

Exercise 2.3 Using Gerunds and Infinitives

A What can you tell the people in these situations? Give advice
with gerunds or infinitives.

Situation	Advice
1. My friends always come late to my parties.	Your friends need _to call you and tell you that they are going to be late_.
2. Heather is always late for class.	She should plan _____.
3. Roberto always turns his homework in late.	He should avoid _____.
4. Time goes so slowly for me at work. I look at the clock again and again, but it never changes!	You shouldn't keep _____.
5. Wei doesn't leave me a message when he's going to be late.	He should agree _____.
6. Lisa refuses to wear a watch.	She needs _____.

B *Pair Work* Compare answers in A with a partner. Is your advice similar or
different?

   A *I think Heather should plan to get to class on time.*
   B *I said Heather should plan to have a friend call her one hour before class starts.*

3 | Verbs Followed by Gerunds and Infinitives

▶ Grammar Presentation

Some verbs can be followed by both a gerund and an infinitive. Sometimes the meaning is the same. Sometimes it is different.	I **stopped e-mailing** the agendas. (For a while, I e-mailed the agendas. Then I stopped doing that.) I **stopped to e-mail** the agendas. (different meaning) (First I stopped what I was doing. Then I e-mailed the agendas.)

3.1 Using Verbs Followed by Gerunds and Infinitives

a. Some verbs can be followed by an infinitive or a gerund without a change in meaning. These verbs include *begin*, *continue*, *hate*, *like*, *love*, *prefer*, and *start*.	*Everyone **began to speak** / **speaking** at the same time.* *Wei **loves to get up** / **getting up** early.*
b. Some verbs can be followed by an infinitive or a gerund, but the meaning changes. These verbs include *forget*, *remember*, *stop*, and *try*.	*Luis **will** never **forget meeting** the president.* (Luis met the president, and he will never forget that he did this.) *Luis **must** not **forget to enclose** his résumé with his application.* (Luis has not enclosed his résumé with his application yet, and he must not forget to do this.)
c. In sentences with *forget*, *remember*, or *stop* + a gerund, the gerund tells what happens first.	SECOND EVENT FIRST EVENT *Jim **remembered making** an appointment.* (First Jim made the appointment. Later, he remembered this.)
In sentences with *forget*, *remember*, or *stop* + an infinitive, the infinitive tells what happens second, after the action of the main verb.	FIRST EVENT SECOND EVENT *Jim **remembered to make** an appointment.* (First Jim remembered that he needed to make an appointment. Then he made it.)
d. In sentences with *try* + gerund, the action of the gerund generally happens.	*Marta **tried setting** her alarm for 6:00 a.m., but she was still late.* (She set the alarm.)
In sentences with *try* + infinitive, the action of the infinitive often does not happen or is not successful.	*Marta **tried to set** her alarm for 6:00 a.m., but the clock wasn't working.* (She didn't set the alarm.)
e. You can use *and* or *or* to connect two infinitives or two gerunds. With infinitives, you don't usually repeat *to*, especially when the sentence is short.	*He **loves planning and attending** meetings.* *He **loves to plan and attend** meetings.* *I **like walking or riding** a bike to work.*
With verbs that can be followed by either a gerund or an infinitive, use the same form for both after the verb.	*I **like walking and riding** a bike to work.* *I like walking and ~~to ride~~ my bike to work.*

▶ Grammar Application

Exercise 3.1 Same or Different Meaning?

A Rewrite the sentences. Change the gerunds in **bold** to infinitives and the infinitives in **bold** to gerunds. If the meaning of the sentence stays the same, write *S* next to the sentence. If the meaning is different, write *D*.

1. I remembered **making** an appointment with the doctor.

    I remembered to make an appointment with the doctor.   *D*

2. My co-workers and I like **to learn** about how different cultures view time.

   _____   _____

3. We began **discussing** our plans for next year.

   _____   _____

4. To manage her time, our colleague Kelly tried **to buy** a calendar.

   _____   _____

5. Our boss started **to accept** that different cultures see time differently.

   _____   _____

6. Kelly and I love **having** a very long lunch break.

   _____   _____

7. Our colleague Bill hates **mixing** work and social activities.

   _____   _____

8. Our co-workers didn't stop **eating** lunch until 4:00 p.m.

   _____   _____

9. We continued **to discuss** our problems until very late at night.

   _____   _____

10. Jill forgot **to contact** Janet last week.

    _____   _____

11. Bo remembered **writing** and **sending** the memo.

    _____   _____

B *Pair Work*   In which sentences in A does the meaning change? Explain the difference in meaning to a partner.

The meaning is different in number 1. In the first sentence, he made the appointment and later remembered that. In the second sentence, he first remembered that he needed to make an appointment. Then he made it.

Exercise 3.2 *Forget, Remember, Stop,* and *Try*

Read the class discussion. Circle the correct answer.

Ms. Vargas   Class, tell me how you did research for this assignment. Did most of you use the web?

Laura   Well, yes. I tried **reading** / **to read** a long article on the web. The conclusion
      (1)
      was good, but I didn't learn much from the rest of the article. I found another
      article on a website about linear time, but I stopped **reading** / **to read** it
      (2)
      because it wasn't very academic.

Wendy   I tried **getting** / **to get** on to a website about
(3)
time and psychology, but I couldn't make it
work. It kept shutting down.

Ms. Vargas   Did anyone else have trouble?

Ahmet   No. Not really. I remember **reading** / **to read**
(4)
one article that wasn't very good. I found
another really good website, though, and I
luckily remembered **bookmarking** / **to bookmark**
(5)
it before I closed it.

Wendy   That was a good idea! I found one good site, but I forgot
bookmarking / **to bookmark** it. I was reading an article, but then
(6)
I stopped **reading** / **to read** and answered the phone. When I got
(7)
back, my computer was off. That was weird because I don't remember
shutting / **to shut** it down!
(8)

Diego   I didn't use the web. In fact, I read a book. I prefer books. I read for a
while and take notes, then I stop **thinking** / **to think** for a few minutes
(9)
about my own ideas. Then I add my ideas to the notes.

Exercise 3.3 Using Verbs Followed by Gerunds and Infinitives

A *Over to You*   Answer the questions about time. Write complete sentences.

1. Where do you like to go when you have free time?

   I like to go/going to the beach when I have free time.

2. What do you prefer to do after work or school?

   _____

3. What do you try doing when you feel bored?

   _____

4. How do you remember not to miss appointments?

   _____

B *Pair Work*   Ask and answer the questions in A with a partner. Are your answers
similar or different?

4 Avoid Common Mistakes ⚠️

1. Do not use gerunds after verbs that require infinitives.

to discuss
They did not expect ~~discussing~~ work during lunch.

2. Do not use infinitives after verbs that require gerunds.

writing
We finished ~~to write~~ our report at 5:00 p.m.

3. Remember: Infinitives include *to*.

to
I want ∧ learn about other cultures.

Editing Task

Find and correct eight more mistakes in this paragraph from a web article about time and boredom.

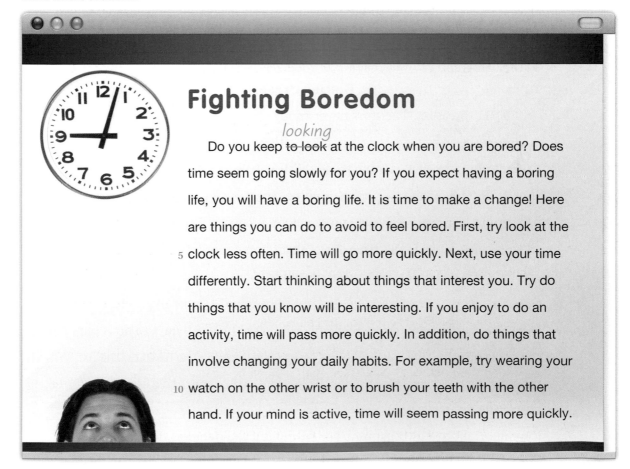

Fighting Boredom

looking
Do you keep ~~to look~~ at the clock when you are bored? Does time seem going slowly for you? If you expect having a boring life, you will have a boring life. It is time to make a change! Here are things you can do to avoid to feel bored. First, try look at the
5 clock less often. Time will go more quickly. Next, use your time differently. Start thinking about things that interest you. Try do things that you know will be interesting. If you enjoy to do an activity, time will pass more quickly. In addition, do things that involve changing your daily habits. For example, try wearing your
10 watch on the other wrist or to brush your teeth with the other hand. If your mind is active, time will seem passing more quickly.

5 Grammar for Writing ✏

Using Gerunds and Infinitives

Writers often use verb + gerund or verb + infinitive combinations to describe people's behavior or habits.

Verb + gerund and verb + infinitive combinations are common in personal stories, letters or e-mails, advice columns, and other texts about people's behavior or habits. Remember:

- **Some verbs take only gerunds after them, while others take only infinitives. It's a good idea to check when you aren't sure.**

  I don't mind <u>waiting</u> for people.   He always <u>seems to be</u> late for things.

- **Some verbs take both gerunds and infinitives, but the meaning can change.**

  She <u>stopped to talk</u> to her friend and was late to class. (She talked to her friend.)

  She <u>stopped talking</u> to her friend after she was late again. (She no longer talked to her friend.)

Pre-writing Task

1 Read the paragraph below. What is one good way to stay organized?

Getting Organized

The expression "There are never enough hours in a day" **seems to be** true more and more these days. Our lives are filled with lots of tasks. To use your time well, **try organizing** yourself. **Learning to do** this **involves organizing** both your space and your mind. Organizing your space **involves creating** a way to organize the piles of
5 papers and mail you receive at home, school, and work. **Try dividing** this paper into separate files, for example, have one each for home, work, and school. If you work in an office, you will probably **need to organize** your papers into several categories. Ones that work very well are "in" and "out" boxes and a "work in progress" box. Next, **start to organize** your mind. Remembering everything you have to do is impossible,
10 so **try creating** a "to do" list. The next step is prioritizing the tasks on the list. Which ones are the most important to finish? When do you **expect to finish** them? After answering these questions, write the tasks on a calendar. Once you are organized, it is important to stay organized. For example, if you **decided to finish** your homework in the mornings and go grocery shopping after class, stick to this plan.

15 Also, **focus on finishing** the most important tasks on the calendar. After a week, check how well this new organization is going and make any changes. You will soon find that by managing your time and space, you have saved a lot of time.

2 Read the paragraph again. Look at the words in **bold**. Underline the verb + gerund combinations and circle the verb + infinitive combinations. Which verbs can take gerunds or infinitives? Does the meaning change for these verbs?

Writing Task

1 *Write* Use the paragraph in the Pre-writing Task to help you write suggestions for organizing your schedule. Use verb + gerund and verb + infinitive combinations from the unit.

2 *Self-Edit* Use the editing tips below to improve your paragraph. Make any necessary changes.

1. Did you use verbs + gerunds and verbs + infinitives to describe people's behavior or habits?
2. Did you use the correct form (gerund or infinitive) after each verb?
3. Did you use any verbs that can take both gerunds or infinitives? If so, did you use the correct form to express the meaning you wanted?
4. Did you avoid the mistakes in the Avoid Common Mistakes chart on page 347?

Gerunds and Infinitives (2)

Civil Rights

1 | Grammar in the Real World

A Are all people treated fairly in the United States today? Read the article about the civil rights movement. What types of discrimination have become illegal since the 1960s?

The 1960s and Civil Rights

BUS DEPOT

WHITE WAITING
— ROOM —
Intrastate Passengers

In the 1960s, a 35-year-old American woman applied for a job as a flight attendant. The airline **was not interested in hiring** her. They told her she was too old.

5 **Discriminating**[1] against people because of their age or for other reasons was common in the United States in the past. However, certain laws make it less common today. The struggle to pass many of these laws began during the
10 civil rights movement.[2]

In the 1960s, laws in many states segregated[3] African Americans. For example, in some states, African Americans and whites went to separate schools. In addition, African Americans couldn't buy houses in many 15 "white" neighborhoods. Civil rights workers opposed this segregation and worked hard **to call** attention to unfair laws. **Changing** the laws wasn't easy. However, in 1964, the U.S. Congress passed the Civil Rights Act. Now, 20 because of this law, **it is illegal to segregate** people.

After the Civil Rights Act of 1964, other groups became **interested in fighting** for civil rights. These groups included women and 25 people with disabilities.[4] This led to many new laws. Today, for example, **it is against the law to build** a school without access[5] for people in wheelchairs. Not **hiring** people because of their age is also illegal. 30

Discrimination is still a problem in the United States today. Hopefully, however, people will **keep on working** for equal rights for all groups. **By working** hard, we can **succeed in passing** even more new laws to stop the 35 spread of discrimination.

---

[1]**discriminate:** treat people differently, in an unfair way | [2]**the civil rights movement:** the struggle for equal rights for African Americans | [3]**segregate:** keep one group of people separate because of race, religion, etc. | [4]**disability:** a physical or mental challenge, such as difficulty walking or seeing | [5]**access:** easy ways to enter

B *Comprehension Check* Answer the questions.

1. What kinds of discrimination were there in the United States in the past?
2. What are two examples of segregation?
3. What did civil rights workers want to change?
4. What other groups fought for civil rights after Congress passed the Civil Rights Act of 1964?

C *Notice* Find the sentences in the reading and complete them.

1. _____ the laws wasn't easy.

2. _____ against people because of their age or for other reasons was common in the United States in the past.

3. Now, because of this law, it is illegal _____ people.

4. Civil rights workers opposed this segregation and worked hard _____ attention to unfair laws.

Look at sentences 1 and 2. You learned that gerunds can come after certain verbs. Where else can gerunds occur in a sentence? Look at sentences 3 and 4. One infinitive shows a purpose or reason for the action. Which one?

2 More About Gerunds

▶ Grammar Presentation

Gerunds can be the subjects of sentences and the objects of prepositions. They can also come after *be*.	SUBJECT GERUND ***Changing*** *the laws wasn't easy.* OBJECT OF A PREPOSITION *We can change the law **by working** hard.* BE + GERUND *His job **is trying** to help people fight for their rights.*

2.1 Using Gerunds as Subjects, After Prepositions, and After *Be*

a. Gerunds can be the subjects of sentences. A gerund subject is singular. It takes third-person singular verb forms.	***Discriminating*** *against people because of age is illegal.*
b. Gerunds can be used after prepositions.	*We can succeed **in passing** more laws against discrimination.*
Note: An infinitive cannot be the object of a preposition.	*They weren't interested **in to hire** her.*
c. Use *by* + gerund to express how something is done.	*You can change laws **by voting**.*

2.1 Using Gerunds as Subjects, After Prepositions, and After *Be* (continued)

d. Certain verb + preposition + gerund combinations are very common.	VERB PREP. GERUND We **believe in fighting** for our rights.
Certain adjective + preposition + gerund combinations are also very common, especially after the verb *be*.	ADJECTIVE PREP. GERUND They weren't **interested in hiring** her.
e. Gerunds can also come after *be*.	VERB GERUND The worst part of her job **was talking** to angry customers.

Data from the Real World

Research shows that these are very common verb + preposition + gerund combinations:

believe in	*forget about*	*succeed in*	*think about*	*worry about*
disagree with	*keep on* (continue)	*talk about*	*think of*	

Research shows that these are very common adjective + preposition + gerund combinations:

afraid of	*good at*	*important in*	*involved in*	*tired of*
aware of	*important for*	*interested in*	*sorry about*	*worried about*

▶▶ Verb + Gerunds and Infinitives: See page A5.
▶▶ Verb and Preposition Combinations: See page A5.

▶ Grammar Application

Exercise 2.1 Gerunds as Subjects, After Prepositions, and After *Be*

A Complete the essay on Rosa Parks with the gerund form of the verbs in parentheses.

Rosa Parks is a hero in the American civil rights movement. Her work was important in _ending_ (end) segregation in Montgomery,
(1)
Alabama. Parks's major contribution to civil rights was one very simple act. That act was _____ (refuse) to stand up and
(2)
move to another seat on a bus.

In Montgomery, Alabama, in the 1950s, African Americans had to stand if a white person wanted a seat on a city bus. This was a law. Rosa Parks did not agree with this law. She worked very long hours every day, and she often had to stand up and give her seat to a white person, even though she was exhausted and her feet hurt. Parks was tired of _____ (do) this. She did not believe
(3)
in _____ (give) her bus seat to a white person for no reason. In
(4)
addition, she was not afraid of _____ (try) to stop something that
(5)
was wrong. Therefore, one day, Parks refused to stand up and move when the bus driver asked her to.

The police arrested Parks. Her arrest angered many African Americans in Alabama. In fact, many people across the entire United States did not believe in _____ (treat) African Americans this way. They were
(6)
interested in _____ (support) civil rights. These people helped by
(7)
_____ (send) money to the civil rights organizers in Alabama. This
(8)
support succeeded in _____ (pressure) the state of Alabama. As a
(9)
result, Alabama changed its laws.

Rosa Parks was involved in _____ (get) an important civil right
(10)
for African Americans. Her one simple act also inspired other people around the country to keep on _____ (work) to end discrimination.
(11)

B *Pair Work* Ask and answer questions with a partner about Rosa Parks. Use a form of the words in the box and a gerund, or your own ideas.

be afraid of	be involved in	disagree with
be important in	believe in	keep on
be interested in	be tired of	succeed in

A *What was Rosa Parks tired of doing?*
B *She was tired of giving up her seat on the bus.*

Exercise 2.2 More Gerunds as Subjects, After Prepositions, and After *Be*

A Complete the sentences in the civil rights time line with the words in parentheses. Use the gerund form, and add prepositions where needed. Note: All main verbs are in the present tense.

Civil Rights Time Line – The Early Days

1948 – _Discriminating_ (discriminate) against people in the military because of race,
(1)
religion, or national origin becomes illegal.

1954 – After much debate and discussion, the U.S. Supreme Court _agrees to ending_
(2)
(agree / end) segregation in public schools.

1955 – Martin Luther King Jr. _____ (be involved / start) the
(3)
Montgomery bus boycott.

1957 – Martin Luther King Jr. starts a civil rights organization, the Southern Christian
Leadership Conference. King and his organization have many ideas about
_____ (fight) for civil rights peacefully.
(4)

1960 – Four African-American students fight segregation by _____ (sit)
(5)
at a lunch counter. No one serves them, but they _____ (keep / sit)
(6)
at the counter. By _____ (do) this, they start the idea of "sit-ins" –
(7)
peaceful demonstrations in the civil rights movement.

1962 – James Meredith _____ (succeed / become) the first
(8)
African-American student to enroll at the University of Mississippi.

1963 – 200,000 people _____
(9)
(be involved / march) in Washington, D.C. They
do this to show their support for civil rights.

1967 – _____ (not allow)
(10)
interracial marriage becomes illegal. African
Americans and whites can now marry each other.

1968 – More and more Americans _____
(11)
(be involved / work) for civil rights.

Crowfoot Library
Self Checkout
August,18,2016 20:37

39065132132042   9/8/2016
Grammar and beyond, 2 [includes audio C
D]

Total   1 item(s)

You have 0 item(s) ready for pickup

B *Group Work* Discuss civil rights in a group. Answer the questions.

1. Are there civil rights issues you are interested in supporting? If so, which ones?
2. Have you ever been involved in marching or protesting to support a civil right? If so, where and when?

3 | More About Infinitives

▶ Grammar Presentation

<table>
<tr>
<td>Infinitives can come after be. They are also often used with in order to show a purpose.

It + infinitive sentences are also very common.</td>
<td>One idea was to organize farm workers.
African-American children had to walk (in order) to get to school.

It was difficult to be an African American in the 1960s.</td>
</tr>
</table>

3.1 Using Infinitives After *Be*, to Show Purpose, and in *It* + Infinitive Sentences

<table>
<tr>
<td>a. Like gerunds, infinitives can follow be.</td>
<td>Her job is to help other people.
The purpose of the demonstration is to get people's attention.</td>
</tr>
<tr>
<td>b. In order + infinitive expresses a purpose. It answers a "Why?" question.

You can use the infinitive alone when the meaning is clear.</td>
<td>People are fighting in order to change unfair laws.

People are fighting to change unfair laws.

Why are people fighting? To change unfair laws.</td>
</tr>
<tr>
<td>When and connects two infinitives of purpose, (in order) to is usually not repeated.</td>
<td>They were working (in order) to change laws and help people.</td>
</tr>
<tr>
<td>c. It + infinitive sentences are very common. It + infinitive sentences often include the verbs be, cost, seem, and take.</td>
<td>It is important to fight against discrimination.
It costs a lot of money to run for office.
It seems difficult to revise immigration laws.
It takes time to change people's minds.</td>
</tr>
<tr>
<td>An It + infinitive sentence usually has the same meaning as a sentence with a gerund subject. The gerund subject is more formal.</td>
<td>It was her dream to have equal rights for everyone.

Having equal rights for everyone was her dream.</td>
</tr>
</table>

▶ Grammar Application

Exercise 3.1 Infinitives After *Be*, to Show Purpose, and with *It*

🔊 Listen to a podcast on an early hero in the women's rights movement. Complete the sentences with the words you hear.

It was difficult <u>to be</u> a woman in the United
$\quad\quad\quad\quad\quad$ (1)
States in the early part of the twentieth century.
Women did not have many rights. For example, they
were not able to vote.

In 1917, Alice Paul organized a group of
women _____ for the right to vote in
$\quad\quad\quad$ (2)
national elections. The group demonstrated in front
of the White House in order _____
$\quad\quad\quad\quad\quad\quad\quad$ (3)
the president's attention. This angered many people. The police arrested many women

_____ the demonstrations. However, this didn't work, so they arrested Paul
$\quad\quad$ (4)
and gave her a seven-month jail sentence in order _____ the other women.
$\quad\quad\quad\quad\quad\quad\quad\quad\quad\quad\quad$ (5)
This was unfair, but Alice Paul was strong. She stopped eating. She went on a hunger strike

_____ attention to the issue of women's rights.
$\quad\quad$ (6)
$\quad\quad$ Paul suffered in order _____ the right to vote, but in the end, this and
$\quad\quad\quad\quad\quad\quad\quad\quad\quad\quad$ (7)
other demonstrations worked. Congress finally gave women the vote in 1920.

Exercise 3.2 More Infinitives

A Complete the textbook passage about César Chávez. Use the correct form of the verbs in the boxes.

focus	get	help	improve

César Chávez was a Mexican-American farm worker.
He was also a civil rights worker. He fought <u>to get</u> equal
$\quad\quad\quad\quad\quad\quad\quad\quad\quad\quad\quad\quad\quad\quad$ (1)
rights for Mexican Americans and _____ the
$\quad\quad\quad\quad\quad\quad\quad\quad\quad\quad\quad\quad$ (2)
lives of farm workers.

Chávez was interested in workers' rights at an early age. He was born in Arizona in 1927. When he was growing up, he experienced discrimination. **For example, it was against school rules to speak Spanish.** If children spoke Spanish, the teacher punished them.

In the 1950s, Chávez joined a civil rights group _____ (3) Mexican Americans register and vote in elections. He gave speeches _____ (4) people's attention on workers' rights. Later, he started the National Farm Workers Association.

| be | help | pay | stop | use |

It was difficult _____ (5) a farm worker in the 1950s. For example, it was common _____ (6) farm workers very low wages. It was also common _____ (7) dangerous pesticides (toxic chemicals) on farm crops.

It was Chávez's dream _____ (8) these things. In the 1960s, he organized a strike _____ (9) farm workers.

| convince | get | help | show |

The purpose of the strike was _____ (10) higher pay for the workers. The strike succeeded, and finally, farm workers got higher wages. In the 1980s, Chávez used another strike _____ (11) growers to stop the use of pesticides on grapes.

César Chávez worked all his life _____ (12) Mexican Americans and farm workers. Today, his birthday is a state holiday in California and in seven other states. The purpose of César Chávez Day is _____ (13) respect for his important work.

B Rewrite each **boldfaced** sentence from the reading. Use a gerund subject.

For example, it was against the rules to speak Spanish.

1. *For example, speaking Spanish was against the rules.*
2. _____
3. _____
4. _____
5. _____

C *Pair Work*   Ask and answer the questions about César Chávez with a partner. Use infinitives.

1. What did César Chávez work for all his life?

   He worked to improve the lives of Mexican Americans and farm workers.

2. Why did Chávez join a civil rights group in the 1950s?

3. Why did Chávez give speeches in the 1950s?

4. Why was it difficult to be a farm worker?

5. Why did Chávez organize a strike in the 1960s? in the 1980s?

6. What is the purpose of César Chávez Day?

D *Over to You*   Think about civil rights today. Are there still problems? What do we still need to work on? Complete the following sentences on a separate piece of paper. Then share your sentences with the class.

Today, it is still difficult to help women get the same pay as men.

It still seems hard for [group] to . . .

People are still fighting to . . .

We are still working to . . .

It is my dream to . . .

4 Avoid Common Mistakes ⚠️

1. Gerund subjects take singular verbs.

Changing laws ~~are~~ *is* a slow process.

2. Use the correct preposition in verb + preposition and adjective + preposition combinations.

They succeeded ~~on~~ *in* getting more rights.

Do not be afraid ~~for~~ *of* standing up for your rights.

3. Do not use an infinitive after a preposition.

They weren't interested in ~~to hire~~ *hiring* her.

4. Do not use *for* in infinitives of purpose.

He worked hard ~~for~~ to help workers with disabilities.

5. Don't forget *It* or *to* in *It* sentences.

~~Is~~ *It is* important ∧ *to* attend the march this weekend.

Editing Task

Find and correct ten more mistakes in this paragraph.

It was more difficult ∧ *to* be disabled in the United States in the

past. It was hard do things like enter buildings or cross the street if

you were in a wheelchair. In many places, it was impossible bring a

guide dog into a restaurant. Many people were interested in to help

5 the disabled. They worked hard for to help people with disabilities.

They finally succeeded on passing an important law. It was the

Americans with Disabilities Act of 1990. Today, sight-impaired

people are not afraid for bringing their dogs into any building.

Making streets accessible to people with physical disabilities are

10 another result of the 1990 law. For example, adding gentle slopes

to the edges of sidewalks help the disabled. Now a person in a

wheelchair doesn't worry about to get from one side of the street

to the other. Making changes like these are a slow process, but an

important one.

5 | Grammar for Writing ✏️

Using Gerunds and Infinitives

Writers often use gerunds as subjects and after prepositions to focus on the importance of an action. They use infinitives to show a purpose when describing people's goals and reasons for doing something.

Gerunds and infinitives with prepositions appear in almost every kind of text and are common in interviews, personal profiles, and other articles that describe people's goals and motivations.

Remember:

- **Focus attention on an action by making it a gerund subject. The gerund is singular.**

  <u>Fighting</u> for your rights <u>is</u> an important thing to do.

- **Gerunds often follow certain verbs + prepositions or adjectives + prepositions.**

  Many people <u>are not interested in making</u> the effort to fight for their rights.

- **You can use infinitives with or without _in order_ when talking about the purpose of an action.**

  I e-mailed my senator (in order) <u>to ask</u> her to help us.

Pre-writing Task

1 Read the paragraph below. What group of people is the paragraph about? What was the problem and what was the solution?

Taking Care of Families

Being a full-time employee and a mother of small children is not easy. What happens when your child gets sick? In the past, you could lose your job for taking time off to take care of a sick child or give birth to a baby. Many people struggled to change this situation, and in 1993, the passing of the Family and Medical Leave Act improved things for pregnant women and for families in general in the United States. This law stopped employers from firing new mothers. Now, employers have to give employees up to 12 weeks off from work in order to take care of their new babies. In addition, after 12 weeks, employers have to give these women a job again. This law is also good for anyone with a sick child, a sick husband or wife, or even a sick parent.

2 Read the paragraph again. Underline the gerund subjects, circle the gerunds that follow prepositions, and <u>double underline</u> the infinitives that show purpose.

Writing Task

1 *Write*   Use the paragraph in the Pre-writing Task to help you write about a group of people who fought for or are fighting for their rights. You can use the Internet to help you. Why was or is life difficult for this group? What rights was or is this group fighting for? Use gerunds as subjects and after prepositions, and use infinitives to talk about purpose.

2 *Self-Edit*   Use the editing tips below to improve your paragraph. Make any necessary changes.

1. Did you use gerunds and infinitives to describe people's goals and reasons for those goals?
2. Did you use the third-person singular after subject gerunds?
3. Did you use gerunds after verb + preposition and adjective + preposition combinations?
4. Did you use infinitives with and without *in order* to show the purpose of an action?
5. Did you avoid the mistakes in the Avoid Common Mistakes chart on page 359?

30 Subject Relative Clauses (Adjective Clauses with Subject Relative Pronouns)

Sleep

1 Grammar in the Real World

A How many hours a night do you sleep? Read the article about scientific research on sleep. Why do some people need only a few hours of sleep?

Sleep and Science

Sleep is important. We need it to live, but not everyone gets the same amount of sleep each night. There are many people **who need eight or more hours of sleep a night**.

5 However, there are also others **who are happy with only four or five hours**. Scientists call these people "short sleepers." Is this simply a lifestyle choice? Not necessarily. Researchers recently found a gene mutation[1] **that might**

10 **control our sleep**.

Recently, a research team studied a mother and her daughter **who are short sleepers**. They only sleep about six hours a night. The researchers analyzed the DNA[2] of the entire family, and they found a gene mutation in both the mother and daughter. The team already knew about this gene, the hDEC2 gene. It controls sleep in animals.

15 They made a guess: People **who have the mutation** might need less sleep than other people.

The researchers then created mice **that had the same hDEC2 gene mutation**. The mice **that had the gene mutation** slept less at night than mice **that didn't have the mutation**. After that, the researchers forced both kinds of mice to stay awake. The

20 mice **that did not have the mutation needed extra sleep**. The mice **that had the mutation did not**.

These researchers think genetics might be more important for our sleeping patterns than lifestyle. If you only sleep four or five hours a night, your lifestyle might not be to blame. Perhaps it's just in your genes!

[1]**gene mutation:** a change in the structure of a gene, the pattern of cell structure that we get from our parents |
[2]**DNA:** chemical in the cells of living things that controls the structure of each cell

B *Comprehension Check* Answer the questions.

1. What might control how much sleep we get?
2. What do scientists call people who do not need a lot of sleep?
3. Why did scientists study a mother and her daughter?
4. What did the experiment with mice show?

C *Notice* Find the sentences in the article and complete them.

1. There are many people _____ need eight or more hours of sleep a night.

2. Researchers recently found a gene mutation _____ might control our sleep.

3. The researchers then created mice _____ had the same hDEC2 gene mutation.

4. The mice _____ did not have the mutation needed extra sleep.

Look at the words you wrote. Circle the noun that each one refers to.

2 | Subject Relative Clauses

▶ Grammar Presentation

> Relative clauses define, describe, identify, or give more information about nouns. Like all clauses, relative clauses have both a subject and a verb.
>
> RELATIVE CLAUSE
> SUBJECT   VERB
> *The team studied people* **who** **slept only four to six hours**. *(**who** = people)*

2.1 Subject Relative Clauses

	RELATIVE CLAUSE			
	Subject Relative Pronoun	**Verb**		
The scientists studied people	**who**	**slept**	**only four to six hours.**	
The mice	**that**	**had**	**the gene mutation**	slept less at night.
It is a gene	**which**	**controls**	**sleep in animals.**	

2.2 Using Subject Relative Clauses

a. In a subject relative clause, the relative pronoun is the subject of the clause.

RELATIVE CLAUSE
RELATIVE PRONOUN
*There are people **who** only need about six hours of sleep.*

RELATIVE CLAUSE
RELATIVE PRONOUN
*A mouse **that** had a mutated gene needed less sleep.*

b. The subject relative pronouns are *who, which,* and *that.*

Use *who* or *that* for people.	*She's the researcher **who/that** heads the sleep project.*
Use *which* or *that* for things and animals.	*They created a mouse **which/that** had the same gene.*

c. Subject relative clauses combine two ideas.

The scientists studied mice. + *The mice had a gene mutation.*

*The scientists studied mice **that** had a gene mutation.*

d. The verb after the relative pronoun agrees with the noun or pronoun before the relative pronoun.

*People **who** have the hDEC2 gene need less sleep.*

*I know a woman **who** sleeps only four hours a night.*

e. A subject relative clause usually comes right after the word it modifies. It can modify any noun or pronoun in a sentence.

SUBJECT
*Someone **who has the hDEC2 gene** sleeps less.*

*The scientists studied mice **who had a mutated gene**.*

*The women participated in a study **that ended last year**.*

▶ Grammar Application

Exercise 2.1 Subject Relative Clauses

Read the student summary of a science article. Circle the relative pronouns and underline the relative clauses.

Many researchers have done studies (that) look at sleep. This article is about a study that compares the habits of good sleepers and bad sleepers. A group of scientists who specialize in sleep research did the study. First, the scientists studied people who sleep well. They learned about the habits that might make these people good sleepers. Then the

5 scientists studied people who do not sleep well. These short sleepers often have habits

which are very different from the habits of good sleepers. From this study, the researchers have developed the following tips for people who cannot sleep. First, do not drink caffeinated beverages like tea or coffee after noon. In addition, eat dinner at least three hours before going to bed, and, finally, get some exercise every day. These are three habits

10 of good sleepers. If you are a person who does not sleep well at night, try to start doing these things. They could help you change your sleep patterns.

Data from the Real World

| Research shows that in informal speaking and writing, people use either *who* or *that* to refer to people. | A Do you know the woman **who/that participated in the study**?
B Yes. She's my aunt. |
| In formal writing, people use *who* to refer to people and *that* or *which* to refer to things. *Which* is more formal. | Participants **who had the hDEC2 gene** slept less.
A report on the study **that/which showed a genetic basis for sleep patterns** appears in the journal Genetics Today. |

Exercise 2.2 *Who*, *That*, or *Which*?

Complete the article about sleep with the correct **formal** relative pronouns. Circle the noun that each relative pronoun refers to.

A Good Night's Sleep

Everyone needs a good night's sleep. This is important for staying healthy. However, (people) _____who_____ (1) have trouble sleeping often worry about their health. Troubled sleepers can get help from recent studies. Researchers _____ (2) study sleep have good advice for people with sleep problems. A study _____ (3) appeared recently showed some interesting results. Not everyone needs the same amount of sleep. Most people need 8 to 8½ hours of sleep a night. However, some people _____ (4) have a special gene need less sleep. People _____ (5) have this gene probably cannot change their sleep habits. They should not worry about sleeping less. However, sleep researchers have some advice for people _____ (6) do not have this gene.

People _____ have trouble sleeping should avoid caffeine after
(7)
noon. Some men and women _____ have trouble sleeping have found
(8)
it helps to exercise. Even walking 20 minutes every day can help. One idea
_____ has helped many people is for them to go to bed only when they
(9)
are tired. This might mean going to bed at 2:00 a.m. and waking up at 7:00 a.m.
Another strategy _____ has helped people is moving bedtime back 15
(10)
minutes each night until it is 8 hours before it is time to wake up.

Exercise 2.3 Using Subject Relative Clauses

A Complete the questions with a relative pronoun and the correct form of the verb.

1. Do you know someone _who/that_ _has_ (have) trouble sleeping? Who?

2. Do you know someone _____ _____ (sleep) nine
   hours most nights? Who?

3. Do you read websites or articles _____ _____ (give)
   tips on sleeping? Which websites or articles?

4. Do you have a friend _____ _____ (stay) up late?
   Who?

5. Do you have a relative _____ _____ (wake up)
   early most days? Who?

6. Do you have friends _____ _____ (take) naps?
   Who?

7. Do you have a favorite sleeping position _____ _____ (help)
   you get to sleep? What position is it?

8. Do you have tips _____ _____ (help) you get to
   sleep? What are they?

B *Group Work* Ask and answer the questions in A in a small group.
Compare answers.

A Do you have a favorite sleeping position that helps you get to sleep?

B Yes, I do.

C What position is it?

B I sleep on my back. What about you?

Exercise 2.4 Sentence Combining

A Combine the sentences from a web article on sleep position and personality. Make the second sentence a subject relative clause.

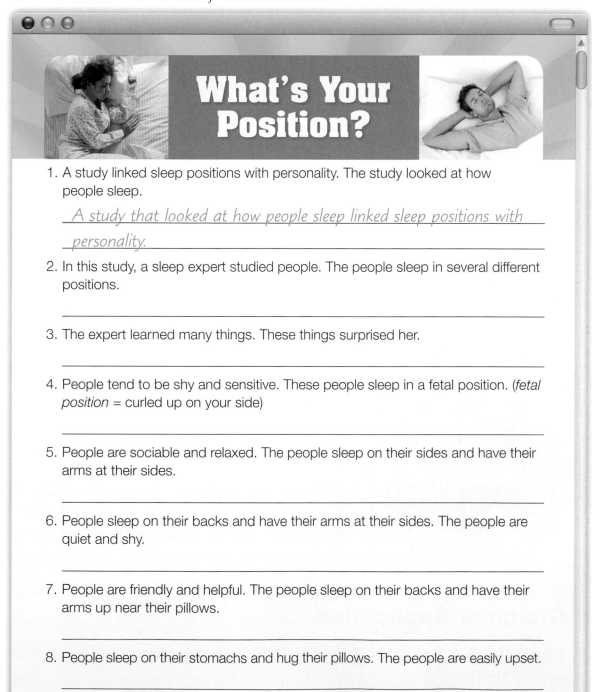

What's Your Position?

1. A study linked sleep positions with personality. The study looked at how people sleep.

   A study that looked at how people sleep linked sleep positions with personality.

2. In this study, a sleep expert studied people. The people sleep in several different positions.

   _____

3. The expert learned many things. These things surprised her.

   _____

4. People tend to be shy and sensitive. These people sleep in a fetal position. (*fetal position* = curled up on your side)

   _____

5. People are sociable and relaxed. The people sleep on their sides and have their arms at their sides.

   _____

6. People sleep on their backs and have their arms at their sides. The people are quiet and shy.

   _____

7. People are friendly and helpful. The people sleep on their backs and have their arms up near their pillows.

   _____

8. People sleep on their stomachs and hug their pillows. The people are easily upset.

   _____

B Underline the subject relative clauses in your new sentences. Circle the noun in the main clause that the relative pronoun refers to.

(A study) that looked at how people sleep linked sleep positions with personality.

C *Group Work* Take a survey of sleeping positions in your group. What is everyone's usual sleeping position and personality? Talk about your group. Give examples. Use subject relative clauses.

I don't think all people who sleep on their backs are quiet. For example, Marcelo sleeps on his back, and he's outgoing and friendly.

3 | More About Subject Relative Clauses

▶ Grammar Presentation

Subject relative clauses can use a variety of verb forms. They can also show possession.	People **who have sleep problems** *can join the study.* People **who are having sleep problems** *can join the study.* People **who have had sleep problems** *can join the study.* *Sally is a scientist* **whose discoveries have helped many people**. (Sally's discoveries have helped many people.)

3.1 More About Subject Relative Clauses

a. Verbs in subject relative clauses can take a variety of verb forms.

The woman **who <u>was participating</u> in the study** *was my aunt.*
People **that <u>have participated</u> in the study** *receive a payment.*

b. The possessive form of *who* is *whose. Whose* + a noun shows possession in a subject relative clause.
A noun always follows *whose.*

NOUN   *WHOSE* + NOUN SUBJECT
The <u>scientist</u> **whose work** *has helped many people won an award.*

c. *Whose* can combine two sentences. *Whose* replaces the possessive form in the second sentence.

The woman *is my neighbor.* + ~~**Her** daughter~~ *was in a sleep study.*
The woman **<u>whose daughter</u>** *was in a sleep study is my neighbor.*

They are **the scientists**. + ~~**Their** study~~ *was on the news last night.*
They are <u>the scientists</u> **whose study** *was on the news last night.*

▶ Grammar Application

Exercise 3.1 Verbs in Subject Relative Clauses

🔊 Listen to a student podcast about sleeping. Complete the sentences with the relative pronoun and the correct form of the verb you hear.

Why do we sleep? This is still a mystery. Scientists <u>*who study*</u> (study) sleep are still
(1)
not completely sure of the reasons. They know some things about sleep, however. Here are some facts:

- People _____ (be) asleep have active brains. Their brains are
(2)
most active during the "rapid eye movement," or REM, phase of sleep.

- Different animals sleep in different ways. For example, a dolphin

_____ (sleep) may continue to swim.
(3)

- Humans and animals _____ (lose) sleep need to make
(4)
it up later on.

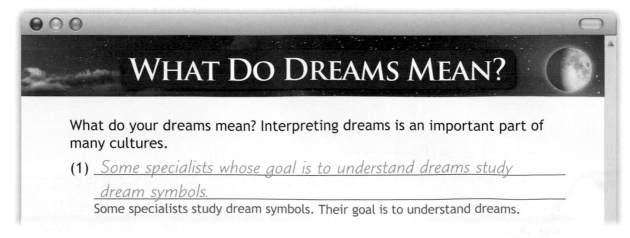

- A person _____ (need) less than eight hours of sleep
(5)
should not worry about sleeping less than other people.

- There are animals _____ (sleep) very little. For
(6)
example, a horse only sleeps three hours a day. There are other

animals _____ (sleep) a lot. For example, a small
(7)
animal called a ferret sleeps about 15 hours a day.

Scientists _____ (study) sleep also have a few guesses
(8)
about the reasons for sleep. There is a study _____ (show)
(9)
REM sleep helps learning and memory. However, there are other studies

_____ (show) the opposite results. For example, certain drugs
(10)
shorten REM sleep. A group of people _____ (take) these drugs
(11)
showed no memory problems in a recent study.

Most scientists agree on one thing. They need to do more research to solve the

mysteries of sleep.

Exercise 3.2 Sentence Combining with *Who*, *That*, and *Whose*

A Combine the sentences to complete a web article about interpreting (giving meaning
to) dreams. Make the second sentence a relative clause. Use *who*, *that*, or *whose*.

WHAT DO DREAMS MEAN?

What do your dreams mean? Interpreting dreams is an important part of
many cultures.

(1) *Some specialists whose goal is to understand dreams study*
dream symbols.

Some specialists study dream symbols. Their goal is to understand dreams.

(2) _____

_____

They believe dreams are about certain things. These things represent important ideas or feelings in our lives.

Here are some examples of dream symbols and their meanings;

▶ (3) _____

_____

People dream about losing a tooth. They are worried about something.

▶ (4) _____

_____

People may have a special wish for freedom. Their dreams are about flying.

▶ (5) _____

_____

People dream about falling. They have a fear of losing control of something.

▶ (6) _____

_____

People sometimes dream about a frightening dog. They have trouble with friends.

▶ (7) _____

_____

A dream can represent extreme emotions. The dream focuses on fire.

Some other meanings seem obvious. (8) _____

_____

For example, a person might also dream of fire. This person's room is too hot.

(9) _____

_____

In any case, most people do not see symbols in a simple way. These people analyze dreams.

Instead, they believe in looking at how the dreamer *feels* about the object in the dream.

B *Group Work* Discuss dream symbols in a group. Use the ones in A or your own ideas. Discuss possible interpretations for each symbol. Use subject relative pronouns. Present your ideas to the class. Use these questions to guide you.

- Which dream symbols are important in a culture you know well?
  Dream symbols that include animals are important in my culture.

- What are some interpretations of these symbols?

- Do you dream about any of these symbols? Which ones?

- What are some positive dream symbols?

- What are some negative dream symbols?

- Whose cultures have similar dream symbols?

- Do they have similar interpretations?

A *I think people who dream about teeth are worried about their appearance.*
B *Something good is going to happen to a person who dreams about a baby.*
C *In my friend's culture, a person who dreams about a dog will have bad luck.*

4 Avoid Common Mistakes ⚠

1. Use *who* or *that* for people and *which* or *that* for things.

who / that
The scientists studied a woman ~~which~~ never sleeps.

which / that
The research ~~who~~ proved the scientist's theory was interesting.

2. Do not use a subject pronoun after a subject relative pronoun.

Scientists study people who ~~they~~ sleep a short amount of time.

3. The verb after the relative pronoun agrees with the noun before the relative pronoun.

have
People who ~~has~~ the hDEC2 gene need less sleep.

4. Do not omit the relative pronoun in a subject relative clause.

who
Two women ∧ were "short sleepers" participated in a study.

5. Remember to spell *whose* correctly.

whose
The scientist ~~who's / whoes~~ work has helped many people won an award.

Editing Task

Find and correct nine more mistakes in a web article about colors in dreams.

Dreaming in Color

Can dreams give us insights into our feelings? Some people who ~~they~~

analyze dreams believe this. There are dream analysts who's interest is the

colors that they are in our dreams. In their opinion, these colors provide clues

about our lives. For example, dreams about people which are wearing black

5 represent sadness. Dreams who have a lot of gray, brown, or tan in them

can represent happiness. A dream who's main color is orange can represent

boldness. Many people who analyzes dreams think green represents life or new

beginnings. On the other hand, there are some people do not dream in color.

These people dream in black and white.

10   Do you remember the colors that was in your dreams last night? The next

time you dream, try to remember the colors. Write down the colors appear in

your dream, and think about how they made you feel.

5 | Grammar for Writing

Using Subject Relative Clauses

Writers often use subject relative clauses to include more information in a sentence about who people are or what things do.

Subject relative clauses are common in scientific articles, product manuals, and other texts that involve definitions or technical explanations.
Remember:

- **Use subject relative clauses to define, describe, or identify nouns.**

  Afternoon naps that are not longer than 20 to 30 minutes are healthy. Longer naps can leave you feeling tired.

- **You can use subject relative clauses to give more information about any noun in a sentence.**

  An alarm clock that didn't work is an excuse that is common from students who arrive late to school because they overslept.

Pre-writing Task

1 Read the paragraphs below. What is the cause of the sleep problems the writer is writing about? What is the writer's solution?

One Useful Trick

People who have sleep problems need tricks that will help them sleep better. Some of these people have problems getting to sleep, while others have problems falling asleep again after they wake up in the middle of the night. One common cause of sleep problems is worrying. People whose problems keep them awake do not always have more problems

5 than other people. Instead, people whose worries keep them awake just cannot switch off their minds. Sometimes they think about important problems which are bothering them. Sometimes they think about appointments, chores, and meetings that are on their schedule for the next day.

One trick which can be very helpful is to make a "to do" list before going to sleep

10 every night. This list helps people feel better because they have a plan that will help them solve their problems the next day. People who do this remove the problems from their minds, and they sleep better.

2 Read the paragraphs again. Underline the subject relative clauses, circle the relative pronouns in the clauses, and draw an arrow to the nouns or noun phrases the relative clauses define, describe, or identify.

Writing Task

1 *Write* Use the paragraphs in the Pre-writing Task to help you write about a particular sleep problem and a solution to the problem. Write about the problem in the first paragraph and the solution in the second. What do you think is the cause of this problem? What is one possible solution?

2 *Self-Edit* Use the editing tips below to improve your paragraphs. Make any necessary changes.

1. Did you use subject relative clauses to write about a problem and solution to a sleep routine?
2. Did you use subject relative clauses to define, describe, or identify exactly the people and things you are writing about?
3. Did you use subject relative clauses in different positions in your sentences?
4. Did you avoid the mistakes in the Avoid Common Mistakes chart on page 371?

Object Relative Clauses (Adjective Clauses with Object Relative Pronouns)

Viruses

1 | Grammar in the Real World

A How do you feel when you get a cold or the flu? Read the article from a health website. Why is it so easy to get a virus?

Viruses

When was the last time you had a viral infection?[1] Almost everyone has at least one a year. If you are like most people **that viruses attack**, you feel
5 pretty miserable once they enter your body. In addition, it can take several days or even weeks to get better. Therefore, it is a good idea to avoid catching or spreading viruses.

10 Viruses are tiny disease-causing particles.[2] The common cold and the flu are two well-known illnesses **that viruses cause**. Infected people can pass viruses easily to others **who they interact with**. This is because they blow small drops of liquid into the air when they cough or sneeze. These drops contain viruses. You can catch a virus from a person **that you touch** or even from someone **that**
15 **you stand near** if these drops enter your mouth or nose. Viruses can also live on surfaces[3] from a few minutes to many hours. This means you can also catch viruses from things **you touch**. This is especially true if you then touch your face before washing your hands.

There are ways to avoid spreading viruses. First, always wash items such as
20 dishes and towels **that an infected person has used**. Cover your mouth and nose when you cough or sneeze. Wash your hands frequently. Also, try to stay home if you get sick, so the people **who you work with** can stay healthy.

Viruses are difficult to control. However, knowing more about them and following the tips above can help you slow the cycle of viral infection.

[1]**viral infection:** illness caused by a virus | [2]**particle:** a very small piece of something | [3]**surface:** the top or outside of something

B Comprehension Check Answer the questions.

1. What are two illnesses that viruses cause?
2. How do viruses spread?
3. How long can viruses live on a surface?
4. What are three things you should do to protect yourself and others against viral infection?

C Notice Look at the underlined words in these sentences from the article. Circle the nouns that the underlined words refer to.

1. The common cold and the flu are two well-known illnesses <u>that</u> viruses cause.

2. Infected people can pass viruses easily to others <u>who</u> they interact with.

2 | Object Relative Clauses

▶ Grammar Presentation

Object relative clauses describe, identify, or give more information about nouns. In an object relative clause, the relative pronoun is the object.

	RELATIVE CLAUSE		
	OBJECT	SUBJECT	VERB
There are many diseases	*that*	*viruses*	*cause*.

2.1 Object Relative Clauses

	RELATIVE CLAUSE			
	Object Relative Pronoun	Subject	Verb	
You can infect people	that who / whom	you	meet.	
The virus	that which	the scientist	studied	was a type of flu.

2.2 Using Object Relative Clauses

a. In an object relative clause, the relative pronoun is the object of the clause.

	RELATIVE CLAUSE	
	OBJECT	
Cold and flu are illnesses	*that*	*viruses cause*.

b. The object relative pronouns are *who*, *whom*, *which*, and *that*.

Use *that*, *who*, or *whom* for people.

	RELATIVE CLAUSE	
	OBJECT	
The professor	*that*	*I met yesterday* has the flu.

2.2 Using Object Relative Clauses *(continued)*

Use *that* or *which* for things.

	RELATIVE CLAUSE
	OBJECT
She has a virus	**that young people often get**.

c. Object relative clauses can combine two ideas.

That is the virus. + Rob gave me the ~~virus~~.
That is the <u>virus</u> **that** Rob gave me.

d. You can omit the relative pronoun in an object relative clause.

The doctor (who) she spoke with had a cold himself!
Wash **the things (that) you touch** if you are infected.

e. The object relative pronoun is followed by a subject and a verb.

SUBJECT   VERB
I wash the towels **that   she   uses**.

SUBJECT   VERB
The flu vaccine **that   they   use** didn't work.

f. An object relative clause usually comes right after the word it modifies. It can modify any noun or pronoun in a sentence.

SUBJECT
The <u>virus</u> **that she studied** was a type of flu.

OBJECT
She washed the <u>towels</u> **that she used**.

PRONOUN
He's the <u>one</u> **who I contacted on the phone**.

2.3 Comparing Subject and Object Relative Clauses

	Subject Relative Clauses	Object Relative Clauses
In a relative clause, the relative pronoun is . . .	the subject.	the object.
In a sentence, the relative pronoun modifies . . .	any noun or pronoun.	
In a sentence, the relative pronoun usually comes . . .	right after the word it modifies.	
In a sentence, the relative clause has . . .	a new verb.	a new subject and verb.
The relative pronoun can be omitted.	no	yes, except for *whose*
The relative pronouns include . . .	*who, which, that, whose.*	*who, whom, which, that, whose.*

2.4 Using Subject and Object Relative Clauses

Subject relative clause	The **doctor** who treated her had a cold.
	SUBJECT
	The **doctor** had a cold. + The **doctor** treated her.
Object relative clause	The **doctor** who she visited had a cold.
	OBJECT
	The **doctor** had a cold. + She visited the **doctor**.

Data from the Real World 🌐	
Which is common in academic writing. It is much less common in informal language.	*The virus copies the host cell **which** it has invaded.*
In informal speaking and writing, *that* is more common in object relative clauses than *who* to refer to people. *Whom* is only used in rather formal situations.	*A Is she the scientist **that you met at the lab**?* *B Yes, she is.*

▶ Grammar Application

Exercise 2.1 Object Relative Clauses

A Read a passage from a history textbook about an epidemic (a disease that spreads quickly). Underline seven more relative clauses. Circle the relative pronouns. Three of the relative clauses do not have relative pronouns. Put a check (✔) above them.

In 1918 there was a global flu epidemic. It spread to almost every part of the world. The regions (that) the flu affected ranged from the Arctic to the South Pacific. In addition, the effects that
5 it had were devastating. The number of people this flu actually killed was between 50 and 100 million. However, the number of people that the virus infected was around 500 million. This was an epidemic scientists could not control. The virus spread very quickly, and it was very powerful. The people
10 who viruses usually affect are very old or very young. However, the people who this virus infected were healthy young adults. The 1918 flu was one of the worst natural disasters the world had ever seen.

B *Pair Work* Compare answers with a partner. Which relative clauses do not have a relative pronoun?

Exercise 2.2 Combining Sentences

Combine the sentences using object relative clauses with *who*, *that*, and *which*.

1. Another name for the flu epidemic was the "Spanish flu." The world experienced this flu epidemic in 1918.

   Another name for the flu epidemic _that the world experienced in_ 1918 was the "Spanish flu."

2. The people were mostly young adults. The flu killed them.

The people _____ were mostly young adults.

3. The people are typically elderly. The flu usually affects these people.

The people _____ are typically elderly.

4. The countries were very far apart. The flu affected countries.

The countries _____ were very far apart.

5. The 1918 flu was an unusual virus. Scientists could not control the virus.

The 1918 flu was an unusual virus _____ .

6. Strange flu viruses also occur today. Scientists do not understand these strange flu viruses.

Strange flu viruses _____ also occur today.

7. SARS, bird flu, and swine flu are recent examples of strange new viruses. Many people fear these viruses.

SARS, bird flu, and swine flu are recent examples of strange new viruses

_____ .

8. Scientists are interested in people. These strange new viruses affect these people.

Scientists are interested in people _____ .

Exercise 2.3 Using Object Relative Clauses

A *Over to You* Complete the sentences about getting sick. Use your own ideas. Write a correct relative pronoun, or Ø for no relative pronoun.

1. The thing _that /which/ Ø_ I usually do when I have a cold is _drink hot lemon juice with honey_ .

2. The thing _____ I usually do when I have

the flu is _____ .

3. I like the doctor _____ I go to when I get sick

because he / she _____ .

4. The best cold medicine _____ I know is

_____ .

5. _____ was the cold remedy

_____ my family used when I was a child.

6. _____ is the flu remedy

_____ my friend uses.

7. _____ is something _____ I avoid when I get sick.

B *Pair Work* Compare the sentences in A with a partner. Then tell the class about some of the interesting home remedies you discussed.

> A *The thing that I usually do when I have a cold is drink hot lemon juice with honey. What about you?*
> B *The thing that I usually do is . . .*

Exercise 2.4 Subject and Object Relative Clauses

A Complete the article about swine flu. Use the correct relative pronoun and the correct form of the verb in parentheses. Use Ø for no relative pronoun. If more than one pronoun is possible, write them all in the blank.

A New Flu

The flu is one of the most common diseases
that / which / Ø viruses _cause_ (cause).
    (1)   (2)
Sometimes the virus _____
                     (3)
_____ (cause) the flu isn't serious.
    (4)
Other times, it is. The number of people

_____ it _____ (attack)
      (5)   (6)
determines this. The number of places around

the world _____ it _____ (affect) also decides this. A
        (7)   (8)
disease _____ _____ (attack) a large number of people
        (9)   (10)
and areas is an epidemic. For example, the 1918 flu was an epidemic. In 2009, another

flu, swine flu, became an epidemic. Some people feel swine flu is still a serious threat.

Regions _____ swine flu still _____ (affect) include
      (11)   (12)
Europe, Africa, North and South America, the Middle East, and Asia. A lot of people

_____ _____ (have) swine flu have mild symptoms.
   (13)   (14)
Others _____ _____ (have) the disease have more serious
     (15)   (16)
symptoms. Swine flu became less serious after the 2009 outbreak, but it could return at

any time.

B *Pair Work* Compare answers in A with your partner. Which sentences have subject relative pronouns?

3 | More About Object Relative Clauses

▶ Grammar Presentation

Object relative clauses can use a variety of verb forms.	He doesn't touch surfaces **that the patient touches**. He didn't touch the surfaces **that the patient touched**. He hasn't touched the surfaces **that the patient has touched**.
They can also show possession.	The student **whose towel she used** had the flu. (It was the student's towel.)

3.1 More About Object Relative Clauses

a. *Whose* + a noun shows possession in an object relative clause.	WHOSE + NOUN The woman **whose husband** the doctor saw also needs an appointment.
A noun always follows *whose*.	WHOSE + NOUN The scientist **whose article** we read is giving a lecture at school.
Do not omit *whose*.	*whose* The scientist ︽article we read is giving a lecture at school.
b. *Whose* can combine two sentences.	The woman is sick. + The doctor saw ~~her~~ **children**. The woman **whose children** the doctor saw is sick.
Whose replaces the possessive form in the second sentence.	That is the scientist. + We read ~~his~~ **article**. That is the scientist **whose article** we read.

▶ Grammar Application

Exercise 3.1 Verbs in Object Relative Clauses

A ◀)) Listen to a podcast about the flu vaccine. Complete the sentences with the relative pronoun or Ø (for no relative pronoun) and the correct form of the verb in parentheses.

A vaccine is a substance _____*that*_____ a health practitioner
(1)

_____ (give) to help a person avoid getting a disease. There are
(2)

two types of flu vaccines. One is a shot _____ a practitioner usually
(3)

_____ (give) the patient in the arm. The other type is a nasal spray
(4)

_____ the practitioner _____ (spray)
(5) (6)
directly into the patient's nose. Scientists develop new flu vaccines

every year. They study flu viruses _____ people
(7)
around the world _____ (had) the previous year.
(8)
Then they choose three critical viruses and make vaccines for

them. For example, in 2009, the viruses _____ they
(9)
_____ (choose) were the most likely to continue to
(10)
cause disease in 2010.

    People often don't like to get their flu shots. However, the

flu shot _____ scientists _____
(11) (12)
(develop) for 2009 was in high demand in the United States. More

people than usual received that shot. According to doctors, getting a flu shot each year

is the most important thing _____ a person _____ (do) to
(13) (14)
prevent the flu. Maybe their message is now being heard.

B ◀)) Listen again, and check your answers.

C *Pair Work* Compare answers with a partner. Which sentences did not have
relative pronouns?

Exercise 3.2 Sentence Combining

Combine the sentences about Louis Pasteur. Use *that, which, who(m)*, Ø, or *whose*.

1. A biologist of the nineteenth century was Louis Pasteur. Doctors today still
value his research.

   A biologist of the nineteenth century *whose research doctors today still value*
   was Louis Pasteur.

2. Pasteur was a scientist. We still use his vaccines.

   Pasteur is a scientist _____ .

3. Pasteur developed vaccines to prevent diseases. Farm animals often get the diseases.

   Pasteur developed vaccines to prevent the diseases _____

   _____ .

4. He also developed a vaccine to prevent a disease. People get the disease from dogs
and other animals.

   He also developed a vaccine to prevent a disease _____

   _____ .

5. This is a disease. People get it from animal bites. The name of the disease is rabies.

   This is a disease _____ . The name of the disease is rabies.

6. Pasteur first tried his rabies vaccine on a young boy. A dog bit the boy.

   Pasteur first tried his rabies vaccine on a young boy

   _____ .

7. The vaccine worked. He cured the boy. The boy became his friend.

   The vaccine worked. The boy _____ became his friend.

8. Another disease is called anthrax. A lot of farm animals still get the disease.

   Another disease _____ is called anthrax.

Exercise 3.3 More Object Relative Clauses

A *Over to You* Answer the questions. Use object relative clauses.

1. In your opinion, what is the best thing that you can do to prevent the flu? Why?

   The best thing that you _can do to prevent the flu is get a flu shot. If you get a flu_ _shot, you won't get the flu, and you won't give it to other people_ .

2. What is the best thing that you can do to prevent the common cold? Why?

   The best thing that you _____

   _____ .

3. When you get the flu or a cold, what is the remedy that you use? Why?

   The remedy that I _____

   _____ .

4. What disease worries you the most? Why?

   The disease that I _____

   _____ .

5. What is the thing you worry about the most when you get sick? Why?

   When I get sick, the thing that I _____

   _____ .

B *Pair Work* Discuss your answers with a partner. What do you agree or disagree about?

A *The best thing that you can do to prevent the flu is get a flu shot. If you get a flu shot, you won't get the flu and you won't give it to other people.*

B *I disagree. Some people get very sick after they have a flu shot. I think the best thing that you can do to prevent the flu is get enough sleep and exercise.*

4 Avoid Common Mistakes ⚠

1. **Use *that / who / whom / Ø* to refer to people in object relative clauses; use *which / that* to refer to things.**

   that / who / whom / Ø
   The scientist ~~which~~ I remember reading about was Louis Pasteur.

2. **Do not confuse *whose* with *who*. *Whose* is possessive.**

   whose
   A person ~~who~~ computer is infected with a virus can use software to solve the problem.

3. **Use *whom* in object relative clauses only (and in rather formal situations).**

   who
   The man ~~whom~~ had the virus was very ill.

4. **Do not use an object pronoun at the end of an object relative clause.**

   The articles that I read ~~them~~ are about Louis Pasteur.

Editing Task

Find and correct eight more mistakes in the web article about computer viruses.

A New Kind of Epidemic

Are computer viruses similar to human viruses? In some ways, they are. A virus

that invades your computer sometimes behaves like a virus that infects your body.

Computer viruses became a serious problem in the 1990s. One of the first types of

that / Ø
virus ~~who~~ computer scientists created was a "worm." A worm is a computer virus that

5 a computer receives it without the user's knowledge. A user who computer is attacked

by a worm may lose data or suffer damage to his or her computer system.

The people which we must blame for the very first worm developed it in 1979.

Much like a human virus, the worm of 1979 gradually spread until it became an "epidemic." A virus who thousands of computers received very rapidly was the

10 famous "Melissa" virus of 1999. Luckily, someone developed a "vaccine" for this

virus, and it is no longer the cause of a computer virus epidemic.

However, people continue to create viruses of different kinds. For example, one

virus attacks people's electronic address lists and sends e-mails to everyone who

name is on a list. The people who you know them may be surprised when they get an

15 e-mail from you that is really an advertisement!

People who computers were infected with viruses needed protection, so

companies began to produce anti-virus software in the 1990s. Nowadays, a user

whom has good anti-virus software doesn't need to worry about a sick computer.

However, people create new viruses all the time. Viruses will continue to be a problem,

20 and new computer virus "vaccines" will need to be developed to fight them.

5 | Grammar for Writing

Using Object Relative Clauses

Writers often use object relative clauses to include more information about the people, objects, and ideas that they are writing about.

Object relative clauses are common in formal academic writing and other texts where writers need to give specific definitions of things.

Remember:

- **You can use object pronouns to help you combine different pieces of information about something into one sentence.**

  My mother taught me home remedies. I use them.
  I use home remedies that my mother taught me.

Pre-writing Task

1 Read the paragraphs below. What remedies does the writer write about in the first paragraph? What prevention techniques does the writer write about in the second paragraph?

Being Sick and Staying Healthy

Everyone I know has been sick recently. The first symptom that everyone gets is a

sore throat. The next thing everyone complains about is achy muscles. The things that

I do to feel better are things which my mother and my grandmother taught me. For example, it is a good idea to drink plenty of liquids. For my throat, I drink a hot ginger

5 and honey tea that my mother used to make for me. It does not taste very good, and
sometimes it burns at first, but after drinking it, my throat always feels better. For aches
and pains, I use hot pads that I put in the microwave. I also take flu or cold medications
that I keep in my bathroom.

To avoid getting sick, I try to take care of myself. One of the most important things is

10 getting enough sleep. Most people I know do not sleep enough. The other helpful thing is
staying fit. Doctors, scientists, and other people whose opinion I respect say that exercise
is very important. They say that if you do not exercise regularly, you are more likely to
get sick.

2 Read the paragraphs again. Underline the object relative clauses and circle the object pronouns. Find the object relative clauses without object pronouns. What object pronoun could you add to each one?

Writing Task

1 *Write* Use the paragraph in the Pre-writing Task to help you write about an illness or health problem. In the first paragraph, write about the illness and the remedies you use to treat the symptoms. In the second paragraph, write about the things you do to prevent this illness. You can write about illnesses or problems such as:

- colds and flus
- frequent headaches
- toothaches

- stomach or back problems
- sunburns or other skin problems
- your own idea

2 *Self-Edit* Use the editing tips below to improve your paragraphs. Make any necessary changes.

1. Did you use object relative clauses to provide more information about the people, objects, and things you wrote about?
2. Did you use object relative clauses to combine different pieces of information?
3. Did you avoid the mistakes in the Avoid Common Mistakes chart on page 383?

32 Conjunctions and Adverb Clauses

Special Days

1 Grammar in the Real World

A What holidays do you celebrate each year? Which are your favorite days? Read the magazine article about "Black Friday" (the day after Thanksgiving). What's good and bad about Black Friday?

BLACK FRIDAY

Black Friday is the Friday after Thanksgiving Day in the United States. It is the start of the holiday shopping season, **so** it is an important day for
5 retailers.[1] It is called "Black Friday" **because** it is the day when retailers go "into the black." That is, they make a profit. Retailers can make 18 percent to 40 percent of their yearly sales in
10 the month between Thanksgiving and Christmas, **so** the holiday shopping season is crucial for them **and** the U.S. economy in general.

Although Black Friday is not an
15 official holiday, many workers have the day off and start their holiday shopping. Shopping on this day is popular **because** retailers offer very low prices on items such as electronics.

20   There is a sense of excitement about Black Friday. Stores advertise their prices in advance and open their doors at 5:00 a.m. Shoppers often line up outside a store hours before it opens

so they can be the first ones in. Some   25
people even camp in the parking lot the
night before.

However, Black Friday shopping is not without its problems. **Even though** the deals sound fantastic, they   30 are often not as good as they seem. For instance, a store will advertise a big screen TV at a very low price, **but** there may be only one in the store. **Since** there are not enough low-priced   35 items for everyone, sometimes people get stressed **and** angry. Shoppers occasionally get into arguments **and** even fistfights. In addition, **since** people are excited and stores   40 are crowded, there are sometimes accidents on Black Friday.

Some people avoid the problems of Black Friday. They shop on the weekend after, **or** they stay home and buy online.   45 Black Friday can mean crowds and bad deals, **and yet** it remains one of the busiest shopping days of the year.

[1]**retailer:** store owner

B *Comprehension Check* Answer the questions.

1. Why is the holiday shopping season important?
2. Why do people want to shop on Black Friday?
3. What are the problems with shopping on Black Friday?
4. What are some ways to avoid the problems of Black Friday?

C *Notice* Complete the sentences from the article. Circle the correct words.

1. It is the start of the holiday shopping season, **but** / **so** it is an important day for retailers.
2. For instance, a store will advertise a big-screen TV at a very low price,
   but / **because** there may be only one in the store.
3. Shoppers occasionally get into arguments **and** / **so** even fistfights.
4. They shop on the weekend after, **since** / **or** they stay home and buy online.

Think about the meaning of each word you circled. In which sentence above does
the word express these meanings?

a. a result ___1___   b. an addition _____   c. an alternative _____   d. a contrast _____

2 | Conjunctions

▶ Grammar Presentation

The conjunctions *and, or, but, so,* and *yet* can connect single words, phrases, or clauses.	WORD WORD *Black Friday causes problems for* <u>shoppers</u> **and** <u>stores</u>. PHRASE PHRASE *They shop* <u>on weekends</u> **but** *not* <u>on weekdays</u>. CLAUSE CLAUSE *He wanted to save money,* **so** *he shopped on Black Friday.*

2.1 Conjunctions

a. You can use *and* to connect related information and add ideas.

*The shoppers were tired **and** hungry.* (words)
*People go out **and** spend money.* (phrases)
*The store opened at 5:00 a.m., **and** shoppers were waiting outside.* (clauses)

b. You can use *or* to give alternatives or choices.

*You can shop today **or** tomorrow.* (words)
*They camp in the parking lot **or** in front of the store.* (phrases)
*You can shop today, **or** you can wait until tomorrow.* (clauses)

2.1 Conjunctions *(continued)*

c. You can use *but (not)* to connect contrasting ideas.	*The store is small* **but** *successful.* (words) *They liked the clothes* **but** *not the high prices.* (phrases) *She has invited Jim for the holiday,* **but** *she has never invited us.* (clauses)
d. You can use *so* to connect causes and results.	*The stores are crowded,* **so** *I'll stay home.* (clauses)
You can use *and* before *so* to show a result.	*Stores cut their prices,* **and so** *they make less money.* (clauses)
It is not common to use *so* to connect words and phrases.	

2.2 Using Conjunctions

a. Use a comma when you connect two long clauses. However, you do not need a comma when the clauses are short.	*This is an important day***, and** *it is the busiest shopping day.* *Stores cut prices* **and** *people save money.*
b. When you connect two clauses and the subject is the same, you do not need to repeat the subject.	*People go shopping* **and** *(people) buy holiday gifts on this day.* *They save money* **but** *(they) don't realize the items aren't new.*
If the verb is the same, you do not need to repeat it.	*People can shop online* **or** *(can shop) at the mall.* *Shoppers start arguments* **and** *even (start) fistfights.* *Stores are cutting prices* **and** *(are) hoping to sell more.*
In addition, you often do not need to repeat prepositions after conjunctions.	*People are not at work on Thursday* **and** *(on) Friday.*
c. You can often use *but + not* to shorten contrasting clauses to words or phrases.	*They shop on Friday* **but not** *Thursday.* (= They shop on Friday, but they do not shop on Thursday.) *They liked the clothes* **but not** *the high prices.* (= They liked the clothes, but they did not like the high prices.)
Do not use *not* if the contrasting ideas are both affirmative.	*The store is small* **but** *successful.* (= The store is small, but it is successful.)

2.3 *Yet, And Yet*

a. *Yet* is a formal word. It has a similar meaning to *but*. *Yet* connects strongly contrasting ideas or surprising information.	*It is often cold, **yet** shoppers still sleep in doorways.* *The deals are often not good, **yet** people still go shopping.*
b. You can use *and* with *yet*.	*There is a downside, **and yet** it is a popular shopping day.*

▶ Grammar Application

Exercise 2.1 *And*, *Or*, *But*, *So*, and *Yet*

Complete a news article about the holiday shopping season. Circle the correct words.

Holiday Shopping in Our City

The malls are decorated **and**/**but** ready for the holiday shopping season.
(1)
The stores are hoping to attract a lot of customers **yet**/**and** make big profits
(2)
this year.

The holidays are a time for giving gifts, **or**/**and** the shopping season is
(3)
important for stores. Black Friday used to be the start of the shopping season,
but/**or** people are starting to shop earlier in November. We talked to some
(4)
retailers **so**/**and** analysts about their expectations for the holiday shopping
(5)
season this year.

"This year, stores are busy, **but not**/**but** as busy as last year," said one
(6)
retailer. "People are tired of the crowds, **but**/**so** they're shopping by telephone
(7)
but/**or** online," he added. "Unemployment in the city has gone up this year,
(8)
so/**and yet** people are still spending."
(9)
An analyst told us, "People are spending, **but**/**or** they are spending more
(10)
cautiously this year. The popular items are electronics **and**/**but** toys."
(11)
She added, "Stores are offering discounts **but**/**or** gifts with purchases.
(12)
They are staying open later on Saturdays **and**/**yet** Sundays."
(13)

Exercise 2.2 Repeated Subjects, Verbs, and Prepositions

Read an online interview with shoppers about Black Friday. If you do not need to repeat a subject or verb, cross it out.

Alex B., Detroit: (1) Black Friday can be a good thing or ~~Black Friday can be~~ a bad thing. (2) There are good deals and there are special offers. (3) For example, at a lot of stores, I can choose free shipping or I can choose a gift with my purchase. (4) I love the deals but I hate the crowds.

Maria S., Chicago: (5) People become over-excited and people become aggressive on Black Friday. (6) People push and people fight to get to the deals. (7) I stay home and I shop online, or I order things over the phone.

Wei P., San Francisco: (8) I can buy all of my gifts and I can save money, too. (9) We go shopping as a family and we enjoy our day out together.

Exercise 2.3 Using *And*, *Or*, *But*, and *So*

A *Pair Work* What do you know about Thanksgiving in the United States and Canada? When are the two holidays? How do people celebrate them? How did the holidays start? Make a list of facts with a partner.

B 🔊 Listen to a radio show about Thanksgiving in the United States and Canada. Complete the chart on the next page.

	Canada	The United States
1. What year was the first Thanksgiving Day?	1578	
2. Who started it (according to history books)?		
3. What month is it in?		
4. What day of the week is it on?		
5. What do people eat on Thanksgiving?		
6. What day of the week do they eat Thanksgiving dinner?		
7. What is the big shopping day?		

C Complete these sentences about Thanksgiving in the United States and Canada. Use the information in the chart to help you. Circle the correct conjunctions.

1. Thanksgiving is a holiday in ___the United States___ **(and)**/ **but** Canada.

2. Thanksgiving is in November in the United States, **but** / **so** the Canadian Thanksgiving is in _____ .

3. In the United States, Thanksgiving Day is always on a _____ , **or** / **but** in Canada, it's on a Monday.

4. In _____ , people get together with family **and** / **but** have a traditional Thanksgiving dinner.

5. People eat turkey **and** / **or** _____ .

6. In the United States, the meal is always on Thanksgiving Day, **but** / **so** in Canada, the meal can be on _____ .

7. Canadians can have Thanksgiving dinner on Saturday, Sunday, **or** / **but** _____ .

8. In the United States, Black Friday is the big shopping day, **but** / **and** in Canada, the big sales are on _____ .

Exercise 2.4 More Conjunctions

Group Work Make a list of favorite holidays and special days in your group. Talk about why the day exists, how people celebrate it, what they wear, what they eat or drink, where they go, and so on. Then discuss the similarities and differences among the days on your list. Use *and*, *but*, *or*, *so*, and *yet*.

A *People get together with family and eat a big meal on Thanksgiving and Christmas. People give gifts on Christmas, but they don't give gifts on Thanksgiving.*

B *People eat candy on Halloween, but they eat some healthy food on Thanksgiving.*

C *You don't get off work on Halloween, so it's not a big holiday.*

3 | Adverb Clauses

▶ Grammar Presentation

Adverb clauses show how ideas are connected. They begin with conjunctions such as *because*, *since*, *although*, and *even though*.

MAIN CLAUSE   ADVERB CLAUSE

CONJUNCTION

*Many people have the day off work **even though it's not an official holiday**.*

3.1 Adverb Clauses

Adverb Clause		Main Clause
Because Since	**there is a big sale today,**	the stores are crowded.
Although Even though	**it is not a holiday,**	a lot of people have the day off.

Main Clause	Adverb Clause	
The stores are crowded	**because since**	**there is a big sale today.**
Many people have the day off	**although even though**	**it isn't a holiday.**

3.2 Using Adverb Clauses

a. Like most other clauses, an adverb clause must have a subject and a verb.

ADVERB CLAUSE

SUBJ.   VERB

People shop on Black Friday **because prices are lower**.

b. An adverb clause on its own is not a sentence. It is a fragment.

They have the day off work **although it's not a holiday**.
They have the day off work. ~~Although it's not a holiday~~.

c. An adverb clause can come before or after the main clause. Use a comma when the adverb clause comes first.

Black Friday is an important day for retailers **because it is the start of the holiday shopping season**.
Because Black Friday is the start of the holiday shopping season, it is an important day for retailers.

d. *Although*, *even though*, and *though* connect contrasting ideas.

Although it is not a holiday, workers have the day off.
Even though some deals sound fantastic, they are not.
Though prices are low, the deals are often not good.

e. *Because* and *since* introduce reasons or causes and connect them with results.

RESULT   CAUSE
It's a popular day **since stores offer special deals**.
CAUSE   RESULT
Because prices are low, the stores are crowded.
REASON   RESULT
Because stores are crowded, many people stay home.

You can use *since* when the reader or listener knows about the reason from general knowledge, or because you have explained it.

Most stores cut their prices on Black Friday. **Since** prices are lower, it is a popular shopping day.

f. *So* introduces results.

The stores are crowded, **so** many people stay home.

So can also introduce a purpose or reason.

They camp in the parking lot **so** they can be first in the store.

Do not start a sentence with *so*.

Data from the Real World

Research shows that *since* is more common in formal writing than in speaking.

Writing ▮▮▮▮▮▮▮▮▮▮
Speaking ▮▮▮▮▮

▶ Grammar Application

Exercise 3.1 *Because*, *Since*, *Although*, and *Even Though*

Complete the magazine article about "Cyber Monday" (the Monday after Thanksgiving in the United States). Circle the best conjunctions.

CYBER MONDAY

The holiday shopping season is important for the U.S. economy (since)/although a high percentage of retail sales occur between Thanksgiving
(1)
and Christmas. **Although/Because** Black Friday is an important day for
(2)
retailers, Cyber Monday has become equally important. Cyber Monday is the first Monday after Thanksgiving Day. It's called "Cyber Monday" **although/because** a lot of retailers have online sales on that day.
(3)

There are a number of reasons why so many people shop on Cyber Monday, **even though/because** they cannot touch or handle the items
(4)
they are buying. For one thing, it's convenient. **Even though/Because**
(5)
most companies have rules against online shopping, millions of people still shop online on Cyber Monday while they're at work and sitting in front of computers. Also, Cyber Monday deals are sometimes even better than Black Friday deals. **Although/Because** Monday is often the last chance for retailers
(6)
to get rid of all the items they had for Black Friday, they often cut prices on Cyber Monday. In addition, some people prefer to buy online **because/although**
(7)
shipping is usually free, and they don't have to carry heavy items home.

Since/Although most people think
(8)
of the Friday after Thanksgiving as the biggest shopping day in the United States, Cyber Monday is now almost as important for retailers as Black Friday.

Exercise 3.2 Adverb Clauses

Combine the sentences to make one sentence. Use *because*, *since*, *so*, *although*, *even though*, or *though*. Sometimes there is more than one correct answer.

1. Researchers study the psychology of giving gifts. Gift giving is an important part of life.

   Researchers study the psychology of giving gifts because/since gift giving
   is an important part of life.
   Gift giving is an important part of life, so many experts study the psychology
   of giving gifts.

2. Stores are crowded during the holiday shopping period. Some people decide not to give gifts.

3. Holiday shopping can be unpleasant and expensive. Sometimes people feel like they can't avoid gift giving.

4. Gift giving in the right situations can make our relationships with people stronger. It can be a nice reminder of how we feel about other people.

5. Gift giving varies from culture to culture. It's a good idea to learn about cultural rules for gift giving.

6. In some cultures, you open a gift as soon as you get it. You wait until the giver has left in other cultures.

7. A certain color can mean bad luck in some cultures. People will avoid using the color as a gift wrap.

8. Both men and women enjoy gifts. Researchers say that gift giving is more important for females.

Exercise 3.3 More Adverb Clauses

A Complete the questions about gift-giving habits with an appropriate conjunction.

1. Do you ever buy gifts for people _*because*_ you want to say "thank you"?

2. Do you ever feel you have to buy gifts _____ you can't really afford them?

3. Have you ever given a gift to someone _____ you felt you had to?

4. Have you ever taken a gift back to the store for a refund or exchange _____ you didn't like it?

5. Have you bought a gift for someone _____ you didn't like that person?

6. Have you bought a gift for someone _____ you wanted to say "I'm sorry"?

7. Have you ever given someone a gift _____ you had no reason?

8. Have you ever pretended to like a gift _____ you didn't like it?

B *Pair Work* Ask and answer the questions in A with a partner. Do you have the same gift-giving habits?

A *Do you ever buy gifts for people because you want to say "thank you"?*

B *Yes, I sometimes buy a small gift for my neighbor when she waters my plants for me.*

4 Avoid Common Mistakes ⚠

1. **Check the spelling of *although*.**

   Although
   ~~Althought~~ the stores are crowded, it's my favorite day to shop.

2. **Do not link three or more clauses with *although*, *though*, or *even though*.**

   I like Black Friday. Although it is very tiring, it's a lot of fun.
   ~~I like Black Friday although it is very tiring it's a lot of fun.~~

3. **Do not forget to use a comma after the adverb clause when it is first.**

   Although we think it is a modern celebration˅ it is an ancient tradition.

Editing Task

Find and correct seven more mistakes in these paragraphs.

Although
~~Allthough~~ Mother's Day is an old holiday it may surprise you to know that
Father's Day is a modern holiday. Some people say the first modern Father's Day
was in 1908, althought most people agree it started in 1910. Father's Day was
born in Spokane, Washington, on June 19, 1910. Father's Day was partly the idea
5 of Mrs. Sonora Smart Dodd. Because her father was a single parent and raised six
children, she wanted to honor him. Although she suggested her father's June 5
birthday she did not give the organizers enough time to make arrangements. The
holiday moved from June 5 to the third Sunday in June. Father's Day is now a popular
holiday. Althogh people laughed at the idea of Father's Day at first it gradually
10 became popular.

Because retailers saw an opportunity to increase sales in the 1930s, they started
to advertise Father's Day gifts. People then felt that they had to buy gifts for their
fathers even though they realized this was commercialization, they still bought them.
Father's Day is an international holiday. Even though people celebrate it on different
15 dates it is an important day in many cultures.

5 | Grammar for Writing ✏

Using Conjunctions and Adverb Clauses

Writers often use conjunctions and adverb clauses to clearly show how ideas are connected to each other.

Conjunctions and adverb clauses appear in almost every kind of text and are very common in academic essays, opinion articles, and other texts that give opinions or describe complex ideas.

Remember:

- **You can connect ideas in words, phrases, and clauses with the conjunctions** *and, or, but, so,* **and** *yet.*

  On Thanksgiving, people look forward to eating a lot, <u>yet</u> they also look forward to spending time with their families <u>and</u> friends.

- **You can show cause and result and connect contrasting ideas with adverb clauses beginning with** *because, since, although,* **and** *even though.*

  <u>Although</u> Halloween is a holiday for children, it is a favorite holiday of many adults.

Pre-writing Task

1 Read the paragraphs below. Which holiday does the writer not like and why? Which holiday does the writer like and why?

The Least and Most Fun Holidays

Super Bowl Sunday is in late January or early February. On that day, two football teams play to see which team is the best team in the country. It is not a national holiday, yet most people think of it as a holiday. People gather together in living rooms or restaurants to watch the game together. The game lasts for several hours. People eat
5 a lot of burgers, hot dogs, pizza, potato chips, and other kinds of junk food on that day. I do not enjoy watching football, so I always get very bored at Super Bowl Sunday parties.

Halloween is on October 31, and it is one of my favorite holidays. Children dress up in costumes and walk from house to house asking for candy. It is a lot of fun answering the door and seeing the children and their costumes. Although this holiday
10 is really a children's holiday, there are always parties for adults to go to. Since most adults wear costumes at these parties, too, it is the one time of year that adults can act like children! Food is important on Halloween, too, but who does not like chocolate and candy?

2 Read the paragraphs again. Circle the conjunctions *and*, *but*, *or*, *so*, and *yet*, and underline the adverb clauses beginning with *because*, *since*, *although*, and *even though*.

Writing Task

1 *Write*   Use the paragraphs in the Pre-writing Task to help you write two paragraphs about two special days. In the first paragraph, write about a day you don't enjoy. In the second paragraph, write about a day you enjoy. What do people do on these days? What do they eat? What do they wear? Why do you like or not like these days? Use conjunctions and adverb clauses.

2 *Self-Edit*   Use the editing tips below to improve your paragraphs. Make any necessary changes.

1. Did you use conjunctions and adverb clauses to clearly explain how your ideas are connected to each other?
2. Did you connect words, phrases, and clauses with *and*, *but*, *or*, *so*, and *yet*?
3. Did you show cause and result or contrasting ideas with adverb clauses beginning with *because*, *since*, *although*, and *even though*?
4. Did you avoid the mistakes in the Avoid Common Mistakes chart on page 396?

Appendices

1. Capitalization and Punctuation Rules

Capitalize	Examples
1. The first letter of the first word of a sentence	*Today is a great day.*
2. The pronoun *I*	*After class, **I** want to go to the movies.*
3. Names of people	***S**imon **B**olivar, **J**oseph **C**hung*
4. Names of buildings, streets, geographic locations, and organizations	***T**aj **M**ahal, **M**ain **S**treet, **M**t. Everest, **U**nited **N**ations*
5. Titles of people	***D**r., **M**r., **M**rs., **M**s.*
6. Days, months, and holidays	***T**uesday, **A**pril, **V**alentine's **D**ay*
7. Names of courses or classes	***B**iology 101, **E**nglish **C**omposition II*
8. Titles of books, movies, and plays	***C**rime and **P**unishment, **A**vatar, **H**amlet*
9. States, countries, languages, and nationalities	***C**alifornia, **M**exico, **S**panish, **S**outh **K**orean, **C**anadian*
10. Names of religions	***H**induism, **C**atholicism, **I**slam, **J**udaism*

Punctuation	Examples
1. Use a period (.) at the end of a sentence.	*I think I can pass this class**.***
2. Use a question mark (?) at the end of a question.	*Why do you want to buy a car**?***
3. Use an exclamation point (!) to show strong emotion (e.g., surprise, anger, shock).	*Wait**!** I'm not ready yet.* *I can't believe it**!***
4. Use an apostrophe (') for possessive nouns. Add *'s* for singular nouns. Add *s'* for plural nouns. Add *'* or *'s* for nouns that end in *-s*. Add *'s* for irregular plural nouns. Use an apostrophe (') for contractions.	*That's Sue**'s** umbrella.* *Those are the student**s'** books.* *It is Wes**'** house. It is Wes**'s** house.* *Bring me the children**'s** shoes.* *I**'ll** be back next week. He can**'t** drive a car.*
5. Use a comma (,): between words in a series of three or more items. (Place *and* before the last item.) after a time clause when it begins a sentence. after a prepositional phrase when it begins a sentence. after an adverb clause when it begins a sentence. before *and, or, but,* and *so* to connect two or more main clauses.	*I like fish**,** chicken**,** turkey**, and** mashed potatoes.* ***Before** I play soccer**,** I do my stretching exercises.* ***Next to** my house**,** there's a beautiful little park.* ***Because** she got a job**,** she was able to get her own apartment.* *You can watch TV**, but** I have to study for a test.*

2. Stative (Non-Action) Verbs

Stative verbs do not describe actions. They describe states or situations. Stative verbs are not usually used in the present progressive, even if we are talking about right now. Some are occasionally used in the present progressive, but often with a different meaning.

Research shows that the 25 most common stative verbs in spoken and written English are:				
agree	dislike	hope	love	see
believe	expect	hurt	need	seem
care (about)	hate	know	notice	think
cost	have	like	own	understand
disagree	hear	look like	prefer	want

Other stative verbs are:				
be	feel	matter	recognize	sound
belong	forgive	mean	remember	taste
concern	look	owe	smell	weigh
deserve				

Using the present progressive of these verbs sometimes changes the meaning to an action.
*Can you **see** the red car?   (= use your eyes to be aware of something)*
*I'**m seeing** an old friend tomorrow.   (= meeting someone)*
*I **think** you're right.   (= believe)*
*Dina **is thinking** of taking a vacation soon.   (= considering)*
*I **have** two sisters.   (= be related to)*
*We'**re having** eggs for breakfast.   (= eating)*

3. Irregular Verbs

Base Form	Simple Past	Past Participle	Base Form	Simple Past	Past Participle
be	was / were	been	keep	kept	kept
become	became	become	know	knew	known
begin	began	begun	leave	left	left
bite	bit	bitten	lose	lost	lost
blow	blew	blown	make	made	made
break	broke	broken	meet	met	met
bring	brought	brought	pay	paid	paid
build	built	built	put	put	put
buy	bought	bought	read	read [red]*	read [red]*
catch	caught	caught	ride	rode	ridden
choose	chose	chosen	run	ran	run
come	came	come	say	said	said
cost	cost	cost	see	saw	seen
cut	cut	cut	sell	sold	sold
do	did	done	send	sent	sent
draw	drew	drawn	set	set	set
drink	drank	drunk	shake	shook	shaken
drive	drove	driven	show	showed	shown
eat	ate	eaten	shut	shut	shut
fall	fell	fallen	sing	sang	sung
feed	fed	fed	sit	sat	sat
feel	felt	felt	sleep	slept	slept
fight	fought	fought	speak	spoke	spoken
find	found	found	spend	spent	spent
fly	flew	flown	stand	stood	stood
forget	forgot	forgotten	steal	stole	stolen
forgive	forgave	forgiven	swim	swam	swum
get	got	gotten	take	took	taken
give	gave	given	teach	taught	taught
go	went	gone	tell	told	told
grow	grew	grown	think	thought	thought
have	had	had	throw	threw	thrown
hear	heard	heard	understand	understood	understood
hide	hid	hidden	wake	woke	woken
hit	hit	hit	wear	wore	worn
hold	held	held	win	won	won
hurt	hurt	hurt	write	wrote	written

*pronunciation

4. Spelling Rules for Verbs Ending in *-ing*

1. For verbs ending in a vowel-consonant combination, repeat the consonant before adding *-ing*.

    get → *getting*   *swim* → *swimming*

2. However, if the verb has more than one syllable, repeat the consonant only if the final syllable is stressed.

    beGIN → *beginning*   BUT   *HAPpen* → *happening (no doubling of consonant)*

3. For verbs ending in a silent *e*, drop the *e* before adding *-ing*.

    move → *moving*   *drive* → *driving*

    For *be* and *see*, don't <u>drop</u> the *e* because it is not silent.

    be → *being*   *see* → *seeing*

    For verbs ending in *-ie*, change *ie* to *y* before adding *-ing*.

    die → *dying*   *lie* → *lying*

Verbs that end in *-ing* are also called *gerunds* when they are used as nouns. The same spelling rules above apply to gerunds as well.

5. Spelling Rules for Regular Verbs in the Simple Past

1. To form the simple past of regular verbs, add *-ed* to the base form of the verb.

    work → *worked*   *wash* → *washed*

2. For regular verbs that end in *-e*, add *-d* only.

    live → *lived*   *like* → *liked*

3. For regular verbs ending in a consonant + *-y*, change *y* to *i* and add *-ed*.

    study → *studied*   *hurry* → *hurried*

4. For regular verbs that end in a vowel + *-y*, add *-ed*.

    stay → *stayed*   *enjoy* → *enjoyed*

5. For regular verbs that end in a vowel-consonant combination, repeat the consonant before adding *-ed*. Exception: Do not double the last consonant for verbs that end with *-w*, *-x*, or *-y*.

    stop → *stopped*   *plan* → *planned*   BUT   *fix* → *fixed*

6. However, if the verb has more than one syllable, repeat the consonant only if the final syllable is stressed.

    preFER → *preferred*   BUT   *Visit* → *visited (no doubling of consonant)*

6. Verbs + Gerunds and Infinitives

Verbs Followed by a Gerund Only	
admit	keep (= *continue*)
avoid	mind (= *object to*)
consider	miss
delay	postpone
deny	practice
discuss	quit
enjoy	recall (= *remember*)
finish	risk
imagine	suggest
involve	understand

Verbs Followed by an Infinitive Only		
afford	hope	pretend
agree	intend	promise
arrange	learn	refuse
attempt	manage	seem
decide	need	tend (= *be likely*)
deserve	offer	threaten
expect	plan	volunteer
fail	prepare	want
help		

Verbs Followed by a Gerund or an Infinitive		
begin	like	start
continue	love	stop*
forget*	prefer	try*
hate	remember*	

*The meanings of these verbs are different when they are followed by a gerund or an infinitive. See Unit 28.

7. Verb and Preposition Combinations

Verb + **about**	Verb + **for**	Verb + **of**	Verb + **to**
ask about	apologize for	approve of	admit to
complain about	ask for	dream of	belong to
talk about	look for	think of	listen to
think about	pay for	Verb + **on**	look forward to
worry about	wait for	count on	talk to
Verb + **against**	Verb + **in**	decide on	Verb + **with**
advise against	believe in	depend on	agree with
decide against	succeed in	insist on	argue with
Verb + **at**		plan on	bother with
look at		rely on	deal with
smile at			

8. Adjective and Preposition Combinations

Adjective + *of*
  afraid of
  ashamed of
  aware of
  careful of
  full of
  sick of
  tired of

Adjective + *by*
  amazed by
  bored by
  surprised by

Adjective + *at*
  amazed at
  angry at
  bad at
  good at
  surprised at

Adjective + *from*
  different from
  separate from

Adjective + *with*
  bored with
  familiar with
  satisfied with
  wrong with

Adjective + *in*
  interested in

Adjective + *for*
  bad for
  good for
  responsible for

Adjective + *about*
  concerned about
  excited about
  happy about
  nervous about
  pleased about
  sad about
  sorry about
  surprised about
  upset about
  worried about

Adjective + *to*
  similar to

9. Modal Verbs and Modal-like Expressions

Most modals have multiple meanings.

Function	Modal Verb or Modal-like Expression	Time	Example
Ability / Possibility	*can*	present, future	I *can* speak three languages. I *can* help you tomorrow.
	could	present, past	She *could* play an excellent game of tennis when she was young.
	be able to	past, present, future	I *won't be able to* help you tomorrow. I'*m not able to* help you today.
Permission less formal	*can* *could*	present, future	Yes, you *can* watch TV now. You *could* give me your answer next week.
more formal	*may*	present, future	You *may* leave now.
Requests less formal	*can* *will*	present, future	*Can* you stop that noise now? *Will* you please visit me tonight?
more formal	*could* *would*	present, future	*Could* you turn off your cell phone please? *Would* you please come for your interview this afternoon?
Offers	*can* *could* *may* *will*	present, future	I *can* help you paint your room. I *could* drive you to work next week. *May* I carry that for you? We'*ll* help you find your wallet.
Invitations	*would you like*	present, future	*Would you like* to come to my graduation tomorrow?
Advice less strong	*ought to* *should*	present, future	You really *ought to* save your money. She *shouldn't* go to school today.
stronger	*had better*	present, future	They *had better* be very careful in the park tomorrow.
Suggestions	*could* *might want to*	present, future	He *could* take a train instead of the bus. You *might want to* wait until next month.

Modal Verbs and Modal-like Expressions *(continued)*

Function	Modal Verb or Modal-like Expression	Time	Example
Preferences	*would like* *would prefer* *would rather*	present, future	I **would like** to take a trip next year. We **would prefer** to go on a cruise. They **would rather** eat at home than in a restaurant.
Necessity less formal	*have / has to* *need to*	past, present, future	We **had to** cancel our date at the last minute. She **needs to** quit her stressful job.
more formal	*have / has got to* *must*	past, present, future present, future	They **'ve got to** study harder if they want to pass. You **must** be more serious about your future.
Lack of Necessity	*don't / doesn't have to* *don't / doesn't need to*	past, present, future	I **didn't have to** renew my driver's license. You **don't need to** worry about your brother.
Prohibition	*can't* *must not* *may not*	present, future	You **can't** attend tonight without an invitation. You **must not** fish without a license. You **may not** board the plane before going through security.
Speculation / Probability	*could* *may* *might* *should*	present, future	He **could** be late because he missed his train. I **may** stay home. It **might** rain later because I see dark clouds. We **should** probably leave now.
	must	present only	She **must** be sick because she didn't come to work today.

10. Adjectives: Order Before Nouns

When you use two (or more) adjectives before a noun, use the order in the chart below.

Opinion	Size	Quality	Age	Shape	Color	Origin	Material	Nouns as Adjectives
beautiful	big	cold	ancient	rectangular	black	American	cotton	computer
comfortable	fat	free	new	round	blue	Canadian	glass	evening
delicious	huge	heavy	old	square	gold	Chinese	leather	rose
expensive	large	hot	young	triangular	green	European	metal	safety
interesting	long	safe			orange	Japanese	paper	software
nice	short				purple	Mexican	plastic	summer
pretty	small				red	Peruvian	stone	training
reasonable	tall				silver	Thai	wooden	
special	thin				yellow		woolen	
ugly	wide				white			

Examples:

I bought a beautiful, new, purple and gold Indian scarf.

There is a tall, young woman sitting next to that handsome man.

We're going to learn an interesting, new software program.

The museum has expensive glass jewelry.

11. Conditionals

The **factual conditional** describes general truths, habits, and things that happen routinely. The simple present is used in both clauses. You can use modals in the result clause, too.

        IF CLAUSE   RESULT CLAUSE

If you use the highway, the drive is much faster.   *(general truth)*

If you enter before 11:00 a.m., you can get a discount.   *(general truth)*

Use the imperative in the result clause to give instructions or commands.

If you don't like the oranges, give them to me.   *(command)*

The **future conditional** describes things that will happen under certain conditions in the future. The simple present is used in the *if* clause and a future form is used in the result clause. You can use modals in the result clause, too.

        IF CLAUSE   RESULT CLAUSE

If it rains tomorrow, they're going to cancel the game.

If I finish my homework early, I'll go to the movies.

If she works hard, she could get a promotion.

Conditionals *(continued)*

You can begin a conditional sentence with the *if* clause or the result clause. It doesn't change the meaning. Use a comma between the two clauses if you begin your sentence with the *if* clause.

RESULT CLAUSE   IF CLAUSE
They're going to cancel the game if it rains tomorrow.

IF CLAUSE   RESULT CLAUSE
If it rains tomorrow, they're going to cancel the game.

12. Phrasal Verbs: Transitive and Intransitive

Transitive (Separable) Phrasal Verbs

Phrasal Verb	Meaning	Phrasal Verb	Meaning
add up	add together, combine	*give up*	quit
blow up	explode	*hang up*	end a phone call
bring back	return something or someone	*help out*	assist someone
bring up	(1) raise a child, (2) introduce a topic	*lay off*	lose a job, end employment
build up	accumulate	*leave on*	keep on (a light, clothing, jewelry)
call back	return a phone call	*let in*	allow someone to enter
call off	cancel	*look over*	examine
cheer up	make someone happy	*look up*	find information
clear up	resolve a problem or situation, explain	*make up*	create or invent (a story, a lie)
do over	do again	*pass out*	distribute (paper, a test, material, homework)
figure out	find an answer, understand	*pay back*	repay money
fill in	write in blank spaces	*pay off*	repay completely
fill out	complete an application or form	*pick up*	(1) go get someone or something, (2) lift
find out	look for or seek information, learn	*point out*	call attention to something
give away	donate, give for free	*put away*	(1) save for the future, (2) put in the correct place
give back	return		

Transitive (Separable) Phrasal Verbs (continued)

Phrasal Verb	Meaning	Phrasal Verb	Meaning
put back	return something to its usual place	*talk over*	discuss
put off	delay, postpone	*think over*	consider
put out	(1) extinguish, stop the burning of a fire or cigarette, (2) place outside	*throw away / throw out*	get rid of something; discard
put together	assemble	*try on*	put on clothing to see if it fits
set up	(1) arrange, (2) plan, (3) build	*turn down*	(1) lower the volume, (2) reject
shut off / turn off	stop (a machine, a light, a TV)	*turn on*	start (a machine, a light, a TV)
sort out	(1) organize, (2) solve	*turn up*	increase the volume
straighten up	(1) make something look neat, (2) stand tall	*wake up*	stop sleeping
take back	return something	*work out*	(1) solve, (2) calculate
take out	(1) remove, (2) obtain something officially	*write down*	write on paper

Intransitive (Inseparable) Phrasal Verbs

Phrasal Verb	Meaning	Phrasal Verb	Meaning
break down	(1) stop working, (2) lose control	*fall down*	fall to the ground
break up	end a relationship, separate	*fool around*	act playfully
come back	return	*get ahead*	succeed, make progress
come from	originate	*get along*	have a good relationship
come on	(1) hurry, (2) start	*get over*	recover from an illness or a shock
dress up	put on nice or formal clothes	*get up*	arise from bed
drop in	visit without advance notice	*give up*	stop
drop out	quit (school, a race, a club)	*go ahead*	start or continue
eat out	eat in a restaurant	*go away*	leave; go to another place

Phrasal Verb	Meaning	Phrasal Verb	Meaning
go on	continue	*run out*	(1) leave, (2) be completely used
go out	not stay home	*set in*	begin and continue for a long time
go up	rise, go higher	*show up*	appear
grow up	become an adult	*sign up*	register for a class or event
hang on	(1) wait, (2) keep going	*sit down*	sit; take a seat
hold on	(1) wait, (2) persist	*slip up*	make a mistake
look into	investigate	*speak up*	talk louder
look out	be careful	*stand up*	stand; rise
make up	end a disagreement	*stay up*	remain awake
move in (to)	(1) take your things to a new home, (2) begin living somewhere	*take off*	(1) leave on an airplane, (2) grow; be successful
move out (of)	leave a place you live in	*watch out*	be careful
run into	meet someone by chance or unexpectedly	*work out*	(1) exercise, (2) go as planned

13. Adjectives and Adverbs: Comparative and Superlative Forms

	Adjective	Comparative	Superlative
1. One-Syllable Adjectives a. Add *-er* and *-est* to one syllable adjectives.	cheap high large long new old small strong tall	cheaper higher larger longer newer older smaller stronger taller	the cheapest the highest the largest the longest the newest the oldest the smallest the strongest the tallest
b. For one-syllable adjectives that end in a vowel + consonant, double the final consonant and add *-er* or *-est*.	big hot sad thin	bigger hotter sadder thinner	the biggest the hottest the saddest the thinnest
Do not double the consonant *w*.	low	lower	the lowest

Adjectives and Adverbs: Comparative and Superlative Forms (continued)

2. Two-Syllable Adjectives a. Add *more* or *most* to most adjectives.	boring famous handsome patient	more boring more famous more handsome more patient	the most boring the most famous the most handsome the most patient
b. Some two-syllable adjectives have two forms.	friendly narrow simple strict quiet	friendlier more friendly narrower more narrow simpler more simple stricter more strict quieter more quiet	the friendliest the most friendly the narrowest the most narrow the simplest the most simple the strictest the most strict the quietest the most quiet
c. Remove the *-y* and add *-ier* or *-iest* to two-syllable adjectives ending in *-y*.	angry easy friendly happy lucky pretty silly	angrier easier friendlier happier luckier prettier sillier	the angriest the easiest the friendliest the happiest the luckiest the prettiest the silliest
3. Three or More Syllable Adjectives Add *more* or *most* to adjectives with three or more syllables.	beautiful comfortable creative difficult enjoyable expensive important independent relaxing responsible serious	more beautiful more comfortable more creative more difficult more enjoyable more expensive more important more independent more relaxing more responsible more serious	the most beautiful the most comfortable the most creative the most difficult the most enjoyable the most expensive the most important the most independent the most relaxing the most responsible the most serious
4. Irregular Adjectives Some adjectives have irregular forms.	bad far good	worse farther / further better	the worst the farthest / the furthest the best

Adjectives and Adverbs: Comparative and Superlative Forms (continued)

5. -ly Adverbs Most adverbs end in -ly. Add *more* or *most*. People usually only use *the* with superlative adverbs in formal writing and speaking.	dangerously patiently quickly quietly slowly	more dangerously more patiently more quickly more quietly more slowly	(the) most dangerously (the) most patiently (the) most quickly (the) most quietly (the) most slowly
6. One-Syllable Adverbs A few adverbs do not end in -ly. Add -er and -est to these adverbs.	fast hard	faster harder	(the) fastest (the) hardest
7. Irregular Adverbs Some adverbs have irregular forms.	badly far well	worse farther / further better	(the) worst (the) farthest / furthest (the) best

14. Academic Word List (AWL) Words and Definitions

The meanings of the words are those used in this book. ([U1] = Unit 1)

Academic Word	Definition
access (n) [U8] [U29]	easy way to enter
achieve (v) [U16]	do or obtain something that you wanted after planning and working to make it happen
administration (n) [U13]	the management or control of an organization
adult (n) [U8]	someone (or something such as a plant or animal) grown to full size and strength
affect (v) [U17] [U23] [U26]	have an influence on someone or something
analyze (v) [U8] [U30]	study something in a systematic and careful way
appropriate (adj) [U3]	right for a particular situation
appropriately (adv) [U3]	in a way that is right for a particular situation
area (n) [U12]	a particular part of a country, city, town, etc.
aspect (n) [U17]	a particular feature of or way of thinking about something
assess (v) [U21]	decide the quality or importance of something
assignment (n) [U3] [U20]	a particular job or responsibility given to you
available (adj) [U5]	ready to use or obtain
brief (adj) [U3]	short, concise, to the point
challenge (n) [U9] [U11] [U22]	something needing a great mental or physical effort in order to be done successfully
challenge (v) [U9] [U11] [U22]	test someone's ability or determination

Academic Word	Definition
chemical (n) [U2] [U10] [U13] [U15]	any basic substance that is used in or produced by a reaction involving changes to atoms or molecules
civil (adj) [U29]	of or relating to the people of a country
collapse (v) [U11]	fall down suddenly, or to cause to fall down; to be unable to continue or to stay in operation
comment (n) [U8]	an opinion or remark
commission (n) [U13]	an official group of people who get information about a problem or perform other special duties
communicate (v) [U3] [U14] [U18]	give messages or information to others through speech, writing, body movements, or signals
communication (n) [U14]	the exchange of messages or information
community (n) [U20]	all the people who live in a particular area, or a group of people who are considered as a unit because of their shared interests or background
computer (n) [U1] [U2] [U4] [U6] [U19]	an electronic device that can store large amounts of information and organize and change it very quickly
constantly (adv) [U24]	nearly continuously or frequently
consumer (n) [U22]	a person who buys goods or services for their own use
contact (v) [U20]	have communication with someone, or with a group or organization
convince (v) [U22]	cause someone to believe something or to do something
couple (n) [U23]	two people who are married or who spend a lot of time together, especially in a romantic relationship
create (v) [U3] [U5] [U12] [U16] [U28] [U30]	cause something to exist, or to make something new and imaginative
creative (adj) [U9] [U22] [U26]	producing or using original and unusual ideas
credit (n) [U7] [U25]	a method of buying goods or services that allows you to pay for them in the future; *academic meaning:* acknowledgment or praise
crucial (adj) [U32]	extremely important because many other things depend on it
culture (n) [U24] [U28]	the way of life of a particular people, especially shown in their ordinary behavior and habits, their attitudes toward each other, and their moral and religious beliefs
cycle (n) [U28] [U31]	a process that repeats
decline (n) [U23]	a decrease in amount or quality
design (v) [U4] [U12]	make or draw plans for something
discriminate (v) [U29]	treat people differently, in an unfair way
discrimination (n) [U13] [U29]	treating people differently, in an unfair way
distribute (v) [U15]	divide something among several or many people, or to spread something over an area
distribution (n) [U15]	the division of something among several or many people, or the spreading of something over an area

Academic Word	Definition
document (n) [U7]	a paper or set of papers with written or printed information
dominate (v) [U26]	control a place or person, want to be in charge, or be the most important person or thing
economic (adj) [U23]	connected to the economy of a country
economy (n) [U23] [U32]	the system of trade and industry by which the wealth of a country is made and used
editor (n) [U8]	a person who corrects and makes changes to texts or films before they are printed or shown, or a person who is in charge of a newspaper, magazine, etc., and is responsible for all of its reports
environment (n) [U18] [U19]	the air, water, and land in or on which people, animals, and plants live
environmental (adj) [U12]	related to the air, water, and land in or on which people, animals, and plants live
estimate (n) [U12]	a judgment or calculation of approximately how large or how great something is
ethical (adj) [U13]	good, correct
expert (n) [U21] [U23] [U24]	a person having a high level of knowledge or skill in a particular subject
feature (n) [U16] [U18]	a noticeable or important characteristic or part
finally (adv) [U3] [U20]	at the end, or after some delay
finance (n) [U25]	the management of money, or the money belonging to a person, group, or organization
flexible (adj) [U28]	able to change or be changed easily according to the situation
focus (v) [U17]	direct attention toward something or someone
gender (n) [U26]	the male or female sex
goal (n) [U9] [U16] [U17] [U25]	an aim or purpose
grade (n) [U26]	a school class or group of classes in which all children are of a similar age or ability; *also:* a score on a test
identity (n) [U7]	who a person is, or the qualities of a person, thing, or group that make them different from others
illegal (adj) [U13] [U29]	against the law
image (n) [U6]	a picture, especially one seen in a mirror, through a camera, in a photo, on TV, or on a computer
income (n) [U25]	money that is earned from doing work or received from investments
instance (n) [U32]	a particular situation, event, or fact
instruction (n) [U19]	advice and information about how to do or use something
interact (v) [U1] [U31]	communicate with or react to each other
issue (n) [U13]	a subject or problem that people are thinking and talking about

Academic Word	Definition
item (n) [U31] [U32]	a particular thing considered as one among others of its type
job (n) [U6] [U9] [U12] [U13] [U21] [U29]	the regular work that a person does to earn money
legal (adj) [U13]	connected with or allowed by the law
link (n) [U8]	a word or image on a website that can take you to another document or website; *academic meaning:* a connection
major (adj) [U27]	more important, bigger, or more serious than others of the same type
medical (adj) [U19]	of or relating to medicine, or the treatment of disease or injury
migrate (v) [U12]	move from one place to another
migration (n) [U11]	movement from one place to another
motivate (v) [U16]	cause someone to behave in a certain way, or to make someone want to do something well; give a reason for doing something
motivating (adj.) [U16]	causing someone to behave in a certain way or to do something well; giving a reason for doing something
negative (adj) [U23]	not happy, hopeful, or approving
network (n) [U27]	a group of computers that are connected and can share information; a group of people who share ideas
networking (n) [U1] [U8] [U27]	the process of meeting and talking to a lot of people, especially in order to get a lot of information that can help you
normally (adv) [U18]	usually or regularly
occupational (adj) [U13]	relating to or caused by a person's work or activity
occur (v) [U11] [U28]	happen
percent (n) [U8] [U32]	for or out of every 100
period (n) [U17]	a length of time
positive (adj) [U3] [U6] [U17] [U23]	without any doubt; certain; good
predict (v) [U23]	say that an event will happen in the future
prioritize (v) [U25]	put things in order of importance
priority (n) [U25]	something that is considered more important than other matters
process (n) [U5] [U15]	a series of actions or events performed to make something or achieve a particular result, or a series of changes that happens naturally
process (v) [U15]	prepare, change, or treat food with chemicals to make it last longer; deal with something according to a specific set of actions
processing (n) [U15]	the preparation, change, or treatment of food with chemicals to make it last longer; the act of dealing with something according to a specific set of actions, such as processing an insurance claim
professional (n) [U3]	a person who has a job that needs skill, education, or training

Academic Word	Definition
professional (adj) [U3] [U23]	having the qualities of skilled, trained, and educated people
project (n) [U21]	a piece of planned work or activity that is completed over a period of time and intended to achieve a particular aim
psychologist (n) [U16]	someone who studies the mind and emotions and their relationship to behavior
psychology (n) [U26]	the scientific study of how the mind works and how it influences behavior
purchase (n) [U25]	something that you buy or the act of buying something
range (n) [U8]	the level to which something is limited, or the area within which something operates
reaction (n) [U8]	a behavior, feeling, or action that is a direct result of something else
recover (v) [U19]	get better after an illness or a period of difficulty or trouble
relax (v) [U25]	become or cause someone to become calm and comfortable, and not worried or nervous
relaxed (adj) [U26]	comfortable and informal
research (n) [U16] [U19] [U30]	a detailed study of a subject or an object in order to discover information or achieve a new understanding of it
researcher (n) [U11] [U26] [U30]	someone who does a detailed study of a subject or an object in order to discover information or achieve a new understanding of it
respond (v) [U3]	say or do something as a reaction to something that has been said or done
response (n) [U6]	something said or done as a reaction to something; an answer or reaction
revolution (n) [U5]	a sudden and great change, especially the violent change of a system of government
role (n) [U27]	the duty or use that someone or something usually has or is expected to have
schedule (n) [U1] [U28]	a list of planned activities or things to be done at or during a particular time
secure (adj) [U7]	safe
security (n) [U7] [U17]	protection from risk and the threat of change for the worse
similar (adj) [U10]	looking or being almost the same, although not exactly
site (n) [U1] [U7] [U8] [U27]	a place where something is, was, or will be
source (n) [U27]	someone or something from which you obtain information; origin or beginning of something
specific (adj) [U3] [U28]	relating to one thing and not others; particular
strategy (n) [U14]	a plan for achieving something or reaching a goal
stressed (adj) [U32]	worried by a difficult situation; being physically tested, like a car part to make sure it is strong
style (n) [U14]	a way of doing something that is typical to a person, group, place, or time

Academic Word	Definition
task (n) [U9] [U24]	a piece of work to be done
team (n) [U10] [U28] [U30]	a group of people who work together, either in a sport or in order to achieve something
technique (n) [U14]	a specific way of doing a skillful activity
technological (adj) [U19]	relating to, or involving, technology
technology (n) [U1] [U19] [U27]	the methods for using scientific discoveries for practical purposes, especially in industry
text (n) [U3]	written or printed material
theory (n) [U11]	something suggested as a reasonable explanation for facts, a condition, or an event
topic (n) [U27]	a subject that is written about, discussed, or studied
traditional (adj) [U5]	established for a long time, or part of behavior and beliefs that have been established
transport (v) [U15]	take things, goods, or people from one place to another
trend (n) [U12] [U23]	direction of changes or developments
volunteer (n) [U20]	someone who does something for other people, willingly and without being forced or paid to do it
volunteer (v) [U9] [U20]	do something for other people, willingly and without being forced or paid to do it

15. Pronunciation Table International Phonetic Alphabet (IPA)

Vowels	
Key Words	**International Phonetic Alphabet**
cake, mail, pay	/eɪ/
pan, bat, hand	/æ/
tea, feet, key	/iː/
ten, well, red	/e/
ice, pie, night	/aɪ/
is, fish, will	/ɪ/
cone, road, know	/oʊ/
top, rock, stop	/ɑ/
blue, school, new, cube, few	/uː/
cup, us, love	/ʌ/
house, our, cow	/aʊ/
saw, talk, applause	/ɔː/
boy, coin, join	/ɔɪ/

Vowels *(continued)*	
p**u**t, b**oo**k, w**o**man	/ʊ/
alone, op**e**n, penc**i**l, at**o**m, ketch**u**p	/ə/

Consonants	
Key Words	**International Phonetic Alphabet**
bid, jo**b**	/b/
do, fee**d**	/d/
food, sa**fe**	/f/
go, do**g**	/g/
home, be**h**ind	/h/
kiss, ba**ck**	/k/
load, poo**l**	/l/
man, plu**m**	/m/
need, ope**n**	/n/
pen, ho**p**e	/p/
road, ca**r**d	/r/
see, re**c**ent	/s/
show, na**ti**on	/ʃ/
team, mee**t**	/t/
choose, wa**tch**	/tʃ/
think, bo**th**	/θ/
this, fa**th**er	/ð/
visit, sa**v**e	/v/
watch, a**w**ay	/w/
yes, oni**o**n	/j/
zoo, the**s**e	/z/
bei**g**e, mea**s**ure	/ʒ/
jump, bri**dg**e	/dʒ/

Glossary of Grammar Terms

action verb a verb that describes an action.
> *I **eat** breakfast every day.*
> *They **ran** in the 5K race.*

adjective a word that describes or modifies a noun.
> *That's a **beautiful** hat.*

adjective clause see **relative clause**.

adverb a word that describes or modifies a verb, another adverb, or an adjective. Adverbs often end in *-ly*.
> *Please walk **faster** but **carefully**.*

adverb clause a clause that shows how ideas are connected. Adverb clauses begin with conjunctions such as *because, since, although,* and *even though*.
> ***Although it is not a holiday**, workers have the day off.*

adverb of degree an adverb that makes other adverbs or adjectives stronger or weaker.
> *The test was **extremely** difficult.   They are **kind of** busy today.*

adverb of manner an adverb that describes how an action happens.
> *He has **suddenly** left the room.*

adverb of time an adverb that describes when something happens.
> *She'll get up **later**.*

article the words *a / an* and *the*. An article introduces or identifies a noun.
> *I bought **a** new MP3 player. **The** price was reasonable.*

auxiliary verb (also called **helping verb**) a verb that is used before a main verb in a sentence. *Do, have,* and *be* can act as auxiliary verbs.
> ***Does** he want to go to the library later?   **Have** you received the package?*

base form of the verb the form of a verb without any endings (*-s* or *-ed*) or *to*.
> ***come   go   take***

clause a group of words that has a subject and a verb. There are two types of clauses: **main clauses** and **dependent clauses** (*see* dependent clause). A sentence can have more than one clause.
> MAIN CLAUSE   DEPENDENT CLAUSE   MAIN CLAUSE
> *I woke up when I heard the noise. It was scary.*

common noun a word for a person, place, or thing. A common noun is not capitalized.
> ***mother   building   fruit***

comparative the form of an adjective or adverb that shows how two people, places, or things are different.
> *My daughter is **older than** my son. (adjective)*
> *She does her work **more quickly** than he does. (adverb)*

conjunction a word such as *and, but, so, or,* and *yet* which connects single words, phrases, or clauses.

*We finished all our work, **so** we left early.*

consonant a sound represented in writing by these letters of the alphabet: ***b, c, d, f, g, h, j, k, l, m, n, p, q, r, s, t, v, w, x, y,*** and ***z.***

count noun refers to a person, place, or thing you can count. Count nouns have a plural form.

*There are three **banks** on Oak Street.*

definite article *the* is a definite article. Use *the* with a person, place, or thing that is familiar to you and your listener. Also, use *the* when the noun is unique – there is only one (*the sun, the moon, the Internet*).

***The** movie we saw last week was very good.*

***The** Earth is round.*

dependent clause a clause that cannot stand alone. Some kinds of dependent clauses are adverb clauses, relative clauses, and time clauses.

***After we return from the trip**, I'm going to need to relax.*

determiner a word that comes before a noun to limit its meaning in some way. Some common determiners are *some, a little, a lot, a few, this, that, these, those, his, a, an, the, much,* and *many.*

***These** computers have **a lot** of parts.*

*Please give me **my** book.*

direct object the person or thing that receives the action of the verb.

*The teacher gave the students **a test**.*

factual conditional describes something that is generally true in a certain situation. The *if* clause describes the condition and is in the simple present. The result clause is in the simple present as well.

***If** it's late, I don't stay online for a long time.*

formal a style of writing or speech used when you don't know the other person very well or where it's not appropriate to show familiarity, such as in business, a job interview, speaking to a stranger, or speaking to an older person who you respect.

Good evening. I'd like to speak with Ms. Smith. Is she available?

future a verb form that describes a time that hasn't come yet. It is expressed in English by *will, be going to,* and present tense.

*I'**ll meet** you tomorrow.*

*I'**m going to visit** my uncle and aunt next weekend.*

future conditional describes something that will happen under certain conditions in the future. The *if* clause describes the condition and is in the simple present. The result clause uses a future form of the verb.

***If** I do well on this final exam, I'**ll get** an A for the course.*

gerund the *-ing* form of a verb that is used as a noun. It can be the subject or object in a sentence or the object of a preposition.

*We suggested **waiting** and **going** another day.*

*Salsa **dancing** is a lot of fun.*

*I look forward to **meeting** you.*

habitual past a verb form that describes repeated past actions, habits, and conditions using *used to* or *would*.

*Before we had the Internet, we **used to** go to the library a lot.*

*Before there was refrigeration, people **would** use ice to keep food cool.*

helping verb *see* **auxiliary verb**.

imperative a type of clause that tells people to do something. It gives instructions, directions to a place, and advice. The verb is in the base form.

***Listen** to the conversation.*

***Don't open** your books.*

indefinite article *a/an* are the indefinite articles. Use *a/an* with a singular person, place, or thing when you and your listener are not familiar with it, or when the specific name of it is not important. Use *a* with consonant sounds. Use *an* with vowel sounds.

*She's going to see **a** doctor today.   I had **an** egg for breakfast.*

indirect object the person or thing that receives the direct object.

*The teacher gave **the students** a test.*

infinitive *to* + the base form of a verb.

*I need **to get** home early tonight.*

infinitive of purpose *in order* + infinitive expresses a purpose. It answers the question *why*. If the meaning is clear, it is not necessary to use *in order*.

*People are fighting **(in order) to change** unfair laws.*

informal a style of speaking or writing to friends, family, and children.

Hey, there. Nice to see you again.

information question (also called **Wh- question**) begins with a *wh-* word *(who, what, when, where, which, why, how, how much)*. To answer this type of question, you need to provide information rather than answer *yes* or *no*.

inseparable phrasal verb a phrasal verb that cannot be separated. The verb and its particle always stay together.

*My car **broke down** yesterday.*

intransitive verb a verb that does not need an object. It is often followed by an expression of time, place, or manner.

*The flight **arrived** at 5:30 p.m.*

irregular adjective an adjective that does not change its form in the usual way. For example, you do not make the comparative form by adding *-er*.

good → better

irregular adverb an adverb that does not change its form in the usual way. For example, you do not make the comparative form by adding *-er*.

badly → worse

irregular verb a verb that does not change its form in the usual way. For example, it does not form the simple past with *-d* or *-ed*. It has its own special form.

go ⟶ *went*   *ride* ⟶ *rode*   *hit* ⟶ *hit*

main clause (also called **independent clause**) a clause that can be used alone as a complete sentence.

After I get back from my trip, ***I'm going to relax****.*

main verb a verb that functions alone in a clause and can have an auxiliary verb.

They ***had*** *a meeting last week.*

They have ***had*** *many meetings this month.*

measurement word a word or phrase that shows the amount of something. Measurement words can be singular or plural.

I bought ***a box*** *of cereal, and Sonia bought* ***five pounds*** *of apples.*

modal a verb such as *can, could, have to, may, might, must, should, will*, and *would*. It modifies the main verb to show such things as ability, permission, possibility, advice, obligation, necessity, or lack of necessity.

It ***might*** *rain later today.*

You ***should*** *study harder if you want to pass this course.*

non-action verb *see* **stative verb**.

noncount noun refers to ideas and things that you cannot count. Noncount nouns use a singular verb and do not have a plural form.

Do you download ***music****?*

noun a word for a person, place, or thing. There are common nouns and proper nouns (*see* **common noun**, **proper noun**).

COMMON NOUN

I stayed in a ***hotel*** *on my trip to New York.*

PROPER NOUN

I stayed in the ***Pennsylvania Hotel****.*

object pronoun replaces a noun in the object position.

Sara loves exercise classes. She takes ***them*** *three times a week.*

particle a small word like *down, in, off, on, out*, or *up*. These words (which can also be prepositions) are used with verbs to form **two-word verbs** or **phrasal verbs**. The meaning of a phrasal verb often has a different meaning from the meaning of the individual words in it.

past participle a verb form that can be regular (base form + *-ed*) or irregular. It is used to form the present perfect and the passive. It can also be an adjective.

I've ***studied*** *English for five years.*

past progressive a verb form that describes events or situations in progress at a time in the past. The emphasis is on the action.

They ***were watching*** *TV when I arrived.*

phrasal verb (also called a **two-word verb**) consists of a verb + a particle. There are two kinds of phrasal verbs: separable and inseparable (*see* **particle, inseparable phrasal verb, separable phrasal verb**).

VERB + PARTICLE

They ***came back*** *from vacation today.* (inseparable)

Please ***put*** *your cell phone* ***away****.* (separable)

plural noun a noun that refers to more than one person, place, or thing.

students   women   roads

possessive adjective *see* **possessive determiner.**

possessive determiner (also called **possessive adjective**) a determiner that shows possession (*my, your, his, her, its, our,* and *their*).

possessive pronoun replaces a possessive determiner + singular or plural noun. The possessive pronoun agrees with the noun that it replaces.

*My exercise class is at night. **Hers** is on the weekend.* (hers = her exercise class)

preposition a word such as *to, at, for, with, below, in, on, next to,* or *above* that goes before a noun or pronoun to show location, time, direction, or a close relationship between two people or things. A preposition may go before a gerund as well.

*I'm **in** the supermarket **next to** our favorite restaurant.*

*The idea **of** love has inspired many poets.*

present perfect a verb form that describes past events or situations that are still important in the present, actions that happened once or repeatedly at an indefinite time before now, and to give the number of times something happened up to now.

*Lately scientists **have discovered** medicines in the Amazon.*

*I**'ve been** to the Amazon twice.*

present perfect progressive a verb form that describes something that started in the past, usually continues in the present, and may continue in the future.

*He **hasn't been working** since last May.*

present progressive a verb form that describes an action or situation that is in progress now or around the present time. It is also used to indicate a fixed arrangement in the near future.

*What **are** you **doing** right now?*

*I**'m leaving** for Spain next week.*

pronoun a word that replaces a noun or noun phrase. Some examples are *I, we, him, hers,* and *it* (see **object pronoun, subject pronoun, relative pronoun, possessive pronoun, reciprocal pronoun, reflexive pronoun**).

proper noun a noun that is the name of a particular person, place, idea, or thing. It is capitalized.

***Central Park** is in **New York City**.*

punctuation mark a symbol used in writing such as a period (.), a comma (,), a question mark (?), or an exclamation point (!).

quantifier Some quantifiers are *much, many, some, any, a lot, plenty,* and *enough.*

reciprocal pronoun a pronoun *(each other, one another)* that shows that two or more people give *and* receive the same action or have the same relationship.

*Mari and I have the same challenges. We help **each other**.* (I help Mari and Mari helps me.)

reflexive pronoun a pronoun *(myself, yourself, himself, herself, ourselves, yourselves, themselves)* which shows that the object of the sentence is the same as the subject.

*I taught **myself** to speak Japanese.*

regular verb a verb that changes its form in the usual way.

live → live**s**

wash → wash**ed**

relative clause (also known as **adjective clause**) defines, describes, identifies, or gives more information about a noun. It begins with a relative pronoun such as *who, that, which, whose,* or *whom*. Like all clauses, a relative clause has both a subject and a verb. It can describe the subject or the object of a sentence.

*People **who have sleep problems** can join the study.*   (subject relative clause)

*There are many diseases **that viruses cause**.*   (object relative clause)

relative pronoun a pronoun *(who, which, that, whose, whom)* that connects a noun phrase to a relative clause.

*People **who** have sleep problems can join the study.*

*There are many diseases **that** viruses cause.*

sentence a complete thought or idea that has a subject and a main verb. In writing, it begins with a capital letter and has a punctuation mark at the end (. ? !). In an imperative sentence, the subject (*you*) is not usually stated.

This sentence is a complete thought.   Open your books.

separable phrasal verb a phrasal verb that can be separated. This means that an object can go before or after the particle.

***Write down** your expenses.*

***Write** your expenses **down**.*

simple past a verb form that describes completed actions or events that happened at a definite time in the past.

*They **grew up** in Washington, D.C.*

*They **attended** Howard University and **graduated** in 2004.*

simple present a verb form that describes things that regularly happen, such as habits and routines (usual and regular activities). It also describes facts and general truths.

*I **play** games online every night.*   (routine)

*The average person **spends** 13 hours a week online.*   (fact)

singular noun a noun that refers to only one person, place, or thing.

*He is my best **friend**.*

statement a sentence that gives information.

Today is Thursday.

stative verb (also called **non-action verb**) describes a state or situation, not an action. It is usually in the simple form of the present or past.

*I **remember** your friend.*

subject the person or thing that performs the action of a verb.

***People** use new words and expressions every day.*

subject pronoun replaces a noun in the subject position.

*Sara and I are friends. **We** work at the same company.*

superlative the form of an adjective or adverb that compares one person, place, or thing to others in a group.

*This storm was **the most dangerous** one of the season.* (adjective)

*That group worked **most effectively** after the disaster.* (adverb)

syllable a group of letters that has one vowel sound and that you say as a single unit.

There is one syllable in the word lunch *and two syllables in the word* breakfast. (*Break* is one syllable and *fast* is another syllable.)

tense the form of a verb that shows past or present time.

*They **worked** yesterday.* (simple past)

*They **work** every day.* (simple present)

third-person singular refers to *he, she,* and *it* or a singular noun. In the simple present, the third-person singular form ends in *-s* or *-es*.

*It **looks** warm and sunny today.*   *He **washes** the laundry on Saturdays.*

time clause a clause that shows the order of events and begins with a time word such as *before, after, when, while,* or *as soon as*.

***Before** there were freezers, people needed ice to make frozen desserts.*

time expression a phrase that functions as an adverb of time. It tells when something happens, happened, or will happen.

*I graduated **in 2010**.*   *She's going to visit her aunt and uncle **next summer**.*

transitive verb a verb that needs an object. The object completes the meaning of the verb.

*She **wears** perfume.*

two-word verb see **phrasal verb**.

verb a word that describes an action or a state.

*Alex **wears** jeans and a T-shirt to school. Alex **is** a student.*

vowel a sound represented in writing by these letters of the alphabet: ***a, e, i, o,*** and ***u***.

***Wh-* question** see **information question**.

***Yes / No* question** begins with a form of *be* or an auxiliary verb. You can answer such a question with *yes* or *no*.

*"**Are** they going to the movies?"*   *""**No**, they're not."*

*"**Can** you give me some help?"*   *"**Yes**, I can."*

Index

Art Credits

Illustration

Photography